STYLE IN ADMINISTRATION

Style in Administration

READINGS IN BRITISH PUBLIC ADMINISTRATION

EDITED BY

RICHARD A. CHAPMAN

Senior Lecturer, Department of Local Government and Administration,
University of Birmingham

AND

A. DUNSIRE

Senior Lecturer in Politics, University of York

PUBLISHED FOR

THE ROYAL INSTITUTE OF PUBLIC ADMINISTRATION

LONDON · GEORGE ALLEN & UNWIN LTD

RUSKIN HOUSE   MUSEUM STREET

First published in 1971

© George Allen & Unwin Ltd 1971

ISBN 0 04 350027 7 cased
0 04 350028 5 paper

Printed in Great Britain
in 10 point Times Roman type
by Alden & Mowbray Ltd
Osney Mead, Oxford

CONTENTS

Contents

Part III. British Administrative Style in Perspective

PREFACE

This book originated in a desire to make accessible to British students a book of readings by British authors using British material, to supplement the books on public administration theory published in the United States and Canada, which naturally use illustrations relevant to these countries and so do not contain the material necessary for an appreciation of the distinctive characteristics of public administration in this country.

It has developed into an exploration of what these characteristics are; in particular, the description of the 'style' of administrative behaviour that has been thought peculiar to, or at least typical of, this country; and of the assumptions that have underlain British organization and practice in the field of public administration.

The present collection has a decided historical emphasis. We have no 'new' theory to peddle, and we have no interest in normative theory about how British public administration should be carried on. There is plenty of room for another book of readings applying organization theory and other modern conceptual frameworks to the understanding of the present administrative structure and working. In this book, we have not attempted either analysis or synthesis, but have simply gathered together a number of pieces of writing connected by their being descriptive of what it is to be distinctively British, in public administration. Many of these will be familiar; some of them will be well known by reference, but difficult to obtain; some, we think, are rescued from undeserved obscurity.

We have been encouraged by the interest shown in our proposal by the members of the Research Committee of the Royal Institute of Public Administration and wish to record our thanks for the particularly helpful comments and advice received from R. J. S. Baker, D. N. Chester, Nevil Johnson, Hedley Marshall and Peter Self. We are especially grateful to Raymond Nottage, the Director of the Institute, who was interested when we first advanced our ideas and who has prodded us to actually do the work; to Ivor Shelley, the Institute's Publications Officer who has seen the book through the press, and to Mrs Gael Heller who made the index and helped with the proofs.

9

PART I

THE STYLE OF
BRITISH ADMINISTRATION

Is there such a thing as a distinctive British administrative style? It seems impossible to deny, though different observers would, perhaps, see it differently. There is the ineffable urbanity of Whitehall establishment manners, which are said to make Americans even today feel colonial, and which to Middle Eastern minds suggest infinite duplicity. South Americans, Spaniards, and others, pay generous tribute to the British administrator's integrity and incorruptibility, to the sense of 'fair play' endemic in British public life. The French in 1945 greatly admired the competitive recruitment and promotion which, allied to internal transferability, produced an Administrative Class of all-round competence and high intelligence, the envy of the world – now so much criticized by so many in Britain itself. British local government is praised for its independence and 'democracy' – which to the British themselves implies not so much widespread popular participation in policy-making as the making of decisions on individual cases by elected representatives in committee. At the centre, too, collegiality in decision seems congenial to an extent ludicrous to a German. Benthamite rationality was and still is somewhat suspect, it seems; expert status may be ascribed, but never claimed, and has until now entailed political abdication; British officials always seek accommodations, never the 'one best way'. Of such observations, perhaps, is the profile of British administrative style composed.

This may be to pursue a will-o'-the-wisp, but it is the theme which links the readings selected for this first Part.

Consider that tiny fraction of the British Civil Service whose faults and virtues tend to characterize the Service as a whole, often unfairly: the Administrative Class. Two theoretical principles, among the earliest to be clearly stated as such,[1] run through a great deal of British thinking in the last hundred years: in the words of Walter Bagehot, that 'non-special minds' are necessary at the head of business, and that

> 'The summits (if I may so say) of the various kinds of business are, like the tops of mountains, much more alike than the parts below – the bare principles are much the same.'[2]

[1] Socrates talking to Nicomachides about the Assembly's choice of Antisthenes, a businessman, to be general in the army, Xenophon, *Memorabilia and Oeconomicus* (trans. E. C. Marchant, the Loeb Classical Library edition, Harvard University Press, pp. 186–7), quoted in Claude S. George jun., *The History of Management Thought*, Prentice Hall, 1968, pp. 15–17.

[2] W. Bagehot, *The English Constitution*, 1867 (Oxford University Press, 1928, p. 175).

Somewhat later, Bertrand Russell was sure that if a man had the 'definite type of ability, namely, that which is called executive or administrative, it makes little difference what the matter is that the organization handles . . .',[1] he will be able to transfer these skills from the Lancashire cotton trade to the air defences of London, or the transport of timber from British Columbia to England.

If further examples are necessary, they can be piled up from early volumes of *Public Administration*. These assumptions seem to be the underpinnings of the British Administrative Class, from 1920. The tradition, however, was not single: it divides in two ways. Among those who agree that the skills called executive or administrative are transferable, there are some who hold, and others who deny, that these skills are analysable and teachable to pupils abstractly, rather than to be acquired only by apprenticeship of practice under a master. Among those, again, who agree that such skills are transferable, there are those who hold, and others who deny, that the milieu, public business or private business, so conditions their exercise that their transfer, and the description of their principles likewise for those who hold this possible, is feasible only within each milieu separately and not in both indiscriminately.

Our first readings illustrate these various positions. Lyndall Urwick is undoubtedly the foremost British writer of the so-called 'scientific management' school, holding that there are isolable, teachable principles: he was early a follower of Henri Fayol who, taking Bagehot's view, urged men in high positions in all walks of life to set down what they judged to be the principles of their own success, for the guidance of the young. Besides his own major contributions to management literature, Urwick made it his business to bring to light a body of nineteenth-century British writing (by, for instance, Robert Owen and the inventor of the digital computer, Charles Babbage) which, if it had been known to and heeded by them, might have saved the American 'pioneers' of scientific management two or three decades of effort and some mistakes.[2]

From a large output we select from his best-known British publication, *The Elements of Administration*. British public administration writing of the middle nineteenth century is probably better illustrated from Sir Henry Taylor or Sir Arthur Helps: in a rather different vein, it derived from Machiavelli through Bacon – direct, realist advice from one practitioner to another with little intervention of

[1] Bertrand Russell, *Education and the Social Order*, 1932, p. 240.
[2] See L. Urwick and E. F. L. Brech, *The Making of Scientific Management*, Pitman, 1945, Vols. I and II.

framework or principles. We print a short passage from Helps, to convey the atmosphere.[1]

The British public service of the 1920s was not, however, either wholly ignorant of or insensitive to the absorption of scientific management theory into the 'new public administration' of Goodnow, White, Gulick and others in the United States. The Institute (now Royal) of Public Administration was founded in 1922, in just this spirit of progressivist hope and trust in the possibility of greater efficiency through rational study. From its journal we include an article by Sir Henry Bunbury of 1928, which has the authentic period flavour and yet makes a point about control and efficiency that is still worth making today.

At once one of the most brilliant results of, and most persuasive advocate of, the apprenticeship-only school was Sir Edward Bridges, Head of the Home Civil Service, later Lord Bridges. He once ended a lecture by saying that many of the things about administration which he had learnt and found of most value had come from watching how more experienced and wiser people handled the problem that came before them. Then came this striking metaphor:

'Thus I suppose that if I was going to learn to row, I might start by reading a book with diagrams which would show mathematically the precise angle behind the rigger at which the oar should be applied to the water in order to give the greatest leverage. I doubt if good oarsmen are made that way. Others think that these raucous noises which the coach shouts through the megaphone have more than psychological value. One gets much nearer the mark when one sees the coach get down into the boat and use his own arms and legs to show the young oarsman what he is doing wrong. But for my part I believe that many of the best oarsmen learned a great deal from the mere fact of rowing in a good crew behind a really good oarsman, for the good style and the good rhythm proved as catching as measles.'[2]

In a more recent comment on some radio discussions, Lord Bridges supported the position taken by Mr Enoch Powell, that the skills exercised by civil servants were not transferable from one milieu to the other:

'A civil servant transplanted temporarily into business could not,

[1] See also B. B. Schaffer, 'Sir Arthur Helps and the Art of Administration', *Public Administration*, 1960, Vol. XXXVIII, pp. 35–47.

[2] Sir Edward Bridges in A. Dunsire (ed.) *The Making of an Administrator*, Manchester University Press, 1956, p. 23.

without a considerable apprenticeship, take on the businessman's job: and the same is true the other way round.'[1]

Both of these views are foreshadowed in Lord Bridges' Rede Lecture of 1950, *Portrait of a Profession*, which we take pleasure in reprinting as the best single authentic source for 'The Civil Service Tradition', its sub-title – though, in our view, it represents only one of the civil service traditions.

For an extended treatment of the issue of transferability from milieu to milieu, whether of principles or of men, we have turned to Peter Self's inaugural lecture of 1965, which cautiously restates the majority British view against the single science of administration.

To deal with collegiality in British administration, the indispensable authority is K. C. Wheare, from whom we select a passage on the reasons for using committees, and the use of experts. What one might call the misuse of committees and of experts, or at least officers, was discussed at length in the Report of the Committee on Management of Local Government (the Maud Committee), 1967, attempting some valid distinction of function between representative member and permanent official. We choose, instead, however, a much older and more pungent discussion of the theme, that from the Minority Report of the Poor Law Commission of 1909. The relationship of policy to execution is dealt with directly by Sir Geoffrey Vickers, using a cybernetic approach, in the stimulating opening chapter of his *The Art of Judgment*, entitled 'The Regulation of Institutions'. Here we reprint instead, as more relevant to the present theme, Chapter 3 of the book, describing the reception of three recent committee reports as 'case studies in appreciation'.

Collegiality in administration extends, it seems to us, beyond the mere use of committees in this country. It is a characteristic of British administrative style to keep rank in the background, to wield authority unobtrusively, even at lower levels. Mary Parker Follett at the London School of Economics in 1933 gave a lecture entitled 'The Giving of Orders', which in our view preaches what, on the whole, British administrators (at least in the public service) practise. Social relations in British public administration are only beginning to be studied; from the very small stock, we choose a passage from one of the pioneers' study of the National Insurance Central Records Office at Newcastle.

R. J. S. Baker has written several articles on administrative practice in the British civil service which would be well worth collect-

---

[1] Lord Bridges in *Whitehall and Beyond*, BBC, 1964, p. 66.

ing together here, if space permitted.[1] We print only a short extract from one of them, which explains the 'air of informality and sometimes casualness which visitors to Government departments notice – whether with approval or disapproval'. The article may also be taken as evidence of the absorption by some civil servants at least of new ways of saying things, new languages which can give new insights.

Style, as seen perhaps in its adjective 'stylish', is probably not the fixed and permanent attribute we have treated it as, so far. The word is best used in the same way as the word 'personality' is used: to indicate the overall impression created by a great number of individual habitual acts and facets of behaviour, each of which has its own rationale and critique, and each of which is a response to its own set of conditions and demands. As conditions and demands change, so responses change – and so, sooner or later, does style. It was Fulton's main charge against the British civil service, as it was Maud's main charge against local councillors, that conditions and demands have changed more rapidly than they have adapted their responses.

But adaptation was taking place; Fulton, perhaps, got credit for what some far-sighted Treasury men (such do exist) were already doing and proposing. Perhaps the most overt single sign of this is the increased employment of economists in government departments, and the permeation of their way of thinking into the work of 'non-specialist minds'. But the annual report of the Civil Service Department[2] will supply many more.

Change in style, it may be agreed, is on the way. But it may be better to recognize that there have been always two styles, two traditions, in the British civil service: a Benthamite and Taylorite (F. W., not Sir Henry) tradition, as well as a Macaulayite and Bridges tradition. As evidence, we may point to the renown of British O & M, and to Sir Henry Bunbury and Sir Frank Tribe, whose 1949 paper on 'Efficiency in the Public Services' we reprint. It is surely not different in spirit, or even style, from the Feldstein article on cost-benefit analysis with which we conclude.

[1] See R. J. S. Baker, 'Discussion and Decision-Making in the Civil Service', *Public Administration*, 1963, Vol. XLI, pp. 345–56 and 'The Art of Delegation', *Public Administration*, Vol. XLIII, pp. 155–73.
[2] London, HMSO, 1970.

1

The Nature of Administration[*]

L. URWICK

In 1942 Lyndall Urwick, a British pioneer of the scientific management movement, gave five lectures in London; his subject was the principles of administration; with minor changes the text of his lectures was published in 1943 as the book The Elements of Administration. *His main concern was what he called the technical skill of administration: 'prolonged experience of a particular kind of group is of substantially less importance as a qualification than ability to administer* per se', *and he explained the importance of the necessary personal and intellectual equipment for an administrator – equipment which included 'a mind well versed in the underlying sciences on which the art of administration rests and thoroughly instructed in the principles and methods of the art itself'. In this extract the general British approach to administrative studies is epitomized in Urwick's general survey of relevant literature and his own approach to the subject.*

THEORY AND PRACTICE

A modern historian wrote of this country in the middle of the last century that

> 'A happy inability to apprehend general ideas appeared to stand between the people of England and their disturbing impact. At their approach the public mind almost invariably ceased to function, or conscious of its limitations, turned eagerly in other directions. In Great Britain the pursuit of theory was left to professed theorists, while an obstinately practical community eschewed the primrose path of general ideas and confined itself austerely to the solution of practical problems.'[1]

This temper is still common among British Administrators of all

[*] From L. Urwick, *The Elements of Administration*, London, Pitman, 1943, pp. 13–19. Reprinted with permission of the publisher.
[1] Philip Guedalla, *The Hundred Years*, pp. 64, 65.

types, whether in business or in other walks of life. Indeed it has recently been claimed as a virtue for the group of higher civil servants who administer our great public departments that their way of looking at things corresponds with that of 'the mass of English professional men'. They have 'much the same working creed in practical affairs, the same ethical standards, political beliefs and working habits'. This official norm has been described as 'stoical realism'.[1]

To discuss Administration in terms of principle is therefore an undertaking of some temerity. It must inevitably encounter the impatience of so-called 'practical men' with theory, with ideas. At the same time he would be a bold man who would venture to claim that the country is satisfied with the organization and administration of its war-time activities, that the best possible use is being made of its productive resources, of the skill of its scientists, and of the enthusiasm and energy of men and women of all classes. On the contrary there is a widespread sense of frustration, abundant evidence of waste and countless instances of muddle and misunderstanding.

There is no quick or easy cure for these difficulties. Patching and improvisation are likely to make the confusion worse confounded. Nor are complacency and self-justification on the part of those in responsible positions, or criticism by those who are not, likely to prove helpful. There is one way and one way only out of a condition of administrative indisposition, a clear determination by all concerned, whether in office or out of it, that administrative practice shall be improved. And such improvement must start with theory, with ideas – clearer thinking by everyone as to the nature of administration and as to the methods by which sound principles can be applied to actual situations.

In other words, lack of administrative skill can only be cured by persuading administrators to become more skilful. And the root of any real progress in this direction must necessarily lie in ideas, in theory – better ideas about how to administer. It cannot start with full-fledged plans and schemes, all complete with model rulings and a photograph of the latest machine. It is not in the nature of administrative skill to germinate in this way.

The ability to administer other people is a skill, an art. It is not just something a man is born with or born without – it is not just a body of knowledge. An individual may have natural disabilities for this particular profession. . . . He may be a successful practical administrator with very little learning in the latest theory of the

[1] H. E. Dale, *The Higher Civil Service*.

20

subject, like the good general practitioner who has forgotten all that the medical schools ever taught him, but in the interval has read deeply in the book of life and death – sufficiently deeply to know how little he can know, which is a great safeguard for his patients. But he will be a better administrator, as a doctor will be a better doctor, if he manages to keep abreast of the latest thought on the subject. Broadly speaking, and for the common run of men and women, administrative skill is very comparable with medical skill. It is a practical art, and practice is essential to make it perfect – much practice. But practice wholly divorced from study is as likely to be limited in its results as study undisciplined by practice is likely to prove sterile and misleading. Francis Bacon put the point a good many decades ago:

'To spend too much time in studies is Sloth; to use them too much for Ornament is Affectation; to make Judgement wholly by their rules is the Humour of a Scholler. They perfect Nature and are perfected by Experience: for Naturall Abilities are like Naturall Plants, they need Proyning by Study. And Studies themselves doe give forth Directions too much at large unless they be bounded in by experience.'[1]

Or to quote a more recent writer, himself a medical man of great wisdom, the fruits of a long and successful career:

'The man of affairs without science is like the physician who has fallen out of the anatomy and physiology he may once have known; within limits he may be a shrewder and abler practitioner than an academic professor; but this he will be at the cost of being stationary. . . . To principles, sooner or later, the subtlest craftsman has to bow his head; for, even while his hand is on his tools, by theory contingencies and complications are being detected and eliminated, and processes shortened and economized.'[2]

THE DANGER OF THE EASY REMEDY

But whether in medicine or administration it is dangerous to rely on 'potted' knowledge. There is more to surgery than the study of a few designs in a textbook of anatomy. To be able to recite a list of symptoms is not diagnosis. All the same, despite these obvious truths, most human beings share a weakness in favour of the quick answer,

[1] *Essays.*
[2] T. E. Allbutt, *On Professional Education.*

the specific, easy remedy which doesn't require the painful discipline of thought as their contribution to the process.

More than one employer has been sold a punched card installation under the impression that by writing a cheque for a few thousand pounds he could 'buy' efficiency. After all, the sorting machine worked so fast and was so systematic, it must of itself overcome the muddle in the office. Administrative skill cannot be bought. There are no hints and tips and short cuts. It has to be paid for in the only currency which is sound in this market – hard study and harder thinking, mastery of intellectual principles reinforced by genuine reflection on actual problems, for which the individual has real responsibility. All books can do is to help towards a first understanding of some of the principles.

FAYOL'S ANALYSIS OF ADMINISTRATION

Henri Fayol was a famous French industrialist. For thirty years he was Managing Director of one of the largest coal and iron combines in the country. When he took it over it was on the verge of bankruptcy. When he retired it was brilliantly successful, with an exceptionally strong balance sheet. Towards the end of his life he tried to reduce to a logical form the principles on which his success as an administrator had been built up. He always insisted that that success had nothing difficult or unusual about it: it followed simply and logically from strict adherence to principle. His *General and Industrial Administration* has probably had more influence on ideas of business management in Europe, and especially in the Latin countries, than any other work. In this country it is less well known, though an English translation is available.

He analysed the operations which occur in business into six main groups – technical, commercial, financial, security, accounting and administrative operations. Thus he regarded Administration merely as one of a group of major functions. 'Administration, regarded in this way,' he wrote, 'must not be confused with government. To govern is to conduct an undertaking towards its objective by seeking to make the best possible use of all the resources at its disposal; it is, in fact, to ensure the smooth working of the six essential functions. Administration is only one of these functions, but the managers of big concerns spend so much of their time on it, that their jobs seem to consist solely of administration.'[1]

He broke down this key function of Administration into five main

[1] *Administration Industrielle et Générale*, p. 59. English edition, p. 35.

aspects – to plan, to organize, to command, to co-ordinate, and to control. But the word he used, *prévoyance*, which has been translated 'to plan', really covers two functions. '*Prévoir* [literally 'to foresee'] as used here means both to foretell the future and to prepare for it.' In other words, the one term meant both forecasting and planning.

These six aspects of administration fall into two main groups related as to process and effect. That is to say:

> *Forecasting* leads to a *Plan*.
> *Organization* has as its object *Co-ordination*, while
> *Command* issues in *Control*.

Now, the most distinguished American authors who have written on the theory of organization, Mr J. D. Mooney, late President of the General Motors Export Corporation, and Mr A. C. Reiley, adopted a logical scheme from a German author, Louis F. Anderson. This postulated:

> First, that every principle has its process and effect, and
> Second, that if these have been correctly identified, the process and effect will, in their turn, be found to have, each of them, a principle, process and effect.

thus completing a logical square of nine items.[1]

Fayol's analysis was simply concerned with aspects of Administration, with operations. But elsewhere he lists, somewhat empirically, sixteen Administrative Duties and fourteen Principles, some of which overlap. The second of his Administrative Duties provides a very sound principle on which to base forecasting, *viz.*, *Appropriateness* – 'see that the human and material organization are suitable.' His Fourteenth Administrative Duty, which is also his Twelfth Principle, equally provides a principle on which to base planning, *viz. Order* – 'ensure material and human order'.

RESEARCH: THE UNDERLYING PRINCIPLE

Thus the logical square is completed with the exception of the principle underlying the whole process of Administration. And here it is not unduly straining probability to imagine that Fayol himself would have inserted *Investigation*. Certainly to students of scientific management, the idea of research into facts as the basis of all activity

---

[1] See *Onward Industry* (Harper and Bros., New York and London, 1931), quoting Louis F. Anderson, *Das Logische, seine Gesetze und Kategorien*, Felix Meiner, Leipzig, 1929.

is fundamental. And every writer of note on the subject is at one on the point. For instance, Mary Parker Follett, in the last lecture which she delivered in public before her death, wrote:

'I have given four principles of organization. The underpinning of these is information based on Research.'[1]

F. W. Taylor, when he first attempted to reduce his practice to generalizations, put first of 'the new duties' devolving on management:

'They develop a science for each element of a man's work which replaces the old rule of thumb method.'[2]

And later:

'Both sides must recognize as essential the substitution of exact scientific investigation and knowledge for the old individual judgement or opinion'.[3]

These three principles, each with its corresponding process and effect, make up the perfect logical square summarizing the main aspects of Administration. The underlying principle on which the whole art rests is *Investigation*. It enters into process with *Forecasting* and the effect is a Plan or *Planning*. Forecasting has its own principle, namely, *Appropriateness*. It enters into process with *Organization*, since the first thing you do when you look ahead is to try to provide the means, human and material, to meet the future situation which you foresee. Its effect is *Co-ordination*. Finally, *Planning* finds its principle in *Order*, enters into process with *Command*, and the effect is *Control*.

This arrangement of the material is shown in tabular form in Figure I.

[1] 'Individualism in a Planned Society' in *Dynamic Administration*, edited by H. C. Metcalf and L. Urwick, Sir Isaac Pitman & Sons, Ltd., London.

[2] *Principles of Scientific Management*.

[3] Hearings before Special Committee of the House of Representatives to investigate the Taylor and other systems of Shop Management 1912, V. iii. F. W. Taylor's evidence.

FIGURE I

THE PRINCIPLES OF ADMINISTRATION

('Administration must not be confused with government. To govern is to conduct an undertaking towards its objective by seeking to make the best possible use of all the resources at its disposal; it is, in fact, to ensure the smooth working of the six essential functions. Administration is only one of these functions.') The general objective and broad policy of any undertaking are therefore 'given' before administration starts.

1. PRINCIPLE	2. PROCESS	3. EFFECT
1. INVESTIGATION	**FORECASTING**	**PLANNING**
All scientific procedure is based on investigation of the facts, which thus becomes the first principle of administration.	Investigation enters into process with forecasting.	And takes effect in a plan.

FORECASTING

must be in terms which correspond with the realities of the situation, i.e. with the general objective and broad policy of the undertaking ('See that the plan of operations is carefully prepared'—A.D.1). It therefore finds its underlying principle in

2. APPROPRIATENESS	**ORGANIZATION**	**CO-ORDINATION**
('See that the human and material organization are suitable for the objects of the undertaking'—A.D. 2).	Forecasting enters into process with the provision of a suitable organization.	And takes effect in co-ordination.

PLANNING

The purpose of planning is to secure systematic action in accordance with the general objective and broad policy of the undertaking ('See that the plan of operations is strictly carried out'—A.D.1). It therefore finds its underlying principle in

3. ORDER	**COMMAND**	**CONTROL**
('Ensure material and human order'—A.D.14 and P.10).	Planning enters into process with command ('Establish a management which is competent and has unity of purpose'—A.D.3).	And takes effect in control ('Subject everything to control'—A.D.15).

NOTES

(*a*) Quotations in brackets are from Henri Fayol's *General and Industrial Administration*. References are to his lists of Administrative Duties (A.D.) and Principles (P.).

(*b*) Fayol does not give the principles of Investigation, Appropriateness and Order. His analysis deals only with actions. But as will be seen they are implied in his list of Administrative Duties.

2

Thoughts upon Government*

SIR ARTHUR HELPS

*One of the traditional debating exercises for students of public adminis-
tration centres on whether administration is a science or an art. In this
connection the Machiavellian writings of Sir Henry Taylor, especially
in his satirical book* The Statesman *(first published in 1836), have been
widely read; but he was not the only English civil servant who in the mid-
nineteenth century was turning his mind from forms of government to
the business of governing. In this extract Sir Arthur Helps, Clerk to the
Privy Council from 1860 to 1875, offers advice on the art of administration, and, with his comments on proverbs makes one wonder whether he
had reached a stage in administrative thought that other scholars did not
appreciate until nearly a century later (see, for example, Herbert A.
Simon, 'The Proverbs of Administration', Public Administration
Review, Vol. 6, 1946, pp. 53–67 and Administrative Behaviour,
Macmillan, New York, 1945).*

There is very little to be said on this great subject, which is not essentially of a commonplace character. In fact, it might also be written
by stringing together a series of proverbs. Men have not been for
many thousand years upon the earth, without finding out their own
faults, or rather those of other people, in the common affairs of life,
and expressing their sense of these faults in pregnant sentences,
which have met with universal acceptation. The worst, however, of
proverbs is that, when you have a proverb embodying one phase of
thought, you generally want an exactly opposite proverb to correct it.

In considering this subject, it will be well to take a particular
instance, and endeavour to work it out thoroughly. Let us suppose
a case of considerable magnitude; not of a legal character, but into
which law enters, as it does into most human affairs; which involves
questions of general policy, and of administration. This case is
submitted to a Minister by his immediate subordinate.

* From Arthur Helps, *Thoughts upon Government*, London, Bell & Daldy,
1872, pp. 198–211. Reprinted with permission of G. Bell & Sons Ltd.

The first thing for the Minister to do, is to begin at the beginning. This of course appears a self-evident remark, but it is an essential one. It will not do for him to be satisfied in taking up any great affair at a certain stage of the proceedings, upon the assumption that he has a perfect account from his subordinate of all that has happened up to that time. He will almost always have his reward in beginning at the beginning, and keeping carefully to dates, which are the backbone, as it were, of every long series of transactions.

The need for this somewhat laborious mode of procedure may be aptly illustrated by what often happens in reading history. I strongly suspect, that when conclusions from history are falsely drawn, it generally results from the enquirer neglecting his dates; and having present to his mind numbers of facts, which were not present to the minds of those who were enacting considerable parts in history. The student, for example, is aware of what was the ultimate result in history, of some long conflict of contending principles brought into action; he knows that Protestantism ultimately prevailed in this country; and does not reflect, that to the promoters of that great work, that final result was anything but self-evident. In few words, he has not the right set of facts before him, at the right dates.

Exactly a similar thing occurs in minor matters – in the current business of daily life; and therefore it is needful, not only to begin at the beginning; but at each stage of the case, to consider what was then the exact state of facts, including also the arguments that had then been brought forward on all sides.

A practice, that should be universally adopted in matters of business is not to accept a reference, or even quotation, without verification. In this heavy case, which I have imagined to be brought before a Minister, reference will perhaps be made to Acts of Parliament, Orders in Council, letters of a former Minister, and other documents. Not only the exact words, but the context, must be looked to in all these references. It is not that men mean to deceive, but that they are terribly prone to inaccuracy, and that inaccuracy is likely to be greatly increased, perhaps unconsciously, by their own prejudices and desires.

There then enters the question of the aid, and direction that are to be gained by precedent. The aid that precedent affords is not to be despised, especially as all mankind are apt to have a great respect for it; but, at the same time, it is a power to which no man, who has any faith in himself, will permit himself to be made a slave.

In the conduct of this case, and in the conclusions which the Minister will have to arrive at, from time to time (for I imagine it to be a case of largeness and continuity), he will probably not act without the advice and suggestions of others, especially his subordinates. It becomes, therefore, a matter of great importance for him to understand the general bent of the characters of those persons, whom he must take into council. Every man has some such bent; and he is seldom, if ever, free from the inclinations of thought which that bent of character determines. One man is nearly sure to take a harsh, or at any rate a severe view, both of persons and of conduct. Being also an accurate and painstaking man himself, he is apt to conclude that other men (the men, for instance, involved in this case) are as accurate and painstaking as he is, and will attribute to other motives, those statements of theirs which merely arise from the ordinary inaccuracy of mankind. There is, of course, the character of an exactly opposite tendency. And indeed, without going further into this matter, it may be laid down as a maxim for the Minister's consideration, that whatever he receives in the way of suggestion or comment, whether from a colleague or a subordinate, is always to be fined down, as it were, by keeping in mind the peculiar character of the man by whom it is made. Moreover, he can thus arrive at the appreciation of an average of thought, and feeling by balancing the views of men of opposite character. With very few men is the dry light of the intellect the only light which they look up to.

Doubtless, too, the Minister – or deciding person – has to beware of indulging too much the bent of his own character; but here a considerable subtlety of observation should enter. Every man should be aware, that he will, ultimately, act in accordance with the bent of his character; and therefore that it is useless for him to assume, by fits and starts, another form of character which does not belong to him. He may resolve to act in direct oppugnancy to what he knows to be the natural inclination of his mind, but if he does so, he must do it handsomely and consistently, and must not play two different parts, in the course of the same transaction.

Then, in any important case, of the kind I am supposing, which is to involve administration, there are certain general considerations, as regards the conduct of mankind, which should ever be present to the mind of the man who has to take action in the case. To enumerate these considerations would be a lengthy and laborious task: it will suffice to point out two of the most serious.

In the first place; the administrator can hardly ever make too much allowance for the indolence of mankind. Where his administration will fail, is in people omitting to do, from indolence, that which he supposes he has given them sufficient means and instructions for

28

doing. Hence, in all matters of administration, continuous supervision and inspection are most needful, and as in also great preciseness of instruction.

In the next place, he must calculate upon a large amount of disobedience, resulting, not from wilfulness, but from misunderstanding, or from the subordinate 'thinking', as he is pleased to call it, for himself, when he has received precise directions from his superior. There is one memorable instance of this kind, which happened to the late Duke of Wellington. It was in the retreat from Burgos.

'Knowing the direct road was impassable, he ordered the movement by another road, longer and apparently more difficult; this seemed so extraordinary to some general officers, that, after consulting together, they deemed their commander unfit to conduct the army, and led their troops by what appeared to them the fittest line of retreat! He had before daylight placed himself at an important point on his own road, and waited impatiently for the arrival of the leading division until dawn; then suspecting what had happened he galloped to the other road and found the would-be commanders stopped by water. The insubordination and the danger to the army were alike glaring, yet the practical rebuke was so severe and well-timed, the humiliation so complete and so deeply felt, that with one proud sarcastic observation, indicating contempt more than anger, he led back the troops, and drew off all his forces safely.'[1]

I now come to that which is perhaps, after all, the most important point in dealing with this considerable case, which I have imagined as laid before a Minister. It especially relates to expression, and will illustrate what I had in my thoughts, when I suggested that expression should be made one of the main objects of the education of a statesman. The particular form of expression, which is now wanted by my imaginary Minister, is concerned with limitation. He will generally find, that when he goes wrong in the expression of his views, or his decisions, it is because the form of expression used has been needlessly wide – in matters, too, where a single extraneous word may pledge him to actions, which he has no intention of undertaking. That the words should exactly clothe the subject-matter dealt with, is one of the greatest aids and safeguards in the conduct of all business, whether it appertains to the high art of statesmanship, or to the work-a-day business of the world.

Another point to be carefully watched in the conduct of business

[1] Napier: *Peninsular War*, iv. 386.

is, not to confuse rules with principles, and especially, that no man should needlessly lay down rules which may hamper himself. His principles may be ever so strict: the rules he lays down should be very elastic, and certainly he should not be prone to communicate to others, needlessly, those rules which he may have instituted as guides to himself. Hence, in making communications upon the subject of the business alluded to, it is seldom wise to say, 'We never do this, or that, or the other – it is contrary to our rules, or our practice.' Perhaps, in a few weeks or months, there may come a case in which it is necessary to violate the rule, or depart from the practice; and then there is an appearance of lamentable inconsistency. The circumstances and conditions of life in any community, where high civilization prevails, are so numerous, various, and difficult to be imagined, even by men of fertile imaginations, that no prudent man shuts himself up in rules made by himself, like a silkworm winding itself up in its own cocoon.

Then there is the general correspondence about the matter to be considered. Herein there must be much continuity of aim and purpose, and, therefore, clearness of expression. If we could trace up some of the greatest errors to their source, we should probably find, that many a decision which has failed to decide, and has, indeed, failed to convey its exact meaning in any way, has been thus made inefficient by its language, in some of the principal sentences, being thorough patchwork: designed by one man; corrected by another; revised by a third, while some little point, merely of diction, has at the last been interlineated by a fourth. The final drawing of any important document should be one man's work, embodying the various corrections made by other men's minds, but having that unity and force which can only be the outcome of a single mind.

Another important point in the transaction of business, and especially in such a case as I have been considering, is to divide the subject-matter into several sections. One of the chief arts in mastering any subject consists in subdivision. It is an art which presupposes the existence of method. In a previous chapter on education, I was able to make only a few suggestions as to how this supreme effort of division and classification, called method, could be taught. It is a thing, however, of inestimable value, and must, somehow or other, be acquired by any man who has to deal promptly with business of much pressure and magnitude. Referring to the case in question, there may be scores of arguments applying to different sections of the case. If these arguments are left as separate forces, as it were, and are not brought, as a mathematician would say, to 'resultants' in their respective sections, the man who has to decide, wanders about in a jungle of unsettled thought, and is perpetually taking up his facts and arguments at wrong times, in the course of forming his determination. Whereas, if the various facts and arguments had been brought to their conclusions in their respective sections, the Minister's labour, in coming to a determination upon the whole subject, would have been almost indefinitely facilitated.

This supposed case has now been considered in much detail; and it has been shown that there are many ways by which the labour of dealing with it may be lightened, while the issue is rendered more felicitous and conclusive. The same methods which are applied to great matters of statesmanship are, no doubt, applicable to all kinds of business.

I shall conclude this chapter with a remark, which also applies to all kinds of business – indeed to almost all forms of human endeavour. It is that the *indirect* results of any course of action are nearly always the most important. Hence it is, that what we call wordly wisdom is so difficult to attain; for hardly any man is sagacious enough, or has that breadth of knowledge, which would enable him to see all the indirect consequences of any course of action he decides upon; although he may perceive very clearly the direct result of that course.

For example, he discerns an evil; he resolves to provide a remedy; but the mode by which he does so is, perhaps, one which indirectly shall be fraught with good or evil consequences, far exceeding in magnitude those direct results that he distinctly foresees, and is resolved to accomplish.

We may turn to natural science for an illustration. There are rays of heat and of actinism, which are not revealed by the spectrum, but which play a vital part in the operations of nature. The statesman who does not take note of the probable consequences of his actions, other than those which are their direct result, resembles the philosopher who should treat the visible light-rays as though they were not accompanied by other rays, for the effects of which he must not fail to make wide allowance, and far-seeing calculation.

3

Efficiency as an Alternative to Control*

SIR HENRY BUNBURY

When, in Administrative Behaviour, *H. A. Simon discussed what he called the review process in administration, he emphasized that there are at least four different functions that a review process may perform: 'diagnosis of the quality of decisions being made by subordinates, modifications through influence on subsequent decisions, the correction of incorrect decisions that have already been made, and enforcement of sanctions against subordinates so that they will accept authority in making their decisions'. He drew attention to the similar, but not identical analysis of the function of review in Sir Henry Bunbury's article 'Efficiency as an Alternative to Control'. That article by Bunbury is reprinted here as an example of the concern for theory in the study of public administration which characterized the early years of the Institute of Public Administration and was reflected in the early volumes of its journal,* Public Administration.

It will be as well to begin by trying to explain what this paper is about.

We have as administrators an inherited and traditional belief in the merits of control. If at times the natural man in us rebels against being controlled by higher authority, his protests become faint and ineffective under the satisfaction of controlling somebody else. The general public is of the same mind. When public expenditure is higher than the public likes, the demand goes up for more control – by Parliament, by Ministers of the Crown, by the Treasury, by any one else who, if armed with an axe, is believed to be capable of wielding, or at any rate of brandishing the weapon. If some essential public service, supplied by private enterprise, is rendered less well or less cheaply than the public demands, the natural solution, in the public mind, is to bring its operations under some form of public control.

The history of the great period of financial reform in this country,

* From Sir Henry Bunbury, 'Efficiency as an Alternative to Control', *Public Administration*, 1928, Vol. VI, pp. 96–105. Reprinted with permission of the editor of *Public Administration* and the Executors of the Estate of Sir Henry Bunbury.

from 1832 to 1866, is the history of the steady construction of a system of effective financial control in place of the disordered and ineffective formalities which had hitherto passed for a financial system.

Now far be it from me to suggest that the principle of control or any particular methods of control are wrong. To an important degree administration *is* control, and if administration is necessary, control there must be. The object of this paper is rather to place in contrast with the idea of control another idea which has of late begun to assert its claims with unusual vigour: to set the two conceptions side by side, and to consider whether there may not be spheres of administrative activity in which the one becomes a rival of the other, and in that sense an alternative. 'The best,' said Plato, 'is enemy of the good.'

That idea is the idea of efficiency. And here again let me guard at once against a possible misunderstanding. It would be absurd to suggest that the introduction or strengthening of control has not in the past been accompanied by an increase of efficiency; or that there is something incompatible between systems of control and efficiency of operation. In so far as the orderly conduct of public affairs is more efficient than the disorderly conduct of those affairs, to that extent the two are at any rate compatible with each other. But there are in the world of administration regions in which orderliness can be bought at too high a price and is not a primary desideratum. These are the regions in which we want, above everything else, enterprise, invention, foresight, far-seeing judgment, a high standard of personal efficiency of performance; and these things an excess of control tends rather to impair than to create. It is in these regions that the idea of control and the idea of efficiency become opposed to each other and in which we may find ourselves regarding them as alternatives in their practical application to particular cases. In actual practice the strengthening of control, and the promotion of efficiency, do present themselves, more often than we might at first sight suppose, as alternatives, between which a choice has to be made.

The modern study of industrial efficiency as an art in itself began in America towards the end of the nineteenth century, though its origin even in that youthful country can be traced back at least to Benjamin Franklin. In the generation which has elapsed since F. W. Taylor began to write, the movement which he originated has passed through many phases. Inspired by engineers, it thought at first of man as a machine and tended to forget that he was a human being. It has made mistakes; sometimes it seemed to have lost its way. It

B   33

has suffered much from charlatans. But all the time it has been learning by its mistakes, enlarging its scope, revising and correcting its methods, until it has become the accepted method of approach to the problems involved in the organization of human effort, and embodies a store of accepted doctrine in relation to those problems. I am confident that posterity, looking back on what has happened in this sphere in the last thirty years, will regard the scientific management movement as a revolution comparable with the industrial revolution of the nineteenth century.

Now the basic idea underlying the scientific management movement is the engineering conception of efficiency. And it is this conception which, for the purpose of illuminating the subject in its application to public administration, I wish to set in contrast with the idea of control which, as I have said, is a leading element in the traditional stock-in-trade of administrative theory. This brings us, however, to the question whether the principles of scientific management are applicable in any material degree to public administration in general; and if so, how far. It is of interest to learn that the Americans have already applied their minds to this question, and that a considerable literature about it is going up. It can, at any rate, be said with some confidence that scientific management has already shown that it can contribute something as regards administration; and one of the objects of this paper is to explore the potential scope and extent of that contribution.

One more reference to America before we get down to our subject. The United States is the home *par excellence* of independent elective administrative authorities. They grow by the thousand. The departments of the Federal Government, the State Governments, and the County and Municipal authorities are far less closely knit together either internally or in their relations with each other than are the corresponding administrative authorities of any important European country. Consequently in current American political thought an acute controversy is proceeding between the advocates of the principle which they call 'integration' and those of the principle which they call 'disintegration'. 'Integration' means the principle of the administrative hierarchy in which various administrative units are subordinated to a common administrative control; 'disintegration' means a system under which each administrative unit operates independently, subject only to its responsibility to the electorate. A Medical Officer of Health responsible to his council would be an example of integration; a Medical Officer of Health directly elected for a period of five years and answerable only to the electorate at the end of that period is an example of disintegration. Now the advocates of disintegration in America base their arguments on the principles and traditions of American political thought and practice, to which anything hierarchical is an abomination. But they are compelled to go further and to attempt to show that a higher degree of efficiency can be attained by a disintegrated system than in a more closely knit and hierarchical organization of authorities. It is this dispute which lends a peculiar reality and liveliness to American discussions of the subject. In that country administration seems to be still almost wholly in the constructive and experimental stage. Advocates of integration have to show that the strengthening of control will not paralyse initiative and enterprise; advocates of leaving things as they are have to devise some means by which the evils of political graft, lack of experience, and want of co-ordination, can be eliminated, while a direct responsibility to the public is preserved. Thus the study of efficiency in administration is beginning to take the place which was previously occupied by the study of constitutional principles in administration. The efficiency engineer has become a formidable rival to the political philosopher.

Control may be the control of one organization over another or the control of one individual by another; but whichever it is it consists essentially in giving or refusing permission to do something which the controlled body or person proposes to do. Control tends to pass into direction, and in so far as it does so it becomes constructive and not merely restrictive or regulatory.

We must next distinguish between the various objects of control. It may be:

        (1) Protective.
        (2) Co-ordinative.
        (3) Directive.

Protective control is created in order to protect particular interests, and the controlling body may represent those interests, as in the case of the Treasury, which represents the interests of the taxpayer as such; or it may be a disinterested and quasi-judicial body such as the Railway Rates Tribunal, whose function is to hold the balance between the interests of railway undertakings and those of the railway user. Protective control is of course always external to the administrative unit upon which it operates.

Co-ordinative control is created with the object of securing consistency of administrative action. Such consistency up to a point is a prime necessity of administration; but it may be that even in these

35

days it is rated a little too highly and that the price paid for it is too heavy. We shall come back to this point later.

Directive control is set up as a means of securing good organization, efficient performance, and right decisions. It is with this form of control that we shall chiefly be concerned.

Let me now try to put the subject in a more elementary and concrete way. Business men are fond of saying that they have no use for elaborate organizations, but go on the principle of giving a man his job, leaving him alone and judging him by results. In the public services, which in the main operate on a much larger scale than most businesses, we cannot proceed on that simple plan any more than an army could operate without a cadre of commissioned and non-commissioned officers. There must be co-ordinated action. This, however, raises the question whether, when once the co-ordinating organization is set up, there is not a tendency to use it for other and less desirable purposes. If my subordinate Mr Smith is doing his work very well and my subordinate Mr Jones making a rather poor job of it, is it the true remedy to set some one of superior wisdom and ability to supervise the work both of Mr Smith and Mr Jones? That is how directive control is apt to come about. Now let us examine the consequences. In the first place it becomes possible to pay both Mr Smith and Mr Jones a smaller remuneration than they could reasonably claim if their responsibilities were greater. On the other hand, it does not follow that the saving on the salaries of Mr Smith and Mr Jones is equal to the cost of the official who is put there to supervise them. In the second place Mr Smith will probably take less interest in his work than he would if he were acting under a fuller responsibility. On the other hand, Mr Jones's errors and omissions will be avoided; but they will be avoided, not by Mr Jones, but by the added labour of the supervising officer who controls him.

Now in a crude example like this, we should say without hesitation that *prima facie* the institution of control does not make for efficient performance, and that a study of the problem from the point of view of efficiency might lead to somewhat different arrangements. Let me quote a statement on this subject, written a good many years ago, which appears to me admirably to express the essentials of the matter:

'In the past too great stress has been laid on executive control and too little upon inspection and advice as a means of securing efficiency. The tendency has been to measure the powers to be entrusted to a class of officers by the capacity of the less capable and experienced members of the class, and to require that all matters falling outside these limits should be referred for decision to a higher authority.... This method has led to undesirable results. The powers to be delegated should be measured by the capacities which may reasonably be expected of the class in question. If in any particular case the powers are not exercised rightly, the failure would be observed by the inspecting officer and endeavour should be made to train the officer at fault by advice and instruction. If this fails, the remedy should be the removal of the individual officer and not the transfer of the work to a higher authority.'

What is true of the individual is equally true of the organization. Control is in itself a costly thing. Not only is there the cost of the controlling authority, but it also increases the cost of the controlled authority. (Mr Hartley Withers estimated some years ago that the aggregate expenditure by the British Railways Companies up to 1910 on the promotion of or opposition to Private Bill Legislation affecting their business was of the order of £90,000,000.) We do well to ask ourselves from time to time as administrators whether the public is not paying too much for the advantages which it gets, or expects but often fails to get, from control. That is why I want in this paper to turn the light, as it were upon the ideal, of which scientific management is the exponent, of eliminating waste of human effort.

But if the waste of controlling effort is in any case and in any degree to be eliminated, what is to be put in its place? For a complex modern industrial community cannot conduct its affairs on principles suitable to the nomad tribes of Tartary. This brings me to the second branch of the subject. Is it possible to reduce the necessity for control by the method of developing primary efficiency?

Let me begin by furnishing a concrete example. In 1868 the Treasury laid down that their sanction should be required for any increase in the establishment of a public department. Since that date the Post Office and the Treasury have gradually developed a system under which active Treasury control of the great manipulative establishments of the Post Office has been almost wholly dispensed with. It was bound in any case to be almost a pure formality; for the amount of staff required by the Post Office varies with the amount of traffic necessary to be handled, and that is a matter entirely in the hands of the public. The system consists in effect of a scheme for measuring efficiency; and the relaxation of control is based on the principle that the Post Office is free to add to its staff, provided that the increase of staff does not exceed the increase of traffic; that is to say, provided that efficiency is at least maintained. The subject-matter is complex and difficult; for traffic conditions vary within very wide limits as between office and office; the work itself is varied in character, and no single and readily ascertainable unit is available. Much depends, for example, on the point whether at any particular office the preparation of night mail despatches is successive or whether one overlaps another. In spite, however, of these complexities the system has in the course of years been steadily improved. It is still far from perfect; but it is not too much to hope that in the course of time it may give not only a measure of the movement upwards or downwards of staff in relation to work, but also an absolute measure of the efficiency of the system as a whole and of particular offices.

This is merely one example out of many that could be adduced, chosen because it very well illustrates the point that methods of measuring efficiency can be used to reduce or modify an external control. There is still the further question how far along these lines the delegation of authority or relaxation of control, whichever you like to call it, can be carried. If then we set out on a voyage of investigation with efficiency of performance, in the engineering sense, as our objective, we shall find ourselves confronted with the questions:

(a) How far in administrative work is it possible to measure efficiency?
(b) How should the measurements be used?
(c) How should inefficiency – *i.e.* performance of function below a reasonable standard – be dealt with?
(d) What are the best means of promoting efficiency?

And when these questions have been answered we shall be better equipped to confront the problem which gives the title to this paper – under what conditions can, and should, a high, or higher, degree of efficiency, in the sense I have indicated, be accompanied by a low, or lower, degree of control. Let us consider these questions further.

No one who is familiar with the development of administrative practice in the last twenty or thirty years would deny that there has been a considerable and steady extension in the public services of the practice of measuring efficiency by objective standards, and that the process has been accelerated since the war. Less is left to be decided by unaided judgment based on general argument or observation, and more use is made of measurement by statistical and accounting data. The processes of cost accountancy – itself a very modern and rapidly developing science – are slowly making their way into the region of public administration. A technique of efficiency measurement is undoubtedly being built up – a little slowly and cautiously no doubt, and this is just as well. So far as the Civil Service is concerned, the Treasury, as the general department of control over personnel and office equipment, has with the aid of specialists added to its staff for the purpose, shown an interest and activity in regard to office efficiency which was not within the scope of the pre-war Treasury. When we turn from the organization to the individual, again we find in the scheme of annual reports and Promotion Boards, working on definite principles and lines of procedure, a new application of the idea of measuring efficiency by definite standards. It is no doubt tentative, and admittedly opinions as to its merits are not unanimous. That it is, however, an important advance in the direction of the just and scientific appraisement of personal efficiency there can be no doubt.

Of the progress that has been made in the Local Government service in the development of standards and methods of office efficiency and in the measurement of individual efficiency I have no personal knowledge; but it may be hoped that we shall receive some information on this aspect of the subject from our Local Government colleagues.

If now we address our minds to the question whether there is room for the further development of the art of measuring efficiency—and here I am thinking rather of the efficiency of organizations than of individuals – we shall find that there are two, and, I think, only two instruments to our hand – personal judgment and statistics. They may be used separately or together, and indeed all statistical method implies the use of judgment at some stage. Under statistics is included costing, and in this connection it is important to remember that cost accountancy, in its practical application, is becoming more and more a method and process of statistics and less and less a method and process of accountancy in the strict and limited sense of that term. This does not imply that cost statistics can be divorced wholly and finally from financial accounts; on the contrary, the more separate the paths which they pursue, the more necessary it is to preserve the union between them and to insist on some form and degree of reconciliation. But it does mean that cost statistics and financial accountancy must be free to live their own lives and to follow each its own bent. But this is a digression.

With the use of judgment in the measurement of efficiency we are all familiar. The annual report system of the Civil Service is an outstanding example, especially where it is combined with some method of placing the officials reported on in a comparative order of merit.

39

Similarly we do in fact say that one department or branch is more efficient than another, although the judgment is apt to be based on subconscious processes rather than on data which are positively present to the mind. I have no doubt that in the Local Government world the same sort of thing happens. In America the process is being carried very much farther, and attempts are being made to appraise the efficiency of Governmental organizations on the basis of definite and measurable statistical data. The first notable example of this process was the investigation carried out by the Federated Engineering Associations of the United States as to the efficiency of some six leading industries both as a whole and as respects individual undertakings in each industry. It would take too long to describe the processes adopted, and it must suffice to say that they were based on definite study by expert investigators on a systematic and co-ordinated plan, and that the results were expressed in statistical form, although a good deal of individual judgment must have been employed both in the selection of the form and in reducing judgment to numerical values. The results of this investigation, which was promoted by Mr Herbert Hoover, were, it may be added, somewhat startling. In the public service field even more ambitious attempts have been made to appraise the relative efficiency of a number of Municipal authorities by means of a series of statistical factors. The choice and the weighting of the factors obviously involve judgment. Methods of this sort are clearly in an early and highly experimental stage; the interesting thing about them is not that they have as yet attained any definite practical value, but that they are a serious attempt to present the idea of efficiency in a form which the public can understand, and to elevate the judgment of it from a somewhat vague impressionism to a definite and concrete process which is of a scientific order, and which is capable of being used as a foundation for administrative action. There is little doubt that the development of means of measuring efficiency, especially in the organization, is an important step in the direction of promoting higher efficiency, and that the subject deserves study by those who are interested in the principles of administration.

Professor White of Chicago University has summed up the position in America in the following words, which seem to contain very sound sense:

'Preliminary steps have thus been taken to work out some standards of measurement in order to be able to evaluate the efficiency of public administration. The subject to be measured is so complex and elusive that it will be many years before the goal has been attained; indeed, some declare that no useful standard can ever be worked out. But practically we are constantly making judgments as to the success or failure of our institutions and their methods, and it is certainly in point to refine those judgments as far as possible. It may be that opinion can never be wholly eliminated; but the area of free play can be greatly diminished. From the scientific point of view, the search for tangible standards is of fundamental importance: and brief experience indicates that it has a practical value as well.' [White, *Public Administration*, p. 76.]

The use of measurements of efficiency should be in the direction of giving greater freedom of action, and relaxing control, wherever the ascertained results justify that course. This after all is merely a parallel to the attitude of the shareholders of a joint-stock company who always leave the directors a free hand so long as the results are satisfactory, and only intervene when things begin to go wrong. It is only human nature. There are, of course, limits to the process of delegation even when openly based on established efficiency. Some minimum of co-ordination must be preserved, and consistency in administration cannot be dispensed with altogether, although as already said we can overdo it and pay too high a price for it. But so far as concerns the Civil Service, the issue turns mainly on the principle of responsibility to Parliament; for it is the demands of that responsibility more than anything else which stand in the way of the fuller delegation of powers to local or subordinate units, however efficient. Mussolini, unless I am mistaken, solved this problem of all democratic Government by doing without Parliament. No one here would suggest so drastic a remedy; but we may, as students of administration, observe with interest the course of the relations between Parliament, the Government and the new British Broadcasting Corporation. Here we have a definite experiment in relaxing Parliamentary control, and if it is to succeed it can only be through the proved efficiency of the Corporation in discharging its functions. The position of the Approved Society under the National Health Insurance Acts is much the same.

Short of relaxing control altogether, a satisfactory system of measuring efficiency can be used to transfer control from an external to an internal authority, as in the Post Office case to which reference has been made – a process which almost certainly makes for economy. There are again questions as to the method of using the system – for instance, whether technical departments should keep their own cost accounts or whether they should be kept for them by accounting departments, a problem the solution of which depends upon a number of factors which have to be studied and weighed in the particular case.

With the third question – that of the means of dealing with inefficient performance when disclosed – I do not propose here to deal further beyond saying that examination into current administrative practice will at once show numerous expedients which have been adopted.

Lastly, there will be the question of the best means of promoting efficiency. There are those who say that full efficiency is not obtainable without adequate incentive; there are others who maintain that the problem of obtaining high efficiency is not a problem of incentive but a problem of organization; that every one naturally tries to do his best, and that if the organization is rightly designed and the right men are put in the right places, the questions of incentive become of minor importance; that the satisfaction of work well done will be an adequate reward.

There is, I think, truth in both contentions; but one of the most notable differences between private enterprise and the public services is the relatively much greater importance which is assigned by the former to incentive, and I cannot but think that the public services have lost something by the limitations under which they are compelled to act in this respect. Every Head of a department must, from time to time, find himself in the position where, if he were able promptly and adequately to reward exceptional effort or quality of work, the cost would amply repay itself, but where he is unable to do so. Yet it is really more important in the public services than in private business, because that other, and I suspect over-rated incentive to efficiency, the fear of discharge, is necessarily very much weaker under the stable and permanent conditions which govern our employment than it is in the commercial world. There are, it is true, the less tangible incentives – interest in work, variety of work, approval, honours. Some of these go further than others, or are more widely available. Perhaps, however, the biggest problem of all arises when none of them is available, and the only incentive left is a man's pride in good work and his satisfaction in serving the public. How far is that going to carry him? This subject of incentive in the public services seems to me to be one which the Institute might very well study, in a scientific spirit. It is a most important factor in the psychology of administration.

These remarks have reference rather to the individual than to the organization; but to pass from the former to the latter is but a short and easy step. To those who would study the question of incentives to efficiency in organizations, there is, for instance, the subject of percentage grants from national taxation to local authorities. Indeed, the whole field of the financial relations between the Central Government and the local authorities is a promising subject for exploration from this point of view.

This is as far as the author of this paper can carry the subject. It contains nothing novel or revolutionary. It is at most an attempt to look at familiar problems and processes of administration in the light of certain general ideas and to lay a special emphasis upon certain aspects of the subject. Perhaps it would be better to have called it 'Some rambling reflections upon efficiency'. The critical reader may say that all it has succeeded in doing is to describe old processes and problems by new and less intelligible names. Even this, however, has its advantages; for it compels us to ask what these names really mean and what they stand for. They set us thinking and prevent us from taking anything for granted. I would hope that they are more closely related to various practical problems of administration, which have not been specifically mentioned, than may at first sight appear. Stress has been laid upon efficiency because in actual administration there is a forced stress upon so many other things that are not necessarily consistent with, and may even be inconsistent with, efficiency of performance. My main object, however, has been to invite attention to the consequences which should follow from the successful application of efficiency measurement to particular cases. When in any particular branch of administrative work, organization and performance have been raised to the maximum attainable efficiency, is relaxation of control practicable and desirable? If so, under what conditions and within what limits? If we think along these lines we may find something worth discovering.

4

Portrait of a Profession*

SIR EDWARD BRIDGES

One of the most controversial issues in British public administration in recent years has been the role of the generalist administrator – a type of public servant who proved himself first in the Indian Civil Service but whose virtues, once recognized, were also accepted as the ideal for the Home Civil Service. In the estimation of some contemporary commentators (whose views were epitomized in the Fulton Report's references to 'the philosophy of the amateur' and 'the cult of the generalist') his standing has now degenerated and he should be replaced by public servants who have specialized knowledge of the subject matter in their particular field of administration. However, other authorities argue that the ideal generalist administrator is, in fact, a specialist in public administration; a specialist in both knowledge of a number of aspects of the science of administration and in practising within an environment which seeks to blend, in perhaps a curiously British way, the elements of democracy with the execution of public policy. Sir Edward Bridges, who was a leading exponent of an alternative approach to that contained in the Fulton Report, expressed his views on the role of the generalist administrator in Portrait of a Profession, *his Rede Lecture, 1950.*

I shall be expected to speak today on a subject about which I may be presumed to know something, by reason of my experience. But I find myself under a strong impulse to speak, not of forms of organization or of administrative techniques, but of things less tangible but more compelling. I would like to describe the inhabitants of Whitehall in terms of the training and tradition, the outlook of mind, and aspirations which play so big a part in determining men's actions.

What I seek to do is to give a picture of the higher staffs of Whitehall, the headquarters staffs of Government, who handle the broader

* From Sir Edward Bridges, *Portrait of a Profession*, London: Cambridge University Press, 1950, pp. 5–33. Reprinted with permission of the Executors of the Estate of Lord Bridges and the publishers.

questions of administration and policy. I have no time to include in my picture the large and important professional and technical staffs who pursue their own specialized duties: nor the far larger numbers engaged in the executive work of Government up and down the country; although much of what I shall have to say applies to them also. I shall start by saying something of each of the main movements or events which have made the Civil Service what it is today, and have built up what could be called the Civil Service Tradition.

I hope this choice of subject will not be thought to be immodest or parochial. I shall not be vainglorious. But I believe that there is something distinctive about the Civil Service Tradition; and, difficult though it may be to describe something so elusive, I shall make the attempt.

I

The real starting-point of any account of the British Civil Service as it exists today must be the reforms instituted by Stafford Northcote and Charles Trevelyan in the middle of the nineteenth century.

But one very important quality of the Civil Service, namely its non-political character, received its main imprint in the eighteenth century and must be mentioned first. The action taken by Parliament in that century to prevent the corruption of Parliament itself by patronage resulted in the series of Acts which limited, and clearly defined, the number of Ministerial offices which could be held by Members of Parliament. These Acts brought into being a sharp distinction between political and non-political offices;[1] and prevented the development of anything in the nature of a spoils system in this country.

But it would be wrong to regard the fact that the Civil Service is non-political, and free from party bias or allegiances, as due solely to the clear statutory distinction between political and non-political offices. It has deeper roots.

Patronage, in regard to first appointments to the Civil Service, continued until towards the end of the nineteenth century. But a characteristic convention was established that, while Ministers could use their patronage to appoint to official posts persons who had some claim upon them, such appointments, once made, were regarded as permanent and were not disturbed by subsequent administrations. More important still, by a process of instinctive good sense, it came

---

[1] Lowell, *The Government of England* (1908), Ch. VII, gives, perhaps, the clearest statement on this point.

to be accepted that permanence carried as a corollary a certain standard of conduct and discretion – namely conduct compatible with loyal service to whatever Government is in power.

II

I have used the term 'Civil Service' as though such a body existed in the eighteenth century. This is an anachronism. Even today there is no statutory definition of the Civil Service or of a Civil Servant save a wholly negative one of certain qualifications for drawing pension.[1] As short a time ago as 1910 the draftsman of an Order in Council could not trust himself to go beyond the collective phrase 'persons serving in His Majesty's civil establishments'. Indeed, though the State has had Civil Servants throughout its history, it is only in the past half-century, or century at most, that it has had anything which could be described as a 'Civil Service'.

I distinguish three main causes which brought about something which can be described as a 'service' in the place of a series of departmental staffs, separated off from each other, distant and jealous.

The first in time was the introduction of a common system of recruitment for all Departments. When Sir Stafford Northcote and Sir Charles Trevelyan were appointed by Gladstone to clean up Whitehall in the middle of the nineteenth century, they saw that little progress could be made until they had abolished a system of appointment which was wholly dependent on patronage and conducted separately by each Department: a system which resulted in recruiting the unambitious and the indolent, whose course was 'one of quiet and generally secluded performance of routine duties'. They sought to substitute for this a system of competitive examinations conducted by a central Board. The examinations were to be of literary character, to test the intelligence as well as the mere attainments of a candidate; the examinations were to be for vacancies at two levels: those of nineteen to twenty-five were to compete for the superior posts, those of seventeen to twenty-one for the junior posts.[2]

[1] The last Royal Commission on the Civil Service, under the chairmanship of Lord Tomlin, gave as a practical working definition of the Civil Service: 'Those servants of the Crown, other than holders of political or judicial offices, who are employed in a civil capacity, and whose remuneration is paid wholly and directly out of monies voted by Parliament'—paragraph 9 of Cmd. 3909 of 1931.

[2] Report on the Organization of the Permanent Civil Service, dated 23 November 1853. Included in *Reports of Committees of Inquiry into Public Offices and Papers connected therewith*. Published by Longman, Green, Longman & Roberts (1860).

The scheme was put forward as a means of recruiting an efficient Service; but it was closely linked with educational ideas and reforms. Royal Commissions on the Universities of Oxford and Cambridge in 1852 and 1853 had stressed the advantage of competition. Thus, the Commission on Cambridge said that the great majority of College Fellowships had long been open to free competition, which had given the University a 'high moral elevation'.[1] The Indian Civil Service was thrown open to competition by the Government of India Act of 1853, and the famous Report of Macaulay (Trevelyan's brother-in-law), recommending the nature of the Indian Civil Service examination, was written in 1854. The Northcote-Trevelyan report owed much to the influence of both Macaulay and Jowett; and its authors, in commending it, said that the inducement of making a Civil Service career open to competition 'would probably do more to quicken the progress of our Universities, for instance, than any legislative measures that could be adopted'.

The Northcote-Trevelyan scheme, although strongly backed in educational circles and in contemporary thought,[2] came up against strong departmental opposition, mainly on the ground that a central system of recruitment would impair departmental efficiency, since Ministers could only accept responsibility for the action of their officers if they themselves had the choosing of them. Their proposals were not, therefore, at once accepted in their entirety. Then followed a period of some years during which the Civil Service Commission, first appointed in 1855, had to be content with a sort of twilight existence of limited competitions, or qualifying examinations, which fell far short of the Northcote-Trevelyan scheme. Indeed, a pretty successful guerilla resistance was waged for some years by many public Departments and it was not until the 1870s that the system of open competitive examination became securely established as the regular method of entry for most of the large Departments. This system of recruitment provided a great bond of unity between the staffs in the different Departments; the bond of having entered by the same gate and of being of the same vintage, or perhaps a year more or less in bottle than Smith of the Department across the road.

[1] Quoted by Sir A. P. Waterfield, 'Competition for the British Civil Service and its relation to the Universities', printed in a special number of *Oxford*, 1949.

[2] John Stuart Mill thought that the proposal to select Civil Servants by a competitive examination appeared to be one of those great public improvements the adoption of which would form an era in history.

III

This bond of unity is closely connected with the second unifying cause, namely transfer between Departments. This was more easy to bring about when those concerned had a common origin in entry by the same examination, and when irritating and minor differences in conditions of service had been done away with. Such transfers began to have real significance when they came about, not very occasionally, and not simply by fluke or favour, but as part of a concerted plan decided upon in the public interest.

How early these moves became common I do not know. The first measure of concerted transfer on a large scale of which I am aware was connected with the setting up in 1912 of the National Health Insurance Commission. This, in any case a heavy task, was made heavier by strong opposition. The work was entrusted to a picked team of young men gathered from nearly all Departments. This 'loan collection' – for this was how it came to be known familiarly – comprised many brilliant men who rose later to the highest positions.

The second such occasion came with the First World War. New organizations had to be set up, and heavily pressed Departments strengthened. This could only be done by drafting trained men from work which was not essential to the war.

After the First World War transferability of staff was strongly fostered by the then Permanent Secretary to the Treasury, who did much in the 1920s to break down barriers between Departments.

In 1920 it was formally laid down that the assent of the Prime Minister was required to appointments to the top posts in all Departments. It was thus made clear that in filling such posts the Prime Minister and his advisers would take as their field of selection the whole Civil Service.

In these ways then, the isolation of Departments was broken down and something in the nature of a real Service came into being. In the last ten or fifteen years the process has been carried much further. In part this is due to the effect of total war on the Government machine, and to the very large scale on which transfers took place in the Second World War. But it is also due to the growing interdependence of Departments as a result of economic factors which affect the whole range of Government. This – the third unifying cause – I shall deal with later.

IV

What characteristics did this Civil Service show as it developed?

One effect of the Northcote-Trevelyan reform was a change – subtle and not easily described – in the relationship of higher Civil Servants to their Ministers. Before these reforms had taken effect many of the higher Civil Servants owed their appointments to the patronage – often in the best sense of that much abused term – the patronage of a particular Minister. Many of the holders of the higher appointments had first been brought into the Service to serve as the private secretary of some Minister and had graduated thence to better posts.

The impression one derives from the autobiographies of such men as Henry Taylor[1] or Algernon West[2] is that many of the higher Civil Servants, in the early or middle nineteenth century, had a far closer allegiance or affinity to the views of particular Ministers, and less attachment or loyalty to a Service, than their successors today: and many of those mentioned in these autobiographies sought or found advancement not in the Civil Service, but in a political career.

But I think that the better organization of the Civil Service which started a hundred years ago showed itself most markedly in the greater capacity of the staffs of Departments to marshal previous experience and bring it to bear on current problems. The clerk who at first had done nothing except copy letters, despatch them and file them, makes himself useful in collecting precedents and previous papers. The next stage is that he becomes a clerk who can describe accurately what has happened in the past, who can collect together the information required by the officer who is going to reach a decision on the matter in hand; and before long you have an adviser who presents his senior colleagues or his Minister with a carefully documented appraisal of the position, who tests all the statements made and sets out what seem to him the possible courses of action and the likely consequences of each. There remains a final step. To sum it all up and say which course has behind it the backing of all the knowledge and experience that the Department can give to its Minister.

But why should I seek to describe in my own words what was so aptly stated by Stafford Northcote and Trevelyan? As they said in 1853: 'The great and increasing burden of public business . . . could not be carried on without an efficient body of permanent officers, occupying a position duly subordinate to that of Ministers . . . yet possessing sufficient independence, character, ability and experience

---

[1] *Autobiography of Henry Taylor*, Longman, Green, etc. (1885).

[2] *Recollections, 1832–1866*, by Rt Hon. Sir Algernon West. Smith, Elder & Co. (1899).

to be able to advise, assist, and to some extent to influence those who are from time to time set above them.'

This transition from the clerk to the administrator was all the more rapid because the competitive examinations were successful in recruiting first-class material from the Universities: men who were determined to escape as quickly as possible from routine jobs by showing that they were fitted for better things; men who brought to their work the happy blend of scholarship and ebullience that one finds in a University.

v

By degrees, then, as Civil Service organization got into its stride, there has been built up in every Department a store of knowledge and experience in the subjects handled, something which eventually takes shape as a practical philosophy, or may merit the title of a departmental point of view.

This is not something which has been imposed on a Department by any one individual, though it may well bear the mark of the mind of some outstanding man who has impressed his personality on the Department. Sometimes the departmental philosophy may be the result of a conflict between two apparently divergent needs or policies: each policy may contain something which cannot be sacrificed, and so a way has been found of making the two go in double-harness.

But in most cases the departmental philosophy is the result of nothing more startling than the slow accretion and accumulation of experience over the years. An original scheme has been altered to meet acknowledged difficulties. Some features of the plan have been found too difficult to administer and have been quietly dropped. Some other point aroused serious public criticism; but means have been discovered of obtaining much the same result in other ways which were more generally acceptable. And so by trial and error something has come about which differs greatly from the original plan; it is something which has been fashioned by many hands. It is quite different from anything which any single man or woman could have produced; it is less logical but wiser and more comprehensive: above all, it is something which works, and which works better than anything else so far devised. And in making and reshaping it, things have been learnt which could only be fully grasped by practical experience; as, for example, that certain problems can only be treated by certain administrative methods; and that if certain limits or marks are overstepped, a public outcry can be confidently expected.

These departmental philosophies are of the essence of a Civil Servant's work. They are the expression of the long continuity of experience which can be one of the strongest qualities of an institution, if well organized. Again they are broadly based, and are the resultant of protests and suggestions, and counter suggestions, from many interests, of discussion and of debates in which many types of mind have taken part. They represent an acceptable, middle point of view after the extreme divergencies have been rooted out.

Every Civil Servant going to a different job, unless it be an entirely new one, finds himself entrusted with this kind of inheritance. He knows that it is his business to contribute something of his own to this store of experience; and that he should play his part in moulding it and improving it to meet changing conditions. Equally he knows that it is something that he will ignore at his peril.

VI

These storehouses of departmental experience have a bearing on one aspect of public affairs which is most frequently misunderstood, namely the relationship between day-to-day administration and policy. The two are often spoken of as though they were wholly distinct; as though decisions in the one field could be taken independently of the other, and as though day-to-day administration had no contribution to make to the framing of policy. It is often added that, while decisions of policy are necessarily taken by Ministers, questions of administration are for the most part best left to their staffs.

This is worth a moment's thought. Let us start by looking at military practice. In the last war the Germans, greatly to their detriment, built up a central organization for military planning, distinct from the Army, Naval and Air Staffs, and superimposed on them. In this country on the other hand the higher professional advisers of Government on the strategic direction of the war were the three Chiefs of Staffs, whose duties have been defined as follows:

'In addition to the functions of Chiefs of Staffs as advisers on questions of sea, land or air policy respectively to their own Board or Council, each of the three Chiefs of Staffs will have an individual and collective responsibility for advising on defence policy as a whole, the three constituting as it were a super-chief of a War Staff in Commission.'[1]

[1] Salisbury Report, 1933 (Cmd. 1938).

Under our system, the Chiefs of Staffs thus carried a dual responsibility therefore, collectively for central planning, and individually for executive action in their own Departments. There was thus no room for the fierce clashes of judgment which occurred in Germany between the Central Planning Staff which dictated a certain strategy and the Services, who believed that the plans drawn up by the Planning Staff were wrongly devised, or even incapable of fulfilment.

We have applied the same principle in the field of battle. It is clearly acknowledged that no Commander-in-Chief would ever be asked to fight a campaign, the plans for which had not been made either by him or under his own direction and therefore carried his full consent.

This principle is of equal validity in civil matters: and it is a cardinal feature of British administration that no attempt should be made to formulate a new policy in any matter without the fullest consultation with those who have practical experience in that field, and with those who will be called upon to carry it out.

Consider now the functions of Ministers and Civil Servants in questions of policy. The constitutional responsibility of Ministers to Parliament and the public covers every action of the Department, whether done with their specific authority or by delegation, expressed or implied. Ministers cannot therefore escape responsibility for administrative matters. They are of course more interested, and rightly so, in issues of policy than in detailed administration. But this does not mean that their advisers have no part to play in framing policy. It is indeed precisely on these broad issues that it is the duty of a Civil Servant to give his Minister the fullest benefit of the storehouse of departmental experience; and to let the waves of the practical philosophy wash against ideas put forward by his Ministerial master. The Minister knows the broad lines upon which his Party or the Cabinet have decided to proceed. The advisers contribute practical knowledge such as no Minister could be expected to possess unless he happened to have exceptionally long experience in that field. The relationship between Minister and adviser thus comprises the essential feature of good partnership, namely that the contribution brought by each partner is different in kind.

'The hand which executes a measure should belong to the head which propounds it . . . ; and there will certainly be something infirm and halting about any measure which is devised by one man and executed by another; or (for it amounts to nearly the

52

same thing) any measure of which the execution is continually revised and corrected by another than the author.'[1]

So wrote Henry Taylor in 1836. But while the principle is sound enough, there is a good deal more to be said about its application to modern large-scale organizations. The hundreds of hands which execute such measures cannot in any literal sense belong to the head which propounds them. It is with the middle ranks of these large organizations that responsibility lies for ensuring that that which the head propounds is thoroughly understood by the hands, and that the hands which execute can communicate back to the head. It is for them to see that the decisions of policy laid down by Ministers and senior officials are thoroughly understood throughout the whole organization. It is for them to appraise everyday happenings and to see that those which are significant from the point of view of policy are brought to the attention of their seniors. Indeed, at the middle levels of the organization at which this work is done it can fairly be said that policy and administration merge and are only distinguished with difficulty. And it is by this kind of process that the administration can be kept in tune with public opinion and the needs of the country.

VII

These working departmental philosophies, of which I have spoken so much – it will be asked, is there not a danger that, being the result of experience gathered within the bounds of a single Department, they may tend to harden into a rigid point of view and to conflict with the needs of Government policy in some other matter of perhaps even greater importance? Are such differences of view serious in practice, and how are they resolved?

Did not Stafford Northcote and Trevelyan speak of the 'fragmentary character' of the Civil Service – of a state of affairs in which each man's experience and hopes and interests were limited to a special branch of the Service; and to the encouragement which this gave to narrow views and departmental prejudice?

That was said in 1853; but I can remember occasions in the 1920s when two Departments – each firmly entrenched in strongly held views, and amply provided with arguments – did long battle over some issue of no great importance; with little or no prospect of coming to a conclusion save by the arbitrament of the Cabinet or some senior Minister. I remember, indeed, one occasion on which the

[1] Henry Taylor, *The Statesman* (1836), pp. 88–9.

two Ministers who were engaged in heated controversy changed places while the battle was at its height. But each, when well established in his new Department, averred that, since his translation, he had had exceptional opportunities of considering the matter anew and had reached an entirely opposite conclusion to that which he had previously held: and so the battle went gaily on, the champions only being transposed.

But all that is changed. Let me explain why.

There is the healthy practice that, particularly in their younger years, men and women should change their jobs within the Department every three years or so. There are also the transfers between Departments of which I have spoken.

These frequent changes of duties, whether within the same Department or between Departments, induce a wider outlook. The first time a man is told to change from work which he has mastered to a new job, he may feel that the special knowledge he has acquired is being wasted. He may grudge the labour of mastering a new subject and may even wonder whether he will be equally successful at it. But when a man has done five jobs in fifteen years and has done them all with a measure of success, he is afraid of nothing and welcomes change. He has learned the art of spotting what points are crucial for forming a judgment on a disputed question even when he has the most cursory knowledge of the subject as a whole.

This widening of experience and transfer from one job to another is a great solvent of the differences between Departments. A man with this experience behind him is likely to look with a critical eye at the departmental philosophy which he has inherited, and to be alert to correct any defects and weaknesses in it which his experience in other fields may suggest.

But it is economic factors more than anything else which have compelled Departments to work more closely together. No Government can today discharge its responsibilities unless it has a coherent economic policy, and such a policy must needs be framed after bringing together the views of several Departments, while its execution demands constant consultation between them. This has increased the interdependence of Departments and it has made necessary much fuller arrangements for discussions and co-operation between them.

These arrangements, I need hardly tell you, take the form of what to an outsider would, I suspect, appear to be an extremely elaborate system of interdepartmental committees, many of them with inter-

locking membership. To some this description alone will be a sufficient condemnation of it. But this system does succeed in enabling a
vast amount of business of an economic nature which concerns
several Departments to be carried through quickly, and with little or
no interdepartmental correspondence. Moreover, it has this great
advantage: that colleagues from several Departments meet and talk
things out before views have had time to harden in each Department
into different moulds.

This habit of early and frank consultation on difficult questions – a
habit which extends outside the economic field – has brought about a
greatly changed outlook: and I would claim that those who work in
Whitehall today look over and beyond the boundaries of their
departmental loyalties and see themselves as part of a much larger
and more complicated organization – an organization engaged in an
enormous variety of tasks, and one in which they recognize that their
own job can only be properly done if it takes its place in the fulfilment of the whole.

VIII

From this somewhat discursive account of the main developments
which have affected the Civil Service in the last two or three generations, let me turn to a summary of what a Civil Servant's job amounts
to.

One is tempted to fall back on paradoxes, as for example that the
Civil Service is a professional occupation yet differs in many ways
from any other profession. If it is a professional occupation, what is
the professional skill that is exercised? This is no easy question to
answer; for in effect most Civil Servants exercise a combination of
two or perhaps three skills or qualities.

There is, first, the long experience in a particular field; the man or
woman who has specialized in labour relations or taxation, and who
can tell you more in a short discussion than you could learn in many
years.

Secondly, there is the special technique of the skilled administrator – perhaps it should be called an art – the man or woman who
may indeed possess special knowledge in several fields, but who will
be a good adviser in any field because he or she knows how and
where to go to find reliable knowledge, can assess the expertise of
others at its true worth, can spot the strong and weak points in any
situation at short notice, and can advise how to handle a complex
situation.

A possible third element – or perhaps it is only another way of looking at the other two – is the need for much the same qualities as are called for in the academic world, namely the capacity and determination to study difficult subjects intensively and objectively, with the same disinterested desire to find the truth at all costs, the same willingness to face the truth when it turns up in unexpected places, and in what may be for practical reasons an inconvenient form, the same readiness to scrap much hard work which has already been done when one finds that one has started out on the wrong track.

But if a Civil Servant is called upon to exercise professional skills, his task differs in two important respects from that of any other professional man. A doctor, when he visits a patient, has to diagnose his complaint and restore him to health. A chartered accountant has to analyse the financial affairs of a company and express a view upon them. A schoolmaster seeks to train and teach his pupils. For each, no doubt, the part which his professional skill can and should play, in the general life of the community, means something pretty important in his general scheme of things. But, viewed in relation to his daily tasks, the end in each case is clear, and his own personal responsibility is clear: it is his job to cure his patients, to teach his pupils, to see that the finances of the company are clearly and truly presented.

But this is not so with Civil Servants. Few of them are ever completely responsible for the work they are doing. On all important questions it is necessary to make sure that the Minister approves what is being done; and, apart from ministerial responsibility, the complications of much Government work call for a far greater degree of consultation with colleagues and consideration for other and wider interests than is commonly found in other occupations. Through the nature of his work, therefore, he has much less consciousness than other professional men that the work he does is his own individual achievement, and is inevitably far more conscious than others that the work he does is part of something greater than himself.

In the second place, though it is possible to regard each job which a Civil Servant does as one of a succession of professional tasks, no one with a single spark of imagination could so regard the range of duties of a Civil Service post. It is impossible not to see the day's tasks in perspective: first, as a contribution – however small – to a particular branch of work which has probably gone on for a long time already and will continue for years after he has gone; secondly, as part of a much broader context, namely the continued well-being of the State.

Then again, another paradox: a Civil Servant is bound to be well aware of the political content of his work. He will not indeed be a trustworthy adviser unless he has studied the general national outlook, as illustrated particularly in Parliament, to any problem he is handling, and accepts this as the general background against which he works. At the same time, he is perhaps the least political of all animals, since the departmental experience of which he is the exponent – although it is an essential element in the Government of the country – is part of the stock of things which are common to all political parties. It is something which stands apart from the creed of any political party and thus makes a Civil Servant avert himself, almost instinctively, from party politics.

Finally, a Civil Servant has to combine the capacity for taking a somewhat coldly judicial attitude with the warmer qualities essential to managing large numbers of staff. Detached, at times almost aloof, he must be if he is to maintain a proper impartiality between the many claims and interests that will be urged upon him.

But at the same time, many of his colleagues are the effective heads and organizers of large staffs whose varying qualities and attainments can only be successfully blended into an effective organization by his understanding and leadership.

IX

It is these paradoxes, these contradictions in the make-up of his job, which give the characteristic flavour to the occupation of a Civil Servant, and make his life so difficult to describe. They also condition his outlook: he must be a practical person, yet have some of the qualities of the academic theorist; his work encourages the longest views and yet his day-to-day responsibilities are limited; he is a student of public opinion, but no party politician.

What manner of creature results from these contradictions? I will list some of his qualities, and, in order that I may finish on a sufficiently elevated note, I will start with the bad ones – real and supposed.

I need not, I suppose, deny the fable of idleness (that belongs to a magic past). Nor need I assert that we are not – to borrow a phrase of the Master of Trinity – used in another and quite different context – a 'strange third sex . . . [created] . . . by training men up from boyhood in a world that is not a world of men'.[1]

[1] G. M. Trevelyan, *Garibaldi's Defence of the Roman Republic* (1908), p. 62.

Our most obvious defects spring from the constitutional position of Civil Servants. They are at all times answerable to some Minister who will get the praise and blame for what they do, and this determines many of their actions and reactions. It was, I believe, this fear of involving Ministers in unnecessary troubles which led to the pernicious tradition of writing letters in language deliberately framed so as to mean as little as possible, in the hope that since so little meaning could be attached to them, they would not lead to embarrassment. Nobody now believes in this ridiculous doctrine, and war was declared upon it several years ago. But, even with the help of Sir Ernest Gowers and *Plain Words*, it will take some years before the disease is wholly rooted out.

It is the same absence of direct responsibility which makes the average Civil Servant uncomfortable and infelicitous in his relations with the Press. The direct quick reply may be the only thing which will satisfy the Press inquirer, but it may result in headlines the next morning which will be far from pleasing to his ministerial master. The tendency of many Civil Servants is, therefore, to hedge or confine themselves to what has already been said. This disease is so endemic that we have had to call in gentlemen from Fleet Street to help us out of our difficulties. I see no remedy for it, unless it be accustoming the younger generation of Civil Servants to face the rigours of the Press from their earliest years.

The same absence of direct responsibility is perhaps also responsible for the Civil Servant's highly developed sense of caution. But it is both natural and right to take more care when you are advising a Minister who will carry the responsibility himself than you would take if any blame would fall on your own shoulders.

There is also perhaps on occasion a tendency to seek a greater degree of logical completeness or of regularity than the matter in hand requires; a tendency which I have heard described as perfectionism or pedantry in action. This habit is but an exaggerated form of the Civil Servant's vigilance in defence of his Minister. For this reason he is at times too unwilling to admit anything which looks like a defect; and he wishes to be certain that the decision made in a particular case will not be used as a lever for other concessions which might embarrass his Minister.

All these are real defects – but they are rather of the nature of occupational maladies which we have to fight against; the housemaid's knee, so to speak, of the profession. They do not touch the essential qualities.

A Civil Servant's life makes him, above all, a realist. He is less easily elated, less readily discouraged than most men by everyday happenings. Outwardly he may appear cynical or disillusioned, and perhaps to be disinclined to put up a fight for things which excited others. But that is because he has learnt by experience that the Walls of Jericho do not nowadays fall flat even after seven circumambulations to the sound of the trumpet, and that many of the results which he wants to see come about in the most unexpected of ways. Once the crust of apparent disillusion is pierced, you will find a man who feels with the fiercest intensity for those things which he has learnt to cherish – those things, that is to say, which a lifetime of experience has impressed upon him as matters which are of vital concern for the continued well-being of the community.

As a Civil Servant's working experience grows and the years go by, his life becomes bound up with some of those wider issues. And it is for this reason that, notwithstanding the disappointments and frustrations inevitable in a life with so many masters, the work provides, and provides to a considerable degree, an intense satisfaction and delight in the accomplishment of difficult tasks, a delight which has much in common with that felt by scholars or even on occasion by artists on the completion of some outstandingly difficult work.

Lest this be thought presumptuous, may I say that this satisfaction and delight are usually accompanied by a sense of humility which is the exact opposite of the avariciousness for power with which we are sometimes credited?

These satisfactions, these disappointments are, moreover, part of a strong corporate life, a corporate life which knows no barriers based on social upbringing or educational background, and which accepts without question as a passport for the higher appointments anyone whose work and approach to problems show that he has learnt how these things should be done. Indeed, the Service recognizes gratefully that it is strengthened and toughened by the greater diversity of experience thus brought within its ranks.

We are, unfortunately, lacking in those expressions of a corporate life found in a College. We have neither hall nor chapel, neither combination room nor common room. But while we have none of these, we share a general recognition that we are seeking to do something more important than the lives of any or all of us and something more enduring. And this in time makes for another characteristic feature, namely an outstanding friendliness and tolerance and kindliness towards colleagues.

x

The Civil Servant is traditionally an object of fun. I take this to be part of the Englishman's reaction against authority. Being a law-abiding person, an Englishman will probably do in the long run what he is told to do; but equally he resents being told, instead of being left to find out for himself. And part of his reaction is to take it out on those who give orders to him, by treating them as figures of fun.

Speaking as one whose first instinct is always to say no when I am told to do something, this attitude seems to me to be inherently right and inescapable; and I confidently expect that we shall continue to be grouped with mothers-in-law and Wigan Pier as one of the recognized objects of ridicule. But, equally, I see no reason why this very proper attitude should not be combined with a rather better understanding of all that goes to make the Civil Service what I believe it to be, namely a calling essential in any state of affairs which I can foresee, and one of the most worthwhile, if also perhaps one of the least understood, of professions.

5

Bureaucracy or Management?*

PETER SELF

In The English Constitution, *Walter Bagehot drew attention to some of the defects of bureaucracy and compared the forms of organization in business and in government. He concluded that the summits of the various kinds of business are like the tops of mountains, 'much more alike than the parts below – the bare principles are much the same; it is only the rich variegated details of the lower strata that so contrast with one another. But it needs travelling to know that the summits are the same. Those who live on one mountain believe that their mountain is wholly unlike all others'. Other writers have also considered the similarities and differences between large-scale enterprise in the public and private sectors; there is, for example, a most useful chapter on this topic in Marshall E. Dimock,* A Philosophy of Administration (Harper & Row, New York, 1958). *A modern approach to the same question is taken in the inaugural lecture of Professor Peter Self, Professor of Public Administration, London School of Economics and Political Science.*

I

The words in my title are flexible ones and their use needs some explanation. Bureaucracy is used here not in the *Oxford English Dictionary* sense of a bureaucrat as 'an official who endeavours to concentrate administrative powers in his own bureau', but as a neutral description of certain features of large-scale organization: while management refers to the skills and the arts needed to make organizations perform their purposes effectively. Thus defined the two terms link the twin interests of most students of public administration – to understand what it is and, if possible, to help to improve it. But more concretely the title also poses a topical challenge to reflection. While both words can be applied equally to all organizations,

* From Peter Self, *Bureaucracy or Management?* London, G. Bell & Sons Ltd., 1965, pp. 7–43. Reprinted with permission of the author and the London School of Economics and Political Science.

bureaucracy is more often used of the processes of government, and management of the activities of private business. Further, management is definitely the more U word. Many believe that public bureaucracies need to be enlivened with a more managerial approach, that there are lessons which they could learn from the best practices of private business, and perhaps that certain broad principles of management exist which should be generally applied. The official head of the Civil Service, Sir Laurence Helsby, has been quoted as saying: 'We tend to use the word administration for the public service, management for business. There is no difference: we want good managers.'[1]

One can approach this question from the stand-point of organization theory. Here one finds new points of convergence between public administration and private management. These have come about through the partial eclipse of the old concepts of bureaucratic man and economic man. We no longer accept that public bureaucracies must necessarily be tied to rigid systems of hierarchy and accountability; instead we stress administrative flexibility, discretion, and initiative. Equally out of favour is the mechanical model of private organization, with its reliance upon screwing together the nuts and bolts in the most technically efficient way and oiling them with the grease of economic rewards. We have learned from social psychology of the importance of non-economic motivations in securing co-operative efforts and satisfactions, and from sociology of the part played by apparently irrational acts in preserving the latent power of groups. Meanwhile, private organizations have become increasingly orientated towards questions of welfare and politics, while public administration has permeated an enormous array of services.

It is natural enough to conclude that the differences between large and small in organizations are generally more significant than those between public and private. And up to a point the conclusion is a true one – far truer than it was fifty years ago. Yet the differences that remain are also enormously significant, and perhaps more inclined to be lost sight of in the current enthusiasm for organization theory and common management practices. For one thing the identification of organization itself – which provides the basis for much writing about supposed laws of organizational growth and competition – becomes a difficult proposition when we turn to public administration. In one sense, each public corporation or local authority can be treated as a separate organization: but there is another sense in which public enterprise as a whole and local government as a

[1] *Sunday Times* magazine, 8 November 1964, p. 23.

whole (and indeed different species of the latter) command joint loyalties. Further, there is another sense in which the whole education service or health service form separate entities with specific goals and professional loyalties. And in central government itself, departmentalism is balanced by the integrative pull of the common traditions of the administrative class and other general groups.

The way in which these organizational balances work out depends quite a lot upon the values of a particular society. American textbooks lay much stress upon the often intense competitive relations between administrative agencies, while British ones largely ignore this subject in their assumption of a common dedication to the public interest. Some may think the American writers over-dramatic, and the British ones over-simple. But my main point is that public administration cannot be easily sliced up into organizational structures and that for certain limited purposes, the whole of government is one gigantic organization.

It is these associated features of great size and great diversity which provide a second set of distinctive issues. Government in Britian currently employs a quarter of the working population and disposes of 40 per cent of the gross national product. It accounts for the bulk of the social services, for most of the largest economic enterprises, and for the lion's share of scientific research and development. It controls and subsidizes industry in a hundred different ways, and it attempts to manage the national economy and the physical environment. These tasks, whether considered individually or collectively, are a great deal more complex than any that private enterprise does. Some might even consider that they are more important. Yet the critical organizational questions are: how far do these multifarious tasks necessarily hang together? how much common co-ordination do they require?

The differences between running a large or small hospital are more significant than any question of who owns it. It is as one moves towards the centre of the system that the distinctive features and problems of public administration appear. Central government and (to some extent) local government dispose of the ultimate powers of the State which consist in the powers to tax, subsidize, and use compulsion. These features set the methods of public administration, at this level, quite sharply apart from those of private management. It is not merely that the use of these powers is at base a political, not a commercial, question. There is also the point that public administrators must act as market compressors, not market innovators. Instead of the business talents required to spot, create, and satisfy

63

new wants, they are perpetually struggling with a surplus of demands.

But most significant of all is the diversity of viewpoints that need to be included in administrative acts. While it would be enough for a private company contemplating a new transport facility to estimate the market, it is necessary for the public authority also to look at the effects on other facilities, consider the impact on traffic and traffic management, analyse effects on town planning, and so on. The greater the stress upon the co-ordinative responsibilities of the State, the more this need increases. So long as regulations were generalized, and local authorities or public boards were left largely alone to perform their work, the central administrator had a tolerably quiet life, save perhaps in the spheres of foreign affairs and defence. But as governmental regulation and aid becomes increasingly specific, as local government becomes enfolded in a network of national social services and public enterprises get caught up in economic planning, the lot of the central administrator becomes almost unsupportable. Inevitably perhaps, he tries to improve his lot by treating as separate matters which have become related: by relying upon interested parties for the advice and information he must have to reach a decision: by using precedent and simplified compromises to resolve questions that appear to call for fresher or stiffer forms of treatment.

II

So far the argument has tacitly assumed that a more managerial and less bureaucratic state is desirable. But this assumption needs questioning. In a recent lecture here Professor Hayek drew an unfavourable comparison between the State's cumulative involvement with particular purposes and its role as the upholder of general laws.[1] Now undoubtedly the call for a more managerial approach in government is linked, at least loosely, with demands that government produce more specific effects. This contrasts with the traditional reliance of bureaucracies upon general rules or laws.

If the Government is to take a greater part in the promotion of economic growth, it is hard to see how more specific interventions can be avoided. The structure of modern industry is such that general measures often cannot be realistically promulgated without awareness of their effects on particular firms. The same pressure towards detailed manipulation can be seen in the central government's growing concern with the pattern of physical development.

[1] Published in *Studies in Philosophy, Politics and Economics*, Routledge, 1967.

Thus the *South-East Study*, prepared by a Conservative Government, proposed that a third of the anticipated population growth in this broad region should be organized in Government-promoted urban projects.[1] Hardly anyone criticized this plan for going too far. The more usual comment was that it still left too much growth to be covered by *unplanned* developments – by which was meant, curiously, developments planned only by the local authorities.

It is not within my compass today to look for justifications, within the broad realms of social theory, for these developments. My concern is with the methods of government: and, within this narrower ambit, one must accept the demand for more positive government as a fact. Yet the questions raised by Professor Hayek still have some relevance. If the ends of government are to be more specific, then sometimes the means must also be so. But is not this connection a little too easily universalized? And are there not too many examples of detailed interventions being undertaken by government before their purposes have been adequately thought through?

Other things being equal, the impersonal suasion of general rules is certainly preferable to the detailed exercise of administrative judgment. But is this rule given the weight it deserves? For example, the Board of Trade considers every application for the location of a new factory 'on its merits', within the framework of a general policy. In this way it can take account of the special needs, and contribution to the economy, of each applicant: but can the administrators (who are few and not highly expert) make these very nice judgments as effectively as would industrialists working under a more general system of rules and incentives? Curiously this alternative is often dismissed upon the grounds that the results would be not less but more 'arbitrary', meaning that they would leave less scope for detailed bargaining on particular grounds. We have become deeply committed to a belief in government by haggle.

The older bureaucratic values also accepted the validity of general (as opposed to specific) compulsion exercised for a sound reason of public interest. Today one may detect a certain willingness to incur administrative complications rather than apply such rules squarely. For example, it is surely accepted that air pollution is an avoidable nuisance of grave dimensions, which is responsible for much bronchial and respiratory illness. Its removal, however, has been left to the piecemeal production of smoke control orders by local authorities which in some badly afflicted areas are going to be spread over a

[1] The *South-East Study*, *1961–81*. Chs 10 and 11, Ministry of Housing and Local Government, HMSO, 1964.

great many years, and which are coupled with a system of compensatory grants. One cannot but suspect that a general prohibition by a stated date, linked with compensation only in cases of proved hardship, would have been both better administration and better civics.

There are also more positive ways of looking at management in government. Whether or not valid general principles of management exist, certain types of practice are now widely commended. These include more care with the advance planning of operations, greater decentralization of decisions so as to reduce strain at the top, and the use of new techniques in central control of finance and staffing. These practices have obvious relevance to the work of government. Indeed the great accumulation of governmental tasks makes their investigation a matter of high urgency. My aim in the remainder of this lecture is to take these questions of planning, devolution, and management, and consider how they appear and might perhaps be improved in a specifically governmental context, it being understood that one can tread over only a few patches of this enormous and sometimes swampy ground.

III

The purpose of planning is to achieve a more consistent pattern of related decisions, based upon careful investigation and evaluation.

Planning is thus a desirable part of the activities of any agency or department. However, particular problems occur with the increasing range of matters of concern to more than one public agency, and it is on these that I shall concentrate.

The traditional framework of means-end analysis still accords fairly well with most of the work of government. Typically, administrative programmes are drawn up with some main end in view, and means are limited proximately by the availability of legal powers and ultimately by the constraining values of the society. However, there are situations, becoming more frequent as the scope of government increases, where a number of conflicting objectives need somehow to be reconciled. New techniques of analysis then become desirable. One can proceed either by trying to order the general goals, and seeing what programme would most accord with their combined ranking: or one can examine a number of concrete alternatives and compare the values yielded by each package. Or one can do both. The latter approach, which is that urged by Herbert Simon, corresponds to the newer picture of a flexibly minded administrator, thinking out a variety of possible alternatives, in place of an old-style bureaucrat ploughing his furrow.

These questions raise more than practical problems of administrative co-ordination, difficult though these be. They entail new tasks of analysis and synthesis, and they go to the roots of political choice.Their solution may require quite radical changes in the system of government.

Take the case of regional planning. Many Ministries are concerned with the location of new developments according to programmes with which they are entrusted. Each has its legitimate viewpoint. The Ministry of Housing and Local Government, which controls the new towns programme, is particularly concerned with the quality of the environment. The Board of Trade, responsible for the development areas programme, seeks to mop up pockets of unemployment where they occur. The new Ministry of Economic Affairs is keen on economic development, particularly in the export field. The Ministry of Agriculture and perhaps the new Ministry of Land are protective, in different ways, towards the countryside.

British departments do not tread rudely on each other's toes. What may be called negative co-ordination, the avoidance of specific points of friction, is well resolved. But departmental programmes can keep along contradictory courses for long periods, although it should be remembered that this is largely a reflection of political ambiguity. Thus the Board of Trade has for long been pumping new jobs into Merseyside and Clydeside while the town planning authorities have been trying to decant jobs and population. But in each case there is an originating political impulse: the one, to cure unemployment on the spot, the other, to establish better conditions for living and working.

But in any case more than co-ordination would be needed to establish a satisfactory regional plan. It would be necessary to test existing aims and to ask new questions. The resulting plan will fly apart in execution if it does not have consolidated political backing: and it will be a purely technocratic set of decisions if public opinion cannot be brought to consider and judge its purposes. From this latter viewpoint, it should be asked whether the practice of presenting the public with a single official plan, persuasively advocated in barristerial manner, is really the wisest. In private life, we are familiar with the process of imagining and evaluating alternative courses of action. Is it really so confusing to try to do the same with possible public programmes, as a preliminary to final decisions? And how else is the public or its representatives to know the possible alternatives: to choose in fact, or at least to endorse administrative choices made on their behalf?

One can test recent administrative innovations by these criteria. The new machinery includes the preparation of broad regional plans under the auspices of the Ministry of Economic Affairs: economic planning boards of civil servants in the regions: and appointed regional councils with advisory status. While this system is clearly an improvement in joint decision-making, I would doubt whether it can satisfy the conditions I have stated. Major decisions about regional development, such as the creation of a new town or the alignment of a motorway, are so politically charged and linked with established Ministerial responsibility, that they could hardly be settled by regional civil servants or their voluntary advisers. They are likely to become, in the technical phrase, 'matters for Cabinet decision', which means that an integrated regional view, if produced at all, will quickly get blurred. I suspect that such a system cannot be really effective unless backed either by an elective regional body or a central Minister with consolidated staff and authority.

Many public authorities, as is well known, function both as general planner and specific developer. This can lead to considerable schizophrenia. Thus recent studies have suggested that local authorities may be led by the structure of housing subsidies into decisions that are completely uneconomic in terms of the deployment of real resources. A more political type of problem is the way in which a strong vested interest (owner-occupiers, for example, or council tenants) may block broader programmes for dealing (in this case) with general housing needs. There is no fully adequate solution to these dilemmas. But their existence does powerfully strengthen the case for creating (within Government departments and local authorities) strong research and planning units that are detached from immediate pressures. At broader levels of public planning, it should stimulate the search for new devices which can somehow maximize the objectivity of the planning agency without making it administratively ineffective. As experience has shown, the gap between ineffectiveness and over-involvement is a very narrow one.

It is fashionable to look across the Channel for a model of economic planning machinery, and such success as the French Commissariat du Plan has had is due to its resolution of this dilemma. Its downward-radiating network of links with industry, and its representation on the various special bodies for applying the economic plan, equip it with vital instruments of consultation and execution. But the Commissariat itself is small and its rather detached, off-centre position helps it to act more as a meeting-place for existing departments than as a jealous rival to them. It has been greatly helped by the ministerial status and high personal qualities of successive Commissioners-General. M. Bauchet can still write that in France 'the conditions governing economic decisions are chaotic and the Ministry of Finance has too much power'.[1] But his words are unjust and testify mainly to the enduring problems of co-ordination under a Cabinet system of formally equal departments, with one a little more equal than the others.

A British equivalent would be to stand the original concept of the National Economic Development Council on its head by placing a small expert staff above the network of consultative bodies, but under the control of a distinguished individual like Lord Franks or Lord Plowden who would sit in the Cabinet. This will be repudiated as a violation of the political character of Ministerial status. One can see the dangers. But perhaps we should ask whether party politics may not have come to occupy such a narrow spectrum, in relation to the actual tasks of government, as to make such expedients worth some consideration.

IV

My second theme is devolution of decision-making. The choice between centralization and decentralization is not of course an absolute one, but represents a whole spectrum of possible arrangements. Viewed as an administrative dilemma, it offers gains and losses in varying proportions. Yet it is an interesting fact that most writers on management and administration subscribe to what may be called a decentralist philosophy. In this respect the business pioneers who have blazed the path of operational autonomy in such vast concerns as I.C.I., Unilever, or General Motors speak a similar language to the harassed politicians and administrators who wish (or say they wish) that Whitehall could shed more of its load. Nor do I believe this congruence of opinion to be accidental. Rather is it an intelligible reaction to the tensions of organizational scale from which many yearn to escape.

Doubtless there is often much false nostalgia in these yearnings. We may regret the passing of the face-to-face society, of the eclipse of town meetings (much mourned in America), or of vigorous borough government (rather less lamented in England), but our notion of the virtues of these institutions may be much exaggerated.

[1] Pierre Bauchet, *Economic Planning: The French Experience*, Heinemann, 1964, p. 100.

In any event, genuinely small-scale government has ceased, save in an advisory capacity, to be a practical possibility. If devolution of powers is to work, then it must be to bodies which operate on what is (historically speaking) a relatively large scale, although not the gigantic one of national government. This creates a cruel dilemma for representative institutions in Britain. For while localism still remains sentimentally quite strong, although practically of declining effectiveness, broader or regional loyalties are distinctly weak for handling the tasks which might be theirs.

Compared with a large business, the patterns of decentralization in government are extremely rigid. In many ways this is obviously right. Local authorities are democratic bodies with separate constitutions: they are dignified bodies with long histories: and their structures and procedures cannot be chopped and changed lightly. On the other hand, they now plainly form part of a single governmental machine. And their performance can be, and is controlled in a great variety of ways. Central control operates with all the weight both of old constitutional conventions and of new social dogmas. The former pressure is seen in a battery of checks upon the local expenditure of central grants which would be the despair of any business: the latter in the conversion of political demands for 'equal standards for all' into cumbersome rules for increasing administrative uniformity up and down the country.

What is the rationale for so much central control? Is it a continuing suspicion that local councils may do something foolish unless closely watched? But the main local councils are heavily earnest bodies with reasonably expert staffs. Is it a burning wish to make sure that Brighton or Wallasey does not spend more than its due proportion of the national tax, plus or minus allowances for its special needs or deficiencies? But this sort of detailed accountability seems rather silly when partners are responsible public bodies, whose citizens contribute to both rates and taxes. One wonders what an operational research exercise might show of the utility of much central checking of local expenditure and local decisions.

Another explanation is the pressure on Ministers and Ministries to 'take responsibility' for the state of the public services everywhere and anywhere. This pressure both reflects and feeds the decline in the standing of local government, but in addition Ministers have perhaps not been as ready as they should be to rebut these imputations of effective responsibility. It is not altogether unpleasant to be a universal Pooh-Bah when local bodies are being kicked for their parochialism, and when the notion that everything ought somehow to be settled 'in the national interest' is still uncontaminated by being put closely to the test. The danger of these arrangements is that the execution of public policies will flounder between Government departments which control without acting, and local authorities which are not always trusted or equipped to act; and that too much staff will be tied up in the exercise of control rather than of initiative.

Consider the case of highways, whose administrative problems have been described by two recent Permanent Secretaries to the Ministry of Transport, Sir James Dunnett and Sir Gilmour Jenkins.[1] According to Sir James, the Ministry suffers in some ways, including its ability to recruit good engineers, from the fact that it does not build roads itself. It plans the motorways and (to some extent) the trunk roads, and it controls the classified roads through a graded system of grants based upon assumed differences in the degree of national or local interest. These controls are largely exercised by the divisional road engineers. According to Sir Gilmour the first rationale of Ministry controls is not the superior technical competence of its engineers – for the local authority ones are agreed to be at least as good – but the need to safeguard Parliament's financial interest in road expenditure. But in what effective sense are the Ministry's divisional engineers the servants of Parliament? And can they ensure that Parliament gets better value for its share of the money? But I have already dwelled upon the archaic nature of this concept.

The other purport of control is (as Sir Gilmour goes on to imply) to get an integrated road system: and this need for vertical integration has to be meshed also with the horizontal integration of roads with town planning. The requirements here differ as one descends. The general pattern of a national motorway system does not imperatively demand (though doubtless it would benefit from) a highly sophisticated analysis. It is largely settled by the facts of economic geography. But the case is very different for roads at the regional level, particularly in and around the large urban regions. Here the view taken depends both upon what other decisions are made about urban patterns and densities, and also upon tricky social estimates of how people will use their cars under alternative conditions, and of how far they can or should be restrained from using congested routes at peak periods. Here elaborate technical studies and social-benefit analysis come into their own (or should do so), but so (equally importantly) does the exercise of social and political judgments.

[1] Sir James Dunnett, 'The Civil Service Administrator and the Expert' in *Public Administration*, Autumn 1961, p. 230. Sir Gilmour Jenkins, *The Ministry of Transport and Civil Aviation*, Allen & Unwin, 1959, pp. 129–30.

It is at this point that the identification of functional needs has to be linked with the choice of appropriate agencies. If there were a Ministry for the Environment, it would be well placed (as the present Ministries are not) to plan and execute a regional development programme through an *élite* corps of engineers and planners. Such a system would be much more efficient than the present one, but even so centralization might not be the most desirable policy. The conditions I have described fit the classic case for experiment. The planning and transportation problems of Tyneside and Merseyside are fairly similar, but does it follow that the attempted solutions should be the same? Given the wide range of possibilities and uncertainties, would not some diversity of policy be fruitful? And should not the citizens of these great areas have some effective say in how their environment is shaped?

The Crowther introduction to the Buchanan Report[1] fixed unerringly upon the need for a clear regional focus of decision-making, but went on to propose the well-worn compromise device of another set of appointed boards. These would partly supervise and partly supplement the local authorities in their tasks of highway improvement and urban redevelopment. One effect would be to attract to the regional boards, with their superior status, such original and creative minds as now exist among local authority planners, architects, and surveyors. The rather few really able and energetic councillors who still exist would also have less to hold them. Have these broader effects been considered? The Maud and Mallaby Committees are currently wrestling with problems of the supply of talent in local government: but, as the National Association of Local Government Officers has rightly told them, local authorities must be big enough and rich enough, and charged with effective responsibilities, to secure the skills they need.[2]

The Herbert Commission's Report on London government expressed, no doubt co-incidentally, the same decentralist philosophy as did the earlier Herbert Report on the electricity industry. One problem that engaged this Commission was how to match the potential supply of competent laymen with a worthwhile work load: and they designed their proposed system of London boroughs with this point very much in mind.[3] It is true that they had no real evidence of what councillors might come forward to work any particular

---

[1] *Traffic in Towns*: Steering Group Report, HMSO, 1963, paras 41–55.

[2] Reported in the *Guardian*, 13 January 1965, p. 3.

[3] P. Self, 'The Herbert Report and the Values of Local Government', *Political Studies*, June 1962.

system of local government: but the evidence is probably not obtainable. Nobody knows who will respond to opportunities which are not yet there.

My point is that any system of decentralized government has to strike a balance between functional needs and the mechanics of management. The classic period of English local government, which lasted from 1888 to perhaps 1939, unified these requirements in a system of elective multi-purpose bodies which performed (with very few exceptions) all internal services. Functional pressures are now disrupting the system. Special regional authorities have already been established for the hospitals, as well as for gas and electricity supply; similar bodies are now being advocated (often for cogent functional reasons) for physical planning, highways, education, housing, and water supplies. It would be mistaken to ignore any longer the basic choices which these developments pose. The question is really not whether to save local government as such, but whether and how to preserve the elective and co-ordinative principles that are part of its conception. For a system of appointed boards, whatever their advantages for specific purposes, inevitably fragments the general machinery of government. It throws a greater load of planning and co-ordination on central government, which already (one might think) has enough to do. It also, to be blunt, sucks the life-blood out of local self-government which is in real danger of being discarded in another of our familiar fits of absent-mindedness.

Connected with these changes is a certain disillusionment with elective institutions as they work at the local level and might work at the regional one. Partly to blame is the narrow range and sometimes mistaken intensity of party politics. By contrast, the more professional air and lower political temperature of appointed boards have a certain appeal. Yet can it be right to build up still further the appointive duties of Ministers and their senior advisers? Government on the outer circle is likely as it expands to become less representative and to yield less initiative from the appointed.

Thus, decentralized government today resembles an unsolved jigsaw puzzle. The larger functional pieces need a broader areal pattern if they are to be fitted together: but the only patterns we have were made from smaller and different pieces. Possibly some new Goschen will eventually appear to diagnose a fresh chaos of rates and authorities, and prescribe a coherent pattern of regional and local institutions. Despite its difficulties this in my belief would be the most desirable solution: but if this conclusion is resisted then I am even surer that the structure of central government will have to be recast so as to produce more integrated regional and local services, and that the pretence that traditional local government can do the work with a little extra help will not last much longer. In support of my own preference, I would say that it is a shade ironic that continental writers are now discovering the importance of Anglo-Saxon local institutions as a means of humanizing the power of technocracy at a time when this heritage is less regarded here.

v

Lastly I turn to what many will consider the core of my subject – the place of management in central government. Opinion on this subject has been much influenced by the Report of the Plowden Committee on the Control of Government Expenditure. This report not only stressed the importance of better management in government, but cast the Treasury for a stronger role in planning the careers of administrators, and in detecting and remedying defects of management in individual departments.[1] The reorganization of the Treasury in 1962 was a step in this direction.

As the Warden of Nuffield has indicated,[2] there is something a little paradoxical about the Plowden Report. It sprang from the disquiet of the Select Committee on Estimates about the methods of Treasury control, but ended by enlarging the Treasury's authority without much scrutiny of that department's capacity for new tasks. To any part that the Treasury's own influence may have had in shaping this report, we should I think add the influence of business analogies. Professor Mackenzie has done a witty 'translation' of the report, in which he compares the Treasury's intended role to that of a holding company, with the departments viewed as operating companies.[3] Loose as the analogy may be, one feels its weight in the attention paid to devising new techniques for checking departmental performance, and in establishing a central pool of mobile managerial ability.

In considering these ideas, we do not start from a *tabula rasa*. The Treasury's style of central management has always reflected the general conception of administrative skill which prevails in the British Civil Service, and which has been described by such prac-

[1] 'Control of Public Expenditure', Cmnd. 1432, 1961, especially para. 17.
[2] D. N. Chester, 'The Plowden Report—Nature and Significance', *Public Administration*, Spring 1963.
[3] W.J.M.M., 'The Plowden Report: a translation', *Guardian*, 25 April 1963, paras 34–6, 46.

titioners as Dale and Sisson as resting upon an expert understanding of the collective machinery of government.[1] The Treasury, as the fount of these special insights, is best placed of all to keep the machine running smoothly, along its traditional lines.

Treasury control of finance well illustrates my point. Professor Beer is an admirer of the style of Treasury control. It works more smoothly and perhaps effectively than that of the U.S. Bureau of the Budget, even though the horde of experts in the latter make the Treasury examiners seem, by comparison, to be few and amateur.[2] But the reason surely is that the budgetary process is grounded in a process of political and administrative bargaining, which it is the job of the Treasury or Budget Bureau to systematize and apply. Thus skills in papering over departmental cracks may well appear to be more important than skills in the comparative measurement of 'value for money' which is an intrinsically tough task and often difficult to isolate from broader issues. And this 'papering over' is of the essence of general administrative and Treasury skills. The Treasury's role has always been limited to that of appraisal at one remove: in the neat explanation of a Ministry of Health witness to the Select Committee on Estimates, it is 'to satisfy themselves that we are properly satisfying ourselves about the economics and soundness of particular schemes'.[3] The limits of this are particularly marked in dealings with the more client-oriented Ministries, such as Agriculture or Aviation. Doubtless it is a basic political choice to give large subsidies to agriculture, and to allow to the National Farmers' Union a considerable say in their size and distribution. Yet when one industry secures annually above 80 per cent of all the public aid voted 'above the line' to the private sector plus handsome payments for research and a free advisory service, exemption from local rates, and the presumed advantages of producer-controlled marketing monopolies, and does all this on terms which (unlike the subsidy to cotton textiles, for example) do not impose any conditions for improved performance, save in a few minor respects, one would at least expect a full appraisal and justification of the sums expended. Yet the Ministry has in fact never published an analysis of the actual effects of any of the sixteen direct farming grants (that is,

[1] 'The one specific excellence of the civil servant is . . . the ability to work the machine of British government', H. E. Dale, *The Higher Civil Service*, Oxford University Press, 1941. C. H. Sisson, *The Spirit of British Administration*, Faber, 1959, says the civil servant 'specializes in the awareness of ministerial responsibility' (p. 13), and even suggests that he is 'most useful' when 'an absolute nonentity' (p. 127)—an unconvincing view, even for pre-managerial days.

[2] Samuel Beer, *Treasury Control*, Oxford University Press, 1956, pp. 58–9.

[3] 'Sixth Report from the Select Committee on Estimates', 1957–8, c. 1092.

75

subsidies additional to price guarantees) which are currently provided, although some of these are individually large enough to shore up the prosperity of a less-regarded industry such as ship-building. The Treasury's part, exercised from two Principals' desks, has certainly included efforts to keep down the total size of the bill; its hand can be detected in the limits put to open-ended subsidies, now backed up by measures of market sharing, minimum import prices, and quantitative restrictions.[1] But this only indicates the heart of the problem. To keep down the taxpayers' bill (slightly), one puts up the price of food rather than looking closely at where the money is going.

It may be said that this system of control by intelligent laymen who ask awkward questions[2] ought to give way to control by technically versed and briefed administrators. Certainly new techniques for measuring departmental performance can be applied with advantage, even though they are bound to stop a very long way short of the tests of economic performance which can be applied by a holding company to its subsidiaries. Even so, skill in what might be called politico-administrative co-ordination will remain of great importance. But when we turn to personnel planning, on which the Plowden Report laid such stress, the desirability of increasing the Treasury's managerial role becomes much more dubious.

The difficulties of doing so spring from the great diversity of departmental tasks, and the widening range of special talents and skills needed for their execution. It is here that the analogy with private big business may be especially misleading.

It is true enough that many qualities of intellect and character are equally requisite for the private manager and the public administrator, and that in both cases width of experience and flexibility of mind are increasingly stressed. Yet while the business manager generally builds upwards from some specialized skill to a broader comprehension of his company's interests, the general administrator (as now understood) is a generalist from the start – and is so within a vastly broader network of public purposes. It is a long step from the sensitive understanding of educational problems to the almost

[1] Details of agricultural subsidies are given in the Annual Review White Papers (HMSO). Comparisons with aid to industry are given in J. W. Grove, *Government and Industry in Britain*, Longmans, 1962, Chs 10–14, and table, p. 265, and a review of agricultural policy and administration in P. Self and H. Storing, *The State and the Farmer*, Allen & Unwin, 1962.

[2] This is the description given by Lord Bridges in *The Treasury*, Allen & Unwin, 1964, pp. 51–3, and criticized by Ely Devons in 'Intelligent Laymen in Whitehall', *The Listener*, 21 May 1964.

buccaneering bargaining skill needed to keep afloat the nation's stake in international civil aviation. Indeed if Government service succeeds in producing this kind of skill (as it has done) the taxpayer should count himself triply blessed. It may be objected that Ministers make these jumps, so why should not senior civil servants? But Ministers are finding happy versatility an increasingly hard exercise: does their attempted versatility need matching or compensating?

That the British system works as well as it still does is due to its dexterity in the deployment of available talent: as Lord Bridges puts it, the task of a Permanent Secretary to the Treasury in advising upon senior appointments is akin to that of a cricket captain (more strictly, I suppose, the adviser to a captain) in placing his field.[1] But is it only the wicket-keeper who now needs skills that are not quickly learned?

By induction a civil servant becomes skilled in understanding his Minister's mind: and Sir Charles Cunningham has told us that one problem is how to convey a proper understanding of these Ministerial thought processes to his junior officers.[2] The disrepectful may wonder how far these exercises in psychology can reasonably be pushed. But the basic doctrine that the Minister must be obeyed if he knows what he wants is well understood. The weak spots occur before and after the giving of loyal but dispassionate advice to Ministers which the British civil servant has always done so supremely well. As Sir Charles, along with others, has also pointed out, the pressure of immediate business is still ousting the work of preliminary investigation and thought whose absence was so strongly lamented by the Haldane Committee forty-five years ago.

Part of the remedy lies in better organization. But the load of political pressure on top administrators would seem to make it more important that they should have adequate experience in the technical, social, and economic aspects of their department's work: and such experience today implies an acquaintance with a range of specialized knowledge which has grown enormously.

I conclude in the first place that any analogy between central government and big business is misleading because of the great diversity of departmental tasks, which extends not only to the skills required but also (though perhaps in lesser degree) to managerial problems. Indeed, to pursue the analogy, some departments such as Power, Transport, or Health are themselves holding companies

[1] Bridges, op. cit., p. 177.
[2] Sir Charles Cunningham, 'Policy and Practice', *Public Administration*, Autumn 1963, p. 235.

which control, with relatively small staffs, the operations of great corporations or of local authorities: while other departments, such as National Insurance, Labour, or the Board of Inland Revenue, are operating companies on a gigantic scale. It would be agreed, however, that there is plenty of scope for the common development and pooling of management techniques in which the Treasury should take the lead.

Secondly, the analogy is particularly misleading if the image of a mobile general manager which one has in mind is that of the traditional general administrator. For this individual, while performing a most valuable part in the co-ordinative work of government, and thus having a natural place in Treasury operations, is decreasingly able to perform departmental tasks without greater specific experience and knowledge. While it may sound sensible to suggest that there should be a still greater degree of talent-spotting by the Treasury, the proposition runs into unsolved difficulties about what talents need to be spotted – and by whom.

VI

This leads me to two reflections. The first concerns the long-standing problem of how to relate the functions of planning, financial control, and general management. Placed all together in the Treasury, as they have been for some time, the machinery of government becomes clogged and over-weighted. One suggestion sometimes made is to hive off personnel and other forms of management to a new department, leaving the Treasury to co-ordinate economic and fiscal policy. But I am sure that this would be slicing the cake in the wrong place. Personnel management and budgetary control are both common housekeeping services to central government as a whole, which require a common co-ordinative technique in which the Treasury is well versed. So long as economic planning was viewed as no more than the erection of a Keynesian super-structure for guiding fiscal controls, it could reasonably remain in the same place. But once viewed as an extroverted and dynamic process for transforming the economy, the style of action required becomes quite different. It no longer accords with even the most exalted kind of housekeeping.

The need for new focal points of decision-making in central government is now widely recognized, and has some reflection in recent departmental changes. I have not the time to pursue current problems further. But I suspect that a critical question for any economic planning authority is whether it can co-ordinate the pattern of aid to the private sector. Thus the problems of agricultural subsidies that were mentioned earlier might be tackled more fruitfully if they were viewed, and required to be justified, as elements in a general budget of aid to industry. I also believe that questions of physical planning cannot sensibly be treated as subsidiary to general economic planning, or be parcelled out among four or five departments; and that housing and road and industrial location subsidies could be conceived and related more rationally if their common focus in environmental problems was recognized, and some specific Ministry with appropriate research staffs could think about these problems.

It will be said that I am posing new problems of departmental co-ordination and reducing the budgetary powers of the Treasury, and both charges are true. But I do not believe that central government can now live without new and necessarily more complicated styles of co-ordination. As to the Treasury, it would still do the ultimate vetting of the budget in line with political priorities and the total size of the cake: and this work is not precluded by a more expert sifting of decisions for broad fields of policy, such as already occurs to some extent with Defence. In some ways Treasury work would be lightened (particularly on the detailed probing where it is weakest), although in other respects it would need to be much more sophisticated. That is the burden of modern government.

Secondly comes the future of general-purpose administrators. That they have a future I am convinced. What may be called the integrative values of the administrative class of the civil service – the loyal, impartial, and hard-working devotion of its members to a collective interpretation of the public interest – is an enormous asset to British government that is rightly admired abroad. The problem is how to relate these qualities to the modern tasks of government, with their increasing demand for a person who might be described either as a generalized specialist or as a specialized generalist.

One possible solution, the one urged by Sir Charles Snow and others,[1] is to increase the scientific equipment of the administrative class, both through the direct recruitment of more science graduates and through what Americans call the 'retreading' of senior scientists into general administrators. For various reasons, including the attitudes of and opportunities before the scientists themselves, I am doubtful whether this particular approach will succeed. The specialist

[1] C. P. Snow, *Science and Government*, Oxford University Press, 1961. See also *The Management and Control of Research and Development* (Zuckerman Committee), HMSO, 1961, p. 93.

classes of scientists, engineers, and others already occupy a more important place in the higher civil service than they did before the war and a more likely development is the creation of more posts of high status for the kind of specialists who have the capacity to interpret a considerable range of relevant knowledge.

A strength of the general administrator has always been his broad-mindedness, his resistance to technocracy. Although the social sciences have their own biases (which are possibly mutually corrective), I am among those who believe that closer acquaintance with these fields of study can do something to impart the appropriate perspective and authority to the modern administrator's work. The French description of the administrator as a social scientist in action puts this point, although it goes too far. Further, there is also a strong case for enabling administrators to study the special issues with which a department or group of departments are concerned. One is often appalled at the gap between ivory-tower contributions to practical subjects and what practical men actually do. Since none of these studies are necessarily best done at undergraduate level, these suggestions envisage a period of post-graduate education for general administrators, with opportunities to pursue more specific research at a later stage.

This brings me to my final point. It is paradoxical that despite the fascinating nature of administrative issues, public administrators – especially perhaps today – often feel frustrated and caught in a narrow round of limited tasks and frequent consultations. Part of the explanation is organizational, which has been discussed. But part is intellectual – a lack of time and opportunity to look freshly at the environment of facts, theories, and opinions with which the administrator (often unconsciously) is encircled.

At a time when new schools of business administration are being created, I believe that it is important to establish some equivalent institution for the advanced study and teaching of public administration. As this lecture has tried to show, public administration and business management share some common ground but there is no subject called management which can adequately comprehend both fields. Administrative issues occur in a distinctive setting, which I have tried to describe, and involve a wide range of academic studies, some of which are rapidly expanding. It is also important, especially at a time when the flow between government and industry is all in one direction, to keep up the 'public interest' end of the argument in the perpetual duologue between government and business. Objectivity is always good. There is an administrative perspective, just as there is a business one, which is worth examining as well as (possibly) simply acquiring.

These aims, if they are sound, call for co-operation between Government, universities, and such bodies as the Royal Institute of Public Administration. There have recently been valuable developments in Treasury training courses: useful as these are the broader aims call for a blending of government's awareness of its practical needs with the universities' capacity for disinterested studies: and it is this latter element that has still to be harnessed.

6

Government by Committee*

SIR KENNETH WHEARE

Sir Kenneth Wheare introduced his book on the use and abuse of committees by saying: 'Committees are to be found wherever people in Britain are working together for some common object – in trade unions, in churches, in musical and literary societies, in sports clubs, in business and professional organizations, in employers' associations, in schools and universities. They are in fact an important part of what is referred to with reasonable pride as "the British way of life". Indeed, in a moment of exasperation during the war, Mr Churchill exclaimed: "We are overrun by them, like the Australians were by the rabbits." '
The following extracts from the first two chapters of Wheare's book deal with aspects of both the use of committees and the role of the specialist in administration.

From the vast field of study which collective group action provides not only for the political scientist, but also for the economist, the sociologist, the social psychologist, even the anthropologist, I have selected for examination a few examples of certain types of committee. I have confined myself mainly to committees forming part of the machinery of government or closely attached to it, and even within this field I deal with a selection only of the many examples of the types of committee involved. I have attempted to bring some order into my exposition by arranging committees into types, and the principle upon which the arrangement has been made is that of the function or process which the committee carries out rather than of the institution of which it forms a part or with which it is connected. Thus I speak of committees to advise, committees to inquire, committees to negotiate, committees to legislate, committees to administer, and committees to scrutinize and control. As examples of committees to advise I choose the elaborate and complicated structure

* From Sir Kenneth Wheare, *Government by Committee*, Oxford, Clarendon Press, Oxford University Press, 1955, pp. 1–2, 5–9, 16–20. Reprinted with permission of the Clarendon Press, Oxford.

82

of bodies operating under a variety of names – panels, councils, working parties, as well as committees – set up to advise the central government in this country. Of committees to inquire I consider again principally bodies acting on behalf of the central government – royal commissions, select committees of the House of Commons, departmental and inter-departmental committees. My examples of committees to negotiate are chosen principally from the bodies engaged in settling questions of hours of labour, rates of wages, and conditions of labour in central or local government service. Committees to legislate are illustrated by the standing committees of the House of Commons; committees to administer, by the committees used in their thousands by the local authorities of the country; and committees to scrutinize and control by three select committees of the House of Commons – of Public Accounts, on Estimates, and on Statutory Instruments. And in studying these examples of the six types of committee I try to make some comparison between them of their effectiveness and shortcomings. . .

It is important to have some idea of what is meant by a committee, if only because there are some bodies called committees which are not really such, and there are many committees called by other names. The essence of a committee is, surely, that it is a body to which some task has been referred or committed by some other person or body. It may be asked or required or permitted to carry out this task. But that is not all. The notion of a committee carries with it the idea of a body being in some manner or degree responsible or subordinate or answerable in the last resort to the body or person who set it up or committed a power or duty to it. It is difficult to state this position precisely. Suffice it to say that if a body or a person commits a power or duty completely to another body, and relinquishes this power entirely, surrendering full and final authority to this body, then this latter body is not a committee. There is inherent in the notion of a committee some idea of a derived or secondary or dependent status, in form at least; it lacks original jurisdiction. It acts on behalf of or with responsibility to another body. Any body which has a task committed to it in this way may be considered a committee, whether it calls itself a council, a commission or royal commission, a conference, a board, a bureau, a panel, or a working party. They are all committees and may be studied as such.

Too much must not be made of this distinction of status. Many committees act in practice in complete independence of the bodies which set them up and to which they are formally subordinate.

Some business could not be transacted at all unless committees exercised exclusive jurisdiction. Their working in such circumstances is directly comparable with that of other groups conducting business collectively whose formal status is higher than theirs. At the same time too little must not be made of the question of status, for it often happens that the proper degree of responsibility or autonomy which a committee should enjoy in relation to its parent body is a question of the greatest importance in the working of a system of committees. Where committees differ from some other bodies engaged in the collective conduct of business is that the question of status *can* arise as a practical problem; it is potentially almost always a matter for argument.

But although our idea of a committee is governed partly by considerations of status – the notion of a body to which some other body has committed a task and to which it is in some sense subordinate – it is governed also by considerations of size. We have some ideas, even if only vague ideas, that if a body is smaller than a certain number or larger than a certain number it can hardly be called a committee. Thus although people speak sometimes of a committee of one, and although indeed the word 'committee' has had the connotation of one person to whom functions were committed,[1] it carries with it today the notion of at least two people acting together. Those who say that they prefer a committee of one are usually taken to be expressing in paradoxical form their disbelief in committees. In practice the whole idea of a committee is that it should be a group and it is seldom conceived of as less than three persons – the lowest number which permits of an exchange of views, of the election of a chairman by majority decision, and of the conduct of business without recourse to the exercise of a casting vote by the chairman. Although a committee of two permits of an exchange of views, it contains the possibility of deadlock in the election of a chairman, and, if that hurdle is surmounted, it permits all questions to be carried by the chairman's casting vote.

If a committee of one is thought of as a contradiction in terms, so also is a committee of a thousand and one. Though, formally speaking, a task may as easily be committed to a thousand and one people as to one, and although those people may be entitled to be called a committee, yet in practice we expect a committee to be smaller than that. We cannot be precise about size, and our ideas on size will certainly be affected by the function that the committee is to perform, but we

[1] It is still so used to describe an individual to whom the person or estate of a lunatic is committed.

have certain upper limits in our minds beyond which a body may be formally a committee but in practice is a public meeting. Yet it is well known that one of the most famous committees in the world, the Committee of the Whole House of Commons, contains over 600 members. How are we to explain this anomaly?

The explanation is to be found in considerations of procedure, which are worth describing because they cover many examples of which the Committee of the Whole House of Commons is only one. A first reason for a numerous assembly referring a matter to a committee consisting of all its members is to ensure that there will be a sufficient attendance at the deliberations. If it is feared that many members will not attend or if it is known that some can come at one time and others at another, it is wise device to make everybody members of the committee and thus have a good chance that a sufficient number will be present. We are told that this was one of the reasons why bills came to be committed in the seventeenth century, to committees of the whole House of Commons.[1] It will be apparent that committees of the whole House in these circumstances are really more like committees than their name suggests, for they would consist in practice of a smaller number of people than the whole House.

A second reason for referring matters to a committee of the whole is that in the consideration of some business by a numerous assembly some members are interested and competent in some matters and some in others. All desire the right to be able to intervene when their interest is aroused, though it is known that it will be seldom that the attendance is very large. In such cases it is wise to refer a matter to the committee of the whole, for it combines equality of opportunity for all the members with a virtual certainty of a smaller and more effective body considering the matter in practice. This is one justification – though not an explanation of the origin – of the practice of the House of Commons of dealing with its financial business in committees consisting of all the members of the House under the names of Committee of Supply, of Ways and Means, and of the Whole House, according to the stage which the business has reached.

When we come to consider the historical origins of this practice we reach a third reason for referring matters to a committee of the whole, and that is the advantage of a different procedure. There are stages in the discussion of a matter when, if it is referred to a committee, an advantageous change of procedure can be effected. Thus

[1] Ilbert and Carr, *Parliament*, p. 54.

in the earlier history of the House of Commons the members wished, when they came to discuss finance and to decide how much money they should vote to the king, to keep their deliberations secret from the king. The Speaker of the House in those days was regarded by the House as the king's man and they feared that, if they deliberated in his presence, he would repeat what they said to the king. So they decided to discuss financial business in committee, which meant that the Speaker left the chair and a chairman took his place. Although nowadays the Speaker is no longer suspect, the procedure goes on as before, with advantages quite unintended by those who devised it.

There are two procedural advantages which large bodies may obtain by going into committee of the whole, The first is privacy. Some public bodies – such as town and county councils, for example – are required to meet in public. If they wish to discuss something privately they may do so by referring the matter to themselves as a committee, and in this capacity they are not required to meet in public. They are not in practice a committee at all; their numbers are unchanged, but they can exclude the Press. A second advantage which may be gained by going into committee is that procedure is often more flexible and informal. Members are often permitted in committee to speak more than once, and if the meeting is also private, a freer discussion may occur. For both these reasons – privacy and freer discussion – many public bodies with large membership refer matters to themselves and thus formally constitute themselves as committees. But they are often committees in no more than name.

It would seem therefore that when a large body calls itself a committee it does so for certain procedural reasons which assist it to perform its work in a particular way, but that these ways of proceeding are not really what we mean by working through committees. There is fairly general agreement that committees are relatively small groups of people, and the exceptions found in the procedure of the House of Commons and of town and county councils are exceptions which prove the rule.

It may be worth while to add that, although committees are often composed of a selection from the members of a larger body, they need not be so composed. It is true that committees of the House oi Commons do in fact consist only of members of that House; the same is true usually, but not always, of committees set up by town and county councils. But committees or commissions may be appointed by ministers, or, as in the case of royal commissions, by the sovereign on the advice of ministers, and in these cases their members

Taxation official / expert misleading.

may be chosen from a variety of places and their claim to the title of committee comes from the fact that a task has been committed to them by the minister. He appointed them; they report to or are responsible to him ...

Pro. General argument.

When we look at the way in which offices are organized, both in the government and outside it, we find that, as a general rule, officials at the top or head of the office are not experts; they are usually general practitioners. This is in most cases a consequence of necessity, for those at the top must deal with a wider range of questions than those lower down and they are bound to be less expert. In British government and in a good part of British commercial and industrial organizations, it is indeed positively asserted that the officials at the top should be general practitioners and not experts. It is not thought odd or unusual to move the permanent head of the Ministry of Supply to be head of the Colonial Office or of the Ministry of Health. A high official of the Treasury is regarded as fit to be head of any department of government. It is general capacity – not specialized knowledge – which is encouraged by the recruitment and promotion policies of the British civil service. In local government, too, a town clerk, a chief education officer, or a treasurer are general practitioners. It is with officials at this sort of level that committees are usually associated and it will be common for them to find that they are dealing not with experts but with general practitioners.

If experts are rarely at the top of offices, they are rarely also at the bottom. Citizens who have been brought into contact with officials in the years since 1939, when so much of the economic life of the country has been subject to control by officials, have formed the firm opinion at certain times that they know a great deal more about these things than do the officials that deal with them. Even if officials higher up may have some technical knowledge of the subject under control, those lower down, dealing with the public at the office counter, are almost certain not to be expert. They are most likely to be laymen in relation to those with whom they have to deal. These subordinate officials usually concern committees only in so far as their work is carried out under the administration or the scrutiny and control of a committee, but it is none the less important to notice that they can usually lay no claim to the title of expert.

Which officials, then, are the experts? They fall into a number of groups. First of all there are those who may be called expert because they have committed to their charge a part of a department's work. Thus in a department like the Colonial Office there are officials who are experts in some part of the world, such as the West Indies, West

87

Africa, the Pacific, or South-East Asia. A similar form of specialization is possible in the Foreign Office and the Commonwealth Relations Office also. Or in departments like the Ministry of Education or the Home Office or the Ministry of Food, officials may specialize in technical education or visual aids, aliens or police, licensing or fish or potatoes or livestock. The area of a department's activities is broken up on some principle of division, varying often with the nature of its work, and officials become experts through being concerned with one of these parts, branches, sections, or divisions.

But there is another group of experts which is of a rather different kind. They are expert in some skill or technique or branch of knowledge which may have a reference to more than one section of the department's work and may be needed anywhere. The legal adviser is the best example of this kind of expert. Most of the experts of this kind are advisers. The need for a legal adviser was early recognized, but with the increasing intervention of departments into many aspects of social life other expert advisers have been added. Economists, agricultural scientists, psychologists, anthropologists, medical men have all been enlisted to advise the official in his task of regulation and control. Some departments, like the Ministry of Agriculture, will have a lot of these specialists, particularly on the scientific side. The Colonial Office makes use of a whole range of experts including sociologists and anthropologists and every type of agricultural scientist.

The work of some departments requires that the scientific and technical experts should be more than advisers to officials and should actually undertake administration themselves. The service departments, for example, and the Ministry of Supply staff certain of their branches with experts in armaments, surveying, building and construction work, and engineering, to name only a few. Most of these administrators would be unable to perform their tasks unless they had a specialized knowledge of the fields with which they deal.

In the service departments and in certain other departments there are groups of officials engaged in inspectorial and supervisory work who have specialized scientific or technical qualifications. They hold positions at a variety of levels in a department's work, ranging from such officials as the senior chief inspector and the inspectors under him in the Ministry of Education, the factory inspectors and the inspectors of constabulary of the Home Office, or the veterinary inspectors of the Ministry of Agriculture down to the clerks of works, supervisors, and foremen on certain types of work done in and for government departments.

The location of the expert has been discussed so far almost entirely in terms of the central government department. Most of what has been said there is true also of the organization of local government departments. The chief officials tend to be general practitioners; the experts are found somewhat lower down. In some departments, like that of planning, say, most of the staff are experts with architectural or some other professional qualification: in the treasurer's department, similarly, most officials will specialize in some branch of the corporation's finance. In the organization of an education department there will be found specialists in areas of the department's work, such as primary schools or secondary schools, and also specialists of the other type – psychologists, advisers on music or physical education, school medical officers, and the like, whose expert knowledge is available throughout the whole range of the department's activities.

Most of the experts of whom we have been speaking so far are administrative officials. But it would be misleading to suggest that the experts in the civil service are always administrators. On the contrary many thousands of those employed in the civil service who could be classed as experts are not engaged in regulatory work at all. They may be engaged upon research or production in governmental employment under such departments as the Ministry of Supply, the Admiralty, the Air Ministry, the War Office, the Agricultural Research Council, or the Department of Scientific and Industrial Research. It is true that some of these scientific and technical officials have organizing work to do in connection with research and production, but the great majority of them are not officials in the strict sense. They are in the civil service because the state has taken over direct responsibility for certain types of research and for the production of certain goods. The Atomic Energy Research Establishment at Harwell is a good example of this kind of organization. It is predominantly an organization of experts, some of whom are responsible for running it, but most of whom do not perform the administrative function. It is these scientific employees of the state who make up the greater part of the scientific civil service.[1] They far outnumber now the specialized inspectorial staffs or professionally qualified regulatory staffs which for a long time constituted the bulk of the technical experts in government service.

From the point of view of committee work it is apparent that these scientific experts who are not administrators are likely to be called upon for their services and should not therefore be disregarded in our analysis. They present special problems also, for in their contacts

[1] See Cmd. 6679 of 1945, *The Scientific Civil Service*.

with laymen and with officials, more particularly with the general practitioners among officials, they find difficulty in presenting their views in sufficiently non-technical language or in the appropriate form to be effective. One of the problems in committee work is to make the best use of the expert and in particular of those experts in the scientific civil service.

But let us remember in conclusion that not all experts are in the civil service. Experts outside government service are to be found, for example, on the various committees to advise that are associated with British government. Scientists, economists, statisticians, philosophers and historians, antiquarians, educationists, lawyers, doctors, architects, chemists, sit along with experts in, say, the retail trade, in the affairs of some trade union, or in the problems of some industry or branch of agriculture. These latter types of expert belong also to the category of 'the interested party' of which more is to be said later in this chapter. But it is worth while at this stage to notice that they have an expert status, though of a distinctive kind.

It will be found, too, that experts outside the government service like experts within it, are sometimes officials, but sometimes not. In many cases they may advise officials both within and outside the government service. They illustrate once more the principle that to equate official and expert is misleading, and if the true function and importance of each is to be rightly understood in committee work the distinction must be kept clear. The principal purpose of the discussion of the expert which I have undertaken in these pages has been to emphasize this distinction.

7

The Many-Headed Tribunal[*]

The Minority Report of the Poor Law Commission, 1909, long recognized as one of the classic texts of social administration in Britain, contains examples of organization analysis with insights that can also be applied elsewhere. The main task of the Poor Law Commission was to study the working of the Poor Law. The Minority Report, now more famous than the Majority Report, was signed by the Rev. Russell Wakefield, Mr F. Chandler, Mr George Lansbury and Mrs Sidney Webb. This extract is concerned with the functions of committees and executives; it particularly draws attention to the committee defect of 'many-headedness' and the advantage of an administrator 'adequately trained for and professionally engaged in the task of hearing and weighing evidence'.

It is, however, to the Boards of Guardians, not to their Destitution Officers, that Parliament has entrusted the ultimate decision as to the grant of Outdoor Relief. We have therefore inquired how it is that these Boards have been so unsatisfactory in their decisions on the evidence presented to them. It was suggested to us by some witnesses that their failure to deal wisely with the problem of Outdoor Relief was to be attributed, in the main, to the character of their membership, and especially to a certain falling-off in social *status* which is alleged to have taken place since the abolition, by the Act of 1894, of the property qualification and the *ex officio* membership of the Justices of the Peace. Putting aside the question as to exactly what changes in social *status* may have taken place in different Unions, we have satisfied ourselves that, broadly speaking, the disastrous social failure of the Outdoor Relief administration neither began in 1894, nor has been increased or appreciably affected by the changes of that year. Moreover, though different Boards of Guardians tend

* From *The Minority Report of the Poor Law Commission, Part I, The Break-up of the Poor Law*, London, The National Committee to Promote the Break-up of the Poor Law, 1909, pp. 59–64 and 80–2.

to err in different directions – some granting Outdoor Relief where it ought to be refused, others refusing it where it ought to be given – we cannot say that, in our experience, we have found the so-called 'strict' Boards appreciably different from the 'lax' Boards, in such fundamental matters as the complete ascertainment of facts, the specialized treatment of the different classes, the enforcement on the recipients of properly considered conditions of life, and, above all, impartial uniformity as between committee and committee, between meeting and meeting, and even between case and case. The cause of so general and so prolonged a failure, common to all parts of the country, and to all periods of the past three-quarters of a century, must, we suggest, lie deeper than any personal characteristics of particular Guardians, or even of particular Boards.

We discover the cause of the failure of the Outdoor Relief administration in the very nature of the Local Authority itself. There is, first of all, the inherent difficulty that a 'Destitution Authority' finds in providing itself with the varied technical advice necessary to the proper domiciliary treatment of so many different classes of persons. Just as the Destitution Authority, as we have seen, inevitably tends to have one General Mixed Workhouse, so it tends to content itself, for all classes alike, with the unspecialized counsel of the one 'mixed official' known as the Relieving Officer. When it becomes conscious of the inadequacy of its staff, the only reform it can conceive is to multiply the number of these Destitution Officers, or to set one above the others as Superintendent, or to have one to check the others as Cross Visitor. It is significant that we have not discovered a single Board of Guardians that has sought to equip itself with a differentiated out-relief staff, in which one officer reported on personal hygiene and the sanitation of the home, another on the educational requirements and progress of the children, whilst a third specialized on the investigation of the financial resources and on the recovery of contributions from relatives. But apart from this lack of specialized officers, which is as inimical to successful Outdoor Relief as it is to successful institutional treatment, the present tribunal for hearing and deciding applications for Outdoor Relief has what, in our judgment, is the fatal defect of being a board – a board, by the way, of as many as twenty, forty, or even 100 members. The Board of Guardians was established mainly for the purpose of administering the Workhouse. But the work of adjudicating upon individual applications for Outdoor Relief differs fundamentally from that of managing institutions. When a committee manages a school or a hospital, it does not decide what shall happen to each particular pupil or inmate. We recognize at once how fatal to efficiency it would be if the managing committee undertook to decide what should be taught to each particular child or gave orders about the treatment of an individual patient. In the administration of institutions, the resolutions of the committee, which are merely general decisions as to policy, do not become instantly and irrevocably operative in individual lives. In arriving at these decisions the suggestions and criticisms, the experience, and even the idiosyncrasies of a number of different persons are all of use. The analogous work in the sphere of Outdoor Relief is the formulation, and from time to time the alteration, of the general rules according to which the relief should be given. This is essentially the work of a representative body.

Most unfortunately, the application of this well-established distinction between the functions of a representative body and those of its executive are obscured in the case of the Poor Law by a strong popular sentiment against officialism, and a general impression that the direct interference of the Guardians interposes a human element between the destitute and the soulless letter of the regulations. The Guardians themselves, jealous of the officers and their powers, and keenly alive to the electoral advantages of being able to oblige individuals and to obtain a reputation for sympathy with the poor in whole neighbourhoods, are naturally altogether on the side of popular sentiment in the matter. Even the educated classes are apt to be under the impression that the Poor Law of 1834 earned the execration of all benevolent men by its sacrifice of human rights to inhuman official theory. It is, therefore, necessary to point out that the restriction of a representative body to its proper function by no means dehumanizes that function, any more than the fact that the jurymen in a criminal case are allowed neither to make the law nor to devise punishments according to their own fancy, withdraws from the prisoner the protection of that human element without which legal institutions would be impractical. It is not suggested that the Destitution Authority should not investigate grievances, or should be denied that access to the relieved without which it would remain in ignorance, not only of the grievances actually complained of, but of the far more important shortcomings of which neither the paupers nor the officers are conscious. Apart from grievances, the main work of the Destitution Authority, that of drawing up the regulations and deciding general questions of policy, must depend for its effectiveness on continuous contact with and observation of its effect on the destitute, as well as on the community at large. There is, besides, the work of choosing the officers and, when necessary, dismissing them. In the exercise of duties thus scientifically limited there would be far more scope than at present for the exercise of that intelligent public-spirited humanity which at present is literally crowded out of the meetings of the Destitution Authority by the intrusion of individual applicants for relief, appealing to the short-sighted good nature, to the desire for electoral popularity, and to the inevitable tendency of the ward representative to be regarded by his constituents, and finally by himself, as a patron saint at whose intercession the Authority must either grant the prayer or slight the intercessor. We have ourselves repeatedly noticed the members of Relief Committees and Boards of Guardians, whilst the cases were being heard, paying very different degrees of attention to the evidence that was being given before them; swayed very differently by considerations other than those given in evidence; and governed by quite different views of social expediency. The joint decision of so composite a tribunal on individual cases can never be a good one. All this is intensified if the Board or Committee is selected by popular vote of the districts in which it has to administer Outdoor Relief. Moreover, the composition of the Board or the Relief Committee, whether elected or nominated, necessarily varies from meeting to meeting, and even from hour to hour. In some cases, to quote the description given by one of our committees, 'the Guardians wander from one (Relief) Committee to the other at pleasure', and 'administer relief to their own constituents'. When the Board does not divide into committees, the effect is much the same. 'Each Guardian's attention,' says a witness, 'is attracted only by cases from his own parish,' and too frequently 'it is turned, during the rest of the time occupied with the relief lists, to other matters, to the loss of silence or orderly prodecure'. Under such conditions it is not surprising to learn, on the testimony of a Guardian in a large urban Union, that Outdoor Relief granted on one occasion may on the next be reversed, without there being any change in the circumstances, but owing to different Guardians being present. This matter ought not to depend on the views held by individual Guardians, but upon a general policy of the whole, otherwise preferential treatment is obtained by some and in other cases the reverse'. 'I find in my own experience,' testifies the President of the Metropolitan Relieving Officers' Association, 'that cases are dealt with differently according to the absence or presence of certain Guardians. Say my Relief Committee consists of eight persons. If Mary Jones comes one week, with certain Guardians present, she will perhaps get 3s 6d in grocery; but if she comes the following week before another batch of Guardians, she will perhaps get 5s'. 'At present,' says an Inspector, the Guardian 'considers every case in his ward as "my case" and speaks and acts as if he was the specially appointed almoner of the ward that he represents. . . . When the case comes on, the Guardian rises and pleads the cause of his client. . . . I have observed,' continues this Inspector, 'that when Guardians have stated their cases, and have indeed acted first as counsel, and then as judge and jury for their client, they too often consider they have done their duty, and leave the room'. All this may be very human; but it is so in the sense in which to err is human; and the notion that such humanity is good either for the destitute or for the community at large must be thoroughly shaken off in reforming our system.

This fatal defect of 'many-headedness', combined with that of mutability of membership, has, we need hardly say, no relation to the manner in which the board or committee is constituted. It is not a question of the name of the body, or of the method of its election or appointment, or the number of its members, or of the size of the area for which it acts, or even of the character and capacity of its membership. The business to be done is, by its very nature, unfit for decision by the votes of a board or committee, whether elected or appointed. There is in it absolutely no room for sentiment about an individual case, personal acquaintance or neighbourliness. It is in fact, 'one of the weak points' of the present 'system of relief,' says an Inspector, 'that it gives opportunity for favouritism, or that preferential treatment which a spirit of neighbourly friendship is sure to engender'. To let in any such considerations – still more to allow the decision to depend on the accidental presence or absence of particular members – is to deprive the community as a whole of its power of control, and to risk non-compliance with the general rules which, by its elected representatives, the community has deliberately laid down. Far from the plan of decision of individual cases by an elected Board being essentially democratic, the chance whim or the accidental non-attendance of one member becomes the means of thwarting the popular will. This is none the less the case because the interference has been caused by a member who has been himself elected. When, however, the intervention is that of an *ex officio* or nominated member, the arbitrary and undemocratic character of this assumption of power by an individual member becomes glaringly apparent. The work of deciding whether or not a given case comes within rules is, in fact, essentially of a judicial character. As such, the only way to obtain effective democratic control, and the only way to secure a uniform impartiality, is to entrust the detailed application of the popularly formulated rules to one responsible person, adequately trained for and professionally engaged in the task of hearing and weighing evidence, who can be definitely instructed to apply even to case after case the principles laid down by the elected representatives of the people . . .

We attribute the almost universal failure of the Boards of Guardians in England, Wales and Ireland, and of the Parish Councils in Scotland, in the matter of Outdoor Relief, in all districts, and in every decade, partly to an illegitimate combination, in one and the same body, of duties which can be rightly done by a board or committee, and those which can be efficiently discharged only by specialized officers, continuously engaged in the task. The 'many-headed' body is exactly what is required, whether for Outdoor Relief or for the management of institutions, for arriving at decisions of general policy; for prescribing the rules that are to be followed in determining particular cases; and for examining grievances and preventing the abuse of their powers by the officers. But if the administration is to be democratic in its nature – if, that is to say, the will of the people is to prevail – it is absolutely necessary that the application to individual cases of the rules laid down by the board or committee should be determined evenly, impartially and exactly according to the instructions, by a salaried officer, appointed for the express purpose. We recognize this at once in the management of a school, a hospital or an asylum, where the most democratic committee finds the best guarantee for the execution of its will in ordering its salaried officials to apply the rules that it lays down. But in the dispensing of Outdoor Relief the same 'many-headed' body that makes the rules, has also attempted to apply them to individual cases; and in doing so inevitably brings in personal favouritism, accident and the emotion of the moment, to thwart the will of the community as a whole. The relative success of the Outdoor Relief administration of some of the best governed parishes of Scotland, is due, we think, to the fact that, whilst the Parish Council makes the rules, their application to individual cases is not left to the chance membership of a particular meeting, but is in practice largely entrusted, as a judicial function, to the Inspector of Poor.

It is, however, not merely that 'many-headedness' of the existing tribunal is the cause of the failure of the Outdoor Relief administration of today. We ascribe that failure quite as much to the fact that the duty is entrusted to a Destitution Authority, served by subordinates who are essentially Destitution Officers. To entrust, to one and the same authority, the care of the infants and the aged, the children and the able-bodied adults, the sick and the healthy, maids and widows, is inevitably to concentrate attention, not on the different methods of curative or reformatory treatment that they severally require, but on their one common attribute of destitution and the one common remedy of 'relief', indiscriminate and unconditional. And just as this Destitution Authority tends always, in institutional organization, to the General Mixed Workhouse, with its promiscuity and unspecialized management, instead of to the appropriate series of specialized nurseries, schools, hospitals, and asylums for the aged that are needed, so it tends also, with its general 'mixed official', the Relieving Officer, to provide, alike for widows and deserted wives, the sick and the aged, infants and school children, one indiscriminate unconditional dole of money or food, instead of the specialized domiciliary treatment, according to the cause or character of their distress, that each class requires.

8

The Art of Judgment*

SIR GEOFFREY VICKERS

In The Art of Judgment, *Sir Geoffrey Vickers writes about institutional decisions taken in the conduct of public affairs. His approach spans several disciplines including psychology, sociology, economics and management theory, and draws on his remarkable breadth of experience. He acknowledges his indebtedness to H. A. Simon, whose writings, especially in* Administrative Behaviour, *pioneered much of the work that has been done in this field. In this extract, Chapter 3 of his book, Vickers considers the way in which Royal Commissions and similar bodies 'appreciate a situation'.*

THREE CASE STUDIES IN APPRECIATION

Royal Commissions and similar bodies provide examples of appreciation which have the advantage of being matters of public record. They are appointed not merely or even primarily to recommend action but to 'appreciate a situation'. By exposing what they regard as the relevant facts and their own value judgments thereon and the process whereby they have reached their conclusions, they provide the authority which appointed them and also all who read their report with a common basis for forming their own appreciations and, it is to be hoped, with a model of what an appreciation should be. They are thus not only analytic but catalytic; and the knowledge that they are expected to be so leads them to expose their mental processes with a fulness which other public bodies seldom equal and are often at pains to conceal.

I have chosen three such reports, differing widely in subject matter – the Buchanan report on traffic in towns; the Robbins report on higher education[1]; and the Gowers report on capital punishment.[2]

* From Sir Geoffrey Vickers, *The Art of Judgment, A Study of Policy Making*, London, Chapman & Hall, 1965, pp. 50–66. New York, Basic Books, Inc., © 1965 by Sir Geoffrey Vickers. Reprinted with permission of the author and the publishers.

Each is concerned with a basic problem of regulation; the problem of how to assimilate a major change with the greatest net gain (or least net loss) of 'value' whilst preserving the balance of the system. The first is concerned with the impact of greatly increased demands for traffic movement; the second with the impact of greatly increased demands for higher education; and the third with the impact of a demand for a change in a critical provision of the penal law. Of these impacts the first falls primarily on the physical system which both generates and must accommodate traffic; the second on the educational system and the third on the penal system; but as the reports show, their impacts cannot be thus canalized. It is interesting to observe how similar are the mental processes made explicit in the three reports.

The terms of reference of the Buchanan Committee were 'to study the long-term development of road and traffic in urban areas and their influence on the urban environment'. The report begins by establishing that, failing restrictive measures not yet dreamed of, the number of motor vehicles in Britain may be expected to double in ten years and treble in little over twenty years, whilst their users may increase even more rapidly; and that this will overwhelm the city street, as now conceived, even as a traffic carrier, as well as multiplying the injuries to amenity already caused by motor traffic – danger, intimidation, noise, fumes, visual intrusion, and squalor. This comprehensive reality judgment is assumed even by the Committee (careful as they are not to impose their own value judgments on others) to be negatively valued by their fellow countrymen. Even those who attach little value to environmental amenity or who are prepared to sacrifice it all for 'better traffic' may be assumed to rebel at a process of development which must be self-defeating even in terms of traffic alone. The report shows that the relation between roads and traffic, still more the relation between traffic and the other activities of human life will not regulate itself at any acceptable level or evoke such regulation by any regulative devices now in use. So a case is made for more ambitious regulation.

The next phase of the enquiry is to find some more adequate and comprehensive way to think about the manifold relations involved. The conflict is reduced to the interaction of two variables by the following analysis:

(1) Traffic is an aggregate of individual journeys, virtually all of which are from buildings to buildings and are generated by the activities in those buildings. Their density is a function of the

density of buildings; their pattern a function of the spatial relation of these buildings to each other.

(2) All buildings need some degree of accessibility. All buildings also need a number of environmental characteristics, to some of which motor traffic is inimical. The conflict involved in reconciling traffic needs and other needs can be expressed as the conflict between accessibility and good environment.

(3) Urban traffic movements take place through streets which still serve the multiple needs which they served in medieval times – vehicles in transit, vehicles arriving and departing, pedestrian traffic, retail trade and personal intercourse, to which parking has now been added. This is an historical legacy, not a law of nature. Dwellings also contained not long ago relatively undifferentiated space. 'As recently as the seventeenth century all sorts of human – and even animal – traffic flowed through the salons of Versailles.'[3] The use of space between buildings, no less than within buildings, could and should be differentiated so as to minimize the conflict between accessibility and good environment.

(4) The conflict, even if minimized, will remain. A given minimum of environmental value implies an upper limit to the amount of accessibility. How high this limit may be depends on the tolerable upper limit of a third variable, cost.

These four propositions state the problem with admirable clarity and perfectly exemplify the 'optimizing-balancing' problem involved in policy making.

The conflict between accessibility and good environment is today, as the report shows, sharper than it need be. Unless reconciled by radical re-design, it will cross one of those thresholds already noticed and result in the progressive deterioriation of both terms of the relation. Re-design, however, can only expand the area within which choice is possible. It cannot remove the need to choose – or let events choose for us – what the balance shall be.

The report proceeds, with a wealth of concrete illustration, to bring home these generalizations. Actual traffic flows are analysed, especially the dominant one generated by the diurnal need of people to move from home to work place and work place to home. 'Through' traffic is distinguished as a separate and relatively soluble problem which complicates but does not create or alter the problem of a city's self-generated traffic. Examples are given of the separation of vehicular traffic from other uses of a city's 'outdoor' space – some by horizontal, some by vertical planning. Her Majesty's Stationery

100

Office, freed from its usual logistical restraints, decorates the broad margins of the pages with telling diagrams and photographs which scarcely need their captions. The report is a major piece of public education and makes clear the dimensions in which education is possible.

It educates the reader's *reality* judgment, stressing the necessary relation between the amounts which can usefully be invested in motor vehicles on the one hand and in facilities for their use on the other; describing the relative orders of magnitude of the factors involved, including the time factor; exploring the degree of certainty attaching to the various forecasts; and inviting him to consider what towns will be like on the basis of present trends and what they might be like on the basis of trends which might be achieved. In doing so, it helps him to break through limitations imposed by his tendency to *see* things in their now familiar categories – to see streets for example, as necessarily serving all the diverse purposes which they serve today.

Further, it educates the reader's *value* judgment – tentatively, as befits a government committee in a society which tolerates the manipulation of its values more readily by private than by public agencies. The Committee limits its own value judgment on priorities to the proposition that good environment *matters*; it has some *value*; accessibility cannot be *all*. When expressing its faith in the potentialities of towns it goes further – '. . . of this there can be no doubt, that there are potentialities for enriching the lives of millions of people who have to live in towns beyond anything most of them have yet dreamed of'.[4] Text and illustrations combine to expose the reader to representations of what is and what might be and invite him tacitly not merely to value but to share the committee's valuation. Will you really put up with this? Would not that be worth striving for? In doing so, they help him to transcend limitations imposed by his tendency to *value* things in familiar ways – to accept what he supposed to be inescapable, to cling to what he believes to be indispensable, without examining those habitual valuations.

Finally, it educates the reader's instrumental judgment by setting a problem before him in its full complexity and showing him some of the innovations already in use – main shopping streets in cities turned daily into pedestrian precincts by barriers of removable posts; precincts and buildings based on a platform high enough above ground level to accommodate all vehicular traffic below; and so on. Such conceptions presented to minds not yet familiar with them, open doors wider than are needed for their own entrance. They help

101

to usher in the concept of traffic architecture, the concept that access to buildings should be as much a function of design as the facilities for circulation within them.

I am concerned here not with the merits of the report as such but with its significance as a step in policy making. It is an admirable example of appreciative judgment; I will draw from it two conclusions which will be of continuing importance to this study.

First, what difference did the report make? Like every effort of appreciation, it posed a problem in regulation and elicited possible executive solutions which it in turn appreciated. It revolved through this circular process sufficiently to identify the main relations to be regulated (a wider set than at first appeared) the kinds of measure which regulation would involve and the scale of effort which would be required. Pursued further – and the covering report of the steering committee pursues it somewhat further – this would lead to progressively more concrete conclusions about the institutional arrangements needed to support the necessary executive actions, the method of finance and so on.

This, however, was not the only aspect of the report. It also enlarged and changed for its readers – doubtless also for its members – the mental organization of which their appreciative judgments are a temporary expression, those readinesses to see, to value and to respond to situations in familiar ways which, while they last, exclude the power to see other possibilities. I will call these readinesses of the mind its appreciative 'setting'. The exercise of appreciative judgment does more than produce an executive solution. It also changes the appreciative setting of the mind concerned, perhaps in fields remote from those of the actual judgment – as Mr Black's abortive plan changed his own and his manager's appreciative setting in regard to each other, no less than in regard to the undertaking's steel supply. This is the educational significance of the mental activity I call appreciation, which is an exercise always in self-education and usually in the education of others also. Since regulation in contemporary societies involves the co-operation of ever more people in sustaining policies of ever greater range and cost, the educative value of appreciations, such as the Buchanan report and the dialogue to which these publications give rise is of major importance and accounts for their increasing use.

How needful and how difficult is the educative task appears even from the comments of the steering committee, a separate committee appointed by the Minister to comment on the report and draw conclusions for public policy.

Referring to limitation on the urban use of vehicles as one possible component in the regulative process, the steering committee commit themselves to two significant comments. 'Distasteful though we find the whole idea, we think that some deliberate limitation of the volume of motor traffic in our cities is quite unavoidable. The need for it simply cannot be escaped.'[5] The committee does not explain why 'the whole idea of limitation should be distasteful' to it. Individually, we must assume that each of these eminent men, in the regulation of his personal life, had long since accepted the fact that limitation is inescapable and indeed necessary to the creation of form. As experienced men of affairs they must also have realized that limitation is essential to the regulation of human institutions. I derive the impression that their 'distaste' for limitation in this connection reflected a long entrenched value attaching to the economic system of Britain in the nineteenth century, that strange epoch when the populations and technologies of Western peoples were expanding among unused resources and unoccupied spaces so vast that the idea of self-limitation was temporarily lost, and the arduous goal of choosing and realizing a 'good', at the cost of all it would exclude was comfortably hidden behind the so much simpler objective of aggregating 'goods'.

The impression is strengthened by a later comment on the limitations which attach even to the possiblity of limitation. Of these

'... perhaps the most decisive is that a car-owning electorate will not stand for a severe restriction. It is a difficult and dangerous thing in a democracy, to try to prevent a substantial part of the population from doing things that they do not regard as wrong...'[6]

Since the steering committee accept the report unreservedly, they presumably accept also its conclusion that unless regulation on a scale unprecedented is introduced at once, the car-owning electorate will have to stand for something more than a severe restriction. (It is standing for it or rather sitting for it already in many public places.) So the committee's comments presumably mean that the electorate will not stand for any restriction *imposed by authority*, rather than by the blind course of event. And the ground for this judgment is that in a 'democracy' people think that state interference should be limited to the prohibition of things which are 'wrong'. The judgment may well be realistic, when applied not to any 'democracy' but to our own today; but the value judgment of which it is a realistic appraisal is itself under fire and in course of change in many contexts.

The regulation of our society requires increasingly the prohibition of acts not because they are morally wrong but because they are socially inconvenient, and it thrusts on to the courts the task of enforcing these prohibitions as part of the criminal law. As Barbara Wootton has recently pointed out[7] this confuses a concept of crime and punishment deeply imbedded in the consciousness of both judges and laymen and leads to incoherent and ineffective enforcement of the law in this area, of which 'traffic offences' form an important part. Clearly 'a democracy' whose citizens do not regard it as 'wrong' to break traffic laws however necessary will not enjoy the pleasure and convenience of car-owning as far as it otherwise might; but to assume it incapable of learning any better seems to me defeatist. (The avoidance of income tax was once regarded very much as the avoidance of parking regulations now is). Legislation in such matters is only one of the triggers of cultural change and cultural change is a possibility which the steering committee seems to me to underrate.

On the need and possibility for organizational change the steering committee has no such reservations. It is clear that existing institutions could not carry out work on the scale required and it recommends the creation of executive agencies, central and regional. Although the committee describe these truly as bodies 'for which there is no precedent', both they and the reader feel themselves on more familiar ground in this part of the report. Public corporations acting as executive agencies have a long history in Britain and elsewhere. The mind has little difficulty in picturing these corporations – much less, at least, than in picturing the towns which they would create.

Finally the steering committee comment on the cost. The true cost, they observe, is 'the real burden of labour and materials that would be entailed'.[8] The money cost would be greater, since so much of the money cost would result from the purchase of land. Raising and paying out the money would present economic problems distinct from those involved in canalizing so much labour and materials to this use. It would, however, earn some indirect return in the increase of revenue from motor and fuel taxation. It is noteworthy that this monumental capital expenditure is never described in the Report as an investment, nor is any reference made to the values of land and buildings which these developments would create, or to the return which these might yield, as distinct from the return to be squeezed from the increased traffic. Something seems already to have muted the Report's clarion call to regard vehicles and the accessibility they need as only one element in the planning of cities as a fit setting for all the activities of civilized urban life. That something is the inertia, necessary yet dangerous, of established ways of seeing and valuing what is and what might be.

Like the Buchanan Committee, the Robbins Committee was required to consider the results of an explosive increase in demand. The expected rate of increase in the demand for higher education, as estimated by the Committee, was about the same as the expected rate of increase in motor vehicles as estimated by the Buchanan Committee – nearly double in ten years, nearly treble in twenty years, with an even sharper rise in the first five years. The Committee, however, was in the happy position of concluding that this demand not only should be met in full (a value judgment) but could be met in full (a reality judgment). The expansion would involve heavy physical development but far less than the rebuilding of our towns; heavy institutional development but on familiar lines. The budgetary problem was marginal, for higher education's share of the national budget, 0·8 per cent in 1962, would need to grow to no more than 1·9 per cent in twenty years. As the Committee cautiously remarked (para 636) ' . . . it is quite conceivable that there are items in the present composition of the (national) budget that on calm consideration may be deemed less urgent than a better educated population'.

None the less the Committee showed itself highly conscious of budgetary problems. Its definition of 'real cost' is significantly different from that of the Buchanan steering committee: ' . . . the real cost of anything is what has to be foregone in order to have it'. It devotes a whole section to 'Education as an investment' and stresses throughout that one main effect of expenditure on 'higher education', most of it being current expenditure, is to maintain a national asset, 'human capital', which is essential even to the merely economic well-being of a community such as Britain in a competitive world. It is at pains to discuss the reality of the return from this investment and the reasons why it cannot be measured. At some point diminishing returns might set in but 'there is a strong probability that the country would have to go a good deal beyond what is contemplated in our recommendations before the return in terms of social net product could be said to suggest general over-investment in this sector'.

The terms of reference of the Committee were

' . . . to review the pattern of full time education in Great Britain and in the light of national needs and resources to advise . . . on what principles its development should be based. In particular . . . whether there should be any changes in that pattern,

105

whether any new types of institution are desirable and whether any modifications should be made in the present arrangements for planning and co-ordinating the development of the various types of institution.'

The Committee was thus concerned with the redesign of an institutional, rather than a physical milieu and none of its recommendations, with one exception, required its readers to make a revaluation so radical as that required by the Buchanan Report, in its estimate of accessibility as a 'good' which every urban environment must limit in order to optimize all its values. Indeed, it sets no difficult problems of valuation as such. That higher education should be available for all who can benefit from it and wish to do so; that it should be almost wholly financed by public funds; that the bodies which receive these grants should be free as they are now to decide how to spend them; that individuals thus freely educated should owe no formal obligation to the society which had done so – all these basic values are either taken for granted or asserted and justified and none of them struck a controversial note.

None the less the Robbins report invites the reader to accept a radical rearrangement of its subject matter, 'for the greater part of their history the universities which were more or less independent of the state, dominated the landscape of higher education' (para. 14). Their isolation had been eroded, partly by their increased dependence on state support (canalized though it was through the University Grants Committee) partly by the rise of near-university level technical colleges, teacher-training colleges, and other institutions which had grown up within the 'state' system of education. The time had come in the view of the Committee to group together these institutions of 'higher education'. This involves a mental adjustment of a peculiarly difficult and complex kind. Institutions previously recognized as part of the state system of education must be taken out of that category, grouped with others (the Universities) which have hitherto strenuously and successfully resisted such grouping in a new category called 'higher education' which must then in turn be related more closely than before to 'secondary' education.

This logical step had its dangers and can be discussed as an educational and as an organizational issue. I am concerned not with its merits but with its psychological and more precisely its epistemological implications. The reader is invited to change his categories of thought and that in a more radical and painful way than anything involved in the Buchanan Report. It is not unduly difficult to subdivide the contents of a given concept, to replace, for example, the concept of a street by a number of concepts each providing for one or more of the many functions of that multi-purpose space. It is much harder to regroup the objects of our attention in new categories which straddle the boundaries of the concepts they replace. Administrators know the difficulty in another form; in reorganizing institutions it is easiest to subdivide, more difficult to combine and most difficult to carve up and regroup the constituents in a going concern. The difficulty illustrates and is perhaps related to the more basic psychological difficulties attending the growth of the categories which underlie our judgments of reality.

A complex net of values attaches to the concept of the University. Any change in this concept – in particular the attempt to include in the category institutions from a category hitherto sharply distinguished – implies a threat to these values. Behind the discussion of merits and demerits this threat adds its often unidentified note of warning. It was this which made so significant the question whether higher education as newly defined should be the responsibility of the minister responsible for other education, or of some other minister. Whichever the recommendation, it would carry a threatening message to numbers of its most concerned readers, in the one case the threat of an intention to 'isolate', in the other the threat of an intention to 'level down'. No words can neutralize such implications. It is significant that this is the only aspect of the enquiry which elicited a dissentient report.

The report, like all such exercises, is not merely a plan for a reorganization of our institutions. It is also a plea for the reorganization of our thought.

One other aspect of the Report deserves attention from the point of view of this enquiry. The Report recognized that the expansion which it proposed depends on an adequate supply of teachers. Since an increase in the numbers of students produces almost automatically a corresponding increase in the number of *potential* teachers, the Committee saw no reason to suppose that their plans would in the long run demand an increase in the proportion of graduates needed by the teaching profession. They recorded however that at the time of their report recruitment was growing more difficult, the proportion of highly qualified teachers in schools was falling and the emigration of academic professionals, especially to America, gave ground for serious concern. They stressed the need to make teaching in higher education sufficiently competitive both in its rewards and in its conditions of work and the ways in which this could be done; but in their estimates of expense they make no provision for these changes in direct and indirect inducements, nor did they refer to the difficulty of ensuring that Universities would or could make these qualitative changes in condition of work, even if the money were available, at a time when they would, as the Report recognized, be overstretched to meet the demands of increased quantitative standards. This was clearly the bottleneck where, especially in the immediate future, the 'optimizing-balancing' skill of the policy maker would be most sharply called on, both at Government level, in giving higher education a degree of precedence which must leave a lasting impression on it and in the Universities, in reconciling quantitative and qualitative demands. It is possible for a reader to feel that the Report does not fully face the most critical area of true cost, namely the problem of ensuring that the potential teachers of the immediate future do what the Report wants them to do, to the exclusion of 'what has to be foregone in order to have it'. Their hesitancy in this regard parallels the hesitancy of the Buchanan steering committee, when faced with regulation demanding a cultural change which cannot be directly achieved by reorganization.

The Royal Commission on Capital Punishment* was required

'to consider and report whether liability under the criminal law in Great Britain to suffer capital punishment for murder should be limited or modified and if so to what extent and by what means, for how long and under what conditions persons who would otherwise have been liable to suffer capital punishment should be detained and what changes in the existing law and the prison system would be required, and to enquire into and take account of the position in those countries whose experience and practice may throw light on these questions.'

Thus the Commission was not concerned, like the Buchanan Committee, with a reorganization of the physical milieu, or, like the the Robbins Commission, with a reorganization of the institutional milieu. It was concerned with the reorganization of a small but important part of the penal law. This was occasioned not by an expected influx of murders (as the others were occasioned by an expected influx of motor cars and of students) but by a change in the valuations current in society. Opposition was growing to the death penalty as such and this new standard of value was shouldering its

* The following summary of the reports is taken from the paper 'Appreciative Behaviour' already cited.

way into the closely organized, traditionally sanctioned ways of classifying and valuing offences embodied in the criminal law and in the social conscience in which that law must rest. The change was not universally accepted; opinion was divided. The Government of the day wished to make some gesture of acknowledgment towards it, without fully accepting it; and at the same time to extend and clarify the public debate on it, which was unusually impassioned.

So it appointed a Royal Commission with terms of reference designed to exclude a recommendation on or even a discussion of the *abolition* of the death penalty for murder.

The Commission prefaces its report with a statement of what it has done, in words which should make a psychologist's imagination boggle.

'Our duty . . . has been to look for means of confining the scope of (capital) punishment as narrowly as possible without impairing the efficacy attributed to it. We had . . . to consider . . . how far the scope of capital punishment . . . is already restricted in practice and by what means; and whether those means are satisfactory as far as they go . . . how far capital punishment has . . . that special efficacy which it is commonly believed to have. We had . . . to study the development of the law of murder and . . . to consider whether certain forms of homicide should be taken out of that category and to what extent the liability . . . might be restricted on account of . . . youth or sex or . . . provocation . . . the extent to which insanity . . . should . . . negative or diminish criminal responsi-bility . . . whether murder should be redefined . . . whether any defects . . . could be better remedied by giving either the judge or the jury a discretionary power . . .'

and so on; leading to the conclusion –

'. . . we thought it right to report at some length . . . in the belief that, *irrespective of our recommendation* [my italics] it would be useful . . . to place on record a comprehensive and dispassionate picture of the whole subject . . .'

The nature of appreciative judgment could not be better illustrated or defined.

By far the greater part of the Report is devoted to describing all relevant aspects of the situation as it is and as it might be, by applying to a great variety of fact and opinion, partly conflicting, the selective, critical and integrating mental activity which I have called reality

109

judgment. This is interspersed with comments expressing the commissioners' own approval or disapproval, their value judgments. Each section ends with recommendations for action, with instrumental judgments.

The reality judgment is voluminous and complex. What homicides fall within the legal definition of murder? What kind and degree of insanity exclude the offence, what kind and degree of provocation reduce it to manslaughter? How varied are the motives and circumstances attending these crimes and the personalities of those who commit them? What is the purpose and what is the effect of death or any punishment in such diverse cases? What are the respective roles of prosecutor, judge, jury, and Home Secretary in deciding which of those convicted shall hang? To these and many other questions answers are offered, definite or tentative, with whatever historical background is needed to make the present explicable.

The report has a double story to tell; the story of the relevant events and the story of the relevant ideas; and it moves easily, unconsciously between the two. The numbers and details of murders committed, of convictions, reprieves, executions belong to the world of event. The attitudes of men to murder and to the death penalty, the interaction of these two in giving murder a special status among crimes, these belong to the world of ideas, a world not less susceptible of factual report. Between the two worlds is an infinity of subtle, mutual connections which the commissioners must disentangle as best they may; for these interactions lie at the heart of the problems committed to them. What is, what should be, the relation between criminal responsibility as a legal fact, defined by the common law; responsibility as a medical fact, defined, they are assured, by the criminal's neural organization at the time and thus no less factual than the law but assessable only by the often divergent judgments of psychiatrists; and responsibility as a normative judgment passed by men on men, a standard of what *should be deemed to be* the scope and limits of their responsibility, yet a standard not without effect on the actual state of minds which know they are to be judged by it.

Based though it is on the present and the past, the reality judgment is concerned primarily with the future, which alone can be affected by any change now made. The death penalty could be limited by changing the definition of the offence or by subdividing it into 'degrees' or by admitting a discretion as to sentence. The reality judgment must arrive at an assessment of the probable effect of these alternatives, collecting what evidence seems relevant about the

110

experience of other countries which have abolished, relaxed or reinstated the death penalty; and about the problems attending the long-term custody of prisoners convicted of crimes of violence.

Some of this evidence is significant in two distinct ways. The commissioners, having collected the views of police officers on whether abatement of the death penalty will increase violent resistance to arrest, must evaluate these statements of opinion both as evidence of what is likely to happen in the world of event and as evidence of what is actually happening in the world of ideas. For the apprehensions of the police about the effect of a change in the law, whether well or ill founded, is both a fact and a force in the present situation and one which may indirectly alter the effect which such a change will actually have – for example, the willingness of police officers in Britain to continue to work unarmed.

The evidence on which the commissioners found their reality judgment varies vastly in certainty and in character. Statistics and estimates; opinions, often discordant, on matters both of fact and of value; the views of different authorities, past and present, on the legitimate purposes of punishment; the views of psychiatrists on human responsibility and its impairment by mental illness; all this and more goes into the mill and out comes the reality judgment, balanced, coherent, urbane, a mental artifact which only familiarity robs of the wonder which is its due.

The Report is also sprinkled with the commissioners' own value judgments – usually expressed as agreement with value judgments found as a fact to exist in the community but none the less their own. Insanity *should be* a defence to murder. The then existing rules defining insanity for this purpose were narrower than they *should be*. Among the sane who are convicted of murder, culpability varies so much that they *should not* all be sentenced to the uniform, extreme and irreversible penalty of death. The abatement of this penalty *should not* be left to so great an extent to the Home Secretary. It *should not* be left to the judge; or (for different reasons) to the jury. It *should be* expressed in the law itself. In these and a dozen other contexts, the commissioners, going beyond the recording of other people's value judgments, commit themselves to value judgments of their own. Whence came the norms which produced these value judgments?

The answer is simple but subtle. The commissioners used the norms which they brought with them to the conference table; but these norms were changed and developed by the very process of applying them; by the impact of the reality judgment which they focused; by

111

the impact, attrition and stimulus of each commissioner on the others; and by the exercise of their own minds as they applied them in one way or another, on one hypothesis after another, in the search for a better 'fit'. As an illustration, consider their debate on the use of the Home Secretary's power of reprieve.

It was their value judgment that, among people convicted of murder, culpability varied so much that punishment should also be variable. This, they realized, could be achieved (within their terms of reference) only by elaborating the definition of the crime or by giving someone discretion to vary the penalty to suit the facts. The first alternative they found in practice to be immensely difficult. The second was already in operation, in that nearly half those convicted of murder were reprieved on the recommendation of the Home Secretary. Was it 'satisfactory' or even 'proper' that so large a discretion should be vested in the Home Secretary? Eminent witnesses were divided. To make the Home Secretary 'an additional court of appeal, sitting in private, judging on the record only and giving no reason for his decision,' said some, 'does not fit into the constitutional framework of this country'. The Archbishop of Canterbury objected on different grounds.

'It is intolerable that this solemn and deeply significant procedure should be enacted again and again, when in almost half the cases the consequence will not follow . . . a mere empty formula is a degradation of the law and dangerous to society.'

Other distinguished witnesses found it not at all intolerable. The late Lord Samuel suggested that 'to maintain a degree of uncertainty as to what would happen in marginal cases may be very useful in retaining a deterrent effect on potential criminals'.

The commissioners' appreciative judgment was that the Home Secretary's discretion was 'undue'; but the only less objectionable alternative seemed to them still too repugnant to recommend. So their appreciative judgments on the point were expressed without any recommendation for executive action. Such recommendations as they did make, they admitted, 'would go very little way toward solving our general problem' (i.e. how to relieve the executive of this undue responsibility). They concluded that

'. . . if capital punishment is to be retained and at the same time the defects of the existing law are to be eliminated . . . the only practicable way of achieving this object is to give discretion to the jury to find extenuating circumstances requiring a lesser sentence to be substituted.'

This appreciation, though without an executive recommendation and indeed all the more on that account is perhaps the most important part of the Report; for it amounts to a finding that there was no satisfactory halfway house between the existing state of affairs and the *abolition* of the death penalty. Their terms of reference precluded them from recommending or even considering abolition; yet a major contribution of their report to the appreciative judgment of their contemporaries was to support the movement for abolition which had in fact occasioned their appointment. The Report made some recommendations for action. Some were adopted in the Homicide Act, 1957; some were ignored. Yet if all had been ignored, the major importance of the Report as an appreciative judgment would have remained the same. The state of the commissioners' minds on the subject of capital punishment, after they had made their appreciation, was different from what it was when they began; and this change, communicated through the Report, provoked change, similar or dissimilar, in greater or lesser degree, in all it reached, from serious students to casual readers of newspaper paragraphs; and thus released into the stream of event and into the stream of ideas an addition to the countless forces by which both are moulded.

Yet their terms of reference, on the face of them, required them only to recommend means to a given end.

REFERENCES

[1] *Higher Education*. Report of a committee appointed by the Prime Minister under the Chairmanship of Lord Robbins, 1961–63, HMSO. Cmnd. 2154.

[2] Royal Commission on Capital Punishment 1949–53, chairman, Sir Ernest Gowers, *Report*. HMSO Cmd. 8932.

[3] BS para. 38.

[4] BW para. 66.

[5] BS para. 30.

[6] BS para. 31.

[7] Wootton, B., *Crime and the Criminal Law*, 1963, London, Stevens.

[8] BS para. 53.

9

The Giving of Orders*

MARY PARKER FOLLETT

In the first two months of 1933, Mary Parker Follett, one of the front rank of political scientists of her time, gave a series of lectures on organization and management to the newly formed Department of Business Administration at the London School of Economics: this extract, about the basis of authority, is from the first of those lectures. Mary Follett was born in Boston in 1868 but had close connections with England which began with a year (1890–91) which she spent as a student at Newnham College, Cambridge. Her main work, The New State, *was published in 1920, and contained an exposition of her theories about the importance of the individual in society and the group process – a group can never be understood as an aggregate of its parts but is an organization with a collective will. The latter part of her life was spent in studying business management and from 1929 to 1933 she studied industrial conditions in England; this attracted her because she saw in business-men some of the deepest thinking at that time, thinking which combined the ideal and the practical. This extract might be regarded as Mary Follett's contribution to the 'human relations' approach to authority.*

I said that tonight I wanted to talk about the giving of orders. There is a very marked and an extraordinarily interesting change taking place in our thinking on this subject. Arbitrary orders are beginning to go out of fashion. One man told me that the word order had not been used in his factory for twenty years. I was much interested last October in the report of an interview with Herr Emil Ludwig when he was here for the production of his play *Versailles*. He had high praise for his London producer and said, 'We work ten hours a day. . . . I have never seen anything like it. And yet he rules without giving orders. He exercises authority without claiming authority.'

* From Mary Parker Follett, *Freedom and Co-ordination*, London, Management Publications Trust, 1949, pp. 17–33. Reprinted with permission of Sir Isaac Pitman & Sons Ltd.

Mr Filene tells us: 'My brother and I do not issue orders. My father never ordered things done, he thought no one got anywhere with such power unless he had his organization with him.' Another business man writes of 'those superintendents and foremen who think of their job as consisting solely in that simple but archaic practice of ordering'. This man, you see, calls ordering an archaic practice.

We find the same thing in the army. A general in the American army tells us that there is a very different idea in regard to orders appearing in military training. He says that when he was at West Point all that he was taught was to look stern when he gave orders, and if he was not obeyed to send the delinquent to the guardhouse. Not a minute of the four years of military training was given to the management of men although that was going to be the principal job of everyone there. He took his first command and not only he wasn't popular, but he wasn't accomplishing what he wanted to do. Then he was sent to teach in the military department of a college. There he found he was really up against the problem of how to handle men for there was no guardhouse there to which to send refractory students. He tells us that that experience taught him how to handle men without forcing them, and he went back to the regular army knowing that he had learned how to control without giving orders. There are many in the army now, he says, who have learned this lesson.

But of course this word is still used in the army and also in industry. In the more progressively managed business, however, it does not today mean an arbitrary command. If anyone doubts this, I should say to him, look at business as it is being conducted today in many plants and watch where the orders come from. What is their origin? Heaven does not privately convey them to the top executive; they arise out of the work itself and many subordinates may have contributed to them. Consider the analysis of executive jobs which is being made in some plants. This can be done in two ways. You can have an expert do it or you can do it as they did in a certain large bank. There they had each man make an analysis of his own work. Out of that analysis rules for his job were formulated. But whether the analysis is made by the man on the job or by an expert, in both cases the rules of the job come from a careful, analytical study of the work itself.

In some factories the same method is used for operating jobs. The job is studied, a conclusion is reached as to the most effective way of performing it, and then that way is standardized until a better way is found. Hence the expression used in many factories today is not orders but standard practice. Men do not 'obey orders' but 'follow standard practice'. In such plants the worker sometimes takes part in the preliminary studies made to determine standard practice. Or if new methods are devised by the research and planning departments, still in many instances they are not finally adopted without a shop try-out, and the workers usually have a chance in this shop try-out to make objections. If they do not make objections, they have practically assented to the new methods. In plants where there are shop-committees, explicit approval is obtained from the shop committees.

I think we may say, therefore, that when the right order is found by research, the orders given by the foreman are coming to be considered not as anything arbitrary on his part, but as information in regard to standard practice, as training in method. Moreover, what is called the work-order is given in some factories by the despatch clerk and not by the foreman. This makes it clear to all that it is part of the whole plan of the factory and not anything arbitrary on the part of the foreman. And an important consequence of this is that the foreman is now released for more constructive work. There is a very marked change in this respect from even a few years ago. Executive intelligence is not today expended in issuing commands, but is released for the solving of new problems, the planning of further developments.

But in all this I am talking of the more progressively managed industries. Many are not conducted in this way. The head of a large engineering firm said to me, 'I tell my people what to do and they have to do it, and that's all there is to that.' And another general manager told me, 'I'm the boss in this place and I stand no interference from subordinates.' As, therefore, we still find arbitrary methods in many places, let us consider their disadvantages. We may say that the first disadvantage is that we lose what we might learn from the man actually on the job if we do not invite his co-operation in deciding what the rules of the task shall be. An upper executive said to me, 'I want the criticism of my men; I can learn a lot from the man on the job.'

The second disadvantage is one which anyone who knows anything at all about industry is fully aware of, namely, the friction between workers and foremen. I said to one girl at a big factory, 'What do you think would be the best improvement that could be made in a factory?' She replied instantly, 'To get rid of foremen.' This was amusing, but it shows, I fear, the usual attitude. Yet it is being found in those plants where orders are part of the general plan, are standard practice, that there is much less friction between workers and foremen.

This is easily understood. The arbitrary command ignores one of the most fundamental facts of human nature, namely, the wish to govern one's own life. 'I don't like being bossed,' a man in a factory told me. Another workman said to me, 'I'm willing to obey but I won't be commanded.' I think that a very interesting remark. Probably more industrial trouble has been caused by the manner in which orders have been given than in any other way. In The Report on Strikes and Lockouts, a British Government publication of a few years ago, the cause of a number of strikes is given as 'illegal harassing conduct of the foremen', 'alleged tyrannical conduct of an under-official', 'the alleged overbearing conduct of officials'. Again, the metal and woodworking trades in a British aircraft factory declared that any treatment of men without regard to their feelings of self-respect would be answered by a stoppage of work.

But even if instructions are properly framed, are not given in an overbearing manner, there are many people who react violently against anything that they feel is a command. It is often the command that is resented, not the thing commanded. I think it is told in the life of some famous man that when he was a boy and his mother said, 'Go and get a pail of water, John', he always replied 'I won't' before taking up the pail and fetching the water. This is significant: he resented the command, but he went and got the water, not I believe because he had to, but because he recognized the demand of the situation. That he knew he had to obey, that he was willing to obey.

I have given two disadvantages of issuing arbitrary directions, namely, that we lose possible contributions from those directed and that such directions are apt to cause friction between workers and foremen. There is a third very serious disadvantage. No one has a greater asset for his business than a man's pride in his work. If a worker is asked to do something in a way which he thinks is not the best way, he will often lose all interest in the result, he will be sure beforehand that his work is going to turn out badly. I have read that it is characteristic of the British workman to feel 'I know my job and won't be told how.' This attitude might be met by a joint study of the particular situation, it being understood that the worker out of his experience has as much to contribute to that study as anyone else. Or if a better way of doing some particular job has been found by the research department, the worker should be persuaded that this really is a better way, not merely told to do it in that way. It

117

is one of the things we should be most careful about – never to interfere with the worker's pride in his work.

Again and again we disregard the fact that workers are usually as
eager to attain a certain standard, as wishful that their performance
shall be maintained at a high level, as their employers. We often tend
to think that the executive wishes to maintain standard, wishes to
reach a certain quality of production, and that the worker has to be
goaded in some way to this. Again and again we forget that the worker
is often, usually I think, equally interested, that his greatest pleasure
in his work comes from the satisfaction of worthwhile accomplishment, of having done the best of which he was capable.

A fourth disadvantage of the arbitrary command is that it decreases the sense of responsibility, and whatever does that just
so far lowers the chance of business success. It has been noticed by
some heads of departments who have encouraged criticisms and
suggestions from their subordinates that instead of getting more
kicks and general unpleasantness, they get less, because now the
man who kicks is expected to suggest something better.

The arbitrary foreman may indeed get hoist with his own petard.
I knew a case where a workman reacting against such a foreman
deliberately carried out a wrong direction instead of taking it back
to the foreman and asking about it, and thus wasted a large amount
of material in order that his foreman should be blamed for the waste.
Thus the man who demands a blind obedience may have it react on
himself. When the accomplishment of a department is the result of a
feeling of joint responsibility on the part of all concerned, that
accomplishment is likely to be of a higher grade.

But while people should not be asked to follow directions blindly,
at the same time a subordinate should not have the attitude of carp-
ing, of finding fault, of thinking things from above wrong. The attitude most desirable for receiving orders is intelligent scrutiny,
willingness to suggest changes, courtesy in the manner of suggesting
and at the same time no prejudice in regard to what is prescribed,
but the assumption that the way prescribed is probably the best
unless one can show some convincing reason to the contrary.

If arbitrary command, the exaction of blind obedience, breaks
initiative, discourages self-reliance, lowers self-respect, how shall we
avoid these disasters? Chiefly in four ways I think. First, by depersonalizing orders. I have already referred to that when I said that in
the more progressively managed businesses orders were being changed to 'standard practice', to 'rules of the job', to merely a way of
doing the work which is accepted as the best way. But then we were

speaking only of routine work, of repetitive work. And a fresh direction may have to be given at any moment. What principle should guide us here? How can we avoid too great bossism in the giving of orders and the inevitable resentment which will follow?

I think the solution is exactly the same for the special order as for the general order, namely, to depersonalize the matter, to unite those concerned in a study of the situation, to see what the situation demands, to discover the law of the situation and obey that. That is, it should not be a case of one person giving commands to another person. Whenever it is obvious that the order arises from the situation, the question of someone commanding and someone obeying does not come up. Both accept what the situation demands. Our chief problem then is not how to get people to obey orders, but how to devise methods by which we can best discover what the order shall be. When that is found the employee could issue direction to the employer as well as employer to employee. This often happens quite easily and naturally: my stenographer or my cook points out the law of the situation to me, and I, if I recognize it as such, accept it even although it may reverse some previous direction I have given.

An order then should always be given not as a personal matter, not because the man giving it wants the thing done, but because it is the demand of the situation. And an order of this kind carries weight because it is the demand of the situation. I found something in a novel which recognizes and expresses this point. The hero of the novel, Richard Hague, was a large-scale farmer in England. And he was a very successful farmer. The author, after telling how Hague got the most out of all his materials down to the very spark with which he lighted a fire, went on to say: 'And it was the same with people. He got use out of them, though not through . . . being personally exigent in any way. It was always the force of circumstances that seemed to make the demand, not himself. He merely made it clear to them what it was that needed doing. . . . So little did it seem an affair personal to him that the sheep needed driving off the corn, or a message carried into the hayfield, that he hardly intervened. He might just call somebody's attention to what was needed, but it was the corn, the cattle, the world that required the service, not he.' And later the author tells us: 'He evidently considered that the task itself made some claim on anybody who happened to come across it, made itself the most interesting and most necessary thing in the world, so that no one could resist it.'

If orders were depersonalized I am sure we should get rid of much of the complaint by workers of tyrannical treatment, but there is another difficulty at the opposite extreme from this, and that is when not enough orders are given. The immediate superior is often so close to the worker that he does not like to give orders at all. If you go into any large shop here in London, you usually find the head of a department sitting at a desk among the salesmen or saleswomen. This person is only a little removed in the scale of authority from those under him or her; moreover, they are working together all day and it is not pleasant to get on bad terms with those with whom you are so closely associated. We often therefore find too great leniency here. Instead of an overbearing authority, we find that dangerous *laissez-faire* which comes from a fear of exercising authority. Of course we should exercise authority, but always the authority of the situation.

I overheard the following conversation in a large shop. The head of the women's cloak department called out, 'You're No. 36, Molly, aren't you? There's someone on the telephone complaining about something you promised yesterday.' 'Well, I like that,' said Molly 'some of these people would complain in Heaven.' I don't know what took place after that, but I think probably, from what I saw, that that was all that happened, except that of course the lady who had not received her cloak had to be appeased. I think probably that head of department did not like to reprimand the saleswoman and so did nothing. And of course she ought not to have reprimanded her. But that was not the only alternative. I think the solution for too little authority being exercised is exactly the same as for too much. I think that situation should have been investigated, not in order to blame anyone but in order to improve store technique. Perhaps the fault was with the saleswoman, perhaps it was in the dressmaking department where the cloak was being altered, perhaps it was in the delivery department, or perhaps, very likely, it was in the organization of the shop which did not provide for that relation between departments which would ensure the best results. A study of that incident in the cloak department need not have resulted in blame, but such study would certainly have given the people concerned better control of such situations in the future.

And that is always our problem, not how to get control of people, but how all together we can get control of a situation.

To find the law of the situation rather than to issue arbitrary commands, I have called depersonalizing orders. I think it is really a matter of re-personalizing. We, persons, have relations with each other, but we should find them in and through the whole situation. We cannot have any sound relations with each other as long as we take them out of the setting which gave them their meaning and value. The divorcing of persons and situation does a great deal of harm. While, therefore, I have said that orders should be depersonalized, a deeper philosophy shows us personal relations within the whole setting of that thing of which they are a part. Within that setting we find the so-called order.

And please remember that in all this I am not merely theorizing and telling you what I think ought to be done, I am telling you some of the ways which I have found in practice in business of avoiding arbitrary commands. If the most important is the depersonalizing of orders (it is convenient to keep to that word), next in importance certainly comes training. The general manager of a clothing factory said to me, 'Times are changing; we don't order people any more, we train them'. They have in this factory what is called a Vestibule School where a girl is trained for her job; she is not expected to pick it up as she goes along through orders given by the foreman. This has made a great difference in the feeling between the girls and the foremen in that factory, and in the cheerfulness of the girls and in their interest in their work.

Such preliminary training is, to be sure, given in many places. Here in London many of the shops have classes in salesmanship. In these classes many things are taught, many hints given, which without such classes would have to be given as 'orders' from the head of the department. In such shops, when a saleswoman is selling a dress, for instance, she is not thinking of orders, she is simply doing her job as she has been trained to do it. And there is a great difference between thinking of what you are doing as the technique of your job or as following commands.

But I am speaking now of preliminary training. Much training also has to be done by foremen and heads of departments as the work goes on – training in regard to new methods, further teaching where instructions have not been fully understood. Censure is becoming old-fashioned in the best-managed plants. When mistakes are made, it is assumed that it is a case for more instruction. We hear little of blame, reprimand, the old weapon of authority. And this point of educating instead of blaming seems to me very important. For nothing stultifies one more than being blamed. Moreover, if the question is, who is to blame?, perhaps each will want to place the blame on someone else, or, on the other hand, someone may try to shield his fellow-worker. In either case the attempt to is hide the error and if this is done the error cannot be corrected.

If the first rule for giving orders is to depersonalize the order, for order-giver and order-receiver together to find the law of the situation, and if the second rule is to replace orders as far as possible by teaching the technique of a job, a third rule might be to give reasons with the order. Some firms make it a rule to do this and I think that the firms who follow this rule find a distinct advantage therein. I know it takes time to give reasons, but I believe it saves time in the end in work done more cheerfully, more intelligently and more alertly.

I do not of course mean that an order should be discussed every time it is given, only that reasons should be given for new orders. And not always then. For many orders are time-saving devices. A superior officer often tells a subordinate officer to do something on the assumption that if he could be given all the reasons for it he would agree, I say only that when possible, reasons should be given with new orders.

An advantage of not exacting blind obedience, of discussing your instructions with your subordinates, is that if there is any resentment, any come-back, you get it out into the open, and when it is in the open you can deal with it. It is the underground come-back that does the harm, both because you cannot deal with it unless you know about it and also because its underground nature increases its intensity.

One fact which helps to show the advantage of giving your reasons with instructions is that factory after factory has had trouble with instructions posted on bulletin boards. Many general managers will tell you that posted orders don't work.

I know a lady who posted over the sink in her kitchen the proper sequence of dish-washing. Her cook did not say what she felt about it, but a few days later she put her own feelings into the mouth of someone else by saying, 'Mrs Smith's cook came to see me yesterday and she said she wouldn't have that in her kitchen.'

This instance throws some light, also, on what I have said of the advantage of the rules of the job being the outcome of joint study. If this lady had said to her cook and maids, 'Let us think out the proper sequence of dish-washing and then stick to it,' all might have been well perhaps. There would have been nothing to resent if they had a share in making the rules.

If we can run our business more efficiently by substituting for arbitrary commands a joint study of the situation, by more training of the worker, and by giving reasons for directions, it is also true that it will be of inestimable help to take measures that all shall know the purpose or purposes of factory, shop or bank, the purpose back of all directions. I am sure that if this were done directions would be more cheerfully and more carefully obeyed. Over and over again this is ignored. but I believe it is going to be one of the largest factors in our future industrial success.

One of the best speeches I ever heard was in York at the Rowntree Cocoa Works. When a number of new girls are taken into the Works, Mr Seebohm Rowntree gives a talk to them. He tells them how one little girl being careless in dipping chocolates may cause the young man who takes a box of chocolates to his best girl on Saturday evening to say that he will not buy Rowntree's chocolates next time. And then he shows the girls how this affects far more than Rowntree profits, how it will make less employment in York for girls and boys and men and women. And so on and so on. He goes on from such simple illustrations to show them their place in the industry of England. I do not believe that the girls who hear one of these talks can ever look at the 'orders' given them in quite the same way as they would if they had not been shown what lies back of the orders. This firm has found a way of making its employees share in a common purpose, of making them feel a joint responsibility, of making them feel co-partners in a common enterprise.

I have given four rules for the giving of orders. We might sum these all up by saying that the one who gives an order should try to bring those ordered into the situation. They should not be kept outside. They should be brought into the same picture. That is not very clear but I will illustrate. A friend of mine told me that he deliberately disobeyed some rule while motoring expecting that he would be fined, but he preferred to do it and pay the fine. To his surprise however, the policeman said, 'I'm not going to get you fined, but I'm going to ask you to take some copies of these rules and give them to your friends, and if you have a chance, talk them over with them.' Now, my friend would much rather have paid the fine, but he was intelligent enough to see that the policeman had found a better way of treating the matter. Instead of considering the rule against speed, or whatever it was, as an arbitrary rule from outside which one either obeyed, or disobeyed and took the consequences, he tried to get my friend inside the situation, the total situation of the needs of other motorists, of pedestrians and so on.

It is the same with orders. You have to get people within the situation, within the same picture, not issue commands to them from outside. They must somehow be made to feel that you and they are on the same job, are co-workers, even if your part is that of explaining the work, informing them of standards, and theirs is the carrying out, two equally important parts of the same thing. I think if we could

123

do this, it might be the solution of the difficult problem of supervision. Many workers object to being watched. In a case in Scotland arising under the Minimum Wage Act an overman was called in to testify whether a certain workman did his work properly. He said he could not tell, for, as he stated, 'They always stop work when they see an overman coming and sit down and wait until he has gone, even take our their pipes if it's a mine free from gas.'

Again, in a Clyde engineering works during the War, one of the blacksmiths became enraged when the managing director in his ordinary morning walk through the works stopped for five minutes or so and watched his fire. The matter was taken up by the trade union, a deputation was sent to the director, and he had practically to say that he would not watch the men's work. To be sure that was during the War when everyone was on edge. Also, I should think probably that particular general manager had not been very tactful, and tact is certainly an important consideration for the giving of directions and the supervision of work.

Moreover, I think a good deal of our language will have to be changed. I don't think that any of us would like to be 'watched'. I think we shall have to substitute another word for that, just as we are substituting other words for 'order'. A good deal of the language of personnel relations in industry could, I think, with benefit, be changed. For instance, Ford has 'trouble specialists', which I think all wrong. Many companies have 'grievance committees' or a 'complaints department'. I think that these 'trouble specialists' and 'grievance committees' are needed, but I don't think they should be called that. I don't think we should be looking for trouble. And what is called a grievance may be a misunderstanding. What is called a complaint may be the stating of some difficulty. I think these words arouse the wrong reaction and should therefore not be used.

And that brings me to almost my last topic, the need for executives to be trained in the giving of orders – taught how to anticipate reactions, how to arouse the right reactions, and so on. This means an understanding of the psychology of the matter, and that subject would take an hour in itself, but I can give a hint of what I mean. If a man under you is to do his work in a certain way, he has to acquire a certain set of habits or attitudes. There are three things you can do about this: (1) prepare the way for orders by creating in advance when possible the attitudes which will ensure their being carried out; (2) provide some stimulus for the adoption of the method suggested (the whole question of incentives comes in here); (3) give opportunity for those methods to become a habit.

In psychological language we should say create attitudes, augment attitudes and release attitudes. There is, therefore, much to think about in making out a new instruction card. It should be so worded that it does not require too abrupt a change of habit, and it should find a way of making an appeal. Moreover, the approach to a new method must sometimes be indirect. A direct approach may put a man on the defensive. We cannot be too careful of the power of previous ideas.

And if we come to realize that the following of directions is from one point of view the acquiring of habits, then we shall realize also that we must be patient until the habits are acquired. Many a time an employer has been angry because an employee wouldn't, as he expressed it, do so and so, when as a matter of fact he couldn't, actually couldn't, do as told because he could not at once go contrary to life-long habits. Couldn't even if he had accepted the direction and wanted to follow it. A general manager in America said to me once: 'There's a curious thing. I find sometimes that one of my executives will accept the suggestion and then not seem to be able to carry it out.' But it is not curious at all. The most elementary knowledge of psychology gives us the reason for this. None of us can change our mental habits in a minute however much we may wish to.

Of course, many rules could be made for the giving of orders. Don't preach when you give orders. Don't discuss matters already settled unless you have fresh data. Make your direction so specific that there will be no question whether they have been obeyed or not. Find out how to give directions and yet to allow people opportunity for independent thinking, for initiative. And so on and so on. Order-giving requires just as much study and just as much training as any other skill we wish to acquire.

The head of a factory told me that in his experience when foremen swaggered and blustered, it was not usually because it was their disposition to swagger and bluster, but merely that they didn't know how to give orders, didn't know how to get work done. It has been suggested that men wishing to become foremen should be specifically trained for their job, and that this should go beyond classes in foremanship, which consist merely of lectures. It has been suggested that they should work for a few weeks under a number of foremen whose methods they should analyse and discuss, and that they should then be given practice in substitute jobs, that is, when a regular foreman is ill or on holiday, before they are considered capable of being put on a regular job. This is, I think, a very good idea.

Business management is gaining something of an accepted

technique, but there still remains, as part of the training of executives, the acquiring of skill in the application of that technique. Managerial skill can not be painted on the outside of executives – it has to go deeper than that. Just as in the case of manual workers, so managerial workers have to acquire certain habits and attitudes.

I can sum up this whole talk in one sentence: orders come from the work, not work from the orders. They have their roots in the activities of the people who are obeying them. There is an active principle in obedience. Obedience is not a passive thing, for it is a moment in a process. There is, as a rule, a very elaborate and complex process going on. At one moment in that process something happens which we call obedience. I have said that it was an advantage to get agreement to instructions, yet it is a fallacy to think that an order gets its validity from consent. It gets its validity long before that, from the whole process to which both order-giver and order-receiver have contributed.

I have written this paper having chiefly in mind the orders given by executives and foremen to those on the operating jobs in the factory, the assistants in the shop, or clerical workers, but all that I have said applies equally well to directions given by upper executives to under executives. Applies even, we might say, more conspicuously to these. For here it is even more obvious that co-operation should be sought in the preliminary study of situations, reasons for policies discussed, the purposes of the company explained, reactions anticipated, and training provided.

I hope, however, there is nothing in what I have said that sounds dogmatic. For while we are trying to get away from a haphazard, hit-or-miss way of performing executive duties to scientifically determined procedure, still not enough study has yet been given to business management as a science for us to be sure that we have worked out the best methods in any one particular. But this we can say, that in business we have always a chance of experimenting, of testing our principles. This is what makes business so interesting. Take our subject of this evening. I am not so much urging you to admit the principles I have put before you as suggesting that you should try them out and decide for yourselves. I am urging that we should all of us take a conscious and responsible attitude toward our experience. In the matter of order-giving this means first that we shall be conscious of the different methods of order-giving, secondly, that we should feel some responsibility in the matter, that is, that we should decide, deliberately which of these methods we think the best, thirdly, that we should then follow those methods as far as the customs of our firm permit, and fourthly that we should very carefully watch results. We should try experiments and note whether they succeed or fail. And one of the most interesting things about business to me is that I find so many business men who are willing to try experiments.

I should like to tell you about two evenings I spent last winter and the contrast between them. I went one evening to a drawing-room meeting where economists and M.P.s talked of current affairs, of our present difficulties. It all seemed a little vague to me, did not seem really to come to grips with our problem. The next evening it happened that I went to a dinner of twenty business men who were discussing the question of centralization and decentralization. There was no academic talk about the necessity for centralization or the advantages of decentralization. Each one had something to add from his own experience of the relation of branch firms to the central office, and the other problems included in the subject. There I found hope for the future. There men were not theorizing or dogmatizing, they were thinking of what they had actually done and they were willing to try new ways the next morning, so to speak. I had felt the night before after the drawing-room meeting, that we had all separated at the end of the evening just the same people as when we had entered that house. But the next evening, with the twenty business men, I felt that we had all learned new possibilities, that at nine o'clock the following morning those men could do things, test out some of the things they had heard, and I felt that some of them were ready to do that.

Business, therefore, because it gives us the opportunity of trying new roads, of blazing new trails, because, in short, it is pioneer work, pioneer work in the organized relation of human beings, seems to me to offer as thrilling an experience as going into new country and building railroads over new mountains. For whatever problems we solve in business management may help toward the solution of world problems, since the principles of organization and administration which are discovered as best for business can be applied to government or international relations. Indeed the solution of world problems must eventually be built up from all the little bits of experience wherever people are consciously trying to solve problems of relation. And this attempt is being made more consciously and deliberately in industry than anywhere else.

One of the best thinkers on business management, Mr John Lee, formerly Controller of the Central Telegraph Office here, told us: 'The old discipline has passed. We are probing a new realm of human

127

relationships which is to take the place of the old relation of sub-ordination and yet is to include subordination (rightly understood).' Mr Lee died before he could carry this idea further, but he and all the deeper thinkers on business management have for some years been feeling the way for this 'new realm of human relationships'.

Business men may be making useful products but beyond this, by helping to solve the problems of human relations, they are perhaps destined to lead the world in the solution of those great problems of co-ordination and control upon which our future progress must depend.

10

What *is* Morale?*

NIGEL WALKER

Students of organization theory will be very familiar with the work of Elton Mayo and the classic account of the Hawthorne experiments by F. J. Roethlisberger and William J. Dickson (Management and the Worker, Harvard University Press, 1939). They tend to be less familiar with similar work undertaken in Britain both in industry, such as in the factories of Robert Owen and in the public service (see, for example, the Final Report of the Health of Munitions Workers Committee, HMSO, *Cd. 9065, 1918); however, such investigations have played a significant part in the history of organization theory. In recent years scholars have been returning to the study of human relations and two notable writers have been J. R. Dale (The Clerk in Industry, Liverpool University Press, 1962) and Nigel Walker. This edited version of a chapter from Walker's book is concerned with one of the fundamental questions in all fields of management.*

The two theories about the nature of morale are not difficult to state. One is that there is such a thing; the other is that there isn't. Perhaps these statements should be amplified a little before we decide between them. Until recently those who have thought about 'morale' – whether they were commanders or psychologists – have assumed that it was something which really existed and which operated as a single force upon human beings They thought of bad 'morale' as something like hunger, which shows itself in symptoms such as pain in the stomach, lack of physical strength, unscrupulous methods of getting food and so on. In much the same way bad morale was supposed to manifest itself in several different ways – for example, in absenteeism, strikes, high labour turnover, a high rate of accidents, and grumbling about minor inconveniences.

This theory – which I shall call 'the condition-with-symptoms

* From Nigel Walker, *Morale in the Civil Service: A Study of the Desk Worker*, Edinburgh, Edinburgh University Press, 1961, pp. 57–63. Reprinted with permission of the publisher.

theory' – is seldom stated in this explicit form. Probably because the notion has such a long and respectable history, investigators who make use of it have tended to assume either that everyone knows what is meant by it, or that everyone will agree with their definition of it.

When investigators began to define the word, it soon became obvious that everyone did *not* agree on what they meant by it. In the first place, some of them treated morale as something which belonged to an individual, whereas some regarded it as a property of groups. For example:

1. 'The term *morale* refers to a condition of physical and emotional well-being in the individual that makes it possible for him to work and live hopefully and effectively, feeling that he shares the basic purposes of the groups of which he is a member; and that makes it possible for him to perform his tasks with energy, enthusiasm and self-discipline, sustained by a conviction that, in spite of obstacles and conflict, his personal and social ideas are worth pursuing'.[1]

2. '*Morale* is obedience to an internal, personal authority (obedience to a sense of duty, it is sometimes called), which arises out of an ideal or value common to the group, the end sought by the group being defined by the ideal or value'.[2]

3. 'As the term is used ordinarily by the employer, labourer and psychologist alike, it refers to a feeling of 'togetherness'. There is a sense of identification with and interest in the elements of one's job, working conditions, fellow-workers, supervisors, employers, and the company. The more a worker possesses such feelings, the higher his morale'.[3]

4. 'Morale refers to the condition of a group where there are clear and fixed group goals (purposes) that are felt to be important and integrated with individual goals; where there is confidence in the attainment of these goals; and, subordinately, confidence in the means of attainment, in the leader, associates, and finally in oneself; where group actions are integrate and co-operative;

[1] Examples 1 and 4 were among the definitions emerging from the Conference on Psychological Factors in Morale held in 1940 under the auspices of the Division of Anthropology, National Research Council (U.S.A.).

[2] T. T. Paterson, *Morale in War*, p. 99, which is influenced by F. C. Bartlett, as the context makes clear.

[3] A. B. Blankenship, *cit.* M. S. Viteles, *Morale and Motivation in Industry*, p. 284.

and where aggression and hostility are expressed against the forces frustrating the group rather than toward other individuals within the group'.

Definitions 1–3 differ from definition 4 in one important respect. If we imagine a squad of factory hands – called, let us say, Henry James, Walter Pater and Ronald Firbank – then the first three definitions would allow us to talk about James's 'morale', Pater's 'morale' and Firbank's 'morale', but not about the 'morale' of the whole squad, whereas the fourth definition would make it sense to refer only to the 'morale' of the whole trio. This is not simply a matter of verbal usage, because definitions 1–3 would allow us to say that James's morale was 'good' or high', but that Firbank's was 'bad' or 'low', whereas the fourth definition would make this nonsense.

On the other hand, it is noticeable that none of the 'individualist' definitions go so far as to exclude all mention of the group to which the individual belongs, while the 'group-property' definitions use such phrases as 'individual goals' and 'confidence in onself'. There are, however, usages of 'morale' which would allow us to talk about the 'morale' of a man on a desert island[1] or in solitary confinement; and attempts have been made to describe situations in which the efficiency and cohesiveness of a group was extremely high although the individuals of which it was composed were each disgruntled and discouraged.[2] Such extreme definitions, however, are somewhat forced, and tend to be found in fiction rather than in psychological case-histories.[3] They serve, on the whole, to emphasize that morale is usually thought of in terms which include references both to the individual and the group.

The other common feature of the definitions which we have so far considered is that all treat morale as if it were what I have called 'a condition with symptoms'. The 'condition' (as definitions 1 and 4 actually call it) is not one which can itself be measured; you cannot measure 'physical and emotional well-being' (definition 1) or 'obedience to an internal, personal authority' (definition 2). It is regarded, however, as manifesting itself in, or causing, behaviour which is to some extent measurable. This behaviour takes the form of high or low productivity, frequency or infrequency of absences, complaints, strikes, quarrels within the group, and so forth.

[1] The unabridged version of *Robinson Crusoe* contains numerous passages dealing with what might be summed up as Crusoe's 'morale'.
[2] See, for example, Herman Wouk's novel *The Caine Mutiny*.
[3] A distinction at least of degree, if not of kind.

131

This theory is, of course, a comforting and optimistic one for the investigator. He is like the doctor who wants to cure a patient's cough, lack of appetite, fever and night-sweats, and knows that he is dealing with several symptoms of one disorder, tuberculosis, which he can tackle by direct methods. If absenteeism, low productivity, complaints and inefficiency are all symptoms of a real disorder called 'low morale', then perhaps this can be treated by some direct method, and so at one stroke remove the underlying cause of all these inconveniences?

As I have said, however, there is also the theory that there is no such thing as morale. According to this theory it is a mistake to assume that there is any single cause underlying all these kinds of industrial behaviour. Even if it were firmly established that there is a very close connection of some sort between them (and, as we shall see, it is not), is there any point in assuming that there exists yet another factor to which they are all linked? Only if you can either measure or manipulate that factor separately. We have just seen how unlikely it is, from the very definitions of the factor which are offered to us, that it will prove measurable; but what about manipulation? If we could show that all the measurable factors could be moved up or down by doing something to the workers that had no obvious connection with any one of these factors, we would have some justification for thinking that we were altering some hidden condition that was causally connected with them, just as a doctor is justified in assuming that he is dealing with a bacillary infection if he succeeds in curing earache by injecting an antibiotic into the thigh. But in order to be sure that one is manipulating something one must be able to measure what one is doing, even if it is only in a rough and ready way; and one is then dealing merely with one more measurable factor. If so, the argument concludes, is there any point in the notion of morale as an unobservable, unmeasurable condition underlying the behavioural symptoms of members of a group?

Investigators who take this view sometimes resort to defining morale instead as a combination of a number of measurable factors. These 'composite definitions,' as I shall call them, usually include two, three or even all of the following four concepts:

Productivity or Efficiency

One or other of these factors usually figures in these combinations. 'Productivity' is of course chosen where the employees are producing something that can be measured, such as a raw or processed material: 'efficiency' where they are performing a service of some sort, such as dealing with enquiries by telephone, interview or correspondence. It is worth noting, however, that not all definitions of morale include one or other of these factors: some investigators appear to use the term in a sense in which it is possible, at least theoretically, for morale to rise or fall in an organization without being accompanied by any corresponding fluctuation in productivity or efficiency.

Job-satisfaction

This, too, appears in most composite definitions. It is the technical term for the extent to which the employee likes his job (as distinct from his attitude towards his employers, supervisors and colleagues). Unlike such things as output or absenteeism, it cannot be measured by counting products or hours worked, but has to be estimated by some sort of communication with the employee himself. This communication may take the form of an interview; but most investigators feel that an interviewer's impression of the job-satisfaction of someone to whom he has talked, even if he attempts to quantify it, is subject to too many distortions from the way in which interviewer and interviewee react to one another; and they prefer to rely on a written questionnaire in which the employee takes his choice from a number of carefully chosen phrases representing various degrees of satisfaction or dissatisfaction with the job. When large enough numbers of employees answer this sort of questionnaire it is possible to compare the job-satisfaction of one group with that of another.

Pride in the Working Group

This is the term invented by Katz, Maccoby and Morse[1] for the 'degree of feeling of attachment to and satisfaction with the accomplishment of the immediate or secondary work group of which the employee is a member' – in other words, the attitude that makes a man maintain that his Section (the immediate working group) or his Company are 'better' than the one next door. Under the rather unfashionable name of *esprit de corps* this is a factor that has been recognized for a much longer time in military groups, who go to great lengths to foster it.

Cohesiveness

This is 'the extent to which members of the group like one another',[2]

[1] Daniel Katz, Nathan Maccoby and Nancy C. Morse, *Productivity, Supervision and Morale in an Office Situation*, Survey Research Center, University of Michigan, 1950.
[2] M. Argyle, *The Scientific Study of Social Behaviour*.

133

although more precise definitions have been offered. It can be measured by observing the extent to which they associate with each other at times like lunch-breaks, and to which, by discussion and agreement, they form common attitudes on questions such as speed of working. Sometimes it is measured by questionnaires asking members to identify those with whom they prefer to work as colleagues, and similar questions; groups whose members tend to select members of other groups are rated low for cohesiveness.

Cohesiveness is thus quite distinct from pride in the working group. Nor should it be confused with 'co-operativeness'. Co-operativeness is the extent to which the members of the group assist each other at the tasks which they, or the group as a whole, are given. No doubt this depends to a certain extent on the members' attitude toward one another; but it also depends very much on the nature of the task and on the attitude of the supervisor towards co-operation. For purely mechanical reasons it is virtually impossible to collaborate with another human being in assembling the parts of a wrist-watch, however cohesive the collaborators may be; again, in any work in which the supervisors encourage a competitive spirit co-operation is bound to suffer. Co-operativeness is not therefore easy to measure in its 'pure' state.

The most ambitious composite definition of morale would include all these factors. 'High morale' would be that state of a group in which its output is above average, its members score high on job-satisfaction questionnaires and evince considerable pride in their group and cohesiveness, and 'low morale' the state in which they produce less than other comparable groups, claim to dislike their jobs, show little *esprit de corps*, and would on the whole prefer to work with members of other groups. Unfortunately, this sort of composite definition assumes that there is a straightforward and positive relationship between these four factors, an assumption which has been found to be mistaken. High output is not necessarily associated with high job-satisfaction; people who enjoy their work are not always the hardest workers.[1] The most that can be said is that low job-satisfaction probably produces high labour turnover and absenteeism, which themselves damage collective efficiency through loss of the time of trained or partly trained workers. Nor are the most cohesive groups always those with the best output; a cohesive group

[1] See for example N. F. Kristy, *Criteria of Occupational Success among Post Office Counter-clerks*, Unpublished thesis, University of London, 1952.

will sometimes agree, explicitly or tacitly, to work at a certain pace which may be slower than the maximum which they are capable of. On the other hand, cohesive groups have higher job-satisfaction. Pride in the working group has been found in one study of office workers[1] to be associated with high productivity *in the groups*; what it does to the individual nobody seems to have asked.

There is of course no point in going to the other extreme and defining morale merely as one of these four factors; and it begins to be doubtful whether enough is known about the relationship between any two of them, let alone any trio, to make any composite definition safe. The only pair between which most of the evidence points to a positive association is cohesiveness and job-satisfaction; but this is getting so far from the ordinary man's idea of morale that to use it in this sense would achieve little but misunderstanding. Like 'the weather' the word 'morale' is best relegated nowadays to the role of a label for a field of study, which is concerned with factors of the sort I have mentioned. To use it as a name for any one of them is otiose; to use it to refer to any combination is at best obscure and at worst assumes relationships which may not exist; and, as we saw earlier, to use it as a name for something which is none of these things but in some ways underlies them all – a sort of personnel manager's Holy Ghost – is almost certainly mistaken.

At this point the employer – any employer – is entitled to ask, 'In that case, what should be the aims of a personnel policy? What am I trying to do, with my attention to welfare, labour turnover, absenteeism, my relations with employees and so on?' The answer out of all the enormous literature on the subject, is that there are only two factors which qualify as ultimate objectives. 'Cohesiveness' is studied only because from the employer's angle it may increase or reduce efficiency[2] and from the employee's angle it may strengthen his hand in his dealings with his employer. 'Pride in the work group' is similarly a means to an end, and not an end in itself. The reduction of absenteeism and labour turnover have some point in themselves, because, whatever obscure condition they are symptoms of, they certainly reduce efficiency simply through loss of trained labour. But the main aim of an employer is bound to be efficiency, both individual and collective.

The other factor that must clearly be considered as an end in itself

[1] In the Prudential Insurance Company, U.S.A. See Katz, Maccoby and Moore, op. cit.

[2] 'Productivity' should of course be understood as included in the term 'efficiency' as a special form of it.

is the employee's enjoyment of his job. To him – if it is not over-shadowed by purely economic thoughts – it is probably paramount. Is there any strong reason why it should not also be the objective of the employer? Nobody has succeeded in demonstrating that to enjoy your work makes you worse at it; and it may even have two or three tangible advantages from the employer's point of view. It will probably make you less likely to take a day off; we shall see that this applies to civil servants too. It may well make you less likely to look for another job, and so waste the time and money that has been spent on teaching you your job (or allowing you to learn it yourself): we shall see that this may be true of clerical officers. The time may even be at hand when competition for recruits to certain occupations – including office work – is so intense that enjoyment of the work may be a deciding factor; for all we know it is already the deciding factor with the literate school-leaver who is thinking of an office job.

All this, however, tends merely to show that attention to job-satisfaction can be justified –if it is not too costly – on grounds of expediency. We have reached the stage, however, when the best kind of employer is no longer the man who is simply not short-sighted or oppressive in his treatment of his employees, but is what is called 'the good employer'. This notion is used in ways which seem to me to imply that he initiates measures which make his employees' working hours pleasanter even if they cannot be shown to produce any tangible advantage from the point of view of efficiency, and indeed even if he is out of pocket as a result. If so, job-satisfaction will no doubt qualify as an end in itself.

In other words, if we are faced with the allegation that some step – such as an increase in the rate of dismissal for inefficiency – will damage morale, we need not become involved in any intricate argu-ment about factors known only to occupational psychologists. All that need be asked are two questions – 'How will it affect individual or collective efficiency?' and 'How will it affect the employees' enjoyment of their jobs?'

11

Organization Theory and the Public Sector*

R. J. S. BAKER

*Public administration is different from private, or industrial adminis-
tration, because it operates in a different environment with different
constraints. Its institutions function internally in a different way
because they have to function consistently and within those constraints.
This extract is from an article in which R. J. S. Baker, an administrator
in the Post Office, explores some of the variety of organization theories
in the public sector. His concern is to survey government departments as
working organizations in such a way that their type of organization can
be compared with the type to be found elsewhere (e.g. in manufacturing
industry).*

GOVERNMENT DEPARTMENTS – OPERATIVE FUNCTIONS

The 'operative' functions of Government Departments can be fairly
clearly distinguished from manufacturing and public utility service
functions in that they are regulatory and based on legal powers over
the citizen. Hence, in this country, they are generally subject to
detailed accountability through Ministers to Parliament – even though
they are in a large proportion routine and non-controversial – at
least until anything goes wrong. They include much of the social
services and the dealings of Government with local authorities,
industry, trade unions and so on. Some of these activities the Government operates by persuasion, consultation, and advice; but nevertheless, in a broad sense, they are all regulatory. Many of them also
involve managing large local and regional organizations and blocks
of staff and also the use of discretion even in the application of formal
rules – just as a policeman uses discretion. But the whole thing must

* From R. J. S. Baker, 'Organization Theory and the Public Sector', *The
Journal of Management Studies*, 1969, Vol. 6, pp. 25–31. Reprinted with permission of Basil Blackwell.

operate within a legally and otherwise precisely defined framework and hence there is some approximation to the classic models of bureaucracy beloved of the theorists. A Government office, local, regional or national, however, operates in the real world of human beings – and not the nightmare world of automata which some of the literature of bureaucracy seems to suggest.

Of course, it is often impossible to separate operative functions from those of adaptation and, indeed, of creation. New Government policies and changes and adaptations in existing policies cannot ever be dreamed up solely by gentlemen in Whitehall – whether Ministers or civil servants – nor, obviously, can they be worked out entirely outside the Government service by experts or pressure groups and then taken over and implemented ready-made. Adaptation and creation of new policy can often arise through the way old policy has worked out – or has failed to work out, and the people responsible for working it out need to be involved in all sorts of ways, in reporting difficulties, making suggestions, consulting and advising. An interesting subject of detailed research would be the means by which any Government Department – particularly one with a large regional and local network – communicates with its own staff and maintains feedback as to how policy actually works and how it might work better. There are many ways in which information moves up and down the official network – not only reports and correspondence, but internal conferences, visits, questions and answers at training courses and selection interviews[1] and interchanges of staff between local and regional and national levels. These formal and informal internal communications systems are probably as extensive and subtle as anything existing in any outside sphere.

ADAPTIVE-CREATIVE FUNCTIONS

Just as adaptive-creative activity can start from below, there is also inevitably much operative and, indeed, almost routine activity at high levels. Nevertheless, the main function of a Department's headquarters is adaptive-creative. Obviously this is not done simply by a number of very clever people sitting back and thinking – nor even by their reading extensively and consulting a few eminent outside experts. Most adaptation and creation of Government policies, large and small, involves the bringing together of groups of people with a variety of information, ideas and pressures of interests.

[1] A process in which I myself and experienced colleagues often find much extremely informative feedback.

This does not mean that it is usually just a matter of seeking compromises between pressure groups – nor that where it is, this is necessarily wrong. Pressure groups can represent people with legitimate interests and rights – and, indeed, ideas. Moreover, inside a large Government Department there are very many different forms of expertise, ideas and information. Major controversial questions of Government policy involve various kinds of new technological development, political questions of the rights of individual groups and people, international questions, aesthetic, legal and sociological questions, and so on. The same sort of conflicts and combinations of ideas from many quarters is involved in many, and perhaps most, of the much smaller problems which have to be solved every day in a Government Department's headquarters. In so far as these problems involve simply the interaction of specialisms there is no doubt much similarity to the problems and conflicts which occur in major research projects and development projects in the academic and industrial worlds. But the special problem of the civil servant is to co-ordinate the considerations arising from the interaction of specialisms with those arising from the mass pressures of the man in the street – or rather the many different pressures from many different streets.

INTERNAL COMMUNICATION – DISCUSSION

The public services – the Civil Service, local government and, indeed, the armed Forces – are often criticized for the amount of time they spend at meetings and committees;[1] but this is unavoidable – unless people with relevant expert knowledge and important group or personal interests are to be ignored when decisons are made. The kind of discussions which civil servants have in such meetings may be broadly divided into those with other civil servants and those with outside interests. Sometimes they are systematized by particular Government Departments or branches of Departments liaising with certain particular outside interests, trade unions, trade associations, foreign governments, local authorities, professional organizations and so on. Their job is to represent the Government to these interests and to represent – equally fairly – the interests concerned to their

---

[1] Schein, E. H., says 'It is widely believed that groups are slow and inefficient, yet case evidence has shown that if a group is composed of members who trust one another and have learned to work well together, it can work more quickly and efficiently than any member alone.' *Organizational Psychology*, Englewood Cliffs, Prentice Hall, 1965.

colleagues in the Government. They will risk being accused by each group of bias towards the other and will sometimes be involved successively in arguing almost contrary points of view – externally and internally.

The adaptive-creative process in Government, therefore, involves a vast amount of argument, much of it oral. The outsider may well ask how it is that this is not completely disruptive of the structural or organic unity of the Department and even personal relationships. The fact that it is not may be attributed to the relatively settled basis on which Civil Service Departments and their staffing are organized.

INTERNAL COHESION AND INTERCHANGEABILITY

Government organization has, of course, changed very greatly in the last two or three generations and is likely to change much more now. So far as I know, however, no important body of opinion suggests breaking down completely the very substantial degree of permanence and cohesion or completely abolishing internal interchangeability. The Fulton Committee, while wishing to open the Service to a greater degree of movement in and out, nevertheless recommended that 'most civil servants should enter at young ages with the expectation, but not the guarantee, of a lifetime's employment and that the great majority of those who come to occupy top jobs will in practice be career civil servants.'[1] They strongly criticized moving a civil servant between unrelated functions with too short a time to master a job properly; but they recommended that he 'should move between jobs, and perhaps between Departments, but usually within the areas of his specialism'.[2] Interchangeability of staff within the Civil Service is a matter of some controversy – which at least until the Fulton Report was conducted largely without agreed facts. It was difficult to say whether practice differed between different Departments, although one would naturally expect that it did. The Fulton Committee's management consultancy group interviewed 77 out of the 2498 members of the Administrative Class and concluded that moves every three years or so were normal. Perhaps these studies will in due course be followed by others over a more extensive field. They could form a useful basis for what will no doubt be the continuing debate on this subject, both inside the Civil Service and within

[1] *The Civil Service*. Vol. 1. Report of the Committee 1966–68, Cmnd. 3638, HMSO, 1968, p. 46, para. 134.

[2] Ibid., p. 40, para. 115.

other large organizations, public and private – where one has the impression that experienced opinion is not yet unanimous. Although certain phrases such as 'amateur' in the Fulton Report have caught the headlines, the Committee did, in fact, give weight to the advantages of internal and external interchangeability. The American authority E. H. Schein suggests that an important means of 'preventing intergroup conflict' is 'frequent rotation of members among groups or departments to stimulate high degree of mutual understanding and empathy for one another's problems'.[1] Likert takes a middle view:

'Rotation and changed personnel assignments are valuable and needed for such purposes as developing personnel, stimulating creativity, pumping new blood into old groups, and handling technological changes and organizational growth, but they tend to prevent work groups from becoming highly effective. In order to achieve and maintain a high level of co-operative working relationships, rapid changes in personnel assignments should be avoided in so far as possible'.[2]

An experienced civil servant has written 'it is a precondition of the functioning of a Department that its Assistant Secretaries should somehow manage to get on with each other'.[3] (Uusually we do a little better than that!) It is indeed a salutary experience to be transferred to another Branch which one had been hitherto criticizing. The mere possibility of this helps to broaden one's outlook. Of course, a transfer should not involve putting a man to a job which he is ill-equipped to master. On the other hand, people can get to know almost too much about a certain kind of specialism – not a professional or scientific specialism, but a specialism in certain policies or rules or regulations. They can know so much about the difficulties of doing anything that it is sometimes valuable to bring in a new man who knows less but takes a more radical view. Obviously individuals vary. Some people have the intelligence, quickness of mind and determination to master the fundamentals of a new subject very quickly, others do not make enough effort to look at the realities behind the policies they are dealing with even if they stay put for years. This, of course, is a matter of selection, training and leadership.

[1] Schein, E. H., op. cit., p. 85.
[2] Likert, Rensis, *New Patterns of Management*, McGraw-Hill, 1961, p. 184.
[3] Dunnill, F. A., *The Civil Service: Some Human Aspects*, George Allen & Unwin, 1958, p. 115.

THE ORGANIC SYSTEM

The informality and extent of oral discussion in Government Departments apply to vertical as to horizontal communication. Indeed, these very terms give an impression of misleading rigidity. Some communication is, in fact, diagonal and all over the place. Subject to the broad framework of organization, which is clearly defined, it is surprising how much of the day-to-day working system is undefined or changing all the time. Of course, legal powers have to be clearly delegated to named persons or defined categories of persons. In some other matters, such as authorities to make appointments the rules have to be pretty formal and precise. But in the great majority, I believe, of Government administrative functions authorities and responsibilities cannot be formally and permanently fixed. This conclusion may seem surprising; but I can only say it is based on well over twenty years' active and varied administrative experience in the headquarters of a Government Department – both in 'Whitehall-type' administrative policy work and other work of a more executive and managerial character. In relatively few instances can I recollect my own authority or that of my colleagues – equal, senior or junior – being defined by formal rules. Most of the time it was not precisely defined at all. It was nevertheless implicit and well understood. One knew that at a particular time a particular type of subject was 'red-hot' and must be submitted above one's own level or possibly to the highest level. On certain other subjects, the views not only of the Minister, but of one's own immediate chief may have been made clear plenty of times before and you knew that it was right to exercise your judgment in a certain way on your own initiative. You should know which of your own staff you could leave to carry on subject to broad direction, and which others, through lack of experience or the difficulty of the subject matter, had to be given a good deal of guidance. You might spend a lot of time discussing basic policies with your chief or your subordinates to establish a clear understanding. Once this was done, particular decisions could be taken without further reference upwards.

It is this sort of thing that produces the air of informality and sometimes casualness which visitors to Government Departments notice – whether with approval or disapproval. In either case the impression is somewhat misleading. Informality is possible because the main bedrock is firm. There is a solid basis of law and of possibly unwritten but very definite policy. It is only subject to this that surface flexibility can exist.

However, one can say generally that in Burns and Stalker's scale the headquarters of a Government Department where the work is mainly adaptive-creative is much nearer to the 'organic' than the 'mechanistic' pole. This conclusion may surprise, or even shock, some organization theorists. I can only add that it is based on experience and I have heard it supported in discussion, both by fellow civil servants and by academics. Yet we should look for something even more complex than Burns and Stalkers' straightforward line of variation between these two poles – something more like Rensis Likert's concept of an 'interaction-influence system' with its inter-locking groups[1] – a concept which must ring remarkably true to anyone with practical experience in a Government Department's headquarters.

THE STABILIZING ELEMENTS

A Government Department has both of the management functions which Sir Geoffrey Vickers[2] has defined – 'balancing' and 'optimizing'. It should be constructive, creative and adaptable but at the same time maintain the regular and systematic functioning of the social and political system. It is the guardian of many of the fixed land-marks in our society. Some of the activities of Government Departments which can very easily be characterized as stuffy are quite essential if the general population are to be able to live their lives in some confidence of the stability of their environment. Yet with our changing society, the rapidly changing scientific and technological background, a fluid and sometimes dangerous international setting, it is essential that Government Departments should be dynamic and creative as well as stable, dependable and secure. It is very easy to imagine that in the environment of public offices public servants are subjected to influences which inhibit originality. They are indeed.

Yet it is not the stability of their environment that makes them cautious but the reverse. They face conflicting, disturbing and even turbulent pressures from all quarters. Parliamentary Questions are usually cited as the prime cause of timidity and lack of delegation in Government Departments; but there are all kinds of other pressures on civil servants and perhaps even more on Local Government officers. The element of legal and administrative rigidity in public

[1] Likert, Rensis, op. cit., pp. 178–91.
[2] Vickers, Sir Geoffrey, *The Art of Judgment*, Chapman & Hall, 1965, pp. 38, 111–2.

authority structures – and it is only an element, because the structures have other characteristics of the opposite kinds – is probably more effective as a protection for initiative than for inhibiting it.

Basic internal stability in an organism is a precondition of creative activity, as Dr Grey Walter argues in his account of the evolution of nervous systems. He quotes the physiologists Claude Bernard – '*La fixité du milieu intérieur est la condition de la Vie Libre*' – and Sir Joseph Barcroft, describing the importance of homeostasis:

> 'How often have I watched the ripples on the surface of a still lake made by a passing boat, noted their regularity and admired the patterns formed when two such ripple-systems meet . . . *but the lake must be perfectly calm* . . . to look for high intellectual development in a *milieu* whose properties have not become established is to seek . . . ripple patterns on the surface of the stormy Atlantic'.[1]

This might indeed be taken as a reasonable analogy for any form of institution whose members have sufficient security of tenure and mutual confidence in one another and the institution itself to be able to think and act creatively – to produce ideas and discuss them freely with their colleagues, knowing that even if they are not eventually accepted they will not get into trouble simply through having ideas, nor feel they are giving away secrets to competitors ready to stab them in the back.

This line of thinking may be out of line with some current notions of 'dynamic' management; but there is plenty of experience that justifies it. The most revolutionary intellectual ideas often develop in a university environment which appears traditional, stable and secure – for instance, the environment within which Rutherford and Keynes in the 1930s respectively challenged the whole foundations of classical physics and classical economics.[2]

---

[1] Walter, W. Grey, *The Living Brain* 1953 (Pelican ed.), pp. 41, 42; Bakke, E. W., 'Concept of the Social Organization' in Haire, Mason (ed.), *Modern Organization Theory*, John Wiley & Sons, New York, 1959, pp. 16–75 particularly p. 58 discusses homeostatic activities in organizations; but all his examples appear to be in the private sector and he does not mention the effect of the legal basis or constitutional framework of a public organization. He expands the idea of an 'organizational Charter' but what he appears to have in mind is an abstract concept – not real charters like that of the BBC or a municipal borough or the statutes creating nationalized industries – even though such documents could largely fulfil the functions he describes.

[2] It is interesting that at the conclusion of their chapter on 'Organizational Change' Katz and Kahn appear to be suggesting that one of the most effective ways of changing an organization is to change its formal structure rather than

144

ORGANIZATION THEORY AND THE PUBLIC SECTOR

As a working community a Government Department, especially its adaptive-creative parts should have a firm basis of confidence – internal self-confidence supported by the confidence of society. A public institution cannot work properly if society simply does not want it to work and does not believe it is doing any good. It should be protected from disruptive influences but nevertheless be fully exposed to outside criticism, stimulus and controversy. Its legal and administrative structures should be firm; but easily capable of adaptation. Internal movement and career development should be planned so as to widen and deepen and not to inhibit the acquisition of knowledge and experience. People inside it must know that they will have some freedom to experiment, to think and to argue, and that when they make vigorous efforts to do things, success will be appreciated, and failure will be criticized at least with understanding. They must feel that their environment is a genuine organism and not a chaos of disparate individuals pursuing conflicting ambitions. (This does not mean they need share the same sorts of educational or social background. It is a great deal better that they should not.)

its informal organization or the individuals that compose it. Katz, Daniel and Kahn, Robert L., *The Social Psychology of Organizations*, John Wiley, 1966, p. 451.

12

Efficiency in the Public Services*

SIR FRANK TRIBE

In 1949 Sir Frank Tribe, then Comptroller and Auditor General, delivered a paper to the Institute of Public Administration in London, in which he discussed the meaning of the term 'efficiency' and its significance in the public service. His paper is interesting not only for the questions it raises about efficiency in public administration, but also for its reference to the words Plato placed over the doors of his Academy: 'Entry forbidden to anyone who cannot appreciate the importance of figures'. Tribe suggested the words should be inscribed over the doors of the Civil Service Commission; similar sentiments about the importance of numeracy are to be found in the Report of the Fulton Committee on the Civil Service, 1968.

INTRODUCTION

I should like to make it clear in the first place that, although I have held the position of Comptroller and Auditor General for some two and a half years, it is not in that capacity that I am addressing you this afternoon. If I have any claim to speak on the subject of efficiency in the public services as a whole it must be due to the fact that it has been my fortune or my fate – however one may regard it – to have served in eight different Departments of the Civil Service in the last twelve years and this has inevitably given me a wider experience than falls to the lot of most Civil Servants. If, however, I had been asked to suggest the name of the most suitable person in the Service to address you on this subject, I should certainly have named your own Chairman, who is the Head of the Organization and Methods Branch of the Treasury. But I understand that in his capacity of Chairman of the Institute he vetoed any such suggestion.

* From Sir Frank Tribe, 'Efficiency in the Public Services', *Public Administration*, 1949, Vol. XXVII, pp. 159–67. Reprinted with permission of the editor of *Public Administration*. Paper delivered to the Institute of Public Administration in London on 10 May, 1949.

EFFICIENCY AUDIT

Perhaps I should explain at the outset why I do not regard the Comptroller and Auditor General as an expert on the question of efficiency. There is in my view much muddled thinking at the present time on the question of the so-called 'efficiency audit', and it has even been suggested that I should audit the accounts of the Nationalized Industries so that I could report to Parliament on their efficiency. An auditor's duties are many and responsible, but they are primarily confined to an examination of the accounts of an undertaking. He has to satisfy himself that expenditure has been properly incurred and is properly vouched, that all receipts have been properly brought to account and that the accounts of the concern give a proper picture of its financial position. He must satisfy himself that systems of financial control are adequate and may appropriately on occasion draw attention to wasteful expenditure or uneconomical methods. But he cannot go further and pronounce judgment on the general efficiency of the undertaking. While cost accounting, as I shall hope to show later, has its proper place in suggesting lines of enquiry, I do not believe that any examination based on figures alone and ignoring such matters as personnel management, installation of machinery and general office or factory organization, can lead to a proper judgment on the efficiency of a concern and still less to the formal certificate required of an auditor.

I have discussed this with a number of Professional Accountants and believe they agree with me. In the case of a commercial concern, the profit and loss account and balance sheet are of course of vital concern to the shareholders and may be taken as a rough and ready indication of efficiency. But even in business highly efficient firms may become bankrupt and inefficient firms may make big profits if conditions are favourable. In the case of a Government Department, even when it carries on trading activities, the question of profit and loss has still smaller relationship to efficiency. We cannot declare a consulate to be inefficient because its fees, fines and other receipts do not cover its overhead costs, nor is the Ministry of Food necessarily inefficient because it loses some £400,000,000 a year on its trading services. On the other hand, a Government Department, which deliberately set out to make a profit every year on its trading activities, would probably meet with more censure than praise in Parliament.

I hope I have said enough to convince you that the purely financial approach will not carry us very far in our consideration of the problem we are to examine this afternoon, which, as I was informed by your late Director, is to be related primarily to criteria of efficiency in the public non-trading services. This I interpret as meaning, not the efficiency of individual public servants nor the efficiency of the equipment and accommodation with which they are provided, but the general efficiency of management, which of course to some extent embraces the other two.

MEANING OF 'EFFICIENCY'

Let us pause for a moment to consider what we mean by 'efficiency'. We all know roughly what the word implies, but it is not too easy to define. I believe economists might describe it as 'the ratio of the degree of attainment of objectives to the amount of resources used', but the word 'ratio', to my mind, envisages an exact measurement, which is frequently impracticable and in any case does not tally with our ordinary conception of the word's meaning. I am not sure that the Oxford English Dictionary is much more helpful. It defines it as 'efficient power; effectiveness; efficacy', and defines 'efficacy' as 'capacity to produce effects; power to effect the object intended'. Whatever definition may be accepted, it is clear, I think, that efficiency is concerned with the relation between means and end. It can be increased by increasing the degree of attainment or by reducing the amount of resources used for a given degree of attainment. The latter method – i.e. making do with fewer resources – is usually known as 'economy'. Efficiency and economy are therefore closely related.

Whatever definition one may adopt, it is obvious that efficiency is a very pragmatic virtue. It cannot be judged in the abstract. There can be no standard of efficiency in itself, unrelated to the objects it may achieve. It is not in the same class as goodness or honesty or any other abstract virtue of which Plato would have said there was an 'idea' in the heavens. No man – not even your Chairman – can walk into an office and see that it is efficient in the way that, according to the book of Genesis, God looked on the world on the sixth day and saw that it was very good. It is possible that an experienced H.M.I. may be able to form a rough impression of a school's general efficiency when he puts his nose inside the door, in somewhat the same way that some experienced auditors by an additional sense not given to most of us can 'smell' a faulty account before they have examined it, or a trained Customs Officer can often spot a would-be smuggler by looking no further than his face. But by and large efficiency can only be evaluated by results; 'by their works ye shall know them' and that makes it all the more important to consider the criteria by which the results can be measured.

It is perhaps typical of modern life that we are all groping after criteria. Why is this? Is it that we are no longer content with inward and spiritual grace, but need and demand outward and visible signs? Is it that in a world which is becoming more and more competitive we are driven to giving more attention to these things? In the field of public service at least the public are becoming more and more critical and the public servant is driven in his own defence – and perhaps to provide himself also with some inner satisfaction – to seek means of proving his efficiency by resort to objective criteria. This may well be a good thing within limits. It is a great mistake for Civil Servants to bask in the pleasing atmosphere of self-complacency and mutual admiration. We must examine ourselves and see if we are really giving the State full value for what we receive. But we must also be on our guard against placing too much reliance on these outward criteria of our efficiency. They must be our servants and not our masters and we must from time to time consider how far they serve a useful purpose.

Before considering further the question of criteria of efficiency on which I was asked to address you this afternoon, I ought to point out that comparison of criteria is not the only way of increasing efficiency. Much can be done by an intensive study, often termed 'time and motion study' of actual processes, followed by experimentation and research. For factory production this method is often very efficacious and there are Institutes with trained staff who devote much of their time to this type of study. I am not sure that we experiment enough in our Public Service; my impression is that the Americans do much more in this way than we do. We are so impressed by the need for securing equality of treatment for all and we recognize that a Minister might not be too pleased if he had to explain in Parliament that his Department had been experimenting on the 'hit or miss' or 'trial and error' system and that unfortunately the Member's constituent had been the victim of one of the errors! In spite of this danger, however, we should, I suggest, be more ready to experiment at times in the hope of increasing our efficiency. But even without new experiments there is much that can be learnt by the study of comparative criteria based on existing practice.

CRITERIA OF EFFICIENCY

There is an almost infinite variety in the criteria that may be chosen,

149

and the greatest skill is required to determine which criteria are the best for valuing the efficiency of any particular type of activity. A thorough knowledge of the work of the Department and of the basic purpose of that work is needed. The speed in replying to letters may be a valuable guide to the efficiency of, say, the Central Record Office of the Ministry of National Insurance at Newcastle, but it would rank pretty low in the criteria of efficiency of, say, the Home Office or the Treasury Solicitor's Department.

As a general rule it seems to me that the difficulty of finding suitable criteria of efficiency varies directly with the amount of pure policy work of the office. To take an extreme example, what criteria can be suggested for the Foreign Office? One can test, of course, the clerical and manipulative duties of the lower staff, but what test can there be of the extent to which the Office is achieving its main purpose? In the first place one must decide what that purpose is. Is it the prevention of war or the creation of better relations with foreign countries or the understanding of the British way of life throughout the world? I doubt if any objective criteria could be devised which would in any way reflect the efficiency of the Foreign Office in any of these purposes.

Let us therefore take some less extreme examples. Could the real efficiency or rather inefficiency of the Ministry of Labour and National Service be determined by the number of persons involved in industrial disputes or by the number of persons unemployed or by the shortage of recruits to the mining industry? Does an outbreak of infantile paralysis or an influenza epidemic prove the inefficiency of the Ministry of Health? Does the number of burglaries or murders vary according to the efficiency of the Police Service? There may be some casual relationship in these examples, and figures taken out over a number of years might give useful pointers, but I doubt if it would be fair to judge the general efficiency of these Services on any such figures. As a general proposition I would advance the view that criteria of efficiency are of far more value when applied to methods of executing policy than to the processes involved in the formulation of policy.

NEED FOR COMPARISONS

As efficiency is itself not an absolute quality but is only to be judged by results achieved, so criteria of efficiency by themselves are of little or no value. They only attain value by comparison. It is, for instance, not of much value with a view to assessing efficiency to know that a typist types X words in an hour; that knowledge only obtains value if one can compare it with the number of words other typists type, and the wider the comparison the better – e.g. the achievement of typists in other offices, in other countries or in other decades. But even then the knowledge is only useful as a pointer for further investigation and enquiry. For a true comparison of efficiency one would need to know whether the other typists or the 'control group' worked under similar conditions, used similar machines, had the same average length of word in their copy and no doubt other factors which must affect any comparison.

As this is a vital point I might give another example. Let us take the vexed question of the length of time taken to reply to letters addressed to Ministers of different Departments. You may have an analysis made and find that in your Department the average time is ten days. That may strike you as excessively long or commendably short, but by itself the information gives no real guide to the efficiency of your Department. But if you find that two years ago in your own Department it was twelve days and that in other comparable Departments it averages thirteen days, then you have some ground for satisfaction. But before you could be really satisfied you would have to probe further and find out whether the type of question now addressed to your Minister is not simpler and more straightforward than it was two years ago, and whether the other Departments do not have to send a higher proportion of their letters to regional offices for enquiry than is necessary in your own Department, before a final reply can be given. And even when you had done all this you would generally, I think, not rest content with these comparisons but would want to satisfy yourself by detailed examination of the processes in the office at every stage that there could not be some further acceleration without interference with other sides of the Department's work.

I have spent some time in pointing out the pitfalls awaiting any student of public administration who may be tempted to place too much reliance on criteria of efficiency. But they undoubtedly have great value – particularly as pointers for subjects of further examination – and we might now consider different types of criteria and the associated and perhaps more important question of the basis of comparison between them. For without comparisons criteria are of very little value. For this purpose comparisons can be classified into four categories:

1. inter-period;
2. inter-national;

151

3. inter-departmental;
4. inter-regional or inter-office.

There may of course be combinations of these, which double their value, but let us consider shortly each in turn by itself.

INTER-PERIOD COMPARISONS

By 'inter-period' comparisons I mean comparisons within an office of criteria for different periods. I have put it first because it is the simplest and most common form of assessing the efficiency of any operation. It requires no comparison with other Departments or other offices and is easy to apply because the nature of the operation has probably not varied much during the period. A typical example might have been the number of man-hours involved in issuing, say, 1000 passports under the old Foreign Office system. If the man-hours had fallen from X to $\frac{3}{4}X$ between 1930 and 1935 the Foreign Office might have derived some satisfaction. But it would not really be a conclusive proof of efficiency. In the first place one would need to know that the work was as carefully performed in 1935 as in 1930, but even if satisfied on that point the test would not prove that by some radical changes the man-hours could not without loss of efficiency have been reduced to $\frac{1}{2}X$ or even $\frac{1}{4}X$. In this particular example, as is generally known, a complete change of system has now been introduced as a result of an examination by O. and M. experts, and not only have the cost and man-power been reduced but a better service to the public has been provided. It is, however, only fair to add that one of the changes introduced has involved a relaxation in the Regulations, and it is possible that, so far as over-all efficiency is concerned, there is still as much room for improvement as there was before. Anyhow, this illustrates the danger of relying too much and with too great complacency on simple inter-period comparisons.

INTERNATIONAL COMPARISONS

My second category, namely international comparisons, is of comparatively little value, mainly because it goes to the other extreme in regard to similarity of material and conditions. If the rate of infant mortality is lower in England than in France it should not give particular satisfaction to our Ministry of Health, though perhaps the Home Office might claim some credit if the proportion of murderers brought to court were higher here than across the channel. International comparisons are more useful in relation to trading services and I should expect the Post Office to get some useful information by comparing the cost of man-hours of various postal services here and in foreign countries. But any such comparisons between one country and another, though they may be useful in providing pointers for further inquiry, are of little real value as criteria of efficiency.

INTER-DEPARTMENTAL COMPARISONS

Let us turn then to the third category, namely inter-departmental comparisons. Here we have a much wider scope for useful inquiry coupled with the zest which can always be derived from legitimate rivalry between one department and another. This category can itself be sub-divided into two, namely comparisons between identical services, mainly in the field of clerical and manipulative duties, and comparisons between allied forms of administration. In the first of these classes it is easy for anyone with a working knowledge of the Public Service to think of a large variety of common services which provide material for comparison. They are the bread and butter material for one side of the O. and M. organization. A few that spring to the mind are:

1. various criteria of typing efficiency;
2. staff time involved in paying salaries;
3. rapidity of delivery by the Messenger Service;
4. average length of time in filing correspondence;
5. average length of time in replying to letters;
6. volume of complaints, such as letters from Members of Parliament.

I believe that it takes twice as much man-power to pay, say, 500 weekly paid staff in one Department as it does in another. On the face of it there is no justification for such disparity. But even in such a clear case as this the criterion should be used rather to point the way to further investigation than as a final assessment of the respective efficiencies of the two Departments. It may be that the apparently more wasteful Department has circumstances peculiar to itself which fully justify the disparity; indeed sometimes a comparison of this sort may reveal merits in the apparently wasteful Department which can be usefully adopted by its rival.

The second class of case is much rarer because it is not often that one finds similar forms of administration practised by a number of different Departments. But where this does occur, a comparison may be very useful and may help to increase the efficiency of both. I will give two examples. First, there are several Departments which have to make weekly a large number of individually small payments. This problem faces the Ministry of National Insurance, the Ministry of Pensions, the Ministry of Labour and National Service and the National Assistance Board. They adopt different systems and different checks. Some pay through their own local offices, some through the Post Office. Some centralize and some decentralize authorisation of payment. It is obviously likely to be of mutual advantage and to increase efficiency all round if from time to time notes can be compared and statistical criteria taken out in regard to such questions as cost, man-power, speed of decision, or proportion of errors and frauds under each system.

The other form of administration that occurs to me as presenting similar problems for a number of Departments is consumer rationing. This affects particularly the Ministry of Food, the Board of Trade and the Ministry of Fuel and Power. Totally different systems have been adopted in dealing with food, clothes, furniture, solid fuel and petrol, but some useful lessons might be learnt by drawing up and comparing criteria of efficiency under the different systems in relation to various common factors such as:

1. extent to which the system guarantees or gives equality of treatment to all consumers;
2. cost of administration;
3. man-power employed per unit of distribution;
4. general acceptance by the public, as indicated by volume of complaints received or number of appeals lodged;
5. proportion of lost books.

INTER-REGIONAL AND INTER-OFFICE COMPARISONS

Let us pass now from inter-departmental comparisons to our fourth main category, namely, inter-regional or inter-office comparisons. By these I mean comparing criteria of efficiency between different regional or local offices of the same Department. It can be applied only to Departments which have a Regional organization, though the Foreign Office could presumably adopt a similar system in relation to Embassies and Consulates abroad. It has the great advantage that comparisons are between standards of work which is either exactly the same or at least very similar in all the offices assessed, and for that reason it is likely to provide a better basis of assessment than an inter-departmental comparison. This type of criterion is in fact widely used in most Government Departments which have regional and local offices and provides in many the main basis of administrative control over numbers of staff. But even this system, though less liable to error than the others, must be used with care and discretion, and it would be unfair to condemn offhand and without enquiry an office with a bad ratio of staff to output. It might be found, for instance, that the office with a ratio much worse than the average had particularly unsuitable premises or had some other special local difficulties. Conversely, the office with the best ratio is not necessarily the most efficient. Nevertheless these inter-regional comparisons are of the greatest assistance to many Departments, particularly when used as pointers for investigation rather than as final and conclusive indications of relative efficiency.

There is one special form of inter-office comparison, possible for Departments which have a large number of local offices. Here what I have called the criteria system can be combined with the experimental system to which I referred earlier. Under this arrangement a particular office is selected; different experiments are tried out in it and the results are compared with those of a normal office of the standard type. All sorts of experiments can be tried – provided they are not very likely to lead to trouble with the Department's clients. It is quite safe, for instance, to experiment with such things as lighting, equipment, rank of officers entrusted with particular duties or lay-out of office accommodation. It may even be possible to experiment with different methods of dealing with the public, provided inequalities of treatment do not result. Sometimes indeed the local public may be taken into the Department's confidence and asked to express their views on the merits or demerits of the various experiments as they affect the user. I cannot help thinking that some Departments might use more imagination along these lines and quite possibly discover improvements which could usefully be applied to the whole of their local offices and thus raise their general level of efficiency.

LOCAL GOVERNMENT COMPARISONS

I have been dealing in the main with national Government Services, but many of the principles are equally applicable to local government. In particular, what we have called inter-regional comparisons can readily be used as between local authorities of comparable size. I believe the cost of services is generally expressed in relation to the product of a penny rate, but this is apt to be misleading because of the existing wide divergence between the level of rateable values in

155

different areas. A more suitable test would appear to be actual cost in relation to the number of inhabitants. The simplest test on this basis is to compare local authorities who have approximately the same number of inhabitants, say Sheffield, Leeds and Dublin or Blackpool, Southampton and Wolverhampton. Supposing the cost of cleaning the streets amounts to, say, £20,000 a year more in the first town than in either of the others; then there is *prima facie* a point for examination by the rate-payers of that town. It may of course be found that their town has a much dirtier atmosphere than the others, or the inhabitants may demand and be ready to pay for a higher degree of cleanliness. But sometimes useful lessons may be learned, and surely comparisons of this sort should tend to increase the all-round efficiency of local government. Now that most rate-borne expenditure automatically attracts exchequer assistance, this is the kind of co-ordinating function which we may hope to see the Ministry of Health develop.

DANGERS OF USING CRITERIA

A word of warning is called for at this stage. There is always the danger that enthusiasts for efficiency tests will use them not merely as pointers for further enquiry but as objective criteria on which to base decisions about grading, promotion, etc. If used in this way, they can become a positive menace and result in inefficiency and waste. Let me give two examples.

Some twenty years ago, when unemployment was the greatest problem facing the Ministry of Labour, there was a staff ratio index for each Employment Exchange and Local Office, relating the number of staff to the number of unemployed in the area. Other sides of the work were not subjected to any similar test, and the idea got around that a good ratio of staff to unemployed affected the Department's views as to the efficiency of the Manager and consequently his prospects of promotion. The result, so it was alleged, was that the Managers were much keener on keeping the unemployed on their books as long as possible than on finding them suitable employment.

My other example has a humorous side. After the 1914–18 War the War Office adopted a complete system of cost accounts. Each Command had its Command Accountant who prepared the accounts showing the full costs of the various units. In the case of hospitals the accounts showed the cost per occupied bed. Fate decreed that one Command Accountant fell ill and was admitted to one of the hospitals, where he was given every care and attention and soon recovered. But although he seemed to be quite well again and was anxious to return to work, the Hospital Authorities would not let him leave. He was puzzled as to the reason for this and began to fear that there was something more radically wrong with him than he had been led to believe. So one day he disclosed his fears to an auditor friend who was visiting him in hospital. Imagine his surprise when he was told by his friend that his retention in hospital was his own fault. 'If you are allowed to leave,' he said, 'the cost per bed occupied will rise, and the hospital will under your own costing scheme get a bad mark.' I might add that this experiment in cost accounting was abandoned after five years as being too expensive.

I don't suppose the War Office will be able to check this particular story, but I have had it on good authority and at any rate it illustrates my point. Incidentally, I was interested to see that the *Accountant*, the official organ of the Institute of Chartered Accountants, not long ago pressed for the abolition under the National Health Service of the use of tests of hospital efficiency based on cost per occupied bed. It said that experience had proved conclusively the futility of this test for purposes of making comparisons between hospitals.

BASES FOR CRITERIA

Let us pass now from considering the way in which criteria of efficiency can be used or should not be used, and examine for a few minutes the way in which they can be compiled. This is where the real art comes in. The compilation of different bases of assessment is an amusing and fascinating job, and it is easy to let imagination get the better of judgment. The important thing is to determine the one, or possibly two, major objectives of the operation and relate the criterion to those objectives only. Too many tests are an encumbrance and a waste of time and money. Take as an example the yearly operation in Employment Exchanges and Local Food Offices of exchange of books. The test might be the number exchanged per hour, or the all-in cost of exchanging 1000 books, or the numbers of mistakes made per 1000 exchanges, or the neatness and legibility of the writing on the new book or the number of books wasted through mistakes. These are all important factors, but should not all be applied at the same time. The officer who decides what tests to apply and what to reject must have regard to the object of the test. For different pieces of administration different types of test will be appropriate. If cost is the prime consideration, as it generally is in industry but not so universally in the Public Service, then cost will be the basis of the criterion and a system of costs accounts will be applied. But in these days man-power is often just as important, and it may sometimes be easier to apply a man-hour than a cost test. Fortunately, there is a close correlation between these two forms of test and it cannot often happen that comparisons on these bases conflict. It is not therefore generally necessary to use both at the same time. But in some operations of the Public Service it may sometimes happen that speed or workmanship outweighs either cost or manpower in importance, and in such cases they should form the basis of the test. In 1940, for instance, it was far more important to turn out fighter aircraft up to the highest standard of efficiency and with the maximum speed of production than to cut costs or stint in man-power. By 1943 the position had changed considerably, and manpower had become perhaps the major consideration. By 1946 cost had probably ousted both speed of production and economy in man-power from their top place.

Once again it becomes clear that efficiency is a relative term and that cost is only one of the factors by which it can be judged. We hear much more about cost accounting than about manpower accounting or speed accounting. But this is only natural because cost, which in most processes has a close correlation with manpower, is generally the simplest and most practical test to apply.

COST CONSCIOUSNESS

In any case I hope nothing I have said will give the impression that I underestimate the value of cost accounting in its widest sense. One of the gravest dangers in the Public Service is that civil servants are not sufficiently 'cost-conscious'. The great majority of civil servants are not concerned with the raising of the money which they spend and therefore tend to ignore that vital side of the public economy. One can have nothing less than hearty contempt for the civil servant who boasts – as some I fear still do – that he – or she – has a mind above figures or cannot understand the simplest accounts. If I had my way I would get the Civil Service Commission to inscribe over the portals of 6 Burlington Gardens the words which Plato placed over the doors of his Academy –

ΜΗΔΕΙΣ ΑΓΕΩΜΕΤΡΗΤΟΣ ΕΙΣ ΙΤΩ

which, being roughly translated, means 'Entry forbidden to anyone who cannot appreciate the importance of figures'.

I am afraid that in many Departments of the Public Service there is still a feeling that questions of cost are matters for the Finance Branch and that it is rather beneath the dignity of the administrative officer to descend from the Olympian heights of policy framing to the mundane question of cutting out unnecessary expenditure. That is an attitude which must be eradicated root and branch before the Service can call itself really efficient. Every officer, both in the Civil and the Defence Services, should take an active interest in the cost of the particular service he administers, and should ask himself at frequent intervals whether that service is giving the State and his fellow tax-payers full value for what it costs. Thus, the Naval Officer commanding a destroyer should know both the capital cost of the ship under his command and the weekly running cost. I believe he will be a more, not a less, efficient officer if he bears these facts in mind and passes them on to his crew. The Officer in charge of, say, a Regional Office of the Ministry of National Insurance should know the annual administrative costs of his region, including staff, premises, postage and stationery, and should take frequent opportunity of telling all his local officers what is the cost of their particular office. Or, to take an example from Headquarters, the Chief Scientific Adviser of the Ministry of Works should know exactly how much his Division costs, in salaries, materials, premises, etc., and should be prepared to justify each item of expenditure, not so much to the Treasury as to his own conscience and to his fellow passengers in the train or the bus, all of whom are contributing to the cost of his organization.

This suggestion may strike some of you as being rather novel and even fantastic, but I wonder how many of my audience could tell me off-hand what is the cost of what they are doing. Would they not take a more intelligent interest in it if they knew? A great number of you are tax spenders but you are all tax payers, either directly or indirectly, and it would be a good thing for the efficiency of our public services if more taxpayers, instead of grousing vaguely about the burden of taxation, took a more intelligent interest in how their money is spent, or it may be, on occasions, mis-spent. If this is true of taxpayers generally, how much more so for those of us who are also tax-spenders?

I know that there are certain practical difficulties in my suggestion, arising largely from the Government system of accounts. Departments do not carry on their own votes a variety of services which are known as 'Allied Services', the most important being premises, fuel and light, superannuation, free postal and telephone services and stationery. But we have now reverted to the pre-war system of giving the estimated value of these services for whole Departments in the published annual estimates. My suggestion would mean splitting up the more important of these bulk estimates into constituent Divisions or regions within each major Department. Intelligent guesses would often be sufficient. Meticulous accuracy is not needed. A little more work might be needed in the Post Office, Ministry of Works and Stationery Office, but I believe the cost would be repaid manyfold by the added interest officers of all grades would take in the efficiency of their work.

PASSION FOR EFFICIENCY

We must get away from the pernicious idea that cost is a matter which concerns only the Treasury and the Finance Department. I believe, thank goodness, that we have largely eliminated the old tradition of taking pleasure in 'diddling the Treasury', but it is not sufficient that administrators should be merely impartial and unconcerned. They should be filled with a passionate enthusiasm for economy and efficiency – for by common consent the two go hand in hand – and a determination that, at least so far as their own work is concerned, all waste, extravagance and other hindrance to efficiency shall be ruthlessly eliminated. If they hold positions of responsibility they should do their utmost to instil the same spirit in all their subordinates. This I believe to be the real key to increasing the efficiency of the Public Service. Criteria such as we have examined have their place and are useful so long as they are our slaves and not our masters. But in the last resort efficiency is not measurable by statistical sliderules or nicely calculated formulae. It is the spirit in which a job is tackled that really counts. *Spiritus intus alit* – 'it is the spirit within us that keeps us alive', is a Vergilian motto adopted by one of our great schools and it seems to me to provide the real clue to the efficiency of the Public Service.

13

Cost-Benefit Analysis and Investment in the Public Sector*

MARTIN S. FELDSTEIN

Whilst more work has been done in the United States than in Britain on the application in the public services of management techniques, there has, in recent years, been a considerable expansion of such activity and interest in Britain. This is reflected, for example, in the highly success- ful Local Government Operational Research Unit of the Royal Institute of Public Administration, and the Operational Research Society's first international conference in 1964, on 'Operational Research and the Social Sciences' (see, R. J. Laurence, Ed., Operational Research and the Social Sciences, *Tavistock Publications, 1966*). There have also been *other significant contributions to management literature* (relevant to the public services as well as business), such as Stafford Beer, *Decision and Control,* John Wiley, 1966. *In this article, Martin S. Feldstein, Oxford University Lecturer in Public Finance and Research Fellow of Nuffield College, Oxford, explains for the administrator the uses to which cost-benefit analysis may be put and surveys the main literature.*

The vast recent growth in the volume and scope of public investment has created a host of new problems for those in charge of planning and directing government activities at all levels. In addition, it has engendered an increasing concern with the efficiency of public spending.[1]

Traditional accounting and budgetary methods are felt inadequate for today's complex management tasks of government departments, nationalized industries and local authorities. To meet this deficiency, public bodies have developed new management accounting and cost- ing methods and have borrowed other techniques of administration and financial control from industry. While these developments are

* From Martin S. Feldstein, 'Cost-Benefit Analysis and Investment in the Public Sector', *Public Administration*, 1964, Vol. 42, pp. 351–72. Reprinted with permission of the author and the editor of *Public Administration*.

making possible a more rational and systematic evaluation of proposed investments, they are often unsuited to the special problems of managing public enterprises. The public administrator is forced to rely on criteria and methods of evaluation that are more appropriate for the commercial undertakings of private firms than for public activities.

The special problems of public expenditure planning have stimulated academic economists to develop analytic methods with which public administrators can make more economically rational decisions. Although cost-benefit analysis, as this approach has been called, can be used to determine efficient ways of operating public services, it has found its greatest use in planning large capital projects. Also it is most easily applied in the quasi-commercial areas of government activity (the nationalized industries), but can, in addition, be used in such non-market areas as roads, defence and the social services. The basic idea of cost-benefit analysis is to supplement the usual financial calculations with measurements of the economic benefits and costs of a project to its consumers and to society as a whole. Financial accounting methods must of course be retained. They provide the information necessary for the planning, control and audit of the actual flow of payments and receipts associated with a project. They do not, however, provide the right information for deciding whether a project should be undertaken. Before proceeding to a general discussion of the problems and methods of cost-benefit analysis, it is worth considering why the usual financial methods and commercial criteria are insufficient in the public sector.

INSUFFICIENCY OF CONVENTIONAL TECHNIQUES

It is most useful to begin with the area of government activities that seems on the surface to resemble commercial operations – electricity supply, rail transport, etc. Here it is possible to prepare financial studies of proposed investments that compare expected operating costs and revenues. Projects may then be selected on the basis of their ability to cover costs with receipts or even to earn a surplus. Nevertheless, this application of private commercial methods to the investment decisions of the public sector may be inappropriate. A private firm's primary responsibility is to its shareholders and its measure of success is the profits that it earns. But the government's responsibility is wider than this: it is to select projects in a way that provides the greatest possible net benefit to society. Some examples will show why applying commercial criteria to estimated money costs and receipts may lead public agencies to select projects that are less than optimal. If railway freight services were improved (say by electrification or better freight yard facilities), some freight traffic would be diverted from the roads to the railroads. The investment would therefore benefit not only the users of railroads, but also those who were able to enjoy less crowded roads. In evaluating the desirability of making investments to improve freight services, both types of benefit must be taken into account. Although it might be possible to assess the benefits to the rail users by estimating the higher charges they would be willing to pay, this would ignore the important benefits accruing to those who still used the roads. Further, since the rates charged would influence the amount of traffic diverted from road to rail, an increase in revenue might actually be accompanied by a decrease in total benefits. Although railroad freight services appear at first to be amenable to commercial management decisions, this example shows that the money revenues of a project can be an inadequate guide for public investment decisions. In this case, as in many others, social benefits that do not produce revenues to the public body incurring the capital expenditure should be separately evaluated and included in the final investment decision.

Similarly, although the market prices that a public body pays for various goods and services are often the best measure of the social cost of the resources used in the investment project, there are important situations in which market prices would be an inappropriate guide. For example, although a commercial firm will always calculate the cost of labour at the wage rate it has to pay, a government agency should make explicit allowance if the labour used on a project would otherwise be unemployed. When this is not the case, the wages paid indicate what the social value of that labour would be in other production. But when labour, that would otherwise remain unemployed, is used to improve a railway line or build a power station, no other production is foregone. It is therefore appropriate to disregard the wages of the otherwise unemployed labour in evaluating the project. In the case of unemployed resources, application of the usual commercial accounting methods would overestimate the true social cost of an investment. In other situations, commercial methods would underestimate social cost. A nuclear power generating plant may use up a great deal of water in its cooling system. Although there may be no money cost to the agency for this water, other water users in the area may suffer or may have to incur costs to assure themselves an alternative supply. If the true social cost of the water used is taken into account in evaluating the construction of the power plant, a more appropriate system (e.g. the building of a dam of the proper size) or method of operation might be adopted.

In the preceding examples we have concentrated on public activities that resemble commercial undertakings. But a number of public investments with significant economic consequences are obviously not amenable to commercial evaluation. Road building is an important example of this. Although no revenues are earned it is important to base the investment decision on an estimate of the economic benefits that alternative road projects would achieve through reducing travel time, decreasing vehicle operating costs, etc. When social benefits and costs are properly evaluated it is possible to appraise the desirability of particular proposed projects, e.g. whether a by-pass should be built, as well as to select among alternative mutually incompatible projects – e.g. to choose between building a six-lane motorway in the present and building it with four lanes and widening it later.

Although investment in roads appears to differ from such quasi-commercial activities as railroad services and electricity generation, we have seen that in both types of cases a proper evaluation of proposed projects requires considering social benefits and costs. When cost-benefit analysis is extended to planning capital expenditure in such fields as defence, health and education, more difficult problems arise in identifying and evaluating benefits. Nevertheless, as in the other areas, cost-benefit analysis can give better measures of the cost to society of different programmes.

The techniques of cost-benefit analysis were first introduced in the 1930s in the United States and were mainly concerned with water resource development projects of irrigation, flood control, and hydroelectric power. More recently, analyses have been directed to problems of military planning, transportation, power, education and health. Regardless of the specific application, the nature of cost-benefit analysis is the same: the evaluation and selection of public investment projects or expenditure programmes. Attention focuses on making efficient use of scarce resources, on selecting among competing demands for capital, labour and land.

It would be impossible to review here either the theoretical controversies that have developed or the exact conclusions that most economists would now accept. Instead, the following sections will briefly outline the types of problems and issues that must be borne in mind when doing cost-benefit analyses. The final part of the paper will review some of the past applications of cost-benefit analysis and suggest some introductory reading on these topics.

164

SOCIAL BENEFITS AND SOCIAL COSTS

The most fundamental difference between cost-benefit analysis and the methods generally advocated for evaluating private investment projects[2] is the definition of benefits and costs. Our concern is not merely with the money costs and revenues of the project but with the social values of its benefits and costs; this is almost always forgotten in British government calculations of the 'rate of return' or other measure of the desirability of a proposed public investment, although there are notable exceptions.

If an investment decision is based on money costs and revenues, it is only necessary to forecast the expected outlays and receipts in future years. When we want to incorporate the social benefits and costs, two types of problems arise: (1) what benefits and costs shall be included?; and (2) how shall these be evaluated?

A number of things must be included in the calculation of social costs and benefits although they do not contribute to the money costs or receipts of the project. For example, an improved passenger train service in the London suburbs is likely to reduce automobile congestion on the roads to London. Although no charge is likely to be made to the road users it is important that these benefits be reckoned into the benefits of the project. It is particularly important to keep such side-effects (also known as 'spillovers' or 'external economies') in mind in the early planning stages; in this case, properly including spill-overs might lead to redesigning the original railroad services to increase the benefits that can be achieved by diverting passenger and freight traffic from the roads. Public sector projects are particularly likely to produce benefits – either direct or spill-over – for which no charge is made. Sometimes, although a charge could be levied, the service is provided free as a matter of public policy or in order to encourage use, e.g. education, health care, museum visits. But often it would be impossible to levy a charge for using the public service or product; for example, although the improved rail services can be sold to individual users, the reduced road congestion benefits cannot be. If anyone is to benefit from the improved road conditions then everyone must benefit whether they are willing to pay or not. Goods and services which have this characteristic are referred to as 'collective goods'. Because of the frequency with which they occur in the public sector it is important to look carefully for such benefits. Of course, negative spill-over effects (e.g. water pollution, road congestion) may occur and must also be taken into account.

Although it is necessary to avoid omitting any benefits, it is equally

165

important to avoid double-counting of benefits and costs. It has not been uncommon in making cost-benefit studies to include mistakenly more than one measure of the same benefit. An irrigation project will increase the value of crops grown on the irrigated land in future years; as a result, the market value of the land itself will increase. It is important to include some measure of the contribution of the irrigation to the productivity of the land; but it would be wrong to include a direct measure of the increased output and also the associated rise in land value.

When the physical quantities of the benefits and costs of the proposed project during each year of its life have been estimated, it is necessary to try to assign 'shadow prices' to them (i.e. evaluate them in terms of money) so that they can be added together and compared with the net benefits of other proposed projects. In transport projects, for example, shadow prices have been used to evaluate the time saved by travellers. In some cases, such assigning of shadow prices may not be possible (e.g. for a road improvement expected to save two lives a year); we return to this problem of intangible and incommensurable benefits below.

In evaluating costs, attention should always be fixed on estimating the *social opportunity cost* of the resources used in the project, i.e. the social value of the goods and services that would have been produced if the resources had been used in the next best alternative public or private use. For most goods and services bought by the government from commercial firms as well as for labour hired in competition with private industry, the market price is an adequate measure of social opportunity cost. An important exception to this is unemployed labour. Although the government must pay wages to attract these otherwise unemployed workers, their employment on these public projects involves no loss in other production; their opportunity cost is therefore zero and their wage should be disregarded in the social cost calculation.

Costs must also be evaluated with care when the government uses some property that is already in its possession, e.g. government-owned land. Here the appropriate social opportunity cost shadow price is the value of the land in the best alternative use to which the government could have put it or its productive value if sold to private users, whichever is higher.

Some of the benefits of government projects will be used directly by individuals as final consumption goods (e.g. coal, electricity, transport); others will be used by industry or agriculture as inter-mediate goods in the manufacture of final consumer goods (coal, electricity and transport may be cited here along with irrigation, flood control, steel, etc.). Any publicly produced good sold on the market in competiton with privately produced goods that are similar or close substitutes may generally be valued at the market price at which it is sold; this is true for both final and intermediate goods. When an intermediate good does not enter into competition with alternative privately produced goods (e.g. electricity in Britain) or when it is not sold (e.g. irrigation), it is necessary to estimate the value of the final consumption goods that will result from its use and assign a social value shadow price on this basis. Such a direct use of market prices is not always possible. If the government project increases the supply of a good by a great deal, its price may fall and an appropriate compromise between old and new price must be estimated.

The most difficult problems of benefit evaluation arise when the final consumption good does not compete with any privately produced good or is not sold at all. A special case of this occurs when a public authority does enter a market in which private firms participate but sells its product at an artificially low price to selected buyers, e.g. council housing. In each of these cases in which the market price of the good is an impossible or incorrect measure of its social value it may be appropriate to evaluate the product in terms of what the consumers would have been willing to pay for it. This raises a number of difficult problems of measurement and interpretation that we cannot now explore.

In many cases, goods that cannot be evaluated by reference to market prices or to the prices that individuals would be willing to pay must be treated separately from the main money cost-benefit calculation as intangible or incommensurable benefits and costs. It is important to clarify this distinction. An intangible benefit or cost, such as the improvement of a landscape by a park or its spoliation by a power line, is characterized by the inability to measure it on any scale. In contrast, incommensurable benefits may be measured in physical units, although they cannot be readily converted to money or any other common unit of measure. They include such things as decreases in death or sickness, or increases in years of schooling. Improvements in health and education have economic effects on productivity which can be calculated in money terms; but in addition there are the non-economic 'incommensurable' components. We may try to find shadow prices by asking what individuals would be willing to pay for these benefits. Often it is better not to use such obviously weak evaluations but rather to admit the incommensurable nature of the benefits and discuss the benefits and costs of alternative projects in terms of not only money but of these other physical effects. A final cost-benefit report would thus contain information about the net social value of those benefits and costs to which shadow prices can be assigned, together with an itemization of the incommensurable physical benefits and costs associated with the project and a description of the expected intangible effects. The presence of incommensurable effects makes the final selection between two projects more difficult than otherwise but a number of techniques can be employed to facilitate the choice, e.g. examining the range of shadow prices of the incommensurables which would make one project preferable.

THE PROBLEMS OF TIME

Until now we have disregarded the problems of time, tacitly assuming that all benefits and costs occur in the present. In practice the problems associated with the timing of benefits and costs are extremely important. Significant public investment choices, arising in both the design and final decision stages, require intertemporal evaluations. Should we use a technique of production that requires large capital investment but has low operating costs (e.g. nuclear generation of electric power) or would the opposite 'time profile' of expenditure (conventional power generation) be preferable? Should we select a project with a constant stream of net benefits or one which produces few benefits in early years but greater benefits later? Should we postpone all or part of a particular investment, such as building a narrow road now and widening later?

Time affects our project evaluation in three ways: (i) changes in the market prices of benefits and costs; (ii) the relatively greater desirability of consumption in the near future to consumption in the more distant future; (iii) the possibility of alternate productive investment of the funds used in a public project and of the benefits received from the project. Each of these aspects of the 'time problem' has been the subject of extensive discussion among economists. Although the literature that has evolved is too complex for summary here, some of the basic issues can be reviewed.

Changes in the absolute level of prices (i.e. a uniform change in all prices), for example a general inflationary trend, can be ignored and all calculations made as if the current level of prices remained unchanged. Not so for changes in relative prices. If some prices are likely to change relative to others this should be reflected in the cost-benefit calculations. For example, it would be reasonable to expect that wages will continue to rise relative to the prices of manufactured goods, raw materials, etc. In calculating the future costs of a public project, this relative price change should be taken into account. Other goods may change in price because of changes in the demand for them (due, for example, to the introduction of other new products or to a change in tastes brought on by higher standards of living) or in their supply (due for example to changes in technology, import regulations, etc.).

Assuming that allowance has been made for future changes in relative prices, we now consider the problem of the relative desirability of consumption in different years. Given the choice of a free trip to the south of France, now or ten years from now, most individuals would select to do it now. In general, we prefer consumption in the near future to consuming something of the same market value in the more distant future. It is reasonable for society as a whole to show the same preference in making public investment decisions, i.e. to give decreasingly less weight to benefits and costs as they occur in the more distant future. The nation will enjoy a higher standard of living in future years; a £1 benefit then will therefore be less significant than it is today. Establishing a quantitative relationship between the significance of a £1 benefit (or cost) today and a £1 benefit (cost) in a future year is an important prerequisite of cost-benefit analysis; doing so is analogous to selecting an appropriate 'discount rate' in private investment analysis.[3] Although economic analysis can help to elucidate the factors that should influence the selection of such a social time preference discount rate, the specific choice is ultimately a matter of public policy involving a balancing of the interests of present and future consumers.[4]

Even if we did not prefer present consumption to future consumption, we would be unwise to ignore the timing of benefits and costs in our analysis. When resources are spent on a public project or when the receipt of its benefits are postponed, we give up the opportunity to make other productive investments in the public or private sectors of the economy. Cost-benefit analysis must therefore take into account the productivity of private investment and/or the alternative uses to which funds could be put in the public sector. The appropriate measure of the opportunity cost of funds used in public projects, or the social opportunity cost rate that measures the productivity of funds withdrawn from private investment, is still a much debated subject.[5]

CRITERIA

One of the most important areas of recent work in cost-benefit analysis has been the development of criteria for project evaluation that take these time problems into account. Considerable attention has focused on the controversy between 'internal rate of return' and 'present value' rules for discounting.[6] Recently, criteria have been proposed that incorporate both the social time preference discount rate and a measure of the alternative social productivity of invested resources (social opportunity cost rate).[7]

Two special conditions that require different types of criteria are worth separate discussions: budgetary constraints and interdependent systems.

The basic criteria of cost-benefit analysis are based on the assumption that if a project is found to be 'worth doing' (i.e. has a positive net social benefit) and is better than any other project with which it is mutually exclusive on physical or economic grounds, the necessary funds for the original investment and subsequent operation will be made available. Often this is not the case. A public agency or department may have a limited budget for use in the present year and may expect some limit to exist in the future. As a result it would be impossible to undertake all projects that would be 'worth doing'. To meet this problem, special criteria have been developed for use in conditions of capital rationing and other budgetary limitations.

Another assumption on which the usual cost-benefit criteria rest is that the costs and benefits of each project are independent of whether or not other projects are undertaken. Again, this is often untrue. The value of a road building project may depend on whether a flood control programme is undertaken in the area. An important case of interdependent projects is the preclusion of a future investment by a current one. A channel tunnel may be a better investment today than a bridge, although the bridge, capable of handling more vehicles, might be a better investment twenty years from now; by building the tunnel today we preclude the opportunity of having a bridge later.

In each case of interdependence, the proper approach is clear. Each interdependent set of projects must be treated as if it were a *single* project, mutually exclusive of the other 'single projects', and the evaluation carried out accordingly. This is simple enough if only a small number of interdependent projects are being considered; e.g. if only A and B are considered, there are three mutually exclusive alternatives: A, B and A-and-B. If a large number of projects must be evaluated simultaneously, complex mathematical methods employing electronic computers may have to be employed.[8]

A different type of interdependence is often important in planning an investment progamme. In the field of electricity generation, for example, a national or regional electricity system as a whole may be required to produce a certain set of outputs (average output, peak capacity, etc.). The task of the cost-benefit analysis is then to determine the proper combinations of plants of different type, size and location to meet these requirements at least cost. Modern mathematical techniques of linear and non-linear programming have been developed for application to such problems. Again, high speed computers make this possible.[9]

RISK AND UNCERTAINTY

Estimates of a project's future inputs and outputs and their appropriate shadow prices cannot be made with certainty. Cost-benefit analyses must explicitly recognize the project's elements of risk and uncertainty. In doing so, it is useful to bear in mind the distinction between problems of risk and those of uncertainty.

In situations of risk, we can enumerate all the possible values that a project's benefits and costs might take (e.g. the amount of flood control that a dam might provide in some future year) and assign objective probabilities to these. These probabilities can be calculated on a basis either of past experience (e.g. previous flood levels at that point) or on an *a priori* consideration about the operation of the project (e.g. the technical blindspot in a radar screen's field of coverage).

When such objective probabilities cannot be assigned, we refer to the situation as one of uncertainty. Here we can only try to enumerate possible outcomes and assign rough 'subjective probabilities' to them.

When probabilities have been assigned to the possible outcomes, techniques of statistical analysis or computer simulation can be used to calculate certainty equivalents, i.e. the 'most probable' or 'expected' values for use in the cost-benefit analysis. Sometimes, in addition to each certainty-equivalent value, a measure of its riskiness or uncertainty (e.g. its variance) may also be incorporated into the analysis. Statistical decision theory, including minimax rules and 'gamblers preference maps', suggests methods for utilizing this additional information.[10]

PUBLIC EXPENDITURE AND GENERAL ECONOMIC POLICY

All public expenditure decisions take place in a climate of national economic activity and against a background of general government economic policy. Since Keynes, public spending (as well as taxation and monetary policy) has been looked on as a means of controlling the level of aggregate demand in the economy. In addition to serving its own specific purpose (e.g. electricity generation), a public investment project is often expected to be an instrument with which the government reduces unemployment, controls inflation, stimulates growth, aids the balance of payments, or otherwise improves the operation of the nation's economy. An important example of this has been the recent emphasis on the location of government activities as a way of reducing regional unemployment and assisting regional development programmes.

The importance of these general aims of economic policy, although they may sometimes conflict with the narrower economic efficiency criteria of project selection, does not decrease the need for cost-benefit analysis. Consider the choice between two alternative projects, both of which are expected to have a significant effect on say the balance of payments or regional unemployment. Although the absolute magnitude of the effects on unemployment may be significant, the difference between the unemployment effects of the two projects may be small in comparison to the difference in their economic efficiency, i.e. selecting the less efficient project may result in 'paying' a great loss in net social benefit for a small reduction in unemployment. It is therefore important to try to make quantitative estimates of the effects of the alternative projects on the general economic aims. Precise estimates may of course be unattainable. But the estimation process itself may be salutary in suggesting how small the expected effect or difference is likely to be. If a substantial net effect, say on regional unemployment, is expected to accompany the selection of the project with a lower net social benefit, this can be taken into account directly in the cost-benefit analysis by showing the expected social opportunity cost of each reduced unit of unemployment, i.e. the amount of net social benefit that is foregone in order to select the project with the greater employment effect. Although this does not automatically indicate the preferred project, it does provide the quantitative information needed for a more rational choice.

One general aim of government policy deserves special mention: reducing extremes of income distribution. Public expenditure programmes are often used not only to provide specific goods and services but also as a means of redistributing income. Although cost-benefit analysis customarily gives equal emphasis to each £1 benefit regardless of who receives it, policy officials may wish to give more weight to benefits received by low income recipients than to those distributed equally throughout the population. The most appropriate way to do this would be by assigning special shadow prices to the outputs of a project according to their final recipients.[11] As with other major policy aims, it could be useful to perform this calculation with and without the distributional shadow prices and thus to calculate the usual social opportunity cost of the distributional policy. Doing this may suggest alternative projects with equally desirable redistributive effects at less of a sacrifice in normal efficiency.

COST-BENEFIT ANALYSIS IN THE ADMINISTRATION OF PUBLIC INVESTMENT

Three questions arise when we consider the problem of employing cost-benefit analysis in the administration of public sector investment. What is the appropriate relation between cost-benefit analysis and the budgetary process? At what level in the planning process should these analyses be incorporated? Who should make the actual cost-benefit studies?

The current method of government budgeting has been one of the major factors impeding the general adoption of cost-benefit analysis in government investment planning. Government budgets have traditionally been prepared for one year at a time; although the Plowden Committee's recommendation of 'forward look' budgets may extend this to several years, public investment projects often have benefits and costs lasting three or more decades. Second, the form of the public accounts requires that current expenditure budgets be prepared in terms of the staff, materials, and other categories of expenditure of administrative divisions rather than by projects or programmes. Instead of posing the question 'Shall this project be undertaken?' the budgetary procedure asks 'How many men shall this agency hire?' and 'How much shall be spent for materials?' In the budgetary process these inputs are not associated with the outputs that they will produce or the particular purpose that they will serve. The costs of a particular project will often be divided among different agencies as well as among different categories of expenditure; several disparate decisions will determine the final availability of men and materials for the project.

This leads to a further difficulty. If a budget has to be reduced it is difficult to review the programmes and projects which compose it, selecting those that can be discarded, postponed or reduced. Instead, attention focuses on the appropriations to administrative divisions or on types of inputs and these may be reduced arbitrarily without regard to how this will affect particular programmes.

173

Although it may be necessary to retain the current method of budgeting for legal or control purposes, careful administrative comparisons among alternative investments can best be done with the aid of a parallel 'programme budget' or 'performance budget' in which expenditures are arranged by the projects on which they will be spent and the programmes that these will serve.[12] Cost-benefit analysis can then be used directly in programme budgeting. When the necessary decisions are made, the results can be translated into the legally required input budget; 'forward look' budgets, for example, could be prepared on programme budget lines and then converted to the conventional annual budgets. Even if programme budgeting is not adopted, cost-benefit analyses can still be used to indicate the projects that should receive appropriations in the regular budget.

The analysis of a project often indicates its wide ramifications and suggests that a better use of resources would be possible if two or more projects were joined and considered as a single system. If two dams in a river basin are planned together they may be able to produce a more effective flood control system for a certain cost than would have been possible if the dams were planned independently. But why just evaluate the two-dam combination when the river basin as a whole may be studied? Why not enlarge the scope even further and consider the entire river system or the economy of the region? Because of this interest in going beyond the single project and considering the entire system of interrelated projects, cost-benefit studies have often been referred to as systems analysis.[13] Unfortunately no general advice can be given about the proper level of decision-making. Only if the analysis is performed for the 'entire system' (i.e. at a high enough level so that there are no ramifications or interdependences outside the system) can the optimal allocation of resources be achieved. But such high level 'optimization' is often impossible in practice; the system is too complicated and too many unknowns remain. Lower level decision-making, 'sub-optimization' as it has become known, is necessary if useful cost-benefit analyses are to be done. Only the experience and judgment of the administrator can help determine the proper way to divide a complex operating system for most effective analysis.

The actual preparation and use of a cost-benefit analysis requires the close co-operation of administrators and technical staff. The final decision on any major project must rest with those politically responsible. It is their judgments about the relative importance of different costs and benefits that must ultimately determine the selection of projects. Similarly, they must be the final authority on the weights to be used for evaluating future costs and benefits, for taking the distribution of benefits into account, etc. But the actual cost-benefit calculations are best prepared by technical members of the department.

For pioneering studies in any field, it is particularly important that an economist participate in the evaluation. In addition to his special knowledge of cost-benefit techniques, his general training makes him best suited for dealing with new problems in the evaluation of costs and benefits, the treatment of time problems, etc. Whenever possible it is useful to use economists who are familiar with the work of the particular department, its technology, the type of risks encountered, the usual problems of benefit evaluation, etc. Only in this way can their technical training be augmented with the necessary experienced judgment. We stress the need to include economists in cost-benefit analysis because of the danger that the recent growth of interest in 'a wider application of mathematical techniques, statistics and accountancy to the problems of public expenditure'[14] may encourage inappropriately trained persons to prepare economically meaningless studies, asking the wrong questions and, with varying degrees of mathematical sophistication, producing misleading answers.[15] Reinterpreting private investment theory so that it can be used in the public sector, developing techniques for dealing with the special problems of a particular public industry, and applying the quantitative methods to individual projects in an economically meaningful way are all technical jobs requiring a trained economist. It is salutary to remember that, as Keynes once noted, economics is 'a matter for specialists, like dentistry. If economists could manage to get themselves thought of as humble, competent people, on a level with dentists, that would be splendid'.[16]

Often, engineers should be fully integrated into the planning process so that it will be possible to adjust and re-design projects in light of economic considerations. In addition, if large numbers of similar types of projects are to be evaluated in a routine manner, it may be possible to prepare cost-benefit evaluation schedules so that a non-economist can gather the data and prepare the necessary computations as part of the technical design process.

READING AND SELECTED APPLICATIONS

Cost-benefit analyses have already been applied in several fields, most notably in water resource development, military planning, electricity supply and transportation. In addition there has been much discussion about applications to public spending for education, health care, and other forms of 'investment in human capital'. Although we shall make no attempt to review individual cases, this section will comment on the problems that have arisen in each of these fields and the methods that have been developed to deal with them. In addition, we indicate some basic reading on each subject.

Water Resource Development

As we noted earlier, cost-benefit analysis first began in the field of water resource development. The interested agencies of the U.S. government used the calculations to appraise proposed investments in flood-control, irrigation, hydro-electric power generation and other forms of water resource development. Since that time, government and academic economists have done much to improve the technique of analysis. Although many of the methods that they have developed are yet to be incorporated into the administrative process, a recent report to the U.S. Bureau of the Budget[17] indicates how seriously they are being considered.

One of the special problems in this field is estimation of the flood control and irrigation services that would be provided by a variety of projects and complex water resource development systems. Faced with the uncertainty of future rainfalls and flood levels, the analysts have developed meteorological records and techniques of computer simulation. Another special problem has been the evaluation of these flood control and irrigation services, both unmarketed intermediate goods.

Several good books on the application of cost-benefit analysis to water resource development are now available. Even for readers not specially interested in this particular field, these works present the best general introduction to cost-benefit analysis. Otto Eckstein's *Water Resource Development: The Economics of Project Evaluation* (Harvard University Press and Oxford University Press, 1958) discusses the theoretical basis of cost-benefit analysis and comments on several general problems before considering in detail the estimation and evaluation of the benefits of flood control, navigation, irrigation and electric power. Although many economists, including Eckstein himself, might now disagree with some of the ideas presented in this book, it is nevertheless a useful introduction.

R. N. McKean's *Efficiency in Government through Systems Analysis, with Emphasis on Water Resource Development* (John Wiley and Sons and Chapman & Hall, 1958) is written more for the administrator or engineer than for the economist. McKean is careful to develop the basic logic of cost-benefit calculations and to relate methods of dealing with uncertainty and the problems of time to the information that will help an administrator's decision. A separate chapter is devoted to each of the major problems of cost-benefit analysis. Two case studies are presented to illustrate the application of cost-benefit analysis in the water resource field.

Addressed to the same audience, *Water Supply: Economics, Technology and Policy* by Hirshleifer, DeHaven and Milliman (University of Chicago Press and Cambridge University Press, 1961) offers an admirably clear presentation of a more limited range of subjects. Two excellent case studies are presented.

For those interested in the problem of spill-overs and the economic theory that forms the basis of evaluating benefits and costs, *Multiple Purpose River Development* by J. U. Krutilla and O. Eckstein (John Hopkins Press and Oxford University Press, 1958) presents an excellent introduction. Much of the book, however, is devoted to calculating an interest rate to represent the social opportunity cost of funds used in public investment; although many of the ideas used in this calculation are sound, the method as a whole is inappropriate.[18] Although the case studies use this interest rate they are well done and add to the value of the book.

The most thorough and advanced book yet to appear on the subject of cost-benefit analysis is *Design of Water Resource Systems* (Macmillan, 1962) edited by Arthur Maass and written by economists, engineers and political scientists who participate in the Harvard University water resource development study group. General problems and special subjects are all covered with extreme care. Although no previous knowledge of economics is necessary, the reader is often expected to be capable of following mathematical derivations and other quantitative discussions. The casual reader or the student might forgo this book or limit his attention to the introductory section; but any government department seriously interested in applying cost-benefit analysis should study it carefully.

Military Planning

The application of cost-benefit analysis to military planning originated in the operational research of World War II. Operational research was developed at that time to improve the use of military resources by selecting routes and schedules that reduced the risk to which shipping was exposed, determining the optimal size of convoys, choosing among designs of military equipment, etc. The operational researchers were scientists, engineers, mathematicians, economists, and others with the appropriate inclinations and abilities. The usefulness of many of their results was beyond question and operational research established itself as a vital part of military decision-making. But viewed in retrospect, much of the wartime work was crude and naive; goals were incorrectly selected, criteria improperly defined and the problems of calculation treated inadequately. Since the war, the use of this type of quantitative analysis in military planning in the United States has increased and significantly improved. This work has been carried on within the several armed services, universities, and such organizations as RAND, the non-profit corporation engaged in long-term research for the Air Force. Much of this is being done by economists who have therefore introduced many of the general methods of cost-benefit analysis into military planning.

Because of the special problems of uncertainty and the importance of the intangible and incommensurable effects of modern warfare, much of the most useful cost-benefit work has been in the form of lower-level 'sub-optimization': choosing components of weapons systems, etc. Nevertheless, a good deal of work has been done on more general problems in the analysis of entire military systems.

Economics of Defense in the Nuclear Age by C. J. Hitch and R. N. McKean (Harvard University Press and Oxford University Press, 1961) presents an excellent discussion of the use of cost-benefit calculations in military planning. It is clear and well written, designed for the administrator or military official as well as the economist. The approach is always practical with emphasis on the logic behind the suggested methods rather than its theoretical foundation or the fine points of application. The authors are well-equipped to discuss this subject; both spent many years as economists in the RAND corporation and Mr Hitch is now Controller of the U.S. Defense Department.

For a shorter introduction to the subject, there is McKean's 'Cost-Benefit Analysis and British Defence Expenditure' (A. T. Peacock and D. J. Robertson (Eds), *Public Expenditure: Appraisal and Control*, Oliver & Boyd, 1963).

Electricity Supply

Cost-benefit analyses have been used to evaluate electricity supply investments in both England and France. Several factors contribute to the government interest in applying the method to this field: investments are large, projects are long-lived, costs are often heavily capital-intensive, and the need to select among alternative fuels, scales of operation and locations is obvious.

The problems of time loom large in these analyses; much of the current controversy in Britain between conventional and nuclear fuels rests on the relative weights to be given to future costs. The problems of time are complicated by the rapid changes in technology that are expected. Two special problems make it difficult to determine the social value of a project's outputs. First, the government is a monopoly supplier of electricity (and often of such close substitutes as coal and gas). Second, the 'output' of a project is not a single product but several interrelated services: average output, peak capacity, etc. Although this would be important for determining the total amount of electricity to be supplied, it does not interfere with what is often the more important problem of finding the minimum cost method of producing a specified output. As we mentioned earlier, there is the further problem of planning a co-ordinated electricity supply. To deal with this, French planners have developed linear programming methods for minimizing the costs of meeting the various planning demands on the system.

In actual application, the studies of investment in electricity supply have not gone beyond the usual cost calculations of engineering economics. Market prices have been used as a measure of the social cost of inputs. Future costs and benefits have been discounted as they would be in evaluating private investments with no special attention given to recognizing social time preference or the social opportunity cost of funds.

The French techniques are discussed in English by Ronald L. Meek in 'The Allocation of Expenditure in the Electricity Supply Industry: Some Methodological Problems' (in A. T. Peacock and D. J. Robertson, op. cit.).This is also an excellent general introduction to some of the other problems in electricity supply planning and contains some interesting material on planning methods in the Soviet Union. The most important French government document on the subject is 'L'Etude à Long Terme des Plans d'Investissement à l'Aide de la Programmation Linéaire' published by Electricité de France in 1960. (*Electricité de France*, June 1960). These methods are further discussed by Masse in *Optimal Investment Decisions* (Prentice Hall, 1962) and by Boiteaux and Bessière in 'Sur L'Emploi des Méthodes Globale et Marginale dans le Choix des Investissements' (*Revue Française de Recherche Opérationnelle*, No. 20, 1961).

Transport Policy

Planning national transport policies requires decisions on all levels from the overall balancing of road and rail to appraising individual road improvement projects or selecting the equipment for a particular railroad operation.

As in all types of cost-benefit analyses, the first problem is predicting the physical benefits that will result from different types of investment. In addition to estimating the immediate effects on the current users of the road or railroad line (e.g. savings in travel and shipping time, increased comfort, reduced costs of motor vehicle operation), one must consider the investment's effect in attracting users from other roads or other rail services as well as in generating increased total use of available transportation. Other 'spill-over' effects are important because of the influence of transportation facilities on regional development.

The evaluation of project benefits has produced some of the most interesting work in this field. Since railway services are not sold in a competitive market and government taxation greatly influences the cost of road transport, market prices must be replaced by shadow-prices calculated to reflect social values. An important example of this is the evaluation of reduced travel and shipping time; this is not only a direct benefit to the consumers of the transportation service but also reduces shipping costs and therefore benefits consumers through lower prices.

Tillo Kuhn's *Public Enterprise Economics and Transport Problems* (University of California Press and Cambridge University Press, 1963) introduces some of the problems of applying cost-benefit analysis in this field and suggests methods for dealing with them. As one of the few currently available studies on this subject, this work deserves the attention of anyone interested in planning transport investments. But many of the subjects are discussed in ways that are both unsophisticated and somewhat misleading. Kuhn seems aware of much of the recent literature on water resource development, but his treatment of transportation problems does not benefit from it as much as it should. Although intended as an introduction to cost-benefit analysis, the book would be read most profitably by someone who is already familiar with the general methods that have been developed. A more suitable book, particularly for non-economists, is C. D. Foster's *The Transport Problem* (Blackie & Son, 1963). Foster pays particular attention to the choice of criteria for evaluating transport proposals. Although the details of his methods might be questioned, he does show the importance of specific and quantitative non-commercial criteria in the fields of road and rail transport.

A group of articles[19] in the *Bulletin of the Oxford University Institute of Statistics* for November 1960 by D. L. Munby, M. E. Paul, D. J. Reynolds, D. W. Glassborow and C. D. Foster can be recommended. Although addressed to economists, much of the material may be read with value by others.

Two useful case studies deserve mention. *The London-Birmingham Motorway: Traffic and Economics* prepared by the Road Research Laboratory (Technical Paper No. 46, HMSO, 1960) illustrates some of the special problems of evaluating road investments and indicates one method of dealing with them. A useful criticism of this document offered by D. W. Glassborow led to a series of papers in 1961 and 1962 by Beesley, Dawson and Glassborow.[20] 'Estimating the Social Benefit of Constructing an Underground Railway in London by C. D. Foster and M. E. Beesley (*Journal of the Royal Statistical Society*, Series A, 1963) shows an imaginative approach to problems of estimating generated traffic flows and of evaluating time savings and improved comfort.

Education and Health Care Expenditure

The economic importance of expenditure on education and health care rests not only on the significance of these services as users of national resources (Britain spends some 10 per cent of the national product on them) but on the contribution they can make to national well-being and growth. The application of cost-benefit analysis can help to determine both the appropriate total expenditure on these services and the best allocation of these funds among competing programmes and projects.

Appraisals of health and education expenditure must take into account that such services represent both investment and consumption. Spending on health and education has been referred to as 'investment in human capital' because it increases future income by raising the productivity of workers and reducing work losses due to disability, sickness and death. These services must also be considered consumption goods because they bring direct satisfaction to those who receive them.

Despite the importance of the consumption aspect of such social spending, most studies on health and education have concentrated exclusively on their desirability as investments. Some have tried to calculate the productivity of education in terms of the higher life income of those with more years of schooling; others have sought to appraise the overall contribution of education to the growth of national income by estimating the unexplained 'residual' growth that remains after allowing for the effects of increased labour and capital. Both of these methods have serious shortcomings and no doubt overestimate the direct productivity of education. Medical authorities have occasionally attempted to estimate the social cost of particular diseases by calculating the national income lost because of illness, disability and death. Although their crude methods, often biased by serious double-counting, have been improved by correcting the notion of individual productivity and introducing better methods for taking time into account, serious problems remain in the treatment of housewives' services, consumption, conditional disease incidence rates, etc. Instead of such general social cost calculations some writers have tried to estimate the economic benefits of particular public health programmes that have been carried out, e.g. Indian malaria eradication. Here in addition to problems of evaluation, there are the difficulties of identifying the specific effects of the health programme; writers eager to justify health spending have often been unduly generous in attributing to a programme all the economic improvements that accompanied it, although often not specifically caused by it.

In neither health nor education have proposed projects been evaluated. To have done so on a basis of the calculation of the investment value alone would be inappropriate; omitting the project's value as consumption would lead to a less than optimal expenditure as well as an inappropriate selection of projects and allocation of funds among different types of health or education programmes. Nevertheless, the lack of specific evaluation of proposed projects has made these studies inapplicable to the actual decisions faced by administrators of education and health care programmes.

If adequate consideration is to be given to specific projects, techniques will have to be developed for estimating their specific effects and for taking into account the uncertainty of these estimates. Studies will have to go beyond evaluating all benefits in money terms and recognize the need for separately including the various incommensurable benefits. If these things are done, cost-benefit analysis can be extended from the more commercial government activities to the health and education expenditures now considered more appropriately 'determined by social need rather than by choices of relative economic advantage' (Plowden Report on the Control of Public Expenditure, p. 22). Choices among alternative programmes of disease prevention or diagnosis, among different methods of treatment, between in-patient and out-patient care for particular conditions, etc. could be made on the basis of statistically derived estimates of the benefits that would be expected from different alternatives and the predicted costs of obtaining them.

The best general survey of the work that has been done on evaluating the social value of education and the social cost of disease is found in *Investment in Human Resources*, a supplementary volume to the October 1962 *Journal of Political Economy*, containing papers presented by several economists at a conference of the National Bureau of Economic Research of New York. Another survey, 'Needs and Resources for Social Investment' by Michael Kaser (*International Social Science Journal*, No. 3 1960), reports on the discussions of a Carnegie Endowment Study Group (Geneva 1959) covering a broader range of subjects with special attention to the problems of developing countries.

Further discussions of the economic value of education appear in John Vaizey's *Economics of Education* (Faber, 1962) and Theodore Schultz's *The Economic Value of Education* (Columbia University Press, 1964). Rashi Fein's *Economics of Mental Illness* (Basic Books, New York, 1958, and Mayflower, London, 1959) and Burton Weisbrod's *Economics of Public Health* (Pennsylvania University Press and Oxford University Press, 1962) present calculations of the social cost of disease. Weisbrod's attempt to find a direct application of these costs as a basis for determining the relative allocation of medical research funds among disease categories must be considered with caution; his approach disregards not only the consumption aspects of improved health but also the important but inexact link between research expenditure and expected improvements. For a discussion of the relevance of cost-benefit analysis to the problems of health service operational research and planning see Martin Feldstein's 'Economic Analysis, Operational Research and the National Health Service' (*Oxford Economic Papers*, March 1963).

CONCLUSION

The Plowden Committee has rightly stressed the need for a 'wider application of mathematical techniques, statistics and accountancy to the problems of public expenditure' (p. 11). But, although there is much truth in their comment that 'economic work on the problems of the public sector . . . has lagged far behind that on other comparably important matters . . .' (p. 30), there is now a growing body of research and experience in the use of cost-benefit analysis to increase the efficiency of public expenditure. There is good reason to expect that the future will bring not only important theoretical improvements in this field, but also a development of practical techniques and a closer integration with the planning and budgeting process.

REFERENCES

[1] See for example: *Control of Public Expenditure* (Chairman: Lord Plowden), Cmnd. 1432, 1961; U. K. Hicks, 'Plowden, Planning and Management in the Public Services', *Public Administration*, Winter 1961.

[2] An excellent summary of these is presented in A. J. Merritt and A. Sykes, *The Finance and Analysis of Capital Projects*, Longmans, 1963.

[3] Discounting is similar to calculating compound interest. If the interest rate is 5 per cent, £1 today is worth the same as £1·05 a year from now; if the discount rate is 5 per cent £1·05 a year from now is worth £1 today. More generally, if the discount rate is 100r per cent., £1 available T years from now is worth $£\left(\dfrac{1}{1+r}\right)^T$ today.

[4] See M. S. Feldstein, 'The Social Time Preference Discount Rate in Cost-Benefit Analysis', *The Economic Journal*, June 1964.

[5] See M. S. Feldstein, 'Opportunity Cost Calculations in Cost-Benefit Analysis, *Public Finance*, 1964.

[6] For a recent comment with particular reference to public sector investments see M. S. Feldstein and J. S. Flemming, 'The Problem of Time Stream Evaluation: Present Value versus Internal Rate of Return Rules', *Bulletin of the Oxford University Institute of Economics and Statistics*, February 1964.

[7] One such method is proposed in *Standards and Criteria for Formulating and Evaluating Federal Water Resources Development*, Report of Panel of Consultants to the Bureau of the Budget (Chairman: M. M. Hufschmidt), unpublished, Washington, D.C., 1961. See also M. S. Feldstein, 'Net Social Benefit Calculation and the Public Investment Decisions', *Oxford Economic Papers*, March 1964.

[8] For a discussion of this problem, see: Stephen A. Marglin, *Approaches to Dynamic Investment Planning*, North Holland Publishing Company, Amsterdam, 1963.

[9] The French experience in this field is appraised by Ronald L. Meek, 'The Allocation of Expenditure in the Electricity Supply Industry', in *Public Expenditure: Appraisal and Control*, A. T. Peacock and D. J. Robinson, (eds.), Oliver & Boyd, Edinburgh, 1963.

[10] A good survey of this problem is presented in Robert Dorfman's 'Basic Economic and Technologic Concepts', Chapter 3 of *Design of Water Resource Systems* by Arthur Maass, *et al.* (Macmillan 1962), see especially pp. 129–58.

[11] This subject is considered by Stephen A. Marglin in 'Objectives of Water Resources Development', Chapter 1 of A. Maass, *et al.*, op. cit., especially pp. 62–87.

[12] Programme and performance budgets are discussed by R. N. McKean in 'Analysis for Performance Budgets', Chapter 13 of *Efficiency in Government through Systems Analysis*, John Wiley and Sons, New York and Chapman & Hall, London, 1958. See also J. Burkhead, *Government Budgeting*, John Wiley and Sons, New York, and Chapman & Hall, London, 1956, especially Chapter 6.

13 McKean, op. cit., discusses this problem, see especially Chapters 1 and 2.

14 *Control of Public Expenditure*, Cmnd. 1432, 1961, p. 11.

15 This problem is discussed in Martin S. Feldstein, 'Economic Analysis, Operational Research and the National Health Service', *Oxford Economic Papers*, March 1963.

16 J. M. Keynes, 'Economic Possibilities for our Grandchildren' (1930), reprinted in *Essays in Persuasion*, Rupert Hart-Davis, London 1952, p. 373.

17 *Standards and Criteria for Formulating and Evaluating Federal Water Resources Development*, 1961.

18 For a criticism of this approach see my 'Opportunity Cost Calculations in Cost-Benefit Analysis', *Public Finance*, 1964.

19 D. L. Munby, 'The Roads as Economic Assets'; M. E. Paul, 'Covering Costs by Receipts'; D. J. Reynolds, 'Some Problems of Planning the Improvement of the Road System'; D. W. Glassborow, 'The Road Research Laboratory's Investment Criteria Examined'; C. D. Foster, 'Surplus Criteria for Investment'. All articles appeared in the November 1960 issue of the *Bulletin of the Oxford University Institute of Statistics*.

20 'The Road Research Laboratory's Investment Criteria Examined', *Bulletin of the Oxford University Institute of Statistics*, November 1960. M. E. Beesley, 'Mr. Glassborow on Investment Criteria', *Bulletin of the Oxford University Institute of Statistics*, May 1961. R. F. F. Dawson, 'A Reply to Glassborow's Criticism of the Economic Assessment of the London-Birmingham Motorway', *Bulletin of the Oxford University Institute of Statistics*, August 1961. D. W. Glassborow, 'A Comment on Mr. Dawson's Reply', *Bulletin of the Oxford University Institute of Statistics*, August 1961.

PART II

ASSUMPTIONS IN MACHINERY
OF GOVERNMENT

'In matters of government, the English have generally been more theoretical than they care to admit', wrote W. J. M. Mackenzie, as the opening sentence in a contribution on 'The Structure of Central Administration'.[1] That is perhaps to say that the English make assumptions which guide their conduct in administrative change, but it is their style not to appear 'doctrinaire' about such matters.

What might such assumptions be? There are two ways of approaching an answer. The first would be to review what various people have said ought to be done next, in this matter of machinery and procedures (as distinct from the major purposes of political action), and why. The second would be to review what the English have actually done in the last century or so in this matter, and as an outside observer postulate a set of beliefs and aims which renders such actions coherent and intelligible. Neither method ensures discovery of 'truth': the first because one could not guarantee that one was quoting all the relevant people; the second because actions will always form a pattern of some kind which, however clearly it stands out to the hindsighted observer, cannot be guaranteed to be the principle which guided the choices of the actors.

What we know as 'The British Constitution' is itself an artefact which, like one of those toys that show two pictures alternately according to the angle of vision, is now descriptive, now prescriptive. At one time, it purports to show 'reality' as distinct from what the legal terminology of our heritage would imply, as with Bagehot's distinction between the 'dignified' and the 'efficient' parts of the English Constitution;[2] at another, it invests that picture of 'reality' with normative force so as to discourage departures from it, as when Dicey thunders about what the 'Rule of Law' demands.[3] It is the charming conceit of the constitutional lawyers that they do not lay down the law, but 'uncover' it, by (let us say, to avoid more metaphysical reasoning) finding the pattern of what is common to the decisions of individual judges in individual cases. This would be acceptable enough, if they were not then such doughty champions of the *rightness* of the principles thus elicited as to make them binding on themselves and their successors. There is a very narrow line between what is usually done and what it is the done thing to do.

[1] W. J. M. Mackenzie, 'The Structure of Central Administration', in Sir Gilbert Campion *et al.*, *British Government since 1918*, Allen & Unwin, 1950, p. 56.

[2] Walter Bagehot, *The English Constitution*, 1867 (Oxford University Press, World's Classics Edition, 1928).

[3] A. V. Dicey, *Introduction to the Study of the Law of the Constitution*, Macmillan, 1885.

Moreover, the 'picture of reality' has to be painted by mortal man, or men, whether the intention be to describe merely, or to set standards; and the distinction is never as clear as the intentions may be, because the painter's perceptions enter into even his description. Conflicts between men may as often be conflicts of perception as they are conflicts of aim. Embarrassed by such philosophical complexity, the British pretend (even to themselves) that in machinery of government questions it is all reducible to what is more convenient for the moment, or what is politically expedient. The extracts in this Part II are selected to unveil, at least a little further than that, the differences of understanding, and of aim, that make them 'questions' worthy of academic study.

We begin with an extract from Wilfrid Harrison's influential text, which may be taken as at once a relatively modern and relatively traditional account of currently received doctrine on the British Constitution. Yet the Constitution is at present itself in question; a Royal Commission is currently sitting, under Lord Crowther. Leaving aside any effects of our entry into the European Community, there is speculation whether Britain already is 'federal' in spirit; whether political resistance to central government policies by local council majorities of the opposite colour ought not to be seen as already providing a British system of 'checks and balances', as it is claimed that we already have a 'Presidential system'. While these may be little more than verbal play, it is a speculation of another order whether a reform of local government on the scale proposed by the Redcliffe-Maud Commission does not (apart from the question of the provincial authorities, specifically referred to the Crowther Commission) involve basic rethinking of central government machinery, so profound must be the effect on central-local relations. Reformist as the Labour Governments of 1964–70 were in machinery of government matters at the highest level, they may be criticized, as by John Mackintosh in the second of our extracts, for not having an overall theory to work from.

If there be, as conventionally accepted, three main parts to the present machinery of government – central departments, local authorities, and the public corporations – the next level of consideration below the constitutional will concern the principles upon which work is allocated among the three parts. Such principles, if articulated axiomatically, would form statements of the 'theory of local government' and the 'theory of public corporations' – phrases familiar enough, though one has never heard the corresponding 'theory of central departments'. Possibly the word 'theory' is loosely used in such applications. For its current value as well as its historical interest, we reprint a lecture on 'Decentralization' given by Sir Charles Harris as long ago as 1925. The complexities of conflict of assumptions about local government are skilfully unravelled by L. J. Sharpe in a very recent article, which we are glad to reproduce here.

A now classic source for principles of public corporations is D. N. Chester's article of 1953, which we reprint in full, along with brief extracts from the 1968 Report of the Select Committee on National-ized Industries, and the section dealing with 'hiving-off' in the Fulton Committee Report on the Civil Service.

The next level of consideration of the machinery of government would logically be the principles upon which work is or should be allocated among units within each of the three sectors separately – including how many units there should be, of what size, and how specialized. For local government, these were the terms of reference of the Redcliffe-Maud Commission; it would be foolish to try to represent that argument, and the debate which has followed the Report, in the space available here. For public corporations, on the other hand, the debate has not been generalized, but applied to particular industries, each of which has had its own other problems. Consequently the arguments have been somewhat various, referring as much to principles of industrial management in general as they did to public corporations.

It is the allocation problem in the third sector, that of central departments and ministries, which is ordinarily referred to by the use of the phrase 'machinery of government questions'. The classic source of normative principles is the Report of the Haldane Com-mittee of 1918, from which we reprint a passage. The indispensable tool for students of this aspect of public administration is F. M. G. Willson's *The Organization of British Central Government*, happily again in print in a second edition and deserving of many future editions. We include a brief extract merely, we hope, to whet appetites for the work itself.

The principles behind recent mergers of ministries in the defence, education, health and technological fields have not been officially spelt out in a Haldane or Fulton type of report, and evaluation has hardly begun. But we are happy to include, as an authoritative exposition of current doctrine (the word preferred among senior civil servants) on the allocation of functions among departments, an address by the Head of the Home Civil Service to a seminar for management consultants – itself a sign of the times.

The last field of conflict of assumptions which ought to be noticed,

191

although it does not usually fall within 'machinery of government' questions, is the longest-standing of all. It goes under various names: *droit administratif*, 'Ministers' Powers', the 'protection of the citizen'. From one point of view, it perhaps ought to be seen as conflict of interest: the struggle between the Executive and the Judiciary goes back to the middle ages and is marked by great battles – Star Chamber, General Warrants, 'New Despotism' – in which (as is usual in demarcation disputes) principle and self-interest are mixed. Less earthily, one may see it as a conflict between emphasis on individual rights, particularly those of property, and emphasis on the collective public interest. It is well known, for instance, that the statutory procedures preliminary to major road construction can take several years longer than the actual building of the road; the then Minister of Transport commented in May 1969 that it was 'difficult to strike a balance between the right of people to object, when their house is going to be pulled down or they are going to suffer inconvenience or lose an open space, and, on the other hand, the demand for more roads'. What might appear, to an overseas observer from a different tradition altogether, as a mere choice between styles of decision – the 'judicial' style and the 'administrative' style – involves in these ways both interest and principle, well brought out in the evidence to the Franks Committee on Administrative Tribunals and Enquiries of 1957 in the discussion of the nature of a public enquiry. We include extracts from two classic documents, the Report of the Donoughmore Committee on Ministers' Powers of 1932, and the Franks Committee's celebrated statement on 'openness, fairness and impartiality': also a forthright editorial from *Public Law* which takes to task the Council on Tribunals for swallowing hook, line and sinker, the 'judicial' view of public enquiries; and D. N. Chester's article on the most notorious scandal in this field of British public administration in recent decades, 'Crichel Down'.

14

The Constitution*

WILFRID HARRISON

The British constitution is the body of rules which prescribes the structure and functions of the organs of government; any theoretical appreciation of the practice and machinery of public administration must therefore include an understanding of the constitutional framework within which it operates. It is for that reason that this reading has been extracted from Professor Harrison's sophisticated introduction to the working of British government; it clearly and concisely lays down the constitutional principles which act as constraints on the day to day management decisions in the public service.

The British Constitution provides the framework of rules within which operate the institutions we are to examine. In discussing the Constitution we are again dealing, but now from a different angle and in somewhat more precise terms, with the question of the essential character of our political system. We are doing so with reference to the more important of the actual principles that are followed in practice by politicians and lawyers. If it were oftener borne in mind that this is what a discussion of the Constitution involves, it would perhaps appear less mysterious than it frequently does. The Constitution is sometimes spoken of as though it meant exactly the same as the political system itself, or as though it were another name for the sum of the various organs of government, lumped together with the electorate and the political parties. The expression is also at times used as though it referred only to the more ancient parts of the government such as the Crown and the House of Lords, and as though the essential character of the Constitution would be lost if any alteration were made in the status of these. In fact, however, the British Constitution is just the same in nature as any other constitution; it is neither a political system as such, nor any selection of the parts of government, but a body of rules indicating the structure

* From Wilfrid Harrison, *The Government of Britain*, Hutchinson, 1948, pp. 22–32. Reprinted with permission of the publisher.

and functions of political institutions and the principles governing their operation. This is a matter that can be much more easily appreciated if we look at countries that have 'written constitutions'; that is to say, in which there is a certain special document referred to as 'The Constitution'. Such constitutions openly purport to give comprehensive and unified expression to 'fundamental laws'; that is, laws that are more authoritative than other laws and require for their passage or their alteration certain special law-making processes that are more difficult and complicated than those involved in ordinary legislation. The Constitution of Great Britain is, however, just as fundamental and just as much a matter of rules as are the written constitutions of the U.S.A., the U.S.S.R., France or the Republic of Ireland.

Of course, in the absence of a single and all-important constitutional document in Great Britain, and in the absence there of any specific and unique process for constitutional amendment, it is rather more difficult to pin down the rules of the Constitution. This difficulty is, however, only relative: no written constitution ever works without requiring some measure of interpretation and adaptation; and these processes take place, in the countries which have written constitutions, as the results of judgments given in the law-courts and of the agreement of politicians to customs and usages. On the other hand, certain parts of the British Constitution are, as we shall see, contained in Acts of Parliament, and are therefore just as much written as are the fundamental laws contained in specialized constitutional documents. The British Constitution thus really differs from the 'written' type of constitution only inasmuch as its written parts do not have the same kind of special origin and are not subject to any special codification. It does not really differ from them in the sense of being completely unwritten, any more than they really differ from it in the sense of being completely written. It may be unusual, and even unique, but it is not different in kind from other constitutions, and, above all, it is not in any way mysterious. It has a history. There are definite sources for its rules. It has central principles that can be given firm expression.

Much of the history of the Constitution is to be found in successive modifications of the royal power or 'prerogative'. Such modifications, even when made by force or threat, have tended to be made in terms of delimitations of the rights of different parts of the government, and therefore at the same time in terms of corresponding duties: and the governed have been held to have rights as well as duties. Thus the process of constitutional development has been two-sided: the greater part of the actual power has been transferred from the Crown to other institutions; but in the process the acquisition of power has been attended by the acceptance of responsibility. The development has also brought about one of the most obvious characters of our Constitution, the divorce between its form and its substance. Governmental power continues to be exercised in the name of the Crown, and this means, literally, only nominally by the monarch. Thus we still have such legal principles as that 'the King can do no wrong' in a country that eschews even bureaucracy and in which any man considers himself as good as any other. This is because the operative sources of our constitutional rules lie elsewhere.

One such source has already been indicated – statutory law, or Acts of Parliament. Many important matters are thus regulated; for instance, the franchise in the 1949 Representation of the People Act and certain of the powers of the House of Lords in the 1949 Parliament Act.[1] Acts which deal with such questions do not differ formally from other statutes: they are constitutional because of what they deal with, and for that reason only. Of course some constitutional statutes have come, in the course of time, to be regarded with a certain reverence: this applies, for instance, to Magna Carta, the Petition of Right, the Bill of Rights and the Act of Settlement. None the less, so far as legal form is concerned, the position of such statutes as these is just the same as that of an Act of Parliament for, say, the regulation of herring fisheries: although it is not very likely to occur, all of these Acts could be repealed in the same way by further Acts of Parliament.

A second source of constitutional rules is to be found in the decisions of judges on cases heard by them in the law-courts. The enactments of Parliament may be interpreted by the judges. Decisions of judges, too, have developed the laws and customs of the realm which we know as the 'common law'; and in this field several matters of major constitutional importance are covered, including some aspects of the royal prerogative and certain questions relating to the

[1] Other important constitutional statutes include the various Acts that altered the electoral system in the nineteenth century, and the Acts settling the form of the local government system. Specific examples are the Habeas Corpus Acts from 1677, the Act of Union (1707), the Riot Act (1714), the Official Secrets Acts (1911–39), the Statute of Westminster (1931).

remedies of the subject in respect of illegal actions of public officers.

The customs of the realm contained in the common law have the force of law because they have been recognized in the courts we accept as having the requisite authority for granting such recognition. Another source of constitutional rules is to be found, however, in usages or conventions whose validity cannot be the subject of proceedings in courts of law. Yet these conventions cover some of the most important parts of our political system. They include, for instance, the greater part of the rules that govern the position of the Cabinet and the working of Parliament; and it is they, in particular, that have served to adjust the operation of these central parts of our government to changes in social outlook. They form the part of the Constitution that is most difficult to study, because they are varied in origin: sometimes they are the subjects of explicit agreements, but at other times they develop more as matters of custom: also, they may sometimes undergo developments that are imperceptible to all save a few contemporaries who are intimate with the inner workings of politics. When Bagehot, who was a close and shrewd observer of the working of contemporary politics, wrote his book *The English Constitution*, he was mistaken about the precise rôle of the monarch in the political system of his day, and we today know more about it than he did because we have available letters and memoirs that were not published in his time. There may thus sometimes be a time-lag in exact public knowledge of particular constitutional conventions. But this does not mean that it is impossible to know anything about them. There has always, in recent times, been broad agreement amongst politicians and amongst students of the subject as to the nature of the greater part of the major conventions; and explanations in Parliament, the correspondence or diaries of statesmen and the published opinions of commentators provide authoritative sources from which we can frame an account of the conventions that is at least approximately correct. Moreover, if there is a dispute of any political importance about the true nature of a particular convention, it is liable to lead to some public discussion and settlement.

Finally, because of the diversity of the other sources of constitutional rules, there has developed the need for systematization; that is to say, for bringing the variety of rules into definite relation one to another and into some degree of unity by reference to central principles. This work has been done by 'authorities', that is, by commentators whose works have come to be regarded as authoritative because they give correct and exact expression to agreed traditions. In certain cases such writers have provided compendious and detailed accounts of the operation of particular classes of rule: an outstanding example of this type of work is Sir T. Erskine May's *Parliamentary Practice*. But in other cases they have been more concerned with the general principles of the Constitution considered as a whole: a classical example of this type of work is A. V. Dicey's *Law of the Constitution*.

To understand the actual character of the Constitution we require to look for the central principles it embodies. These principles can be expressed in a variety of ways, but it is convenient to summarize them as three: Supremacy of Parliament, Rule of Law, Cabinet Responsibility.

There are two sides to the principle of Parliamentary Supremacy: the first is the rule that the law made by Parliament (that is, Acts of Parliament) always overrides any other law (that is, that Parliament can change the common law or overturn judicial decisions); the second is the rule that the right to this legislative supremacy resides in Parliament and in Parliament alone. (Thus the royal prerogative may be limited or defined by Act of Parliament, but neither through the royal prerogative nor by any other means can any legal limitation be placed upon Parliament.) As a corollary, the right to impose taxes resides with Parliament alone. Again, Parliament alone has the right to legalize past illegalities.

This is a very formal characteristic of our Constitution, and by itself it throws no light on whether it is, for instance, democratic or otherwise. It is none the less important, because it lets us know quite clearly where to look for ultimate legal authority. It should be noticed that when we say 'Parliament' in this context we do not mean, as is sometimes meant in other contexts, simply the House of Commons or the two Houses of Parliament together, but the "Crown-in-Parliament"; that is to say, the Crown, the House of Lords and the House of Commons in their capacity as acting together. For it is normally only by the joint action of these three that legislation in Great Britain is possible, as is indicated in the words with which an Act of Parliament opens: 'Be it enacted by the Queen's Most Excellent Majesty, by and with the advice of the Lords Spiritual and Temporal, and Commons, in the present Parliament assembled, and by the authority of the same . . .'. The supremacy referred to here is however, legal supremacy only. It inheres in the institutions just described and these are controlled by determinate persons, but the control exercised by these persons is, as we shall see, itself controlled: other constitutional principles are honoured which in practice limit the actual powers of those whose collective legal powers are without limit.

The principle of the Rule of Law throws more light on the concrete character of the Constitution. It is the principle that the ordinary law of the land is of universal application, that there is to be no arbitrary authority, and no divisions into separate systems of law (for instance, into one for officials and another for ordinary citizens); and it carries with it the rule that the remedies of the ordinary law will be sufficient for the effective protection of the constitutional rights of ordinary citizens. The conception of the Rule of Law was given classical formulation sixty years ago by one of the commentators previously mentioned, A. V. Dicey. It has since been questioned whether it ever did apply exactly, for instance (as we shall see) in respect of the immunities of the Crown in litigation. It has also been suggested that it is honoured less today than when Dicey was writing, since for instance, it has become common to create special departmental tribunals outside the ordinary courts. It does, none the less, still represent a central characteristic of the Constitution. The ordinary citizen in Great Britain is not liable to be punished except for breaches of ordinary law; there are no extraordinary tribunals for trying 'offences against the State'; no officials or departments have arbitrary power to arrest us; officials in order to perform their duties may have special powers which ordinary citizens do not have, but these are defined by law, and abuses of them are subject to control by the courts; and while there is an increasing amount of delegation of authority to departments and officials, governments still appear to try to ensure that such authority will not be exercised arbitrarily, since they lay down rules for its exercise and provide for the payment of compensation in cases in which it causes suffering to legitimate private interests.

The significance of the Rule of Law as a legal principle is that it is recognized in the working of the courts of law. (In the same way recognition is also given to the 'Rules of Natural Justice': for instance to the rule that no man should be judge in his own case.) It might be held that the Rule of Law can remain a cardinal principle of the Constitution only so long as Parliament agrees that it should do so. For practical purposes, however, this consideration is less important than the truth that Parliament in fact does choose to do so. To put it another way, Parliamentary supremacy is, in part, only tolerable because the Rule of Law is recognized. Thus the two principles are connected; and they are further connected with the third principle.

I have called the third principle 'Cabinet Responsibility'. This

198

principle is political in character. Again, while of the other two principles, one relates specifically to Parliament as such and the other to the position of the individual citizen, this principle by itself links Parliament and citizens, and, by reference to the relation between the two, delimits the essential mode of operation of our form of government.

The Cabinet is the 'Executive' part of our government, as distinct from the 'Legislative' part, which is Parliament (in the sense of the Crown-in-Parliament). The Executive is not confined, however, simply to the literal execution or carrying-out of the laws made by the Legislature. It supervises that execution (which is mainly in the hands of the government departments), but it also has, as we shall see, the power of initiative in respect of legislation. That is to say, while it cannot itself legislate, it can, and does, choose the issues to be put before Parliament, and, further, it has, most of the time, the power so to influence Parliament, through its control of the House of Commons, as to be able to ensure that what it proposes will in fact pass into law. This is a very considerable concentration of power; much greater, indeed, than would have suited some of the older constitutional theorists, who considered that there should be a 'Separation of Powers', because any concentrations in the same hands of the executive and legislative powers must lead to tyranny. Thus, for instance, in the American Constitution the powers of government were carefully separated. 'All legislative power herein granted,' reads the first section of Article One of that constitution, 'shall be vested in a Congress of the United States,' and the first section of Article Two continues: 'The Executive power shall be vested in a President.' In the Cabinet system, however, the executive is in the legislature, and leads it.

But this concentration of authority is offset. In the first place, the Cabinet is responsible to Parliament. It is governed by the doctrine of Collective Responsibility, whereby for all that is agreed in the Cabinet all of its members who do not at once resign are thereafter individually responsible. It must explain itself to Parliament: the Prime Minister or another spokesman must speak for its policies, and time must be allowed for criticism of its policies. Individual ministers can also be questioned about the activities of their departments. And the Cabinet is in power, and remains there, only in virtue of being able to count upon a majority of the votes in divisions in the House of Commons. But this presses the question a stage further back; for a majority of votes in the House of Commons is obtained only by obtaining a majority of seats at a General Election. At a

General Election electors are choosing which of the rival parties shall be returned to power. It is, as a rule, very clear who will be Prime Minister if one party is victorious and who will be if the other party is. To quite a degree, too, the election chooses members of the Cabinet: no one could doubt in 1945 that if the Labour Party won the election of that year the Cabinet would contain Mr Bevin and Mr Morrison, or that, if the Conservative Party won it, it would contain Mr Eden and Mr Butler. Moreover, at a General Election, a retiring Cabinet is being judged at least in part, on its previous performance in office; and the leaders of the party that is victorious at the election do not go to Westminster with a completely free hand to behave as they wish: they are tied in various ways and in varying degrees by their own and their party's pronouncements and promises. They are charged by the people with responsibility for carrying on the government of the country at least broadly in a character consistent with their own representations of themselves. They will answer at the next General Election, and the question of responsibility to Parliament will not arise for them if the result of the election is such as to place the 'trust of the people' elsewhere.

These questions of responsibility indicate that the Cabinet is an executive with limited authority. There is a further side to this. The concentration of the powers of government in Great Britain has traditionally stopped short with the executive and the legislature: the judiciary has remained outside. It is true, of course, that the highest court of appeal is one part of the legislature, the House of Lords. It is also true that the ordinary courts have at times been excluded from considering orders made by ministers and that some justiciable issues have been entrusted to administrative tribunals. But there is no confusion between the legislative and judicial functions of the House of Lords, and, to whatever extent the judiciary may have suffered or be suffering encroachment, there is no question of direct parliamentary or executive interference. Subject to the supremacy of Parliament, the courts remain independent, free from control or influence by the Cabinet.

Cabinet Responsibility thus supplements the juncture already noticed of Parliamentary Supremacy and the Rule of Law. It provides both the practical pattern for the operation of Parliament and the means whereby the citizens, whose liberties Parliament is to respect, may exercise an influence upon Parliament. It is in this way the most fundamental principle of the modern Constitution.

Some people think that discussions of the Constitution and of its principles are a waste of time because they have nothing, or very

200

little, to do with practical questions of politics or of the machinery of government. Anyone who takes such a view is making a big and a dangerous mistake. It is important, in the first place, to be clear what the Constitution is, because there have been times when the word has been used to colour political controversy. Some Conservatives have at times implied that they have considered their party to be 'constitutional' in some sense in which the Labour Party apparently was not. This is just a confusion of issues. It is doubtful whether the word 'constitutional' so used has any meaning at all. It is certainly no more constitutional to oppose attacks on the House of Lords than it is to oppose attacks on the Trade Unions: the use of the Union Jack as an election emblem is neither constitutional nor unconstitutional; whether you are for or against free enterprise or nationalization gives no indication whether you can be counted upon to act constitutionally. The Constitution is not the property of any one of the political parties; and there have in fact been occasions when some Conservatives have appeared to behave with doubtful constitutional propriety.[1]

In the second place, there is considerable point in appreciating just what the central principles of the Constitution are taken to be. We sometimes say, with heat, that a Government, or a department, has 'no right' to do this or that. As a rule we do not mean that there is no constitutional right but simply that there is a policy of which we do not approve. Again, it would be advantageous if there were a more general understanding of the extent to which political leaders are agreed on a body of constitutional principles. Time is often wasted in private political debate in arguing points on which no leading politicians would differ. Further, the detailed rules should themselves be better known, because, if they are not, the significance of many mechanisms of government will be misunderstood.

[1] In opposition to the Liberals, 1906–14. See A. B. Keith, *The Constitution of England from Queen Victoria to George VI*, Vol. I, pp. 400–21.

15

Piecemeal Reform[*]

J. P. MACKINTOSH

*In surveying the weaknesses and examining the performance of the
contemporary local government structure, J. P. Mackintosh, M.P.,
previously Professor of Politics at Strathclyde University, was reminded of Dr Johnson's reaction in another context. It is 'like a dog's
walking on his hinder legs. It is not done well; but you are surprised to
find it done at all'. His, however, was only one of a number of books
and articles focusing attention on problems of devolution in Britain in
the late 1960s: see also W. A. Robson,* Local Government in Crisis,
George Allen & Unwin, 1966; Local Government: A Report to the
Liberal Party, *Liberal Publications Department, 1962; L. J. Sharpe,*
Why Local Democracy, *Fabian Society, 1965; Bow Group,* New Life
for Local Government, *CPC, 1965. In this extract Macintosh focuses
attention both on some of the essential features of local democracy and
on the accepted government methods of approaching administrative
reform.*

It is typically British to imagine that it is possible to reform local
government – or any other institution – without first being clear
about its purpose, without first settling the value judgments and
working out the objectives of the reformed institutions. It is assumed
that by looking at the particular machinery, by taking evidence about
how the present arrangements work, inconsistencies will emerge,
obvious changes will suggest themselves and the problem will be
solved.

Recent Governments have broken up the question of institutional
reform into segments almost as if to ensure that the broader issues
will not be discussed. At the moment of writing, some ministers,
M.P.s and members of the public are considering methods of Parliamentary reform. Meanwhile, totally disconnected, the Fulton com-

[*] From J. P. Mackintosh, *The Devolution of Power, Local Democracy, Regionalism and Nationalism,* London, Chatto & Windus, 1968, pp. 39–45. Reprinted with
permission of the author and the publisher.

PIECEMEAL REFORM

mittee examined the personnel, professional structure and recruitment of the civil service. Both parliamentary and civil service reform closely affect local government but it is being reviewed in a totally separate compartment subdivided into three boxes labelled London (which has been 'done' by the Herbert Commission), England (the Maud Commission) and Scotland (the Wheatley Commission). There was a further sub-division, since staffing (in England only) was examined by a special Committee under Sir George Mallaby, and the management of local government was reviewed by a Committee under Sir John Maud, both of which reported in 1967. Yet for both staffing and management, a crucial question is the attitude of the civil service to regional and local administration. Is it better to give up the idea that central departments can only act through agencies such as *ad hoc* boards and local government? If Whitehall departments wish to control a policy, perhaps they should execute it themselves and leave local government the task of administering only those matters which can be totally entrusted to the local councils? On the other hand, if it is considered that the central government cannot handle the details of local investment programmes and if there is to be some real power given to reformed local or regional government, this will have major repercussions in Whitehall. At present the departmental structure and loyalties are a major reason for the failures in regional government. The answer may have to be a new ministry or new structures in the existing ministries. Perhaps officials in the top-tier local authorities should be part of the central civil service or at least there should be periods of secondment from Whitehall. Similarly one of the factors inhibiting regional variations of central government policy is the present system of responsibility to the House of Commons. If it is wished to alter this and to give M.P.s some creative work or actual influence in their areas, it might be possible for M.P.s to sit on regional or top-tier local authority councils.

By subdividing the consideration of reform and failing to state the overall objectives clearly, many of these possibilities and interconnections were omitted. In addition, the terms of reference of the various committees and Royal Commissions were carefully limited so that there were areas of each of the separate aspects of the problems put before the committees which they were not allowed to consider. For instance, the Committee on Staffing were restricted to 'the *existing methods* of recruiting local government officers and of using them; and what changes might help local authorities to get the best possible service and help their officers to give it'. (My italics.)

203

That is to say the Committee were asked to work on the assumption that there would be no major reforms in the structure of local government (after all, these were being handled by another Commission) and they were not expected to consider alternative methods of recruitment even if the present structure was retained. Thus there was no examination of the virtues of a single local government service with a body which would recruit, fix the levels and grades of training and the pay for categories of posts while leaving the councils to select officers from this unified service for appointment to their staff. This system has been tried in countries overseas that have otherwise adopted the British pattern of local government. As has been said, there could be no consideration of how far it would be desirable to have civil servants from the central departments seconded for periods to local government and vice versa, nor could there be any examination of such questions as whether it was desirable, from the staff point of view, to keep the present tripartite structure of the Health Service. All that the Committee on Staffing could do in this last instance was to produce two stirring recommendations. The first was to local authorities to 'Note the changes which affect the recruitment and use of medical practitioners in the other two' (branches of the Health Service) and then to the Ministry of Health: 'The relative positions of medical practitioners in the local authority service and in the other two branches of the National Health Service should be re-examined.'

The Committee on Management had similarly restricted terms of reference, its task being 'to consider in the light of modern conditions how local government might best continue to attract and retain people (both elected representatives and principal officers) of the calibre necessary to ensure its maximum effectiveness'. This Committee, however, took a somewhat wider view of its task and examined local government procedure and internal organization abroad. It felt able to make a radical appraisal of the committee system, of departmental organization, of relations with the central government and the public, and conducted some research into the categories of persons elected to local councils. But again it was hampered by the need to start with the existing structure and system, so that there was no thorough consideration of the city manager or directly elected sole executive. Nor was there any examination of the problems that might arise in attracting suitable persons to serve on fewer larger councils, should there be a reform of structure. But within these limits, the Committee did produce a thorough and useful report.

The most striking and potentially serious restrictions were, how-

204

ever, imposed on the most important of the reviews, that undertaken by the two Royal Commissions on Local Government, They were told

'to consider the structure of Local Government in England, outside greater London (or in Scotland), *in relation to its existing functions*; and to make recommendations for authorities and boundaries, and for functions and their division, having regard to the size and character of areas *in which these can be most effectively exercised* and the need to sustain a viable system of local democracy.' (My italics).

The first and greatest weakness of these terms of reference is that they limit the examination to the most suitable areas for the conduct of the *existing functions* of local government. Yet the present functions are not in any sense the pure essence of what local government ought to do; they are the entirely arbitrary collection of tasks left after some had been removed on the grounds that the existing units were too small, too poor or simply inappropriate. In this way over recent years local authorities have lost responsibility for main roads, some civil airfields, hospitals, public assistance, passenger road transport services, electricity supply and gas undertakings. It may be that these functions are better out of the hands of local authorities, but surely it was wrong to omit any consideration of whether larger units could resume them with general advantage.

Even more serious, the terms of reference prevented the Royal Commissions weighing the desirability of local government units big enough to take over the functions now given to the boards, bureaux and commissions of 'intermediate government'. A far better approach would have been to ask the Royal Commissions to consider not only the existing tasks of local government but to extend their survey to examine all functions which were conducted either by local government, by bodies outside the central departments or by central government itself, if these functions might usefully be devolved. The most obvious example is the work of the regional economic planning councils. Although these bodies are only advisory, if their plans include land use planning and are accepted, all the most important decisions about the local environment are settled. The more recent of these elaborate documents set out the location of new towns and roads, recommend which existing roads should be developed, earmark land for industrial estates, recreation and new housing, and suggest sites for technical colleges and the whole range of principal amenities. If the work is done properly and is endorsed by the local authorities and the central government, it pre-empts all the key lines of development. Refusal to consider this kind of planning, its progressive adaptation to circumstances and its implementation as proper functions for local government, might well take much of the meaning out of any reformed system.

The terms of reference do not mean that evidence on these issues was not presented to the Commissions or that they did not talk over this problem. The author gave evidence that included these questions, both in writing and orally, to the Scottish Royal Commission, and the D.E.A. also mentioned regional planning in its evidence to the English Royal Commission. But the terms of reference do require the Commissions to ignore any arguments relating to the performance of functions other than the existing functions of local government in coming to their conclusions. Because most of the functions that require large regional units have already been taken away from local government or, if they are new functions, were never awarded to local government, this has effectively removed all the strongest arguments for really large units from the purview of the Commissions. In effect it would be possible to propose a reformed system for conducting the existing activities of local government, and central government might (it is at least theoretically possible!) be reformed both in Westminster and in Whitehall, and yet one of the major weaknesses of the present system would remain in the form of regional or national boards, advisory committees, development commissions, planning councils and so on, all performing important duties yet untouched by these reforms and outside the effective democratic control either of M.P.s or of local government councillors.

The question of democratic control occurs in the last line of the terms of reference: 'the need to sustain a viable system of local democracy'. It is not clear what 'viable' means in this context but evidently a factor to be taken into consideration is whether any new structure of local government can attract and hold public interest, and excite participation more effectively than the present range of councils. Yet there is considerable evidence that while the public are not very interested in the circumscribed functions at present performed by local government, they are much more ready to take an active part in the strategic decisions affecting the life of a locality which are not at present entrusted to local government. The best example again is the regional planning councils. When these began it was thought that they presented an opportunity for shaping a whole locality or region from the point of view of those resident in the area. The result was a great clamour for appointment and precisely the sort of leading professional, industrial and trade union personalities were coming forward whose absence from the existing councils is so much lamented. Yet if these functions cannot be considered by the Royal Commissions as suitable for local government, then electors and potential councillors cannot be blamed if they show little interest.

This aspect is particularly evident in the cases of Wales and of Scotland where one form of reformed local government would be a single unit assembly or council for the whole country. There are arguments based on function (to be examined later) which would point to three regions in Wales and to six or seven regional divisions in Scotland, but there are also arguments which would point to a single unit in each case. It would be a pity if the latter arguments were discounted merely because they depend in part on the importance of transferring functions which do not at present lie with local government. What ever is thought of the merits of the case for total independence in Scotland and Wales, the rise of the nationalist parties has shown that there is far more interest in such nation-wide decisions and therefore in a single unit government, than in a series of internal regions: the former is far more democratically viable and it would be a great mistake if the Royal Commission on Local Government in Scotland were not able to take this into account. There is no Royal Commission on Welsh Local Government but any decision on its future would be profoundly affected by a recommendation that the top-tier unit of elected local government in Scotland should cover the whole country.

16

Decentralization[*]

SIR CHARLES HARRIS

Decentralization, the delegation of decision-making power as a part of the areal division of powers, is now usually regarded as having two forms. One is known as devolution, where authority to make decisions is delegated by law to sub-national territorial assemblies (e.g. a local authority); the other is deconcentration, where delegation is of authority to make administrative decisions on behalf of central administration to public servants working in the field (see Brian C. Smith, Field Administration, Routledge & Kegan Paul, 1967). In this article, written nearly half a century ago, Sir Charles Harris is primarily concerned with using his administrative experience to analyse deconcentration. Such decentralization is an important feature of the machinery of government in Britain, both in the way departments of central government have large numbers of regional and local offices and because the degree to which devolution is actually practised through British local government is questionable.

Without attempting a formal definition of decentralization, I ought to explain why the title of devolution, under which through a mis-understanding this paper was first announced, was changed. I do not know how far a lexicographer would agree, but I think we may distinguish between decentralization, as a characteristic of the rela-tions between higher and lower authorities resting on the same basis, or, as a soldier would say, in the same chain of command, and devolu-tion or the entrusting of powers and duties by a higher authority to lower authorities, resting on a different basis; as when Whitehall, resting on the taxpayer, devolves powers and duties to the Town Hall, resting on the ratepayer. With devolution in this sense I shall make no attempt to deal, for the very good reason that I have practically no

[*] From Sir Charles Harris, 'Decentralization', *Public Administration*, 1925, Vol. III, pp. 117–33. Reprinted with permission of the editor of *Public Administration*.

personal experience of it. At the present stage of that scientific exploration of the sphere of administration which is the object of our Institute, it seems to me that we want travellers' tales rather than attempts at systematic geography, and that the most useful contribution a humble individual can make to the common stock of knowledge and ideas, is to present the results of his own practical experience. Devolution as distinct from decentralization does, it is true, exist in one region of Army administration, that is, in the relations between the War Office and the County Associations created by the Act of 1907 to administer the Territorials; but the position is very special, and it would be dangerous to attempt to draw any general conclusions from that experience.

If I appear before you as a thoroughgoing advocate of decentralization, it is as a convert to that faith in middle age: and I venture to hope that the fact that the missioner has himself occupied a seat on the penitents' bench, may be accepted as some evidence, if not of the truth of his faith, at least of the conviction with which he holds it. At the beginning of my service I was greatly impressed by the lack of general knowledge and of grasp of central principle displayed in the local decisions and actions that came under my notice. For years the conviction grew upon me that a larger measure of active control from the centre would conduce to both efficiency and economy of administration; and today, if I were to confine my view to particular details and to immediate results, I should still feel on that point no possible doubt whatever. It is when one falls back to Capability Brown's view-point, and tries to see the wood as well as the trees, that the certainty disappears. And I think the very fact that the word 'decentralization' is logically a negative points in the same direction as my own little pilgrim's progress, suggesting that centralization is the natural condition and that the administrator when found in the wild state, and especially when caught young, will exhibit the characteristic markings of the centralizer, while those of the decentralizer must be sought among the older individuals, and – may we perhaps say? – the more cultivated strains. I am going to attempt to suggest to you some reasons why in this matter we should try to transcend the natural and obvious view.

As I have just said, decentralization is a negative idea and therefore a bad starting-point for exploration. We shall do better if we transfer our attention to the positive idea of centralization and the forms in which it is to be found existing. It seems to me that there are two principal forms, and I have been at some pains to find labels for them. I shall call them simple and compound, because the second

209

form, like compound interest, includes the first, only more so. Also, like compound interest, it is perfectly logical, may seem to a well-ordered mind to need no defence and has the same supreme quality of reducing its victims to paralysis and despair. The main difference is, that while simple centralization drives up the functions of decision and authorization to the head centre, it leaves action, when decided upon, to be carried out by the subordinate authority, while the compound form removes from him action as well. Of the simple form, perhaps the best-developed example is to be found in the military organization, where the War Office, the headquarters of a Commander-in-Chief, those of the Commander of an Army Corps, a Division, and so on are all organized on the same general plan, with departments of the General Staff, the Adjutant General, and the Quarter-master-General, each dealing with its proper group of subjects, and where questions for decision, if beyond the powers assigned to the subordinate commander, go up the chain, and orders come down it. But at whatever point the order or decision is given, it comes down finally to be carried out by the executive authority at the lower end of the chain. A less complete example is afforded by the Post Office organization, where there is, under the General Post Office, a system of officers in charge of areas; but the chain is shorter than in the Army, and there is the important difference that the Engineering department does not come under the general area chief, but has a separate local organization of its own; so that whatever may be the reason why the head of a postal area is called a Surveyor, it is not that he is monarch of all he surveys. I am not presuming to indicate any opinion on that thorny question, when I say that if some one department stands out of the main chain, so that no decision affecting it and other departments can be taken, unless by consent, at any point short of the head office, it makes for centralization.

Centralization or decentralization of the simple type is a question of degree. I think it is Bertrand Russell who has said that discussion of such subjects should be conducted as far as possible in quantitative terms and that, for want of this precaution in political controversy, if the point at issue were the proper temperature for a sitting-room, one party would go to the country advocating absolute zero, while the other would stand out for the temperature of red-hot iron – and perhaps in these days he might have added that a third party, without naming any definite temperature, would content itself with saying that the eternal principles of thermal hygiene would shortly reassert themselves. Unfortunately, in administration generally it is not easy to mark degrees of centralization in plain figures, though in one very important branch of the subject, financial decentralization, figures naturally present themselves – of which more a little later.

Before illustrating what I mean by compound centralization, let me digress for a moment. It is difficult to write concisely or clearly on the subject, because of the complete lack of any accepted technical vocabulary and of the ambiguity of many of the terms in common use. 'Department' for instance, may mean a whole organization like the War Office and Army combined (the War Department), or a Department of State like the War Office without the Army, or a section of the organization like the Quartermaster-General's department, or an executive body like the Army Ordnance department, carrying out services not essentially military, as distinguished from the Staff which is essentially military, thinks, but does not itself execute. Staff, again, has also the quite different meaning of the whole body of persons employed in a department or office or other establishment; and establishment also has several distinct meanings. But probably the word 'Service' holds the record for ambiguity. Think of its different meanings in such phrases as civil, sea, land, or air service, a service *Department*, meaning the Admiralty, War office or Air Ministry, length of service, valuable service, service of the debt, a service of trains, a Part I works service, a service rendered by one department to another, and in this connection a *service* department in the sense of a purveying department. This list is not exhaustive, but I will content myself with asking whether so ambiguous a word is of service at all to those who need to speak exactly. I would venture to suggest, for the consideration of the Council, whether the Institute might not perhaps take up the task of standardizing the technical vocabulary of administration, so that in course of time the personnel of the Civil Service might use words in a defined sense.

Well, I found that what I wanted to say about compound centralization was that it consists in replacing certain departmental services of the service *departments* by services performed for them by *service* departments. I hope that to those who have followed me so far that is clear; but perhaps it would be well to supplement it. A department of State like the Admiralty or War Office, in pursuit of its main object of defence, exercises many different activities such as building, occupation of land, supply of stores in very great variety, medical services, and so on. Compound centralization withdraws these several activities or services one by one from such Departments of State and places them in the hands of central technical departments which exist for the special purpose of these particular activities.

In some comparatively unimportant matters, such as the supply of

211

books and stationery, this has long been the established practice, and I should not suggest disturbing it; though to carry it so far as to lay down that no printer may be employed anywhere under government except by the Stationery Office is another story. But of late years there has been much advocacy of a great extension of this type of centralization in far more important matters; for instance, the establishment of a permanent Ministry of Supply to provide material of all kinds for all purposes; the creation of a central Lands Department to buy, sell, and manage lands for all government departments, Crown lands only excepted; the amalgamation of the Medical departments of the three fighting Services, and so on. Here we have no longer a mere question of degree, to be argued quantitatively; it is a question of the kind of administrative system to be employed.

So much by way of definition and illustration. Let us now look a little critically at simple centralization. At the first glance one sees its evident merits and falls captive to its symmetrical beauty. As Euclid would have stated it, in any organization the man that is at the head is the wisest and, of the others, he that is nearer to the head is wiser than he that is more remote; so that the higher up the chain a decision is given, the better it should be intrinsically; and moreover, decisions given by final authority possess in addition that special merit pertaining to the judicial decisions of the House of Lords: that at all events they are final, and one can make one's account with them. Further, central decisions mean uniformity; and that, in public administration, and especially in that important sphere the remuneration of the individual, has come to be regarded as the highest good, not because it corresponds in any way to the facts of life, but because it is found to expose the least target to criticism. The conditions under which the Civil Servant works continually press him towards centralization, and particularly the two very wholesome institutions of Parliamentary questions and Treasury control. Questions are the recognized constitutional machinery for eliminating bureaucracy and enforcing the fundamental principle of British administration: that no Civil Servant is to decide a question involving any human interest. They and the kindred institution of letters from constituents bring the Minister into touch with detail, and it is one of his most important functions to bring a whiff of the healthy open air of the constituencies into the devitalized atmosphere of a government office. Questions largely relate to personal grievances and claims, and I often used to feel how impossible it was to put the sum total of human knowledge about some complicated personal detail into a very hurried minute, addressed to a very hurried and perhaps new and suspicious minister, to justify the cause quite rightly taken by some subordinate official, which to the minister looked like mere red-tape, but which in fact could not be reversed without opening flood-gates; and how natural it was for the minister to say, 'Well, I suppose I must give that answer this afternoon, but I must have more time to go into these things in future, and should like them brought up to me for decision before refusals are given.' Then, when a case is brought up, the minister is very likely to want to take a course which, under the principle of uniformity, will have reverberations unsuspected by him, and reference to the Treasury becomes necessary. The Treasury, of course, knows by long experience the danger that one department may make concessions without regard to the claims that may result in another, and that ministers might not be adequately impressed by such consequences, even if their attention was drawn to them; and so it centralizes control in itself, and not unnaturally tends to work in the direction of uniformity, as all central departments do. Such uniformity and the closer organization of government employees and beneficiaries now prevailing, increase the danger of consequential claims arising, and the reply to this is to tighten the central control still further, so that centralization leads to uniformity, and uniformity leads to more centralization, and a vicious circle is generated.

Of course, the effect of this is felt all down the chain; for if the head office has to submit a matter to the Treasury, it obviously cannot decentralize it, whatever its intrinsic unimportance. And so an official anywhere is taught to regard individual cases as raising large general questions for decision by central authorities; and if anyone, greatly daring, ventures to act for himself he is not unlikely to find that by going outside regulation, or acting in the absence of regulation, he has only exposed himself to a demand from the Comptroller and Auditor-General to produce Treasury sanction after all, and, further, I have invariably found that the Public Accounts Committee starts from the view that Treasury sanction ought to have been obtained, though on occasion it will accept a good defence.

So the stars in their courses fight for centralization, and the Press calls out for larger doses of Treasury control, though at the same time it girds at official delays and red tape. With what prospect of success shall we struggle against a natural instinct reinforced by such potent influences? Is there no real alternative to a fatalist acceptance, or should we take our stand against it, lest one good custom should corrupt the world? The answer to these questions depends on the mode of action of central bodies – of the sun on its planets, and the planets in turn on their satellites. In our system, the Treasury holds a peculiarly central position, different from that of the Ministry of Finance in any other country; and moreover as Lord Bradbury once put it to me, Treasury control is just whatever the Treasury likes to make it. I am proud to have spent my whole official life as 'an outpost of the Treasury', and an old commander of outposts may be allowed, in a technical paper, to express his limited ideas on the theory of the relations between the outposts and G.H.Q., but nothing I may say about central bodies must be taken as attributing any position or policy to the actual Treasury of today. Premising, then, that a Treasury does not mean *the* Treasury, this is how the position appears to me.

I start from the distinction between parsimony, the principle of not spending, or doing without things – a virtue once esteemed more highly than in these progressive days – and economy, the science of getting value for money. A Treasury, in our sense, is the High Priest of parsimony, and at Estimate time is enthroned in all its mystic vestments; but when the government has fixed the money to be assigned to a department and the Chancellor has arranged to find it, the first duty is no longer to pursue parsimony within that limit and surrender as much as possible, but to practise economy by getting the best value for the money; and as value is a technical judgment, this duty must lie primarily with the spending department. I do not suggest, of course, that economy is no concern of a Treasury, or parsimony of the spending department, which has to impose it on its sub-departments (to which it is in turn the central body), to do all it can to reduce its Estimates, and to accept Treasury decisions loyally; but I suggest that, reciprocally, it should be given the freest possible hand in laying out its rationed total, and all experience shows that this is the way to secure the best results. It is easier to make a nation sober by Act of Parliament than to make a spending department economical by Treasury correspondence.

This view is not in any way inconsistent with the duty of a Treasury or other central body to control: it is all a question of degree and method, of which the Treasury has unfettered choice. If the central body distinguishes clearly between control and supervision – a line, like Lord Morley's elephant, which we cannot define, but recognize when we see it – and adopts that line as the frontier between its own sphere and that of the inferior departments, it will aim at avoiding overlap with them, while maintaining oversight. Its method will be, not to go into details afresh, but to find means of integrating them and dealing with broader features. If it has no such means at hand, it may find itself driven back on the alternative line of trying to do the

work of the inferior departments over again, so creating a centralization that may become a tyranny in detail. A good deal, therefore, will
depend upon suitable methods of integration. Two such methods are
well established: inspection and accounts. The former does not mean
waiting until details are submitted and then holding inquisition on the
spot; that is only a way of doing work over again. Inspection is best
suited to technical matters, and a good example of what it does mean
is afforded by military training. The general staff officer does
not stand at the elbow of the commander and check him if he is
not putting his men rigidly through a prescribed course; he gives him
his head and tests the results by setting the troops to accomplish
some practical task. For administration, reducible to the least common denominator of money, all business men rely on accounts – not
mere indexes to vouchers proving that every payment, whatever its
merits, is duly authorized, but accounts summarizing results which
the mind can grasp as showing whether the stewardship on the whole
has been good or bad. By such means a central department can not
only preserve control, but improve it; for at present, all the criticism
and control are applied to the prospectus, and the dividend, the actual
result, is never brought to light.

My answer, then, to the question whether centralization of details
is inevitable, is 'No; so far as each central department, beginning
with the centre of all, will choose the line of integration, and can
develop the machinery necessary to that end.' But if this is held to be
impossible, then indeed we are in a parlous state; for we must
recognize that the higher wisdom, the finality, the universality of
centralized decisions are bought at a price, and of that price the components are the paralysis of action, the multiplication of delays and
the psychological effect upon the great majority of officials. It is true
that my experience has lain in regions where action and the time-
factor are of special importance: but the man who first said 'Bis dat
qui cito dat' was not an Army administrator, and there are many
instances in civilian affairs in which a less enlightened decision,
promptly acted upon, is better than the quintessence of human
wisdom deferred till the twelfth hour has struck. Do not think that I
want to see everything remodelled on military lines, or that I claim
decentralization to be a part of military tradition – far from it.
Centralization has long been known as one of the besetting sins of all
armies in peace time; and though the vast scale of modern war has
made it impossible in the fighting of battles, and though all soldiers
are now (at all events in theory) advocates of decentralization, and not
least in matters financial, so human is the heart that beats under a

215

red coat, that it is a common experience to find a soldier enthusiastically keen on decentralization, down to the particular place he holds in the chain, but much impressed by the practical difficulties involved carrying it any lower.

It will be instructive to glance at the history of decentralization in our Army. Originally, there was no centralization of the administrative services (as we should call them) because the regiment in peace was a self-contained organization. It provided its own food, which was paid for out of the soldier's shilling; the Colonel farmed the clothing to his own profit, bought his own horses and forage out of an allowance, and so on. Then followed an era of departmentalization, leading to a sort of compound centralization within the War Department, through the formation of administrative departments to deal with such matters, not under the orders of the Commander-in-Chief, but civilian in status. In 1870, a regimental indent for things like barrack furniture or cooking utensils passed all the way up through the Brigade and Division to the Commander-in-Chief at the Horse Guards, whence his Quartermaster-General transmitted it in due form to the War Office, which sent it on (if approved) to the Commissary General and so on down the chain of the Ordnance Department to the Store Officer who actually had such things in his hands; and he, if the regiment had not by that time left his jurisdiction, issued the things. The then Commander-in-Chief and his staff defended all this as necessary; for, said they, it was their duty to see that the troops were properly found, and how were they to do it, if such matters were transacted without their cognizance? But Lord Northbrook, the enlightened assistant of that enlightened minister Cardwell, arranged a system by which general regulations defined what the troops were entitled to, and men on the spot saw that they got it from the local magazines.

When, later on, the Commander-in-Chief became responsible for the material as well as the personnel of the Army, the feature of compound centralization dropped out, and the generals in commands were given powers of ordering extra-regulation issues in temporary emergencies, subject to reporting for sanction to the War Office. So far decentralization progressed; but in spite of repeated efforts, any further advance in administrative matters found itself in the main blocked by the requirements of Parliamentary finance. For in those days the ruling notion of pursuing economy was to parcel out funds in watertight compartments, and allow no *virement* without superior authority. Army estimates were divided, as Navy estimates are still, into fifteen separate votes, *virement* requiring Treasury authority covered eventually by an Act of Parliament; and these votes were further divided into some 200 or more sub-heads, *virement* between which required Treasury authority; and, in theory at all events, failing such authority anything unspent on any sub-head reverted to the Exchequer. I say 'in theory', because with an Army all over the world, it was impossible to know exactly how any sub-head would come out, until months after the end of the year, when of course it was too late to remedy an excess; so that one constantly found oneself driven back on the Nelsonian theory of monocular vision at telescopic ranges, and a good many of the 200 little annual surrenders failed to materialize. Moreover, these watertight compartments referred to formal classes of expenditure, such as pay, food, fuel, and so on, all over the world, and not to any particular branch of the Army, or geographical area, so that the only account that could show how any particular sub-head stood as compared with the estimate, was the central account kept at the War Office itself, from which the annual Appropriation Account was prepared. On such a plan, where the account is, there also must the financial control reside; and how could the heads of administrative departments at the War Office, each under strict orders to keep the expenditure within this intricate cellular structure of limits, give any real decentralized spending power to local military authorities? To have made each such authority an annual allotment under each sub-head, would only have intensified the evil. So it came about that whatever attempts were made to decentralize, centralization always crept back. In fact, the whole system of appropriation by votes and sub-heads put the Treasury virtue of parsimony, not spending, into the place that ought to be occupied by the administrative virtue of economy, or getting value for money; not by lopping off limbs with half-shut eyes and an axe, but by scientifically measuring the ratio of return to expenditure, and concentrating effort upon improving that ratio.

There is now only one Army vote, and the expenditure is so grouped that each head of a regiment, a hospital, a store depot or any other establishment gets a monthly account setting out the expenses of his particular 'show' under all heads, reduced to cost per some suitable economic unit; and he is expected to use his wits so that if he wants to spend on this, he saves on that, without being told every minute that he is overstepping one or more of 200 meaningless limits. By accepting this change, the Treasury has at all events made real financial decentralization formally possible, though much remains to be done before a finished superstructure on that basis has been built.

217

As I said, advance towards decentralization was blocked in the main; but something was accomplished from 1901 onwards, and it will be worth while to see just what it was. In the first place, branches of the War Office finance department were planted out at the headquarters of military commands, to examine accounts and to act as financial advisers to the generals in command, though not under their orders. About the same time, an annual sum of £5000 was placed at the disposal of the Secretary of State to cover minor expenditure of a non-recurring character, which could otherwise from its nature have required Treasury sanction, and other sums amounting in all to £6500 were similarly placed at the disposal of generals commanding, to obviate correspondence with the War Office. After the war, these grants were increased in view of the diminished value of sterling. They afford a useful relief from correspondence of a petty kind, but it is significant that so accustomed is everyone concerned to sending matters on for sanction as the law of official life, that some vigilance is required to ensure that the extra-regulation powers (as they are called) do not fall into abeyance.

Expenditure on building services, which naturally appeared in estimates on a geographical plan, was decentralized as far as maintenance and minor new services were concerned; but as each Part I service, of £2000 and over, formed a separate treasury watertight compartment, not much could be done in that quarter. After the war, the £2000 was raised to £3000, but at the present price of building work, that apparent relaxation is really a turn of the screw toward centralization.

These last two changes give a quantitative meaning to decentralization, and the fourth direction in which something was done – the write-off of losses of public property – is even more illuminating on that score. In the Army, such losses are matters of military system and discipline rather than of finance, the main issue being whether anyone concerned failed to do what might properly be expected of a careful man under the practical conditions of Army life, and cases are accordingly dealt with on the basis of a military Court of Enquiry. In theory, all losses require Treasury authority for write-off, and must be reported to Parliament in the annual accounts; but the Treasury delegates power within certain money limits to the Army Council, and allows the Council to delegate within certain other limits to local generals, provided that the local finance branch of the War Office agrees.

For legal reasons, if it is considered that any officer should make good part of the loss, the case must be dealt with by three members of the Army Council (of which one is always a financial member), so that War Office consideration of these cases falls on the highest authorities there. Having spent many months of my life on these post-mortems, I am fully aware of their value (within limits) for administration, as showing the way in which the flesh and blood Army reacts to the instructions so continuously showered on it; but their financial value is another story, and it is from that point of view that the limits of delegation must be considered. There is an elaborate classification of such limits, running to some 40 heads, with which I will not bore you, but I will take a few examples only. For losses by fraud, suspected fraud, or gross carelessness, for stores lost in a contractor's hands, and for nugatory expenditure such as failing to use a passage taken up in a ship, no one outside the Treasury had any power whatever in 1914. For theft, the Council's limit was £5, the general's £1. For over-issues to an individual, the Council's limit was £20, and the general's the same. For stores lost or deficient in account, the limit was £100. In 1922, the general's limits were doubled, for higher prices, which now means some real increase; while the Council got powers up to £25 for cash and £50 for stores where it had none before; its £5 for theft was raised to £25 cash and £100 stores, the £20 for over-issues to £100, and the £100 for deficient stores to £200. That was real progress. But still, remembering that all this writing about spilt milk employs officers of the highest rank all up the chain, that it is primarily administration, and that on its financial side it might well be left to statistical integration and audit, except in cases of real importance; remembering that, with supply expenditure standing in the Budget at £400,000,000, and with the War Office finance branch at the general's elbow, he is still limited to £2 for some things and nothing at all for others, I think you will realize that the decentralizer has not exactly brought off a break-through.

Now consider the psychological effect on a human being of a life spent under conditions of centralization – I do not mean the quill-drivers and office-wallahs, but the men from whom the commanders of the forces and the heads of civil departments will be chosen. In those positions they will be wanted to show initiative, to love responsibility, to act promptly, to look outside departmental blinkers. And yet, by concentrating all real responsibility at the head, and even removing it very often to an outside department, we secure that in the case of the great majority, before a man's chance of real responsibility comes, the greater part of his life will have been spent in unfitting him for it and teaching him to avoid it; to wait till things are brought up to him and then pass them on for higher decision; to accept delays as the law of official life; to represent his own narrow sectional view of a question to those above him, and leave them to harmonize it with wider considerations. We make work as meaningless as possible by so arranging it that a man does not see the results of his own actions. Wanting him to be economical, we take care not to let him know the cost of the things he uses, not to enlist his brains in the cause of economy, but to force it on him from afar, with an air of knowing what he wants, or ought to want, better than he can – and then we wonder that he does not respond. I will not attempt to give illustrations of the effect of this psychological factor from War Office experience, though I could give many, lest I should seem to have forgotten the French scientist's warning to his research students, 'if you are not very careful, you will find what you are looking for'; but here is recent and independent evidence.

Our classical accountancy frowned on interdepartmental payments, and when in 1919 the Army accounts were remodelled to include items of cost like stationery and postal services, in the sure faith that economy would result, principle was still held to forbid payment from Army to Civil votes, and these services had to be rather awkwardly written off on the face of the accounts as 'items of cost for which no cash payment is made'. But from April 1922, the Treasury tried the experiment of making all government departments pay the Post Office for telegrams, and the last report of the Public Accounts Committee gives the result. It says, 'the authorities of the Post Office have reported to the Treasury that the change resulted in a reduction of about 50 percent in the number of telegrams sent, and that the average number of words in each telegram was less'. That is just the sort of result that follows as soon as you let a man see the result of his own actions, and appeal not to his obedience but to his intelligence. But if you deny him the exercise of the faculty of contrivance, the adaptation of limited means to measurable ends, the measurement of his results against those of other men – things which give zest even to dull work, and stimulate keenness where the incentive of direct gain is absent – if you will not let Tommy make his own mistakes and learn by them, but are always sending nurse to 'see what he is doing and tell him not to', then before long he comes to hug his chains, to feel that provided he can quote regulations or precedent for everything he does himself, and sends on to higher authority everything else, he has done what is expected of him and is blameless, whatever happens – 'safety first'. Thus, instead of training administrators we breed red-tape worms, and ludicrously defeat the high aims of efficiency and economy with which we embarked on the course of centralization; just as a man in a fog, having lost the distant view and looking at his own feet, may find himself heading straight back to his starting-point. And the heads of departments, instead of having time to think ahead, find themselves in the condition described by Lord Wolseley, when he was Commander-in-Chief, as 'buried in silly little papers on silly little subjects'.

Now let us turn to compound centralization; and that opens the wider question of the general lay-out of our administrative system, for a survey of which we naturally turn to the report of the Machinery of Government Committee of 1918, under our Chairman of tonight. After a review of the whole position, that Committee found that the choice lay between two main principles on which business might be distributed; according to the class of persons whose interests are being dealt with, or according to the nature of the services to be rendered; and they chose the latter as the main principle to be followed, on the broad ground that the former would lead to 'Lilliputian administration', and could not reach the high standard of specialized service which the latter promised. But it would be a mistake to conclude that they recommended what I have called compound centralization, for the report goes on to say that for great nationalized services such as defence, or postal or (as then appeared possible) railway communications, the work of dealing with the large personnel employed was of such importance that the two distinct principles of *persons* and *services* led to the same result, viz, the existence of separate ministries (which I will call Class A ministries) for such undertakings; while the conflict between the two principles became acute only in dealing with ministries of administrative supervision and control (which I will call Class B) such as education, trade, agriculture, and so on. The Class A ministries would be largely self-contained, and the report explicitly recognizes that if, for instance, a ministry of supply had been maintained, its relations with the defence departments would have required very special study and adjustment. My own experience makes me heartily agree with these conclusions, though I reach them by a somewhat different path. To me, Class A ministries differ from Class B not in the large numbers of persons they directly employ, but in the nature of their work; and the distinction presents itself to my mind as between ministries of action and ministries of direction. It is because Class A ministries are immediately responsible for action in matters of vital importance, that it is necessary to give them powers fairly commensurate with their responsibilities, even at some sacrifice of symmetry in organization.

221

It is fundamental with us that the ministers at the head of the Admiralty, the War Office and the Air Ministry are responsible to the nation, not for a high standard of *expertise* in this and that, but for the integral fighting efficiency of our defensive services; and the man in the street interprets this very crudely as meaning that he will have somebody to hang if there is failure in the day of battle. In the Crimean war there was failure but no one to hang, because the responsibility for the campaign was divided between half a dozen different authorities and departments. Compound centralization had proved disastrous, and it was found essential to create at once a self-contained War Office by pitchforking the various sections together in the middle of the war, and appointing a Secretary of State for War to run it as a whole-time job. In this process, the War Office absorbed the old Ordnance Office which from Tudor times had supplied weapons to both Navy and Army; and some thirty-five years later the Admiralty, on the ground of its responsibility for the fighting efficiency of the fleet, created a Naval Ordnance department to take over from the War Office the naval side of the work, so affording a good instance of that overlapping of departments performing similar services, on which the advocates of compound centralization have concentrated so much attention.

The case for a self-contained Post Office is not, of course, a matter of national life and death, like these; but we probably all feel that if our letters are not punctually on the breakfast table and our telephones efficient, there ought to be some one responsible minister who in the last resort can be driven from office. No maze or web of interdepartmental committees from specialist departments, can give the necessary guarantee that such services as these are kept efficient and progressive.

Putting it pictorially, one may say that in the administrative field there is an area of action, stratified vertically, and an area of direction, stratified horizontally; and compound centralization is an attempt to extend the horizontal stratification to the area of action, not in substitution for the vertical – for that would be going back to the Crimean muddle, and the public simply will not have it – but in addition to it, on the plea that in this way you get a higher standard of efficiency as well as economy. And incidentally – I do not for a moment suggest design – all these horizontal centralized departments tend to stand in a specially close relation to the Treasury. With purveying departments like the Stationery Office, having no minister, this is inevitable. I have seen it stated that the Office of Works, to which it has more than once been suggested that Army building work should be transferred, is in some special historical sense a sub-department of the Treasury, though it has a minister who may be of Cabinet rank. Any reference to the Government Actuary was originally to have been made through the Treasury. Whether this is the actual practice I do not know. What position the Ministry of Supply would eventually have held, if it had continued, can only be surmised, but its selling department ended in the Treasury. Thus, our lay-out would resemble one of those wooden gratings you see in a boat, consisting of bars crossing one another at right angles, mortised together at every crossing, and the whole gripped firmly in a stout frame. For rigidity and resistance to any slipping, it is not to be surpassed, and there are many positions in which that is the most important quality. But I think, if this plan were adopted, some unfortunate minister of Class A might some day have occasion to recall that in the good old days men found themselves tied up to just such a grating to take a flogging.

But, coming closer, there are difficulties of a more immediate kind. Since, under our political system, a minister's responsibilities are broadly defined by his Parliamentary estimates, how is expenditure conducted on compound centralization principles to appear in estimates and accounts? For instance, with a Munition or Supply Ministry outside the War Office, how is provision to be made for Army munitions? Is the expenditure to rest finally in the accounts of the Supply Department, or is the War Office to provide for it in Army estimates, and repay the Ministry of Supply? In the Great War, of course, the Army got unlimited quantities of anything it asked for – sometimes even more than it asked for – without knowing or caring anything about cost; but that could not continue. From 1855 to 1888, the War Office supplied the Navy with munitions free of charge, though with strict limitation; but when Europe had accepted the view that peace is an interval for preparation between wars, that plan was found unworkable and, as I said, the Admiralty took over the duty.

A return to the old independent Ordnance Department had been mooted, but a very high authority, after studying the question, summed up the position by saying that under modern conditions it would pass the wit of man to define the relations of the Admiralty and the War Office to such a department. In 1919–20 it was ordered that the War Office should provide in its estimates for paying the Ministry of Supply for whatever it had. As the ministry disappeared before the war muddle had been cleared up, this plan was never tried out, but while it lasted it promised to develop all the difficulties that my early experiences in connection with Naval Ordnance had led me to anticipate. Anyone who has himself administered a Store vote, not for ordinary goods like stationery, which are in common use and can be stocked by the purveying department, but for highly technical and costly specialities like modern weapons, knows what those difficulties are. The department responsible for estimating and working the vote on which the charges finally rest, has no earthly chance if it has no first-hand touch with prices, no control over priority, contract policy, contracts, factories, inspection and the other ingredients, the deft blending of which is essential to a successful dish-up at the end of the year. I am not merely flogging the dead horse of the Ministry of Supply. Similar difficulties arose over Army Sea Transport while a separate Ministry of Shipping existed; and experience of the buying and selling of land on any considerable scale on annual estimates, points to acute difficulty with an independent Central Lands Department. Our whole system of Parliamentary finance pre-supposes that the administration of a vote lies effectively in the hands of some one minister. Neither in theory nor in practice have I been able to find any satisfactory solution of this problem.

Before passing on, let me mention a pernicious form of compound centralization, in which the activity withdrawn from a Class A ministry is not transferred to a central department *ad hoc*, but remains in commission. For example, it was proposed to amalgamate the medical services of the three fighting forces. The movement towards assimilating in detail the pay codes of the three forces, which has been in evidence since the war, makes in the same direction. Of course, a general balance of advantages, as seen from the recruiting market, must be maintained between the three, but there could be no greater mistake than to work towards a joint pay code, not only because the conditions of life in sea and land forces are essentially different, but also because the closer you get to a joint code, the closer you will be driven to joint administration. If the uniformity complex in the central mind should have that result, the fighting ministries would find themselves running a sort of eternal four-legged race, each unable to stir without the other two. The position as regards civilian employees is quite different, for, though it is all becoming much too centralized, the Civil Service proper is to a large extent one service, though in many departments, and there is a central administrative branch in the Treasury.

Are we, then, between the devil of disintegrated responsibility and the deep sea of Lilliputian administration and loss of specialized efficiency? Well, to some extent we are; but after all, that region is our normal habitat, and has a healthy climate for an active man. We must sacrifice something; but, as Ruskin says somewhere, a shrub remains a shrub just because it lacks the forest tree's habit of sacrificing some branches to others. If we go back to the Machinery of Government Report, we shall there find the elements of a solution which should keep the sacrifice within the limits of toleration. The report, you may remember, recognizes that a service or interest such as education, health, finance, is in some connections dominant and in some subordinate; and lays down that, where it is subordinate, it should be committed to a special section or department within the ministry of the dominant interest. If a question arises in a particular case as to which is the lady and which the tiger, we must go back to practical life. For instance, where should agricultural education come: in the Ministry of Education, or of Agriculture? That depends on whether we want to see the best farming taught, though possibly by old methods, or a possibly out-of-date style of farming, taught in the most modern and compelling manner. The question answers itself. Finance is a very strong and dominant interest, but in national defence it is subordinate because in the last resort, when all the possibilities of economy have been exhausted, safety must come before parsimony; and therefore defence finance is rightly committed to separate departments in the ministries of defence and not, as in India, to the Treasury itself. But, with an organization on these lines, the report insists on the necessity for the branches of subordinate interests to keep in close touch with one another, and with the ministry in which their particular interest is dominant, whether by standing committees or by other means, so that they may reciprocally share their experience, and keep in the van of progress in their special subject. The point on which I would insist is that such committees, technical associations or discussions are not to be a link in the chain of action. In all ordinary matters, the King's government in any ministry must be carried on by the authorities of that ministry, with such help and advice as its own sections of subordinate interests can give; and the true function of the collaboration with similar technical sections or departments outside, is not government by general consent, but the improvement of the quality of that advice. If it is really expert and is fearlessly given, it will not fail in the long run to carry the weight it deserves. And here I seem to see a great sphere of usefulness for our Institute. By these methods, though you may drop a point here and there, you will preserve the possibility of action, maintain personal responsibility, and avoid the bottomless pit of administration by interdepartmental committees.

And now, do these lines of thought lead up to any practical rules of conduct? I think they do, but it must be frankly recognized that they involve swimming against the stream, forsaking the shrub habit, and sacrificing present convenience to future good, and such proceedings will not commend themselves to everyone. As the subject is negative, the rules present themselves naturally in the form of 'Don't'. For instance, as regards simple centralization:

(1) Don't regard centralization as anything but a necessary evil at best – not even if you are at the centre; and if you are not, don't think decentralization should stop at yourself.

(2) Don't think the central point of view must be right in every case because it is central. Like other generalizations and abstractions, it may have lost touch with the concrete particular. Don't forget that the executive man on the circumference sees things that the centre doesn't, but give him his head whenever you can. Any chambermaid can put a man into the room where Procrustes keeps that famous bed.

(3) Don't wait for the man below to extract from you a little freedom, grudgingly given, but develop your integrating machinery and then give him all he can carry.

(4) Don't forget that precept of Bacon, the greatest Englishman who has written on administration, 'Interlace not businesse save of necessitie,' and, in particular, don't consider yourself debarred from treating an exceptional case exceptionally and promptly, by some far-fetched analogy with some different case in another department.

(5) Don't fall into the snare of unifying pay where the conditions of it are essentially different. If equals be added to unequals, the whole are unequal. (Euclid again!)

(6) Don't cut down the discretion of the man below, or his class, by requiring submission to higher authority in future, because he has made a mistake. Teach him and try him again; but if he is unteachable, shunt him. Delegation cannot be successful unless there is power to select and to weed. All branches and grades of the public service suffer from carrying passengers in the boat, because it requires less determination to go on than to stop and put them ashore. And for this reason, don't let Whitley Councils or anything else deprive a Head of the control of his staff. Remember that 'selection men' are always in a minority.

It is easy to multiply such maxims, and even to secure mental

226

assent to them, but, just because simple centralization is a matter of degree, it is not easy to keep them to the fore in practice. *Video meliora, proboque; deteriora sequor.*

But when you come to compound centralization, it is quite simple. There is only one rule: DON'T.

17

Theories and Values of Local Government[*]

L. J. SHARPE

In this article L. J. Sharpe, Fellow of Nuffield College, Oxford, and Director of Intelligence for the Royal Commission on Local Government in England, which reported in 1968, surveys recent (and earlier) theoretical writings on local government and considers how local government can be justified at the present time. A shortened version of this essay, together with four other valuable articles on theories of local government, appears in Lionel D. Feldman and Michael D. Goldrick (Eds), Politics and Government of Urban Canada: Selected Readings, *Methuen Publications, Canada, 1969.*

Whatever the dangers may be in politics of arguing from 'an abstract principle, or a set of related abstract principles which has been independently premeditated',[1] it is evident that the British as a nation, if not their academics, are well aware of them. Few countries can be as reluctant to theorize about their political institutions and their local government in particular. We have usually managed to get along with what W. J. M. Mackenzie in the best historical account of British ideas, if not theories, of local government has dubbed 'an ethical commitment to an extremely vague notion of local self-government'.[2] Here the validity of past theories for modern conditions in a democracy rather than their history will be examined

[*] From L. J. Sharpe, 'Theories and Values of Local Government', *Political Studies*, Vol. XVIII, pp. 153–74. Reprinted with permission of the Clarendon Press, Oxford.

[1] M. Oakeshott, 'Political Education' in *Philosophy, Politics and Society*, Laslett (Ed.), Blackwell, 1956.

[2] W. J. M. Mackenzie, *Theories of Local Government*. Greater London Papers, No. 2, LSE, 1961. For a more comprehensive and systematically argued discussion of local government theory see Hugh Whalen, 'Ideology, Democracy, and the Foundations of Local Self-Government' in *The Canadian Journal of Economics and Political Science*, Vol. 26, No. 3, 1960. It is reprinted in L. D. Feldman and M. D. Goldrick (Eds), *Politics and Government of Urban Canada*, Methuen, 1969.

and, tentatively, additional theories suggested. The discussion will be mostly confined to the British experience although foreign experience will be discussed where it seems to be relevant. Probably much of it will be applicable to 'advanced industrial' democracies, and at the very least, the foregoing seems unlikely to be applicable to societies dominated by subsistence farming. The last point needs perhaps further emphasis. There is clearly a very powerful link between urbanism and local government; the great bulk of the activities of most local government systems are closely associated with providing common services for people living in close proximity to one another who could not provide these services for themselves individually. This is not to say that local government is of no account in a wholly rural society, there is still at the very minimum a need for schools and roads in even the most widely dispersed rural society. But it does mean that most of the following discussion is applicable to urban and mixed societies more than it is to predominantly rural societies.

If such an exercise requires a justification it is that proposals for the first complete overhaul of the present local government system of the United Kingdom have appeared,[1] and it therefore seems appropriate that something a little more substantial than an ethical commitment may be in order, especially since that commitment may be getting a little threadbare. The Maud Committee's dictum that 'The local administration of public services is essential, that the local organs of administration should be democratically elected bodies is not'[2] is, after all, merely the more articulate expression of what may be taken to be a fairly widespread public sense of indifference and bewilderment to local government.

So as to keep to open country as long as possible and avoid the thickets of infra-sovereignties, areal hierarchies, decentralization, devolution and so on, a potential problem must be fended off by defining what is meant by local government. Hedley Marshall's Stamp Memorial Lecture[3] provides as good a working definition as

[1] Royal Commission on Local Government in England—*Report* (RCLGE), 3 vols, Cmnd. 4040, 1969.
Royal Commission on Local Government in Scotland—*Report*, 1 vol. and Appendices, Cmnd. 4150, 1969 (Wheatley).
White Paper, *Local Government in Wales*, Cmnd. 3340, 1967.
White Paper, *The Re-shaping of Local Government*, Cmnd. 517, HMSO, Belfast, 1967.
[2] *The Report of the Committee on the Management of Local Government*, HMSO, 1967, p. 68.
[3] A. H. Marshall, *Local Government in the Modern World* (Athlone Press, 1965).

any. He defines a local authority as having three essential characteristics: 'operation in a restricted geographical area within a nation
or state; local election or selection; and the enjoyment of a measure
of autonomy, including the power of taxation'.

One reason why local government has not attracted the political
theorist's interest, and a brief glance at the literature suggests that
this may apply to other countries as well, is that it exists and has
existed in some form for a long time. To quote Mackenzie again,
himself paraphrasing a hallowed Whitehall rubric: 'It is justified
because it is an effective and convenient way to provide certain
services. It is justified because we like to think that our central
government needs the kind of qualities which are best trained by local
self-government.' Local government's position as an almost primordial feature of the political landscape was such that even an
incorrigible weaver of abstractions as Harold Laski was 'almost'
persuaded to forgo the temptation to premeditate some principles on
its behalf: 'The case, indeed, for a strong system of local government
in any state is clear almost beyond the needs of discussion.'[1] In the
sense that above the Monte Carlo and San Marino scale of states,
Laski seems to be right: local government in some form seems to be
in existence everywhere. The most plausible explanation would appear
to be that no national government wants to cope with everything and
it is possible, as Mill demonstrated, to define functions that are
purely local in character and therefore should only concern those
living in the locality:

> 'The very object of having local representation, is in order that
> those who have an interest in common which they do not share
> with the general body of their countrymen may manage that joint
> interest by themselves'.[2]

There can be little serious objection to this claim for local government, indeed it is the least ambiguous and the most concrete of all the
justifications of local government. But it embraces a very limited
range of activities which it is difficult to envisage as sufficient grist for
a full-dress elected and tax-raising system enjoying 'a measure of
autonomy'. It may be called the sewage without tears value of local
government and it leaves out of account those services – the more
important – about which it is not self evident that the local common

[1] H. J. Laski, *A Grammar of Politics* (Allen & Unwin, 5th edn, 1949), p. 411.
[2] J. S. Mill, *Considerations on Representative Government*, World Classics
Edition, Oxford University Press, 1912, p. 368.

interest plays a greater part than, say, the need for national minimum standards or national economic management.

Linked to this functional value is the knowledge value of local government. Not only is it irrational to involve anyone else in the local problems of the local area, central government is not equipped to grasp the inimitable conditions of each locality. Local government is preferable precisely because locally elected institutions employing their own specialist staff are better placed to understand and interpret both the conditions and the needs of local communities. This is what Laski called 'the genius of place'.[1] It is clearly an important function of local government and together with the sewage without tears value it constitutes an important though limited justification for local government and will be picked up again later.

Arthur Maass and Paul Ylvisaker, in what remains the most exhaustive systematic discussion of the division of powers by area, have defined the values inherent in local government as being: liberty, equality and welfare.[2] Local government promotes liberty in the sense, following Montesquieu, that it is a division of powers on an *area* basis which mitigates the power of the sovereign. It promotes equality in the political sense that it provides broad opportunities for citizens to participate in public policy. Finally, it promotes welfare in the sense that it provides agents that are apt for meeting the needs of society.

The first doubt about this trio arises out of the use of the word equality to describe what is in effect better described as participation. It is true that political equality rather than economic or social equality is meant, nevertheless there is a particular problem arising from the use of equality in this context for it invites unnecessary confusion since local government may promote economic and social *inequality*. The existence of quasi-independent areas responsible for major services must conflict to some extent with the pursuit of equality nationally. Indeed it is as a promoter of inequality that local government has come under heavy attack, in particular from those who place a high value on equality but it may also be seen in the public's attitude of indifference and bewilderment to local government mentioned earlier, which reflects increasing public demand for greater social and economic equality. Georges Langrod addressing himself not to the theoretical justification for local government but to whether or not it is a necessary condition for democracy nationally, has made its tendency to promote inequality

---

[1] *A Grammar of Politics*, p. 411.
[2] A. Maass (Ed.), *Area and Power*, Free Press, 1959.

one of the cornerstones of his contention that local government and democracy are incompatible.[1] The conflict between economic equality and local government will be discussed later, at this stage of the discussion participation has clear advantages over equality for describing this value of local government.

Similar doubts arise about the appropriateness of Maass' choice of the word welfare to describe the service-providing role of local government. Apart from the essentially ameliorative overtones attached to welfare that do not quite square with one of local government's traditional roles as the regulator and rationing device for the provision of services, if welfare is retained it is difficult to find a place for the value of efficiency. Although efficiency is itself ambiguous, it does convey all that welfare in this context is intended to convey but much more besides in relation to the practical advantages of local government for providing services. Since this is possibly one of the major justifications for local government in modern democracies, efficiency has clear advantages for describing the third value of local government. For these reasons the Maass formulation is discarded in favour of Stefan Dupré's trio of: liberty, participation and efficiency.[2]

LIBERTY

But in favouring the Dupré approach it must be emphasized that the value of liberty which he shares with Maass is the least convincing of the three values. Dupré is himself unhappy with it and points out that Montesquieu was after all discussing individual liberty in a somewhat different context. Whatever the tendencies, real or imagined, of modern democracies to infringe individual liberty they can hardly compare with those of the France of Louis XV. Dupré therefore settles for its very persistence as a value attributed to local government as his justification for retaining it and quotes an advisory committee of the United States Commission on Intergovernmental Relations to the effect that the task of local government is to soften the impact of arbitrary State and National laws and regulations'.[3] The word 'arbitrary' seems, at the very least, questionable in the context of a democratic system. It is certainly difficult to see this as one

[1] *Public Administration*, Vol. XXXI, p. 28. Langrod also effectively quote Tocqueville in support of his contention.

[2] J. Stefan Dupré, *Intergovernmental Relations and the Metropolitan Area*, Paper No. 5. Centennial Study and Training Programme on Metropolitan Problems, Toronto, 1967.

[3] *An Advisory Committee Report on Local Government*, U.S. Government Printing Office, Washington, D.C., 1955, p. 9.

of the tasks of local government in the British context where it is central government that is cast in the role of softening arbitrariness, that is to say, as the guardian of the rights of individuals and of groups against the possible depredations of local authorities. It has too, statutory backing for such activity for a whole range of services. Of course it would be nonsense to assume that governments in a democracy never infringe individual liberty, but it is difficult to see in what way a local authority is less likely to err than central government except in the sense that local government is likely to be less bureaucratic than central government because lines of communication are shorter and because, under the British system at least, it is possible to establish greater surveillance by the elected representatives over official activity than is conceivable for a central department.[1] But what is being protected is not so much individual rights as corporate policy decisions. We see here a mistaken identification of the liberty of individuals with the liberty of communities. It is certainly possible for local government to promote individual liberty, but just as central government does not have a monopoly of arbitrariness, equally a local authority's interests are not necessarily those of its individual citizens. After all, one of the justifications of local government on the participation side, as we shall see, is its ability to generate attitudes which recognize interests that lie beyond mere self interest and family interests.

There is another important variant of the liberty value that demands examination. This is propounded by the free market school of economists who see local government as the political equivalent of the free market. Local government is not as effective as the free market itself to be sure, but if a service cannot be provided by private firms then local government is the next best thing, for central government is always potentially, perhaps even inherently, a threat to individual liberty. Thus F. A. Hayek, the doyen of this school, has put it:

'While it has always been characteristic of those favouring an increase in governmental powers to support maximum concentration of those powers, those mainly concerned with individual liberty have generally advocated decentralization. There are strong reasons why action by local authorities generally offers the next best solution where private initiative cannot be relied upon to provide certain services and where some sort of collective action is

[1] This advantage of local government is given special emphasis by J. H. Warren, *In Defence of Local Democracy*, Conservative Political Centre, 1957.

therefore needed; for it has many of the advantages of private enterprise and few of the dangers of the coercive action of governments'.[1]

More precisely, local authorities are 'the next best solution' because they will compete with each other in the services they provide and so raise the quality and effectiveness of these services. This assumes that consumers are as mobile as between local authorities as they can be between producers in a market situation. This seems on the face of it improbable and Hayek, unlike some free market economists – D. S. Lees[2] for example – who promote this justification for local government, is not altogether happy with it and suggests that the mobility effect will only apply to 'the young and more enterprising'. But even with this limitation this value of local government is a fairly rickety one. In reality local authorities are much more like area *monopolists* for the service they provide. Far from providing the optimum level of service under the lash of consumer mobility, local authorities tend to supply a bewildering variety of levels of services.[3] Lees actually argues that this tendency to variety is an additional reason why local government promotes liberty since it widens choice, but he fails to reconcile this with its other alleged tendency to provide an optimal service because individual local authorities are in competition. It must be concluded that what may be called the market view of local government as a promoter of individual liberty is as weak as that which sees it as a bulwark against possible central tyranny. Perhaps for Britain at least, the preservation of individual liberty as a value of local government may be given a decent burial (alongside the separation of powers and parliamentary sovereignty?) in the liberal individualist graveyard. Certainly if it is to remain it must take a poor and dubious third to the other two values.

PARTICIPATION

The first of these is participation which is now a vogue word and as such is shrouded with all sorts of inarticulate major premises. But

[1] F. A. Hayek, *The Constitution of Liberty*, Routledge, 1960, p. 263.

[2] '. . . if someone doesn't like the "bundle" of local services or the level of local rates, he can move to another area more closely suited to his preferences', 'The Place of Local Authorities in the National Economy' in *Public Administration*, Vol. 39, Spring, 1961, p. 32.

[3] Bleddyn Davies, 'Local Authority Size' in *Public Administration*, Vol. 47, Summer 1969, p. 247.

this should not be allowed to clog the discussion unduly for, unlike liberty, its persistence in the celebratory literature of local government seems to have a sounder basis. In its extreme form the starting point of the argument for participation as a value of local government is rooted in the assertion of the primacy of the community, the town. The nation, so the argument runs, is an artefact of man but the municipality is an artefact of nature. Tocqueville puts it with characteristic appeal and force: 'man creates kingdoms and republics but townships seems to spring from the hand of God'.[1] There is little doubt that this value has exerted a powerful influence on the development of British local government and is one of the two dominant traditions that have co-existed in this country over the past one hundred years or so; this is the 'fundamental antithesis between centralization and "autonomous" decentralization' detected by Redlich.[2] Briefly, it is a view of local government which sees it primarily as a series of representative institutions with a high degree of autonomy that exist in their own right irrespective of what services they happen to be providing at any particular point in time.

The other tradition is the Benthamite, or more accurately, Chadwickian tradition that sees local government primarily as a series of agencies for providing national services as efficiently as possible to national minimum standards. This tradition will be discussed later, suffice it to say here that it is difficult to reconcile the two traditions and this accounts, amongst other things, for the persistent ambiguity which envelops central–local relations in Britain, and of course makes it very difficult, though not hopefully impossible, to evolve a consistent theoretical justification for local government that claims to bear some resemblance to actual practice. The community autonomy tradition has a lot to be said for it; it is possible, though not always easy, to define over most of the country self-conscious communities and to argue that their citizens should have some mechanism for promoting and protecting their collective interests. In its extreme form the community autonomy tradition sees local authorities, because local communities are prior to national government, as being superior to it as well. The best known protagonist of this view is Toulmin Smith but since he was not concerned with promoting democratic participation so much as preserving the common law vestry in order to resist the onward march of Benthamism he need

[1] Alexis de Tocqueville, *Democracy in America*, J. P. Mayer and Max Lerner (Eds), trans. G. Lawrence (Fontana), Vol. I, p. 73.

[2] J. Redlich and F. W. Hirst, *Local Government in England* ,Vol. I, Macmillan, 1903, p. 10.

not detain us.[1] However, it may be claimed that in democratic terms, local authorities are also superior since it is only at the level of the municipality – the city state – that the individual can really participate in his own government, and so government is truly democratic. For Robert Dahl, the most recent protagonist of this view, representative government at the national level is merely a substitute designed to give the nation State democratic plausibility and has usurped real democracy, by a sleight of hand so to speak, perpetrated in the nineteenth century: 'with John Stuart Mill, who in Representative Government dismisses as irrelevant in a single sentence at the end of a chapter, almost as an after-thought, the two-thousand-year-old tradition'.[2] Dahl questions the notion of any primacy attaching to the nation state. We must he urges:

'. . . drop the belief that there is a single sovereign unit for democracy, a unit in which majorities are autonomous in respect to all persons outside the unit and authoritative with respect to all persons inside the unit. Instead we begin to think about appropriate units of democracy as an ascending series, a set of Chinese boxes, each larger and more inclusive than the other, each in some sense democratic though not always in the same sense, and each not inherently less nor inherently more legitimate than the other.'

Current developments in technology and communications, Dahl maintains, will place the city, at least in the United States, as 'the optimum unit of democracy in the 21st Century'.

There is little doubt that Dahl's central concern, the relation between scale and democracy, and his consequent exposure of the spurious primacy of the nation state in democratic terms is a vital one. Clearly local government does have a democratic primacy over national government because it does enable more people to participate in their own government. Like it or not, it is an ineluctable fact that participation is a diminishing function of scale. The key question is participation in the government of what? A parish council is impeccably democratic but may be incapable of doing anything of any importance. Some sort of balance has to be struck between functional capacity and the requirements of democracy. Dahl asserts, with perhaps a misguided faith in the literature on the relation between scale and performance, that a city of between 50,000

[1] See Redlich and Hirst, op. cit., p. 145, for a brief outline of Toulmin Smith's theories.
[2] Robert A. Dahl, *The City in the Future of Democracy*, APSR, Vol. LXI, No. 4.

and 200,000 is about the optimum for meeting the needs of democracy and of functions.

Assumptions that the future lies inevitably with the ever larger nation or federal state have had a long and on the whole forlorn innings and Dahl's discussion comes as a refreshing and timely change. Nevertheless the nation state, though apparently decreasing steadily in scale – the majority of the member states of the U.N. now have a smaller population than Scotland – still seems likely to be with us for the forseeable future. It therefore seems otiose to pursue this particular aspect of participation any further except perhaps to note that if the nation state is here to stay, in the larger democracies at least, the role of local government in mitigating their participatory inadequacies will presumably remain.

The participation value of local government then, emerges as a strong one, unquestionably stronger than liberty. But there remain at least three further and related facets of participation as a value of local government that merit discussion.

The first is the role of local government as a political educator, as a means of civilizing men through the medium of self-government. For some it has been seen as *the* agent, and for Dahl it is at least 'a great indispensable and comprehensible pre-requisite'. For Tocqueville at his most quotable it seemed to be *the* agent:

'However, the strength of free peoples resides in the local community. Local institutions are to liberty what primary schools are to science; they put it within people's reach; they teach people to appreciate its peaceful enjoyment and accustom them to make use of it.'

Mill shared similar sentiments:

'I have dwelt in strong language – hardly any language is strong enough to express the strength of my conviction – on the importance of that portion of the operation of free institutions which may be called the public education of the citizen. Now, of this operation the local administrative institutions are the chief instrument.'[1]

Mill's views, if in a less magisterial tone, have been carried forward by many hands including those of James Bryce[2] and Laski.[3] Latterly

[1] *Considerations on Representative Government*, p. 365.

[2] 'An essential ingredient of a satisfactory democracy is that a considerable proportion of the people should have experience of active participation in the work of small self-governing groups, whether in connection with local government, trade unions, co-operatives or other forms of activity.' Quoted in S. Verba, *Small Groups and Political Behaviour*. Princeton U.P., 1961.

[3] *A Grammar of Politics*, p. 411.

it featured prominently in C. H. Wilson's discussion of the values of local government ('political capacity is deeply and widely nourished by organs of local self-government'),[1] and in the rather different context of 'developing' societies by Henry Maddick.[2] There is undoubtedly a great deal of plausibility in this view; at the very least it would be extremely difficult to actually refute it point blank. As Dahl points out, it is after all merely our new friend political socialization in a more concrete and dare it be said, comprehensible context. This problem is not so much whether local government does or does not educate, but how *many* it educates. Tocqueville was of course talking about local democracy *en masse*, the New England Township meeting. In modern Britain where the only remaining survival of direct democracy is the parish meeting, the role of local government as political educator can only touch a tiny fraction of the population. According to current estimates, about 43,000 people are local councillors in England and Wales[3] and even if we add co-opted members, we must also allow for the non-participant, for we are assured in all studies of small groups, local authorities included, that within them participation in any meaningful sense is confined to a minority.[4] It may be contended that the 43,000 extend the educative process by carrying the message of democracy to the wider public, although it is difficult to envisage this in practice.[5] If it does happen however, there is very little evidence that the wider citizenry are very attentive pupils.[6]

There are in any case aspects of the educative value of local government that raise one or two doubts about its complete acceptability in a modern democracy. The first is its powerful overtones of paternalism. It derives in essence from a rather pessimistic view of human nature directly descended from Aquinas' view of self-government as a means of subjecting individuals' 'irascible and concupiscable

[1] C. H. Wilson (Ed.), *Essays in Local Government*, Blackwell, 1948.

[2] Henry Maddick, *Democracy, Decentralization and Development*, Asia Publishing House, 1963.

[3] *The Report of the Committee on the Management of Local Government*, Maud, Vol. 1, p. ix. This figure excludes parish councillors of whom it is usually estimated there are about 50,000.

[4] S. Verba, *Small Groups and Political Behaviour*, p. 3.

[5] J. H. Warren introduces the notion of the 43,000 'leavening . . . the mass of citizenship'. In the sense that this could be interpreted to mean 'to make rise up' intriguing possibilities are suggested but the case for local governments' educative function is hardly advanced much further. *In Defence of Local Democracy*, p. 12.

[6] See B. C. Smith, 'The Justification of Local Government' in Feldman and Goldrick, op. cit. Also RCLGE, *Research Study No. 9*, Section C and *Report*, Vol. III, Appendix 7.

powers to the royal and politic rule'.[1] If this sounds a bit far-fetched the modern variant still has a distinctly Gladstonian, schoolmasterish tone that sees the special task of local government as being that of teaching the great unwashed that money does not grow on trees. This is certainly Mill's view, who wanted to exclude non-ratepayers altogether from the fold. It also crops up later and is clearly evident in a suitably modified form in Wilson and others.[2]

Linked with this paternalist element is another, peculiarly British strain, which seems to give the need for local government as a political educator a more urgent appeal in this country. This is the fear, again stemming directly from Mill, that those who are to receive the direct benefits of training in democracy are pretty poor stuff anyway. The low calibre of councillors was for Mill, 'The greatest imperfection of popular institutions.' He places great emphasis on how important it is for 'the very best minds of the locality' to be on local councils so that they may confer on the lower grade minds 'a portion of their own more enlarged ideas and higher and more enlightened purposes'. One finds similar sentiments in the Webbs and it also seems to have infected foreign observers, notably Ostrogorski.[3] The persistence of this attitude in Britain is perhaps another example of cultural lag from an aristocratic past still lurking in an erstwhile democratic system. In this instance widespread unwillingness to accept the full consequences of democracy where it involves the man in the street actually taking part in government. At the parliamentary level this attitude is not nearly so evident because the fine sieve of selection procedures eliminates most manual workers irrespective of party, and even where M.P.s from working class backgrounds are elected they seldom reach ministerial rank before becoming absorbed in the wider political ruling group.[4] Local government on the other hand, has no such screening devices, hence apparently the obsession with the calibre of its representatives.

[1] Quoted in Anwar Syed, *The Political Theory of American Local Government*, Random House, 1966, p. 160.

[2] 'The local councillor has to learn that the world in which he acts is a world of scarcity and that all the resources at his disposal are limited.' *Essays in Local Government*, p. 18. Also S. K. Panter-Brick, 'local government . . . tends to guard against too much enthusiasm, against that disinterested but misguided benevolence which in its enthusiasm fails to count the cost. The administrative and financial difficulties of bright ideas can be learnt at the parish pump level'. *Public Administration*, Vol. XXXI, p. 347.

[3] He noted a 'decline of the intellectual and, to some extent, moral standards of the personnel of the Town Councils'. *Democracy and the Organization of the Political Parties*, Vol. I, p. 490.

[4] W. L. Guttsman, *The British Political Elite* (MacGibbon & Kee, 1965), Ch. XII.

A further participatory value that is claimed for local government is its role as a training ground for democracy. In Bentham's view, admittedly in a mere footnote to his grand design, local government provides 'a nursery for the supreme legislature; a school of appropriate aptitude in all its branches for the business of legislature'.[1] This claim has been exhaustively examined so far as Britain is concerned by Brian Smith[2] but it does not emerge as a very significant one. Much depends on the emphasis placed on the difference between the respective roles of local councillor and M.P. and equally on the extent to which private politics are seen as providing a comparable training to local councils. Nevertheless, after a careful examination of the available evidence Smith's conclusion is: 'Local government experience then, is relevant to central government practices because it is political experience . . . (but) . . . we should not overestimate the value of local political experience for national legislators and leaders.'

The remaining aspect of participation as a justification of local government which must be noted is that which sees local government not so much as a (or *the*) training ground for civic virtue or for the national legislature – the breeder of better individuals as it were – but also as the essential element for establishing a stable and harmonious national state, the breeder of better societies. For Tocqueville and Mill these two aspects of participation were very closely linked. It is only by participating in and learning the arts of self-government at the local level that the individual had a stake in and came to appreciate the virtues of free government at the national level.

But as we saw in relation to the difficulty of accepting liberty as a value of local government, local community interests do not necessarily coincide with individual interests; nor do they with national interests. Self-government may or may not nurture civic virtue, but if it does, there is no guarantee that this will always enhance the citizens' perception of the national interest and it is likely to enhance local loyalties. However, if the nation state is viewed in non-territorial terms, there is a variation on this theme that has a certain plausibility. This sees the stabilizing and harmonizing functions of local government in terms of reconciling class, religious and sectoral interests. The most eloquent exponent of this view is J. H. Warren: '. . . local government has been a great agency of reconciliation in

[1] Quoted in Mackenzie, *Theories of Local Government*, p. 13.
[2] Brian C. Smith, 'The Justification of Local Government' in Feldman and Goldrick, op. cit.

240

our national life, taking much of the sharp edge of the war of class and creed. You do not bring men and women of every class, creed and station in life into necessary co-operation in practical tasks without some mutual adjustment of ideas and feelings'.[1] Also G. D. H. Cole who, despite overtones of the peculiarly English brand of paternalism just discussed, seems to get nearer to the reality of the modern situation:

'Our problem ... is to find democratic ways of living for little men in big societies. For men are little, and their capacity cannot transcend their experience, or grow except by continuous building upon their historic past. They can control great affairs only by acting together in the control of small affairs, and finding, through the experience of neighbourhood, men whom they can entrust with larger decisions than they can take rationally themselves. Democracy can work in the great States ... only if each State is made up of a host of little democracies, and rests finally, not on isolated individuals but on groups small enough to express the spirit of neighbourhood and personal acquaintance.'[2]

Each of these variations on the harmonizing role of local government has its appeal and it would be difficult to refute any of them out of hand. Doubts arise on the degree of emphasis that the proponents put on them; clearly it is possible for the main elements of a stable democracy to be achieved nationally before democratic local government has been established locally. In Britain, democracy in the one man one vote sense was achieved nationally before it was locally, and many parts of rural England were bereft of any local representative institutions until 1888. As Brian Keith-Lucas has reminded us the local government franchise was not finally assimilated to the parliamentary franchise until 1948.[3] Similarly Langrod, in the article cited earlier, asserts: 'When a State has long since passed from the absolutist age to that of the constitutional regime, local government has often remained (for example in Austria from 1866 to 1918) as a veritable fortress of anachronistic privilege.'[4] In other words local government may be viewed as being possible only where there already exists some national cohesion and sense of national identity, if not

[1] J. H. Warren, *In Defence of Local Democracy*, p. 12.
[2] G. D. H. Cole, 'Democracy Face to Face with Hugeness' in *Essays in Social Theory*, Macmillan, 1960, p. 94.
[3] B. Keith-Lucas, *The English Local Government Franchise*, Blackwell, 1952.
[4] *Public Administration*, Vol. XXXI, p. 27.

democracy. Such a distinguished authority as Fesler is inclined to this view.[1]

To retrace the path for a moment, the New England townships Tocqueville so engagingly portrayed may have owed as much to the fact that the American union was stable because it emerged out of a revolution against what could be portrayed as an external enemy (whereas in France both sides of the revolution could legitimately claim a place within the state) as the stability of the states and the union owed to the townships. This is not to cast Cole out entirely, we probably have a familiar cause and effect problem: both local and national representative institutions, amongst other things, together contribute to the maintenance of a democratic climate. Even Langrod, who questions most of the justifications of local government in a democracy so far discussed, grants local government this modified role albeit with some reluctance.[2] The importance of other avenues to political education and national harmony that together with local government create a national climate, was emphasized with more than a hint of flag waving by Bagehot when commenting on Tocqueville's view on the educative function of local government:

'. . . it was natural that in France, where there is scarcely any power of self-organization in the people . . . a solitary thinker should be repelled from the exaggerations of which he knew the evil to the contrary exaggeration of which he did not. But in a country like England, where business is in the air, where we can organize a vigilance committee on every abuse and an executive committee for every remedy – as a matter of political instruction, which was de Tocqueville's point – we need not care how much power is delegated to outlying bodies, and how much is kept for the central body. We have had the instruction municipalities could give us: we have been all through that. Now we are quite grown up and can put away childish things.'[3]

To sum up so far, participation in its different forms emerges as an undoubted value, if not in the full glory of some of its promoters at least as an important justification for local government in a democ-

---

[1] J. W. Fesler, 'Centralization and Decentralization', in *International Encyclopedia of the Social Sciences*, Macmillan, 1968, p. 372.

[2] As do Panter-Brick and Leo Moulin in response to the Langrod article. See *Public Administration*, Vol. XXXI, p. 344, Vol. XXXII, pp. 433 and 438.

[3] W. Bagehot, *The English Constitution* (World's Classic Edition), pp. 256–7. I am grateful to Owen Hartley for allowing me to see his unpublished paper on the history of English local government theory from which this quotation is taken.

racy. It may well be that it is a value of increasing importance in the future. All the indications, sparse though they are admittedly, point to formal education as having the foremost influence in determining the extent of an individual's interest in and willingness to participate in local institutions.[1] On the assumption that education is likely to continue to expand in the future, the demand for participation in representative bodies at the local level is likely to grow too. Judging by the rapid expansion of local pressure groups in recent years this growth is already occurring.[2]

EFFICIENT SERVICES

There remains the third and final justification or value of local government and that is as an efficient agent for providing services. Again our starting point must be John Stuart Mill, who as we saw earlier, provided a fairly cast iron case for local government on the grounds that it was the most efficient agent for providing those services that are essentially local in character. The problem was that it did not take account of all those services local government has gained since Mill wrote that do not fit into his neat local and central formula because they have both national as well as local implications. If local government is to be justified in functional terms for modern conditions that justification has to rest on something a little more substantial than its efficacy for the disposal of sewage and refuse. There are strong grounds for assuming that there *is* a more substantial functional case for local government since if it did not exist something very much like it would have to be created in its place.[3] The argument begins at the central level. The point was made earlier that one advantage of local government over central government was that it is more likely to know the inimitable characteristics of each locality and adjust the administration of the service accordingly. This assumes that local government already exists, but if it did not it is perfectly possible for central departments to organize field agencies manned by staff resident in the locality who could acquire all the necessary local knowledge. What out-stationed field agencies could

[1] See RCLGE, *Report*, Vol. III, Appendix 7.

[2] M. Broady, *Planning for People*, Bedford Square Press, 1969, and L. J. Sharpe, 'Leadership and Representation in Local Government', *Political Quarterly*, April–June, 1966.

[3] In the discussion of this value of local government, I must acknowledge a profound debt to the work of James Fesler on the relationship between area and function, in particular his *Area and Administration*, University of Alabama Press, 1949.

not do however, is to co-ordinate their activities with each other. It is this factor together with the need to accommodate local opinion that constitute the main functional case for local government.

The need for co-ordination is derived from the fact that the central departments are responsible for clusters of services usually of a similar character. In this they are exploiting the advantages of specialization. The picture is not clear cut because departments are not merely functional agencies but are also corporate 'personalities' in their own right, particularly the older ones. Nevertheless in general the departmental system is based on specialization of tasks. But if specialization is an administrative convenience at the central level it creates serious problems for some services at the point of consumption at the end of the administrative line in each locality. This is because people do not live in the ordered categories in which central administration is organized (deprived children, expectant mothers, old age pensioners) but in mixtures of these categories, in communities, and the mixture varies from one community or area to another. This variation means that although each department may lay down policies for its service or group of services and achieve some local adjustment perhaps, there must be some compendious, horizontal coordinating agency which can gather together the separate vertical services coming down from the centre and adjust their content and character to the particular needs of each community; to determine the appropriate mixture of services for each community. In short, the social and economic unity of each locality should be matched by an equally unified service providing agency.

This co-ordinative function is crucial in the British context because alone among advanced industrial democracies it does not have an intermediate level of administration responsible for the bulk of public services within its area between central government and local government proper. Federal systems have it by definition and most other comparable states follow, with variations, the French prefectoral pattern. Some, West Germany for example, appear to have both. So in Britain it may be argued, if local government did not exist, in functional terms at least something very much like it would have to be put in its place. There would have to be groups of specialist field agencies of the central departments who were subordinate at the local level to some common generalist superior.

Such a system would entail a complete reorganization of central government involving the creation of a Ministry of the Interior which would have *primus inter pares* status to the other home departments. It would also mean a fundamental change in the traditional role of central departments so that, in addition to being controller, adviser, and policy maker, they would also have to manage the execution of policy, to be actual builders of houses and educators of children. It would have to be a fundamental change because British central government is not by tradition or nature an operational authority except for one or two services, the biggest being defence. This is probably what Mill meant by his bold assertion at the opening of his chapter on local representative bodies that has no doubt caused raised eyebrows for generations of his readers: 'It is but a small portion of the public business of a country which can be well done, or safely attempted, by the central authorities.'

But if we assume for a moment that Mill's assertion is no longer valid and that central government relations with local authorities could be transformed into something roughly comparable to the district commissioner system of the former Colonies, there still remains the second function of local government as an efficient provider of services. This is the need to accommodate local opinion.

Communities not only vary in the mixture of needs and therefore services they require in an objective sense, but there is often disagreement within the community as to what this mixture ought to be. In other words, it is not enough to be able to define the characteristic of the locality objectively (assuming that this can be done anyway), account must also be taken of subjective views within the community as to what the objective facts imply in terms of needs. And having settled them there remains the problem of deciding the relative priorities of each major service given the varying conditions in each locality. Understandably, no central government has the tenacity, the energy or the time to cope with the reconciliation of these conflicts within each community up and down the country. There are more important tasks for it to do in any case, tasks which it alone can and must do. It seems likely that here we see the main reason why most countries have some kind of local government.

But if the localities are to be left (probably *have* to be left) to adjust the mixture of services to their own taste, within limits set by the centre, on what basis are they to be allowed to do it? Clearly they must have the power to choose, and the power to choose must also be the power to command resources; to have some control over public finance. The way this finance is raised may vary, the key point is that the right to decide the size of the local cake and the way it is to be sliced is inevitably linked with the right to command resources.

Central government field agencies then, even where they are subject to overall supervision by a general common superior, would not be sufficient unless those differences that inevitably arise in any community as to the needs of the community are reconciled and priorities agreed between the competing demands of the services for the inevitably limited resources available. And such a system would also have to have some command over these resources, i.e. to raise taxes. These are three fundamental aspects of political power, particularly the right to raise taxes, and it seems improbable if not inconceivable that they could be wielded by bureaucratic local agencies co-existing within a democratic national system. Some form of election seems essential.

Local government emerges then with strong claims as an efficient provider of services, but surprisingly this has been seldom acknowledged, rather the reverse. Whereas the value of local government as a bulwark of liberty, or at least as a handmaiden of democracy, has as we have seen been recognized, its role as an agency for providing services has evoked no comparable enthusiasm. More often than not, it has been attacked for its deficiencies in this sphere. This attack has mainly focused on the tendency of local government to create and perpetuate inequality. Whereas central government field agencies, it is claimed, can lay down minimum standards and ensure equality of service, local government encourages diversity and with it inevitable inequalities. That local government does encourage diversity and inequality is surely true and in that sense it clashes with the tendency to economic and social equality that is inherent in democratic societies. This is the main burden of Langrod's claim, noted earlier, that local government and democracy are incompatible:

'Democracy is by definition an egalitarian majority and unitarian system. It tends everywhere and at all times to create a social *whole*, a community which is uniform, levelled and subject to rules . . . On the other hand local government is by definition a phenomenon of differentiation and individualization, of separation. It represents and strengthens separate social groups enjoying a relative independence, sometimes autonomous, constituting parts of the public power.'[1]

Although Langrod is prone to indulge in Hegelian melodrama elsewhere, ('local government has within itself, inevitably, the seed of its own death once the process of democratization is accomplished') he gets nearer in this quotation to the spirit of modern democracy

[1] G. Langrod, *Public Administration*, Vol. XXXI, p. 28.

than some critics have given him credit for. Certainly it seems a little far-fetched to accuse him of advocating totalitarianism.[1] But the egalitarian spirit of modern democracy may be misplaced in so far as it sees local government as a barrier to the achievement of equality, for a number of reasons. In the first place it is extremely difficult to conceptualize equality, let alone measure it, for those services that involve complex inter-relationships between institutions and staff rather than cash payments; that is to say for the bulk of the major services at present the responsibility of local government in this country. A high degree of equality is certainly possible for social security payments or unemployment benefits, but as a service becomes more complex and involves a combination of heterogeneous factors that go to make up its effectiveness, so it becomes more difficult to achieve equality in any measurable sense.[2] Nor is equality, whether measurable or not, a realistic objective, partly because it is impossible to begin with a *tabula rasa* or to move at the same pace over the whole country at the same time; and partly because what is regarded as an acceptable level of service is constantly changing as new needs are generated.

It is difficult to escape the conclusion that inequality is an inevitable feature of a wide range of public services. Even supposing it were not, the tendency to diversity inherent in local government is not the only possible source of inequality; central government is after all not only an impartial arbitrator but the supreme political agent in the state and as such may be vulnerable to pressures that can produce inequalities to match any that might be generated by local government. The link between inequality and local government is neither obvious nor unique and there are other aspects of local government as an efficient provider of services that perhaps outweigh any tendencies it does have to promote inequality.

The first is that local authorities, unlike any other public bodies are independent in the sense that they are elected separately from central government and have independent sources of revenue. They are not of course entirely independent; the central departments in

[1] 'Langrod's stipulative definitions of democracy and local government constitute a curious blend of selective empirical observations and rigid apriority. These particular conceptions appear to give expression in institutional terms, to Rousseau's doctrine of the general will, and to a tradition of political thought which we style "totalitarian democracy".' H. Whalen, *Ideology, Democracy, and the Foundations of Local Self-Government*, in Feldman and Goldrick, op. cit.

[2] See Bleddyn Davies, *Social Needs and Resources in Local Services*, Michael Joseph, 1968, for a contrary view which nonetheless provides an informative discussion of this problem.

Britain as in most other comparable countries,[1] exercise a considerable range of controls over the activities of local authorities and in Britain provide about 37 per cent of their total expenditure. Equally local authorities are not the agents of the centre; the relationship is a more complex one in which Redlich's 'fundamental antithesis' between centralization and decentralized autonomy still lurks and competition and conflict modified by co-operation co-exist. Any discussion of the value of local government as an efficient provider of services must be viewed in this setting. As John Griffith has put it: 'In the broadest terms their interests may be the same; to promote the public welfare. But they are also stationed in opposition to one another. Each local authority must seek to obtain for itself the best possible treatment from the departments.'[2] This relationship of competitive co-operation makes local authorities very different from any other agency with whom the central departments have to deal. In a system where a Minister can only comprehend the broad outlines of national policy and for anything less the democratic process expresses itself through Parliament and through competing pressure groups, local authorities, because they are independent but within the public sector, are pressure groups of a very special and valuable kind. This is because producer pressure groups (employers and employees) whose interests are fundamental to the economic well-being of their members are for this reason always much stronger than consumer groups. Of course all producers are also consumers anyway; the problem arises for those consumers who are not producers, such as the retired, the young, married women and those producer groups that for different reasons are unorganized. These groups are only weakly represented, if at all, in the pressure group system. One of the primary tasks of democratic government is to redress this inherent imbalance within the system. Local authorities are preeminently consumer pressure groups who help redress this imbalance and thereby are important and probably irreplaceable elements in a modern democratic political system. They are the ultimate allies of central government even though they may be in conflict with it.

There is a further aspect of the efficiency value of local government which merits discussion. Local authorities not only help to redress the imbalance in power between producers and consumers, they also

[1] See *Local Government in the XXth Century*, International Union of Local Authorities, The Hague, 1963.

[2] J. A. G. Griffith, *Central Departments and Local Authorities*, Allen & Unwin, 1966, p. 18.

248

provide an alternative basis for responding to demand for public services that have no market. On the initial assumption that central government cannot cope with everything, and because it lacks an intermediate level or a tradition of operational responsibility British central government may be more limited than most, the basic alternatives open other than local government are two: the public corporation or the private sector. There are various forms of public and quasi-public agency that lie between these two, nevertheless they all fall within one or the other category. But ultimately both the public corporation and the private sector depend for their successful operation on the existence of the market. The private sector does so by definition, the public corporation because the market provides a criterion of performance which makes its independent status feasible. There remains, however, a long list of public services in most industrial democracies that are not sold in the market and which cater for an ever changing and expanding demand.[1]

These services pose a new and formidable administrative problem since if they are to respond to demand the institutional arrangements for their provision must be such that some sort of balance is struck between the competing demands of flexibility and initiative in the field; professional autonomy; and public accountability. This is a difficult not to say impossible task, yet in so far as it is achievable, local government may offer a better prospect than the only other alternative which is some form of direct central control. Local government is, in short, a form of public agency which can respond to demand without the external discipline of the price mechanism. This is not to say that local government is a kind of *ersatz* free market. As we have seen, local authorities are local monopolists, and although competition and emulation may take place between authorities, the key characteristic of local government is that it is subject to the discipline not of consumer sovereignty but of the ballot box. Where local authorities are dominated by the national parties, as is the case in most of urban Britain, and the national parties themselves are highly centralized, as is the case in Britain as a whole, the discipline of the ballot box may be obscured. This does not mean that it has ceased to operate however. It may be true that in the urban areas national issues appear to dominate the outcome of local elections,[2] but it does not follow that the value of elections in this context is lost. Voters

[1] See Enoch Powell, *Medicine and Politics*, Pitman, 1966, for one of the very few discussions in print of this problem.

[2] See P. J. Fletcher, 'The Results Analysed' in L. J. Sharpe (Ed.), *Voting in Cities*, Macmillan, 1967.

may cast their vote on the basis of all manner of motives – sensible, judicious, bigoted or capricious – what matters is that an elected body is produced that acts *as if* it is a representative of its constituents' interests. If the motives of the electorate in making their choice are to be the basis for questioning the efficacy of the system then we must logically extend the argument to all forms of democracy and not just the local variety.

The advantages of local government over other forms of administration for non-market services may be seen in an extreme form in relation to capital renewal and growth. Rapid growth is now a characteristic of a wide range of services that usually fall within the ambit of local government. In Britain over the period 1956–7 to 1965–6 total revenue expenditure at real costs has increased by more than 50 per cent.[1] Over the period 1963/4 to 1967/8 the percentage expansion at real costs for individual services has been: housing 42 per cent, education 26 per cent, health and welfare 23 per cent and child-care 31 per cent.[2] The precise reasons for this remarkable expansion are not known and some of it may be due not to change in demand but to inefficiency or to over production, but there seems to be general agreement about three other causes that are the result of actual changes in demand.[3] The first is the growth in the numbers of those age groups that consume the lion's share of these services, the young and the old. Second, there is the rise in expectations generated by rising living standards; and third on the supply side, rising standards generated by the services themselves. This last may be the most decisive of the three and broadly takes the form of last year's most advanced increment to standards becoming next year's basic need. Similarly, improvements in one service can create new demands in another, for example, improvements in secondary education creating a demand for more university places.

It seems unlikely that any of these factors is likely to diminish significantly in the future and there is good reason to suppose that the effect of the third is likely to intensify for two reasons. First, because of improvements in their accessibility to the public and in the amount of information about them.[4] Second, because of rising education standards which seem to have the most decisive effect on

---

[1] RCLGE *Report*, Vol. III. Appendix 6.

[2] R. H. S. Crossman, *Paying for the Social Services*, Fabian Society, 1969.

[3] Ibid., pp. 7–9, see also Association of Municipal Corporations: *Statement to the Royal Commission on Local Government in England on Local Authority Expenditure*, 1967.

[4] This will be even more likely when the recommendations of the Seebohm

public interest in local government. It seems plausible to assume that there is a similar relationship between interest in all education and public services. A better educated public is going to be a better informed public and a more demanding one.

It therefore follows that rising demand is likely to be a permanent feature of a large slice of the personal health, welfare and education services. The ability to respond to it then, becomes an important, possibly even vital, consideration in assessing the relative merits of alternative administrative arrangements.

If the service is not run by local government nor is it in the market, that is to say all the reins are in central hands, expansion in response to constantly rising demand can only be effected by a crisis sufficient to shift public opinion at the national level and can only be sustained if that opinion does not shift elsewhere. Without such a shift in opinion, steady expansion will be difficult and capital starvation is likely to set in as the service languishes at the tail end of the capital investment queue. For in the competition for resources the centralized service faces formidable rivals for public support, not least defence which has stood at or near the head of the national queue for the past third of a century absorbing a major proportion of public sector expenditure.

This is not to say that expansion can not take place, it can, but rather that it is spasmodic, and therefore inefficient. Inefficient because during the long static intervals the skills and experience that are required for capital development atrophy, existing facilities are over-worked and resources may be absorbed in expensive patching up and steadily rising running costs. In Britain, the likelihood of capital starvation of centralized services is increased because of the recurrent need for successive governments to deflate the economy so as to protect the balance of payments. Faced with the need to do so rapidly, capital investment that is directly controlled by the centre is the most vulnerable to the axe. The post-1945 history of the hospitals, the national road system, and in a slightly different context, the prison service, the national airports, the universities and the Post Office provide instructive illustrations of this problem and in a negative sense reflect the efficiency value of local government. It does not follow that all of these services ought therefore to be made the responsibility of local government. There may be other, more compelling reasons for running them by other means. But their common

Committee which are designed to improve public access to and knowledge of these services, are implemented. See Dr R. Parker, *The Problems of Reform*, Loch Memorial Lecture, Family Welfare Association, 1967.

failure to keep pace with demand illustrates this defect of centralization; the recent change in the status of the Post Office to that of a public corporation and the emergence almost unnoticed of a new university system – the Polytechnics – run by local authorities suggest that the defect has been officially recognized.

There remains one further aspect of the efficiency value of local government. The growth in the technical complexity of public services and the consequent specialization of function has meant a parallel growth in the power of professional groups. Where the service involves largely formal, unambiguous duties that can be laid down and enforced by the centre, this does not matter since the area of discretion and therefore the degree of professional autonomy is weaker and in any case the professional group is consequently weak too. But where there is a high degree of discretion involved and professional autonomy is essential, a potential threat to effective democratic government is posed. The service gradually comes to serve objectives set by the professional group or groups running the service rather than those of its recipients or society at large. In short, public services that require a high degree of professional autonomy and are not subject to the discipline of the market are always in danger of incipient syndicalism.[1] This is not to say that the objectives of the professional group will necessarily conflict with the national interest; clearly the two will often coincide. Nor is a conspiracy theory implied; it is simply that it cannot be assumed that the two interests will always coincide. Some form of control external to the professional group is therefore necessary. At a national scale the possibility of such control is not feasible except at the broadest level of policy or in response to a national scandal. This means that unless there exists a system of decentralized generalist agents of the central government in each locality to which the local units of the service are responsible, and this is ruled out for reasons discussed earlier, local government offers the best possibility of counteracting incipient syndicalism. It does so by creating an additional focus of loyalty for professional group members – the local authority itself – on a scale that makes political control feasible and subjects the group to the moderating influence of a face-to-face relationship with other comparable and competing professional groups.

To sum up: the participatory value if not the liberty value still remains as a valid one for modern local government. Not perhaps in the full glory of its early promoters but as an important element in a

[1] See R. M. Titmuss, 'Social Administration in a Changing Society' in *Essays on the Welfare State*, 2nd end. Allen & Unwin, 1963.

modern democracy nonetheless. But as a co-ordinator of services in the field; as a reconciler of community opinion; as a consumer pressure group; as an agent for responding to rising demand; and finally as a counterweight to incipient syndicalism, local government seems to have come into its own.

18

Public Corporations*

D. N. CHESTER

*Public corporations are a type of governmental institution for adminis-
tering publicly owned industries or services. In Britain, where government departments have been regarded as likely to hamper efficiency
and restrict initiative in undertakings of an industrial or commercial
character, public corporations have been established to secure a
sufficient degree of accountability without requiring them to be subject
to ministerial control in respect of managerial decisions and many
routine activities (see, for example, W. A. Robson,* Nationalized
Industry and Public Ownership, *Allen & Unwin, 1962, 2nd edition).
In this article Mr Chester examines the use of the term and compares
public corporations with other types of governmental institution.*

I. GROWTH OF THE TERM 'PUBLIC CORPORATION'

'Public corporation' is now part of our vocabulary and is in use
overseas. Though the characteristics which it is meant to convey are
very much older, it is, I think, first found in the Report of the Craw-
ford Committee on Broadcasting (Cmd. 2599, 1926) which recommended 'a public corporation acting as Trustee for the national
interest'. It was used in this way in the Preamble to the first Charter
of the B.B.C. The Liberal Yellow Book (*Britain's Industrial Future*)
published in 1928 used the term in quite a different sense – as one to
be applied to a new category of Limited Liability Companies[1] which
because of their size and preponderance in a particular industry
should be required to conform to certain extra statutory conditions.
This report, a landmark in British thinking on industrial organization, uses the term then common – public board – for such bodies as

---

* From D. N. Chester, 'Public Corporations and the Classification of
Administrative Bodies', *Political Studies*, 1953, Vol. I, pp. 34–52. Reprinted with
permission of the Clarendon Press, Oxford.
[1] Mr. Ernest Davies in his *National Enterprise*, p. 24, is mistaken in implying
that the Liberal Report used the term 'public corporation' in its present sense.

the Port of London Authority. Harold Laski in the chapter on Economic Institutions in his *Grammar of Politics* (1st edition 1925 and subsequent editions) talks about Governing Boards and makes no reference to 'public corporations'. The Bridgeman Committee on the Post Office (Cmd. 4149, 1932) talked about the Independent Corporation or Statutory Authority. Marshall Dimock, writing in 1933[1] (*British Public Utilities and National Development*), does not speak of the 'public corporation' but refers to 'a public utility trust, as represented by the Central Electricity Board'.

The term was gradually coming into use in the Labour party between 1926 and 1930 and was popularized and developed by Mr Herbert Morrison in the debates on the London Transport Bill and particularly in his *Socialization and Transport*, published in 1933. Academic writers began to follow suit. Terence O'Brien, in his *British Experiments in Public Ownership and Control* (1937), speaks of the CEB, the BBC, and the LPTB as three public corporations,[2] and Lincoln Gordon published in 1938 *The Public Corporation in Great Britain*. Professor Robson, however, in *Public Enterprise* (1937) had a final essay headed 'The Public Service Board: General Conclusions', and in his preface he referred to public boards and commissions but did not use the term 'public corporation'. Yet he was clearly dealing with the same bodies as O'Brien and Gordon.

Since 1945 Professor Robson and most other writers have used the term 'public corporation', though such terms as 'semi-autonomous authorities' and 'public boards' still continue to be used. Is this just a change in fashion? Are public board, corporation, commission, statutory authority, *ad hoc* board, public utility trust, public service board, government corporation, autonomous authority,

---

[1] By 1936, however, Professor Dimock was using the term 'public corporation' —see his 'Public Corporations and Business Enterprise', *Public Administration*, Oct, 1936, pp. 417 ff. He there used the term to cover three corporate types – public utility trusts, mixed undertakings, and government owned corporations. He also used the term 'semi-public corporation' apparently to cover such large-scale private concerns as General Motors and United States Steel. See also his *Modern Politics and Administration*, 1937, Ch. XIII.

[2] On p. 24 he justifies the use of the term in these words: 'No settled title which conveys the essential nature of these institutions has yet come into use; and the titles most commonly employed—"Public Boards", "Semi-Public Bodies", and "Independent Statutory Authorities" seem to the writer unsatisfactory, at least for his purposes. Since the use of the word "corporation" to describe an incorporated *political* unit is long established in England, and the institutions discussed in this study are fully public bodies, the title of "Public Corporations" has been adopted; and where closer definition is required the qualifying adjective "Semi-Independent" seems to the writer the most accurate one available.'

public authority, and others a group of synonyms from amongst which, for one reason or another, 'public corporation' has emerged as the most fashionable in contemporary use? The answer is not clear, for this term is used with a variety of meanings and content.

II. EXTENSIVE AND LIMITED USE

'Public corporation' was first used to cover the CEB, BBC, and the LPTB, with the Port of London Authority brought in as an after-thought. After 1945 the boards of the newly nationalized industries were included and on occasion the term has been used as a synonym for 'nationalized industry'. Sometimes, however, a number of other bodies are mentioned, though it is not always clear whether the writers regard them as public corporations or only as bodies similar in form. Thus Sir Arthur Street in *The Public Corporation in British Experience* (1947) included the British Sugar Corporation and the United Kingdom Commercial Corporation and finished his survey by saying: 'I have had to omit references to scores of other bodies such as the Agricultural Mortgage Corporation, the Commissioners of Crown Lands, the Forestry Commission. . . . Enough, however, has been said to illustrate the flexible character of the Public Cor-poration. . . .' (p. 13). In his essay in *British Government since 1918* (1950) Sir Arthur Street discussed a much larger number of bodies, including the National Assistance Board.

Professor Robson has recently mentioned a number of bodies.

'The public corporation [he says] is not an entirely new insti-tution. There have long existed numerous organs exercising official or governmental functions, yet possessing varying degrees of independence from the executive and distinguishable from the great departments of state under the direct control of ministers of the Crown. There are bodies such as the Public Trustee, the Charity Commission, and Trinity House . . . the Tithe Redemption Commission, the Air Registration Board, and Medical Research Council . . . the Arts Council, the British Council, . . . the Prison Commissioners, the Board of Control, the Commissioners for Crown Lands, and the State Management Districts for Liquor Control in Carlisle. . . . These organs are, however, quite different from the new public corporations concerned with the operation of great socialized industries or services.'[1]

[1] *Problems of Nationalized Industry*, pp. 15–16.

Dealing with the legislation of 1945–50 he includes, as public corporations, the Central Land Board and the New Town Development Corporations.[1] He adds: 'Several other public corporations have been created during the past 5 years. There are, for example, the Regional Hospital Boards . . . [and the] . . . National Research Development Corporation. . . .'[2]

The lawyers appear to be as uncertain as the political scientists about the scope of the term. Professor Friedmann[3] includes the Regional Hospital Boards, New Town Development Corporations, Central Land Board, and others as well as the more usual industrial or commercial corporations, and has influenced Dr Glanville Williams's *Crown Proceedings* (1948). Griffith and Street in their recent *Principles of Administrative Law* have a similar classification, and Griffith[4] appears to apply the term to every public body not a government department or a local authority. On the other hand, Wade and Phillips, in their now standard *Constitutional Law* (4th edition, 1952), use the collective expression 'Independent Authorities' and distinguish 'the many statutory authorities with executive and regulatory functions of government which for various reasons are not directly under the control of a Minister answerable to Parliament for their administration' from 'the public corporations which have been created since 1945 for the main public utility services (except water) and for the coal and iron and steel industries' (p. 205). They include the R.H.B.s not with the 'Independent Authorities' but with the 'Boards under Ministers', and call these 'specialized agencies of government which for convenience of administration have been severed from the general departmental organization' (p. 212).

In striking contrast a report of the Central Statistical Office, *National Income and Expenditure, 1946–51*, published in August 1952, defines a public corporation as 'a trading body which is publicly controlled to the extent that the Sovereign, Parliament, or a Minister appoints, directly or indirectly, the whole or a majority of the board of management, but which is established as a corporate body with its own legal existence and with financial independence' (p. 72). A list of the bodies which satisfy this definition includes the Scottish Special Housing Association and Festival Gardens Ltd. The Regional Hospital Boards are included with the Central Government (as

[1] Ibid., p. 20. [2] Ibid., p. 21.

[3] 'The New Public Corporations and the Law', *Modern Law Review*, 1947, p. 233; 'The Legal Status and Organization of the Public Corporation', *Law and Contemporary Problems*, Autumn 1951, p. 576.

[4] 'Public Corporations as Crown Servants', *University of Toronto Law Journal*, 1952, pp. 169–93.

'grant-aided bodies . . . having no financial independence'). And the Port of London Authority and other Harbour Boards are included with Local Authorities largely because of the wording of the Local Taxation Returns Act, 1860.

Recent writings thus indicate two possible extreme meanings for the term, *viz.:*

(i) confined to the National Coal Board, British Transport Commission, and other boards with a statutory responsibility for the management of self-financing industrial or commercial undertakings;

(ii) extended to mean all governmental bodies not otherwise classified as a government department or as a local authority.

Some writers appear to take up an intermediate position by including bodies which are not trading, e.g. the Regional Hospital Boards, but still leaving out a large number of boards.

So far I have done nothing more than to show that the term is being used in widely differing senses. This is inconvenient, to say the least. Let us take an example of the possible confusion which may arise. It has often been said that the public corporation is the Labour party's chosen instrument of nationalization. Recent writings have described the following bodies as public corporations: National Coal Board, Port of London Authority, Forestry Commission, Central Land Board, National Assistance Board, and Regional Hospital Boards. Can each of these be said equally to be the chosen instrument? Most of the members of the governing body of the Port of London Authority are elected by the wharfingers and other users – may it be assumed, therefore, that this was part of the Labour Government's scheme of management? Until 1945 one member of the Forestry Commission had to be an M.P., and he answered questions in Parliament about the work of the Commission; since 1945 no M.P. can be a member – which provision guided the Labour Government? The staff of the National Assistance and Central Land Boards are civil servants – is this a normal feature of the chosen instrument? The Regional Hospital Boards are financed almost wholly from annual parliamentary appropriations; the statute constituting them declares that they act 'on behalf of the Minister', and questions can be asked in the House of Commons about their work – are these also features of the chosen instrument? The constitutions of the National Coal Board, British Transport Commission, and of the boards of the other nationalized industries have none of these features.

There are perhaps two lines of defence against this criticism. The simpler is to say that what is significant in the general statement is that the Labour Government decided not to use either ministerial departments or local authorities but some other kind of body one or more stages removed from a popularly elected assembly. A public corporation would thus be any government administrative body which is neither a ministerial department nor a local authority. This is fair, but if that is all that it is, why not say it in this simple way? And is it implied that so long as this particular (and somewhat negative) characteristic is present, none of the other constitutional features has any significance? A second possible defence is to draw a distinction between significant features and incidental details and imply that the latter may vary considerably without affecting the claim of a body to be called a public corporation. There is obviously something in this: the number of members of a board and their tenure of office may vary without changing the constitutional character of the body. But are all the above differences of this kind? Is it purely a matter of detail whether the board has an independent source of finance or receives all its money by way of annual parliamentary appropriations, or whether its members are appointed by the Minister or elected by consumers or workers? In fairness to recent writers it should be said that most of them are aware that there are significant differences. This explains, in part, various attempts to distinguish industrial and social service corporations and references to 'more modern types'[1] or the 'modern "classical" public corporation'.[2] An article in *The Times*[3] called the BBC 'a unique hybrid not possessing all the attributes of a public corporation', and Mr Gladden[4] has said that the National Assistance Board is not a 'real' public corporation and the Forestry Commission is a 'quasi' one.

We are still a long way from being out of the wood. There are two problems. (1) Even if we admit that public corporations are neither government departments nor local authorities, how do we in practice distinguish these three classes of administrative authority? (2) If there are important constitutional differences between the large number of bodies included in the public corporation class, should we not subdivide or somehow indicate more clearly the particular set of characteristics we have in mind when making general statements involving the use of the term?

[1] W. A. Robson, *Problems of Nationalized Industry*, p. 21.
[2] A. M. de Neuman, 'Some Economic Aspects of Nationalization', in *Law and Contemporary Problems*, Autumn, 1951, p. 722.
[3] 20 Jan. 1947.
[4] *An Introduction to Public Administration*, 2nd edition, 1952, pp. 129, 136.

Both these problems arise whether we adopt the more limited or the more extensive use. The more limited use does not run up against the second problem to quite the same extent, for certain differences are likely to be excluded by definition and the group will be smaller. But significant differences would still remain because I assume that the differences in the methods of electing the Port of London Authority and the National Coal Board or in the financial basis of the BBC and the CEB are important enough to make it unwise to conceal them by using a single group-name without qualifications. What follows, therefore, does not depend on whether we use the term 'public corporation' in its limited or extensive meaning or even on the term being used. Instead I assume that there is a wide range of administrative bodies other than government departments or local authorities which, until we have agreed a group-name or names for them, I will call the 'rest'.

III. ANALYSIS AND CLASSIFICATION

(a) *Bodies Excluded*

Before attempting to deal with these two problems I propose to exclude two kinds of bodies: (i) those which are not legal entities, and (ii) those which are private or non-governmental.

(i) *Corporate and other bodies.* It is convenient to exclude bodies which are not corporations or legal persons but are only part of a corporation.[1] The Divisional Coal Boards, for example, are parts of the National Coal Board, but the Area Gas and Electricity Boards, are legal entities. Regional or Local Offices under a Minister and the committees of a local authority would also be excluded. A number of advisory committees, particularly local ones, would not be included, but I suspect that such statutory committees as the Central Advisory Councils for Education and the Health Services Advisory Council and also the statutory Consumers' Councils would be included.

(ii) *Public and private bodies.* Sometimes 'public' and 'governmental' are used as synonyms, but it is preferable to speak of governmental and non-governmental bodies instead of public and private (or non-public) bodies. The words 'public' and 'private' have a considerable emotive content for many people and bring in matters not strictly relevant to the classification of governmental bodies.

---

[1] A corporation is an artificial person endowed with the capacity of perpetual succession. It can sue and be sued, grant or receive, and perform any act, by its corporate name.

Thus some might argue that Oxford University was a public body in a way that Unilevers could not be said to be. It would be less easy to argue that it was a governmental body.

What test(s), then, can be applied to decide whether a body is governmental? One test might be whether the body was set up by an Act of Parliament or Royal Charter. This is too general. Most companies which operated gas and electricity undertakings before nationalization were 'statutory', and so were railway and canal companies, but I do not think that anybody claimed them to be governmental bodies. Another possible test might be whether the body obtained all or part of its annual revenues directly or indirectly from either national or local taxes; but by no means all bodies which receive Exchequer grants can be said to be governmental, for example the Universities, the British Institute of Management, the Institute of Public Administration, the Royal Society, and the National Council of Social Service. And I do not think the non-profit-making test is particularly helpful (the Post Office is not the less a government body because it has a surplus each year); neither is the test whether the stated object of the body is the achievement of some public good – the Royal Society for the Prevention of Cruelty to Children (or to Animals for that matter) is not a governmental body.

My inclination is to say that a governmental body is one in which the governing person or body is either elected under the usual electoral system of the State or is appointed by one or more persons who have been so elected. There are certain minor difficulties with this definition, e.g. the appointing person may be Her Majesty or a member of the House of Lords. Both these cases could be taken as implied in the British system or the definition could easily be altered to cover them. More difficult is the London Passenger Transport Board, which would fail to qualify as a governmental body because its members were appointed by Appointing Trustees.[1] Perhaps the fact that the members were removable by the Minister 'for inability or misbehaviour' after consultation with the Appointing Trustees should be given due weight, for the right to remove may be as important as the right to appoint. If so, the definition should be altered to read 'appointed or removable by'. Perhaps I should be prepared to let this one stick out like a sore thumb. At least my test

---

[1] My definition must be interpreted to include corporate bodies appointed by governmental bodies, e.g. the publicly-owned iron and steel companies, the boards of directors of which are appointed by the Iron and Steel Corporation. The Appointing Trustees and the LPTB can hardly be said to have been in this relationship.

261

throws up sharply the problem of public accountability when members of governing bodies are neither elected nor appointed by the elected.

With whatever definition there will be an overlap between government bodies and the non-government bodies. These are often called 'mixed undertakings' or 'mixed corporations'. Popular on the Continent, there are also examples in Britain. Thus the Manchester Ship Canal has a board of up to twenty-one directors of whom those appointed by the Manchester City Council must always be in a majority of one. The chairman is appointed by the private shareholders and the deputy chairman by the City Council. The Port of London Authority is also a mixed corporation according to my definition, for though nine of the members of the board are appointed by a Minister or a local council, the remainder are elected by the wharfingers and certain other users of the port. I am not worried by this result, for I have thought for some time that it was misleading to include the Port of London Authority, and for that matter the Mersey Docks and Harbour Board, in exactly the same category as the National Coal Board and the British Transport Commission.

(b) Administrative Bodies

There are many more governmental bodies than can be covered by the three terms – governmental departments, local authorities, and public corporations (even with the widest definition). I am dealing with Administrative bodies. There are also Judicial and Legislative bodies and bodies whose sole function is to inquire and report or to advise. Advisory bodies could be treated either as a completely separate group or could be attached to the category of Administrative body which they advise. But it is very doubtful whether there is any point in mixing them with Administrative bodies for the purpose of this classification. No broad classification can avoid some bodies appearing in two or more categories. Ministerial departments are primarily administrative, but may also have judicial and legislative functions. But the purpose of this exercise is not to force all British institutions into tidy boxes and to make the 'boxes' the main aim of discussion.

It seems to me that what most people have been trying to stress in recent years is that there are three[1] main categories of administrative bodies: (1) ministerial departments; (2) local authorities; and (3) the

[1] In the 2nd edition of his *Cabinet Government* (1951) Sir Ivor Jennings divides the Administration into Departmental, Local Government, and Independent Authority Administration (p. 90). In Appendix III he classifies such bodies as

rest – the 'rest' going under a variety of titles often involving the use of the words 'independent', 'autonomous', 'semi-independent', or 'quasi'. What tests can we apply to particular bodies to decide in which category they should be put?[1]

The names of the bodies, e.g. the Board of Trade, the National Coal Board, and the Board of Guardians, do not help. The area covered is also not an infallible guide even as between departments and local authorities; few, if any, would classify the New Town Development Corporations or the Area Gas and Electricity Boards as local authorities.

What people are emphasizing when they speak of public corporations, semi-autonomous boards and the like, is that such boards do not have full and direct responsibility to an elected body, usually Parliament. In the British Constitution it is an individual Minister who is normally responsible; nowadays powers are not usually given to a department as a corporate body, e.g. they are given to the Minister and not to the Ministry of Health. When, therefore, powers are given to a Minister and are exercisable in his name we have a ministerial department. If, however, the statutory powers are given to some named body other than a Minister, the assumption is that this body belongs to the 'rest' unless it is a local authority. In a unitary State a local authority can be distinguished by the functions being exercised by or in the name of a council elected by the electors for an area less than the area of the whole country. In other words the Minister and Parliament and the Local Council are directly responsible to the electors, whereas the other administrative bodies (i.e. the rest) are not.

So far as the central government is concerned the major difficulty in applying this distinction is that convention has made particular Ministers wholly responsible for the work of certain administrative bodies even though the powers are given to a board and not to a single, named Minister. This presents little difficulty when the convention is quite clear, e.g. in the case of the Board of Trade and Treasury, or where a Minister's responsibility has been formally indicated, e.g. for the Board of Admiralty, Air and Army Councils, and for the Boards of Customs and Excise and of Inland Revenue.

the British Council, Central Land Board, and National Assistance Board as departments not represented in Parliament (p. 529).

[1] Professor Friedmann says the public corporation is distinguished by its 'functional character' from the Crown and from local authorities which are multi-purpose authorities. But are the New Town Development Corporations and the Colonial Development Corporation really less multi-purpose than the small Borough or Urban District Council or than the Ministry of Civil Aviation?

But what of the National Debt Office, the Commissioners of Crown Lands, the Public Works Loan Board, the Tithe Redemption Commission – are these also in effect a Minister under another name and, therefore, to be excluded from the 'rest'?

There are two possible lines of approach here. The first would be to stick to what was laid down in the Acts, charters, or other instruments which established the body and set out its constitutional position. If there is a board with its own powers and duties and there is no declaration to the effect that all these powers and duties are exercisable in the name of a Minister, then it is not a ministerial department. We need not go to the length of treating the Board of Trade and Treasury in this manner where there is a clear and well-understood convention that the departmental name usually means a particular Minister. But otherwise we would classify according to an examination of the statutory position of the body and not inquire how this worked in practice. The advantage of this approach is that it avoids the need for judgment on just how influential in practice is the Minister – a method which if adopted for these bodies might well have to be applied to many other bodies in the 'rest', e.g. the NCB. The big difficulty is that the outward and visible statutory signs may not reveal the real position.

A practical approach, which at the same time avoids the difficulties associated with a detailed inquiry into the precise degree of ministerial responsibility would be to classify according to whether questions could be asked of the Minister in the House of Commons about the day-to-day affairs of the body. (This would be a test applicable only in Britain and countries having our system of the Parliamentary Question.) If the Minister or the Clerk at the Table could on any matter[1] refuse to accept the question on the ground that the matter was the responsibility of the body, then that body must be included in the 'rest'. In practice there might not be a great deal of difference in the two lines of approach, for where a board has clear statutory responsibility for some function a Minister will not normally accept responsibility to Parliament for the board's exercise of its discretion.

The local authority category is less difficult, though there may be marginal cases. The Local Government Act, 1933, defines a local authority as 'the council of a county borough, county district or rural parish'. The Rating and Valuation Act, 1925, defines it as 'any body

---

[1] Only if the Minister is totally and not merely partially responsible for the board can it be said to be part of a ministerial department. A Minister will usually have some statutory powers of control over the board and for these he cannot escape responsibility to Parliament.

having power to levy a rate or to issue a precept to a rating authority'. The former definition is too limited, the latter too wide. The two key characteristics are, I suggest: the jurisdiction of the body is limited to an area less than the area of the country and its governing body is elected by the people of that area, though the right to levy a tax on the citizens in its area may be regarded by many as another essential feature. Joint Boards would be part of the local 'rest' as being bodies appointed by and therefore owing some responsibility to the local authorities. The New Town Development Corporations being appointed by a Minister and not by a local authority would be included in the national 'rest', even though their jurisdiction is limited to a particular locality. The former School Boards and Boards of Guardians would, of course, be included in local authorities, as would the London Passenger Transport Board have been had the board been elected by the local government electors for its area.

To sum up:

i. A ministerial department is a Minister of the Crown to whom powers have been given either explicitly by name of his office or in the name of a body which by convention or declaration is clearly understood to mean that Minister.

ii. A local authority is a council with its powers and duties confined to a local area and elected by the electors of that area.

iii. Any governmental administrative body which has its own statutory powers and responsibilities and is neither a Minister nor a local authority is part of the 'rest'. It does not matter if this includes a number of bodies which are in practice completely or very nearly subordinate branches of a ministerial department. It will be the purpose of the remaining part of this essay to discuss the range of independence which bodies in the 'rest' may have.

It will be seen that by this method a public corporation or whatever the 'rest' is called is defined negatively. In part this is due to certain positive characteristics having been disposed of when the distinction between governmental and other bodies was discussed. In part it is that these bodies are so diverse that until analysed no simple definition is of much use.

IV. THE REST

There are several hundred governmental administrative bodies which are neither ministerial departments nor local authorities, and their characteristics are too diverse to warrant generalizations being made

265

about them as though they were a homogeneous group. There is, therefore, an obvious need to classify them so that general statements may be made which will be true of all bodies in a particular category. Professor Friedmann has suggested[1] a threefold division:

(1) commercial corporations 'designed to run an industry or public utility according to economic and commercial principles . . .';
(2) social service corporations 'designed to carry out a particular social service on behalf of the Government';
(3) supervisory public corporations having 'essentially administrative and supervisory functions'. They do not engage in commercial transactions either to fulfil their main objective or incidentally to the performance of a social service.

Griffith and Street[2] give the three types the titles of 'managerial-economic', 'managerial-social', and 'regulatory-social' bodies. In a footnote they appear to add a fourth category – the 'regulatory-economic'.

Sir Arthur Street has discussed quasi-government bodies under three headings:

(i) Regulatory bodies (non-industrial) – i.e. bodies used for departmental administration carried on by other means, e.g. Central Land Board.
(ii) Regulatory bodies (industrial) – bodies concerned with the relationships between Government and private industry, e.g. the Marketing Boards.
(iii) Managerial bodies – including the large State industrial and trading corporations.

He thinks, however, that though the classification is convenient for purposes of exposition it is 'imperfect and artificial' and that it is unsafe to generalize about quasi-government bodies, for 'a new species often suggests a new genus'.[3]

H. R. Greaves has put forward a different classification.[4] He dislikes the attempted distinction between economic and social services as being on occasion artificial or arbitrary. He prefers a classification based on an analysis of the reasons for setting up such bodies. He says there are four types: Regional, e.g. the many Port Authorities;

[1] 'The Legal Status and Organization of the Public Corporation', *Law and Contemporary Problems*, Autumn 1951, p. 579.

[2] *Principles of Administrative Law*, 1952, pp. 271–5.

[3] *British Government since 1918*, p. 160.

[4] *Civil Service in the Changing State* (1947), pp. 105 ff.

Quasi-Judicial, e.g. the Civil Service Commission, the Import Duties Advisory Committee, and the Electricity Commission; Trusteeship bodies (for the management of property on behalf of others), e.g. the Charity Commission; and Administrative or Managerial (of a national service), e.g. the National Coal Board.

Wade and Phillips mention four categories of 'independent authorities':

(i) authorities which administer purely governmental services and make discretionary payments out of public funds, e.g. the National Assistance Board;

(ii) authorities which receive grants from public funds to expend at their discretion on cultural activities, e.g. the British Council (said to be in a comparable category to (i));

(iii) authorities[1] concerned with the production of coal, electricity, gas, and iron and steel;

(iv) a most diversified group concerned with a variety of economic controls of enterprises, the ownership of which remains in private hands, e.g. agricultural marketing boards. They also include in this category 'a number of licensing, registration and rate-fixing bodies, exercising powers of a quasi-judicial character', e.g. Area Traffic Commissioners and the Transport Tribunal.

Classification by purpose or function has its uses. For some matters it is obviously important to deal separately with trading and regulatory bodies, just as earlier we distinguished between judicial, administrative, and advisory bodies. The classification suggested by Professor Friedmann would seem to be the most useful, though his definitions are rather loose and not altogether happy. And I suspect that there are many bodies which would fall outside his three categories, e.g. the Civil Service Commission, the War Damage Commission, and the Charity Commission. His third category by no means includes everything left after the commercial and social service corporations have been taken out. In such a functional classification the commercial corporation corresponds to the public corporation in its early meaning. As the adjective 'public' applies equally well to all these bodies, there is something to be said for the descriptions 'commercial' (or 'industrial'), 'social service' (or just 'social'), and

[1] Of these they say rather startlingly: 'the new authority does not fit naturally into the age-long triple classification of governmental functions—executive, legislative and judicial; this classification is unsuited to any industrial or commercial undertaking'.

'regulatory' (or 'supervisory'). Until there has been much more analysis of the functions performed by these bodies some such broad analysis will have to suffice.

The weakness of the functional classification from the viewpoint of the political scientist (and, I suspect, of the lawyer) is that constitutional characteristics do not correspond with functional. True, the separation of commercial from other corporations is almost equivalent to the important distinction between bodies with independent sources of revenue and those which obtain revenues from parliamentary appropriations. But that is about all the constitutional characteristics which are so revealed, and even this conceals the fact that the Electricity Commission (which presumably would be called a regulatory corporation) had its own source of revenue by way of a levy on electricity supply undertakings.

We must also have a system of classification which throws further light on or pays regard to the main characteristics of the 'rest' – their 'independence' or 'semi-independence' or 'autonomy'. We have seen that the main distinction between the ministerial department and local authority on the one hand and these other bodies is that the former are under the direct management of elected representatives whereas the latter are at one stage removed from this. In the British political system there has developed a clear if perhaps over-simplified view of the position of the elected representative – he is accountable to the electorate, and they have a chance to remove him at an election held periodically. Moreover, there have been developed well-accepted methods of controlling the departmental activities of Ministers and councillors and the finances of their departments and of bringing home their accountability. However many reservations may be added, there seems to be an important difference in quality between the position of the Minister, M.P., or councillor and of the appointed members of the various boards.

The giving of statutory powers and duties to bodies not under the direct management of elected representatives places these bodies outside the normal system of control and accountability. The extent to which they are outside will depend, however, on two things: the extent to which they have characteristics similar to those which provide the opportunities for parliamentary control of the departments, and the extent to which the Minister has statutory powers of control over or intervention in their affairs. What we must analyse and assess, therefore, are these key points. (For purposes of simplicity I am concerned here with the contrast between the ministerial department and bodies appointed by Ministers, though the same kind of contrast could be made between local authorities and independent bodies appointed by local authorities.)

There are a number of possible elements. I have room to deal briefly with four:

1. *Finance*

Finance is a far-reaching element in all forms of political control. So far as annual revenue for current expenditure is concerned there are three simple forms of the finance of governmental bodies: (*a*) own, independent source, e.g. from sales (NCB) or levies (Electricity Commission); (*b*) parliamentary appropriation in the normal manner (detailed estimates, &c.); and (*c*) parliamentary Grant-in-Aid – usually this need not be accounted for in detail to Parliament nor need the unspent balance of the money secured be surrendered at the end of the year.[1]

Bodies in category (*b*), e.g. National Assistance Board and Civil Service Commission, must submit detailed estimates to the Treasury and to Parliament, are covered by the rules governing *virement*, etc., are audited by the C. and A.G., and are subject to the detailed scrutiny of the Estimates and Public Accounts Committees. Bodies in category (*c*), e.g. the Arts Council and the Medical Research Council,[2] are subject to a modified and much more limited form of this control. But bodies in category (*a*), e.g. the British Electricity Authority, offer no such opportunities.

Some bodies come into two categories. Thus the two Airways Corporations receive Grants as subsidies to their income from operations. The position of the BBC is peculiar in that its main revenue from the sale of licences is collected by the Post Office and paid to it in the form of a Grant and it also receives a substantial Grant-in-Aid for its Overseas Services (perhaps it was the uncertainty of its financial position which caused the author of *The Times* article to call it a hybrid corporation).

So far as borrowing for capital expenditure is concerned, here again there are important differences: (*a*) Borrowing on the body's own credit by way of its own named stock (e.g. British Electricity Stock). (Such borrowing may be with or without a Treasury guarantee.) (*b*) Borrowing from the Treasury with an obligation to repay (e.g. the

[1] For recent developments in this device see Fourth Report, Public Accounts Committee 1950/51, and J. W. Grove, 'Grants-in-Aid to Public Bodies', *Public Administration*, Winter 1952.

[2] A recent Treasury memorandum (Appendix 4 to the Fourth Report of the Public Accounts Committee 1950/51) lists 150 bodies in receipt of a Grant-in-Aid. Many of these are not governmental bodies according to my definition.

NCB). Such loans appear in the Annual Estimates and Appropriation Accounts. (*c*) Finance of capital expenditure out of a Parliamentary Grant-in-Aid (e.g. most bodies which receive such Grants-in-Aid). (*d*) Finance of capital expenditure by way of the ordinary parliamentary appropriation (e.g. all bodies whose annual expenditure is financed in the normal departmental manner). And for the sake of completeness I should add: (*e*) Finance of capital expenditure out of the board's independent annual income (e.g. the BBC until quite recently).

Obviously, other things being equal, a body which has its own independent source of annual income and can finance its capital expenditure by borrowing in the market on its own credit is likely to be subject to much less parliamentary (and therefore ministerial) control than is a body financed wholly out of annual parliamentary appropriations of the usual departmental kind. This is, of course, what Professors Robson and Friedmann and others have been stressing in distinguishing between public corporations operating commercial and industrial enterprises and all other 'semi-independent' boards. This is why the former can be so independent. It is this method of analysis rather than a functional analysis which throws up the significant constitutional differences. Moreover, it indicates that there are different degrees of financial independence.

2. *Character and Tenure of the Board*
This is a complicated and little-explored aspect of the matter. In the space available I will content myself with three illustrations of what I have in mind:

(*a*) In Canada and Australia, and possibly in other countries, it is not uncommon for serving civil servants to be appointed to membership of governmental boards. It is not the practice in this country. If, however, the Minister of Fuel and Power were to appoint the Permanent Secretary of his Ministry and several other of his senior civil servants to membership of, say, the British Electricity Authority and they continued to serve him in his department, the implication would surely be that the BEA would then be less independent.

(*b*) It is possible that the Minister or M.P.s may be members of the body. Our constitutional rule that M.P.s cannot hold offices of profit under the Crown, and the statutory provisions in many of the Acts establishing the boards prevent M.P.s being members. But in some cases M.P.s and even Ministers could be members (and in some countries this is the practice). We have the interesting example of the Charity Commission, a governmental body represented in

Parliament by an M.P. who is also a Commissioner. Where a Minister is a member, e.g. the National Debt Office, there may be an inference that the body is part of the ministerial department, but the Church Commission contains a number of Ministers and yet none is answerable for its decisions. There are obviously possible variations in the relationship between a board and Parliament, depending on the position of M.P.s as members of the board.

(c) Sometimes the members of a board are given no statutory security of tenure and are removable at the will of the Minister, whereas in other cases the Statute lays down a minimum period of years or in other ways gives them security. Security of tenure is obviously a difficult concept to pin down, for much depends on convention; the British civil servant, for example, has no statutory security of tenure though in practice it is difficult to dismiss him once he is established. Even so, if on examining the statutory provisions governing the membership of two different governmental boards I found that in one case the members could be removed only by a special and complicated process and tenure in the other case was at the Minister's sole discretion, I would be inclined to say that the former would be likely to be the more independent body.

3. *Ministerial Powers*

Most Acts establishing governmental bodies, in addition to prescribing the constitution, powers, and duties of the body, also enable or require some Minister to exercise some control over the operations of the body. Thus the Minister's approval may be required before the board can do certain necessary things, e.g. acquire land, or borrow for capital expenditure. Sometimes the Minister must participate in the action before it can become effective, e.g. approving schemes prepared by the Electricity Commissioners or by the Coal Commission (prior to the recent nationalization Acts abolishing these two bodies). Occasionally, as with the recently nationalized industries, the Minister may issue general directions which a board must carry out; and Statutory Instruments may require to be submitted to Parliament by a Minister, e.g. the National Assistance Board's scale of assistance. The statutory powers of Ministers in respect of the various boards may vary in two ways. On the one hand, the number of points at which he may exercise control varies from board to board and quite substantially. In some Acts the Minister is hardly mentioned (e.g. in the London Transport Act, 1933), whereas in others there is little of significance that the board can do without the Minister having some say (e.g. the National

Health Service Act, 1946, and the Regional Hospital Boards). On the other hand, each point of control is not of equal significance. The power to issue general directions may be more important than the power to prescribe the form of accounts. And there is the further question whether the Minister can exercise any major control not specifically provided for by Statute but arising out of custom or some general weakness in the position of a board.

We know both from the contents of the Acts and from observation that the powers of control exercised by Ministers over the various bodies included in the 'rest' vary considerably. Therefore if we are to classify these bodies according to their degree of independence, some method will have to be found to allow for these variations, but it may have to be a rough and ready assessment.

Perhaps I should add one other point. Ministers are responsible to Parliament for the exercise (or the non-exercise) of all their statutory powers and duties. Thus the more statutory powers of control possessed by a Minister in respect of a particular board the more the affairs of the board are directly the concern of Parliament.

4. *Staff*

A small point but one frequently stressed by supporters of the 'public corporation' is freedom from Civil Service rules. This is at present true of the nationalized industries but not of all the 'rest'. Most if not all the bodies financed by parliamentary appropriations are staffed by civil servants, e.g. the Central Land Board and the National Assistance Board. But those with their own sources of income are outside the Civil Service system, as indeed are most of those bodies which receive only a Grant-in-Aid. In some countries (e.g. Australia) some of the commercial corporations are subject to a Civil Service Board. In other words, freedom from normal Civil Service arrangements is not an inevitable or inescapable characteristic of these bodies.

v. CONCLUSIONS

To what purpose can we put this kind of analysis? Its humblest use would be to make us chary of all generalizations about 'public corporations' which are true only of bodies which have particular constitutional characteristics. The statement that a public corporation is a financially autonomous and independent body sounds like a definition. If one then proceeds to use the term to cover a wide range of bodies, without having made certain that they possess the characteristics of financial automomy and independence, one is in danger of confusing both oneself and the reader. A fuller awareness of the difference and a study of their significance should therefore in time lead to a more precise use of words.

More ambitiously it may be possible to develop this kind of analysis as the basis of a much more exact system of classification. Most writers on the subject stress the variety in form and in the degree of independence. If this variety is significant to the political scientist he must find some classification which takes account of it either within each functional group or for the 'rest' as a whole.

I have been sticking my neck out fairly far and a little farther is not likely to matter. There is already plenty of hostage for the hatchet. Let me sketch in a fanciful way a possible method of assessment or grading. Supposing by further research we could agree on what were the key points in control and independence and what were the significant variations in them. Would it be possible, with a greater degree of assurance than at present, to grade the bodies in some rough order of independence? We are willing to talk of quasi or semi-independent bodies: should we be willing to go further and talk of 'quarter', 'half', or 'three-quarter' independent bodies or 'most', 'middling', and 'least' independent bodies?

Supposing there are two corporations or bodies in the same country with the following key characteristics:

	Corporation A	Corporation B
Annual Income:	Parliamentary appropriation	From Sales
Borrowing:	Parliamentary appropriation	Own Stock
Composition of Board:	Mainly serving Civil Servants	Part-time business men
Tenure of Members:	Removable at Minister's discretion	Appointed for minimum period of 15 years
Minister's powers of control:	Can issue general directions and his approval required at many points	Can only control at a few minor points
Staff:	Civil Service	Not under Civil Service

Would anyone be likely to deny that, other things being equal, Corporation A would be likely to be less independent than Corporation B? Obviously the difficulty comes when the differences are not so extreme. On that I can at this stage only throw open the problem for discussion. Perhaps my academic colleagues[1] may think that solution

---

[1] I am reassured to find that Mr J. A. G. Griffith is searching for a somewhat similar kind of analysis to test whether particular public corporations are Crown

is not worth the effort or they may have a simpler approach, or more terrifyingly they may want to add a lot of reservations and complications.

Two other final points. Such terms as 'public corporation' and 'autonomous bodies' are now in international use. I have confined myself largely to British examples and my analysis is based on British constitutional arrangements. If we are muddled about the use of these terms when confined to British conditions, how much more difficult it must be to use them internationally. How far would my analysis fit the arrangements in the Commonwealth and the United States, let alone France, Russia, Sweden, and other European countries?

The other point is: how should we use the term 'public corporation' in future – in its limited sense or in its extended sense? I have a feeling that recent writings have made it difficult to continue using the term within its pre-war limits. At the same time, as it is associated in many minds with this limited meaning, I greatly hesitate to go over to its extended use. It is not a revealing title for such a large and mixed class of bodies, and I think I would prefer to use some such term as 'Independent Authorities' to cover the 'rest', with perhaps 'industrial corporation' (or even 'public industrial corporation'), and so on, to indicate particular functional groups. It would be worth while getting an agreed nomenclature.

Servants. After applying certain tests, e.g. financial dependence, he comes to the conclusion that the Central Land Board, the Regional Hospital Boards, and certain other boards are sufficiently dependent on a Minister to be regarded as Crown Servants (*Toronto Law Journal*, 1952).

19

Nationalized Industries and Parliament*

In 1968 the Report of the Select Committee on Nationalized Industries considered aspects of the accountability to Parliament of nationalized industries; in particular they were concerned with their own terms of reference. Within the British system of government the work of the Committee is, in fact, only one of about ten means of controlling nationalized industries, but its activities were being questioned in the late 1960s primarily in relation to the 'Specialist' Select Committees then introduced. For a comprehensive account and analysis of nationalized industries as agents of government see W. A. Robson, Nationalized Industry and Public Ownership (Allen & Unwin, 2nd edition, 1962).

The Select Committee appointed to examine the Reports and Accounts of the Post Office and of the Nationalized Industries established by Statute whose controlling Boards are appointed by Ministers of the Crown and whose annual receipts are not wholly or mainly derived from moneys provided by Parliament or advanced from the Exchequer, have agreed to the following Special Report:

THE COMMITTEE'S ORDER OF REFERENCE

INTRODUCTION

1. Between 1951 and 1955 the House of Commons paid attention on several occasions to the question of possible machinery for the control of nationalized industries. A short account of the various proceedings appears in Erskine May's Parliamentary Practice (Seventeenth Edition, pp. 671–2).

2. A Select Committee on Nationalized Industries (Reports and

* From *Special Report from the Select Committee on Nationalized Industries*, The Committee's Order of Reference, HMSO, H.C. 298, 1968, paras 1–23.

Accounts) on the present pattern was first set up at the end of 1956. The Order of reference of that Committee was 'to examine the Reports and Accounts of the Nationalized Industries established by Statute whose controlling Boards are appointed by Ministers of the Crown and whose annual receipts are not wholly or mainly derived from moneys provided by Parliament or advanced from the Exchequer'. The Orders of reference of Committees of succeeding Sessions have remained unaltered, except only that from Session 1965–66 onwards the Post Office was specifically included by name.

3. The term 'Nationalized Industries' does not appear to have been further defined to or by succeeding Select Committees on Nationalized Industries (although in answer to a written question on 27 July 1954 the Prime Minister gave a list of the industries which would fall within a different Order of reference then under discussion, *viz.* BOAC, BEA, the National Coal Board, the British Electricity Authority, the Gas Council, the North of Scotland Hydro-Electric Board and the British Transport Commission). But Your Committee believe that, whatever bodies might be held to be included by that term, where the assets of a whole industry or the major part of an industry have been statutorily acquired by the state, the industries concerned have, beyond dispute, been within their Order of reference. In addition, the Order of reference has been applied without difficulty to BEA and the North of Scotland Hydro-Electric Board (which had only a limited history of private ownership behind them), to BOAC which was the successor Corporation to Imperial Airways and to London Transport, although that is not a whole industry; and Your Committee have regarded the British Airports Authority as within their Order of reference, although the Authority does not manage all United Kingdom airports, and the management of the assets of the Authority was originally the direct responsibility of the various Departments in charge of civil aviation, and until the passing of the Airports Authority Act 1965, provision for the management was carried on the Estimates.

4. The Post Office was specifically added to the Order of reference by name; until legislation is passed establishing a controlling Board for it, it remains statutorily subject to administration direct by the Postmaster General, and whether or not the Post Office is a 'nationalized industry', since it has no 'controlling board' and was not 'established by Statute' it does not meet the definition of the original Order of reference.

5. Since 1956 Select Committees with this Order of reference have reported on the North of Scotland Hydro-Electric Board, the National

Coal Board, the two Air Corporations (BOAC and BEA), British Railways, the Gas Industry, the Electricity Supply Industry, BOAC, London Transport, the Post Office and BEA.

6. In addition to the British Airports Authority already mentioned, Your Committee consider that their present Order of reference also clearly covers the British Steel Corporation, the South of Scotland Electricity Board and (at any rate until the Transport Bill now before Parliament comes into effect), the Transport Holding Company, the British Waterways Board and the British Transport Docks Board. But these bodies have never been the subject of an investigation by any Nationalized Industries Committee.

7. But can any other bodies owned or controlled by the Government be held to be already within the Order of reference? Or alternatively, if all other bodies are held to be excluded, should future Committees be given a different Order of reference which would include some other bodies? In this Special Report, Your Committee do not wish to argue an answer to the first question at length. Future Committees will not wish to act otherwise than within the intentions of the House in appointing those Committees; and they will accordingly not wish to start inquiries in an atmosphere of doubt as to the propriety of their proceedings.

8. This Special Report therefore takes the more radical course of considering which, if any, other bodies ought to be included within the Order of reference of future Committees. But in considering the position of particular bodies, comments are made as to why the body concerned might be held to be outside the present Order of reference; and it will emerge from these comments that the application of the Order of reference has been somewhat haphazard in its effect, simply because 'nationalized industries' have been defined in the Order of reference only in terms of their legal structure.

OBJECTS OF PAST INQUIRIES OF SELECT COMMITTEES ON NATIONALIZED INDUSTRIES

9. Just as the term 'nationalized industries' is less than clear, so there has been no definition of what is meant by 'examine the Reports'. Your Committee believe that the House's original intention in setting up Select Committees on Nationalized Industries was to meet the wishes of Members who desired to study the affairs of the industries, but were largely prevented from doing so by means of Questions in the House, owing to the rule that Questions could not be asked about the day-to-day working of the industries. A further

major consideration was the amount of state capital committed to investment in the industries, and the attendant liabilities of the Exchequer.

10. At that time provision on the Estimates for anything related to the activities of the industries was a rare occurrence, as it still is for many of the industries. It was thus not, in general, open to the Estimates Committee to hold inquiries into the activities of the industries.

11. It was recognized, when a Nationalized Industries Committee was first appointed, that the Committee of Public Accounts could, if they so wished, examine the Accounts of any of the industries whose Accounts are laid before the House, for that Committee are *required* under Standing Order No. 79 (Committee of Public Accounts) to examine the 'Accounts showing the appropriation of the sums granted by Parliament to meet the public expenditure', and *may* examine such other accounts laid before Parliament as they think fit. In practice, however, the Committee of Public Accounts had confined their activities mainly to examining the Appropriation Accounts and such other accounts as they had examined had almost invariably been those subject to statutory audit by the Comptroller and Auditor General. The Accounts of the nationalized industries are not subject to the Comptroller and Auditor General's audit, and accordingly very little information on the industries' activities arose from the Reports of the Committee of Public Accounts.

12. It appears that successive Nationalized Industries Committees have seen their first and primary task as to understand the general principles on which the industry under review conducts its affairs, with special reference to any instructions or guidance that it may have received from the Government of the day, to the industry's pricing and investment policies (as well as any elements of cross-subsidization implied in the policies), to the quality of the service provided by the industry and to any particular problems or difficulties with which the industry finds itself confronted.

13. At the same time successive Nationalized Industries Committees have hoped to give the industries an opportunity to answer in detail any criticisms which have been consistently raised against them in a way which is rarely possible in debates in the House, and, of course, quite impossible at Question time.

14. Former Nationalized Industries Committees appear to have considered that their object should be not to confine their Reports to spheres of activity where criticism might arise, but generally to give as much information to the House as might be thought of interest to

it, so long, of course, as the commercial interests of the industries concerned were not prejudiced.

FUTURE REVIEWS OF ACTIVITIES OF PUBLIC BODIES

(a) 'Non-Specialist' Select Committees

15. Your Committee believe that the process of seeking information by means of Select Committees has been helpful to the House. They further believe that it should be possible for the House to use its Select Committees to seek information about all areas of activity for which Ministers are ultimately responsible both where the Government is acting directly and where it is acting through agents which it actually controls or could control if it chose to do so. (In this connection they distinguish between the older-established Select Committees (Public Accounts, Estimates and Nationalized Industries) which traditionally select subjects for enquiry from a fairly wide range, and the more recently established 'specialist' Select Committees which confine their enquiries to particular subjects in science, agriculture and education.)

16. This Report (see paras 10–11) has already referred to the work of the Committee of Public Accounts and to the work of the Estimates Committee; it is clear from the Standing Orders (Nos 79 and 80) which give those Committees their Order of reference that as a matter of course direct activity by the Government is likely to fall within their field, because in general direct activity by the Government has to be paid for by the Government and will appear in the Estimates and the Appropriation Accounts accordingly.

17. In addition to the activities which are a direct charge on the Estimates, there are a considerable number of bodies financed largely by periodic advances from the Exchequer; and Parliament has frequently provided by statute either that the accounts of these bodies should be subject to audit by the Comptroller and Auditor General, or at any rate that an Account of the Exchequer advances should be so audited and separately presented to Parliament. Consideration of these accounts has commonly been regarded as within the traditional field of the Committee of Public Accounts; and it may be thought that, in providing for audit by the Comptroller and Auditor General, Parliament has clearly shown its intention to make suitable arrangements to obtain information as may be appropriate on the working of bodies of this nature.

18. There remain, however, a number of bodies set up by the

Government or acquired by the Government with substantial trading or commercial interests which provide these bodies with an income which is not 'provided by Parliament'; and some of these bodies have not so far come within the Order of reference either of Your Committee or of the Estimates Committee, nor have they been within the traditional field of the Committee of Public Accounts. It is true that many of them are required to lay their Accounts before Parliament, and may thus theoretically be subject to examination by the Committee of Public Accounts; but in fact since 1956, when a Nationalized Industries Committee first began inquiries, the Committee of Public Accounts have reported on only two accounts not subject to the Comptroller and Auditor General's audit, namely the Independent Television Authority's Accounts in Session 1958–59 and the Accounts of a particular new town corporation in Session 1963–64. In the case of the new town, it may be noted that while the accounts of the new towns corporations are not themselves subject to the Comptroller and Auditor General's audit, receipts and payments by the Government under the New Towns Acts are so subject; accordingly it may be said that the Report on the Accounts of the Independent Television Authority is the only example since 1956 of the Committee of Public Accounts making a report upon a matter outside its traditional field.

19. Your Committee refer to the traditional field of the Committee of Public Accounts at some length because it has to be remembered that the Order of reference of that Committee not only enables them to consider the Accounts of the present nationalized industries and other bodies, but actually requires them to consider, for example, the provision on the Estimates for grants to the British Railways Board which are brought to account in the Appropriation Accounts.

20. Your Committee draw attention to this potential overlap between Select Committees merely in order to emphasize that so long as the activities of any particular body can be agreed to be within the ordinary field of inquiry of one Select Committee or another, the fact that Orders of reference would theoretically enable more than one Select Committee to examine any one body should not be thought to be a serious disadvantage.

(b) 'Specialist' Select Committees

21. The recent appointment of 'Specialist' Select Committees raises again the question of possible overlapping of Select Committees. In this connection Your Committee note that the appointment of the Select Committee on Agriculture in Session 1966–67 did

not prevent the Committee of Public Accounts of that Session from considering the Appropriation Accounts of the Ministry of Agriculture with witnesses from the Ministry; and in their fifth Report (H.C. 647 (1966–67)) paragraphs 93 to 96 dealt with the wheat subsidy and paragraphs 97 to 100 dealt with the cattle subsidy.

22. Similarly the fact that the Select Committee on Science and Technology reported last Session on the United Kingdom Nuclear Reactor Programme (H.C. 381 (1966–67)) and examined witnesses from the Central Electricity Generating Board did not prevent the Select Committee on Nationalized Industries of last Session from examining the Chairmen of the Electricity Council and the Central Electricity Generating Board in the course of their own inquiry.

23. Your Committee do not believe that the present or future appointment of 'Specialist' Select Committees has much bearing on the Orders of reference of the present non-specialist Committees; the 'Specialist' Select Committees are primarily concerned with the question of what the Government's policy in their field is, and how it might be changed; but the approach of the 'non-specialist' Committees is altogether different.

20

'Hiving-off'*

*In considering how central government departments might be restruc-
tured for greater efficiency, the Fulton Committee on the Civil Service
discussed the proposal that large-scale executive operations cannot be
effectively run by government departments and that they should be
'hived-off' wherever possible to independent boards. The Committee
recommended a number of measures to increase efficiency (including
the application of accountable management and changes in the internal
structure of departments). In this extract from the Fulton Report the
Committee explains the meaning of the term and how it might be
applied in British Government.*

We return now to the question referred to in paragraph 145, whether
there are areas of Civil Service work that should be 'hived off'
from the central government machine and entrusted to autonomous
public boards or corporations. It has been put to us that accountable
management is most effectively introduced when an activity is
separately established outside any government department, and that
this solution should be adopted for many executive activities,
especially the provision of services to the community. These boards or
corporations would be wholly responsible in their own fields within
the powers delegated to them. Although they would be outside the
day-to-day control of Ministers and the scrutiny of Parliament,
Ministers would retain powers to give them directions when necessary.
There are a number of commercial enterprises within the public
sector that are already run on this principle, and it is also shortly to be
applied to part of the Civil Service by 'hiving-off' the Post Office.
There are also non-commercial activities in the public sector that are
similarly organized, for example, the Atomic Energy Authority.

* From *The Civil Service, Vol. I, Report of the Committee, 1966–68*, HMSO,
Cmnd. 3638, 1968, pp. 61–2.

We have seen such a system operating in Sweden where the principle of 'hiving-off' is much more widely applied than has so far been attempted here. In Sweden central departments deal in the main with policy-making; they are quite small and are predominantly staffed by younger men. The task of managing and operating policies is hived-off to autonomous agencies whose senior staff are mainly older men of mature experience. This system is used not only for activities of a commercial kind, but also for public services in social fields. We were much impressed by it. On the other hand, we are aware that in the United States the application of the 'hiving-off' principle, as evidenced in the work of the independent regulatory commissions, has attracted a good deal of criticism.

Much new policy is a development of that which already exists and springs from practical experience in its operation. Any complete separation of policy-making from execution could therefore be harmful. However this does not appear to happen in Sweden, and we see no reason why the risk should not be provided against. There is indeed a wide variety of activities to which it might be possible to apply the principle of 'hiving-off'. They range from the work of the Royal Mint and air traffic control to parts of the social services. We have not been able to make the detailed study which would be needed to identify particular cases; but we see no reason to believe that the dividing line between activities for which Ministers are directly responsible, and those for which they are not, is necessarily drawn in the right place today. The creation of further autonomous bodies, and the drawing of the line between them and central government, would raise parliamentary and constitutional issues, especially if they affected the answerability for sensitive matters such as the social and education services. These issues and the related questions of machinery of government are beyond our terms of reference. We think however that the possibility of a considerable extension of 'hiving-off' should be examined, and we therefore recommend an early and thorough review of the whole question.

Meanwhile, we believe that the other recommendations in this Chapter should make it possible to gain some of the benefits that could arise from 'hiving-off', even where activities and services remain the direct responsibility of Ministers, by making it possible to allocate responsibility and authority more clearly. In this connection, we attach particular importance to our proposals:

(a) to distinguish those within departments whose primary responsibility is planning for the future, from those whose main concern is the operation of existing policies or the provision of services;

(b) to establish in departments forms of organization and principles of accountable management, by which individuals and branches can be held responsible for objectively measured performance.

21

The Machinery of Government*

Lord Haldane believed that in philosophy as well as in science no systematic knowledge is sufficient in itself unless it leads up to and points to first principles; indeed, it is said that his highest praise for a colleague was that he looked for a clear principle before advising action. The Report of the Machinery of Government Committee, which he wrote himself, is one of the most important documents in the development of central administration in Britain – it was the first official report dealing with central government to review the whole system of the central executive and to propose its arrangement in accordance with a rational plan. This extract considers the principles upon which responsibilities are allocated between departments, and the way in which the functions of government are brought together in the Cabinet: 'the mainspring of all the mechanism of government'.

We have endeavoured to define in the first place the general principles which should govern the distribution of the responsibilities in question, and in the second place to illustrate the application of these principles in sufficient outline. Part I of this Report deals with the results of our enquiries under the first of these heads, and Part II with the results under the second. As regards the latter, it should be explained that we have not attempted to deal exhaustively with all the Departments of State, or to do more than give illustrations, in such detail as seemed practicable, of the manner in which the general principles laid down in Part I might be applied; the reason being that, in present circumstances, there must necessarily be great uncertainty as to the extent to which the sphere of action of the central Government may be enlarged or restricted after the war, and as to the number and functions of the Departments which will be required.

Our investigations under the first head have made it evident to us

* From *Report of the Machinery of Government Committee*, HMSO, Cd. 9230, 1918, paras 3–7 and 12–27.

that there is much overlapping and consequent obscurity and confusion in the functions of the Departments of executive Government. This is largely due to the fact that many of these Departments have been gradually evolved in compliance with current needs, and that the purposes for which they were thus called into being have gradually so altered that the later stages of the process have not accorded in principle with those that were reached earlier. In other instances Departments appear to have been rapidly established without preliminary insistence on definition of function and precise assignment of responsibility. Even where Departments are most free from these defects, we find that there are important features in which the organization falls short of a standard which is becoming progressively recognized as the foundation of efficient action.

THE CABINET

But before dealing – either generally or in detail – with Departmental organization, some reference must be made to the functions and procedure of the Cabinet, which is the mainspring of all the mechanism of Government. Its constitution and the methods of its procedure must depend to a large extent on the circumstances of the time, on the personality of the Prime Minister, and on the capacities of his principal colleagues. But we may be permitted to offer some general observations on the purposes which the Cabinet is, in our view, intended to serve and the manner in which these purposes can most effectually be carried out.

The main functions of the Cabinet may, we think, be described as:

(a) the final determination of the policy to be submitted to Parliament;

(b) the supreme control of the national executive in accordance with the policy prescribed by Parliament; and

(c) the continuous co-ordination and delimitation of the activities of the several Departments of State.

For the due performance of these functions the following conditions seem to be essential, or, at least, desirable:

(i) The Cabinet should be small in number – preferably ten or, at most, twelve;

(ii) it should meet frequently;

(iii) it should be supplied in the most convenient form with all the information and material necessary to enable it to arrive at expeditious decisions;

(iv) it should make a point of consulting personally all the Ministers whose work is likely to be affected by its decisions; and

(v) it should have a systematic method of securing that its decisions are effectually carried out by the several Departments concerned.

Org of enquiry + research.

FORMULATION OF POLICY

Turning next to the formulation of policy, we have come to the conclusion, after surveying what came before us, that in the sphere of civil government the duty of investigation and thought, as preliminary to action, might with great advantage be more definitely recognized. It appears to us that adequate provision has not been made in the past for the organized acquisition of facts and information, and for the systematic application of thought, as preliminary to the settlement of policy and its subsequent administration.

This is no new notion. There are well-known spheres of action in which the principle has been adopted of placing the business of enquiry and thinking in the hands of persons definitely charged with it, whose duty is to study the future, and work out plans and advise those responsible for policy or engaged in actual administration. The reason of the separation of work has been the proved impracticability of devoting the necessary time to thinking out organization and preparation for action in the mere interstices of the time required for the transaction of business.

But the principle ought by no means to be limited in its application to military and naval affairs. We have come to the conclusion that the business of executive Government generally has been seriously embarrassed from the incomplete application to it of similar methods. It will not be possible to apply these methods as fully in the sphere of civil government, because the exact objectives of civil administration are less obvious and less easily defined than those with which the Navy and the Army are confronted; and the elaboration of policy cannot be so readily distinguished from the business of administration. But we urge strongly (*a*) that in all Departments better provision should be made for enquiry, research, and reflection before policy is defined and put into operation; (*b*) that for some purposes the necessary research and enquiry should be carried out or supervised by a Department of Government specially charged with these duties, but working in the closest collaboration with the administrative Departments concerned with its activities; (c) that special attention should be paid to the methods of recruiting the personnel to be employed upon such work; and (d) that in all Departments the higher officials in charge of administration should have more time to devote to this portion of their duties.

The establishment in 1915, under the Lord President of the Council, of a new Department to develop and organize the knowledge required for the application of Science to Industry,[1] to keep in close touch with all Departments concerned with scientific research, to undertake researches on behalf of Departments, and to stimulate the supply of research workers, marked a stage in the recognition of a need which is not merely local or departmental, but national, and there is in our opinion good reason for extending what has been done here to other fields in which thinking is required in aid of administration.

A Cabinet with such knowledge at its disposal would, we believe, be in a position to devolve, with greater freedom and confidence than is at present the case, the duties of administration, and even of legislation. Even in countries where, as in the United States, there is a Federal Government with but little power to interfere in local administration, the value of systematic investigation and accumulation of general knowledge by Departments of the central Government, though unaccompanied by the power to apply it administratively, is regarded as of great importance; and we have come to the conclusion that where, as in this country, Parliament and the Cabinet are supreme, the analogy applies still more strongly.

The general question of devolution we do not regard as within the scope of our reference. However far in the direction of devolution Parliament may decide to go, the principle of providing the supreme Government with exact knowledge of the subject-matter to be dealt with is not the less essential. The possession of such knowledge would not, in our opinion, hinder free devolution, but would really facilitate it. We may here add that the gradual introduction of the co-operation of the Ministers of the Dominions in affairs which belong to a Cabinet now charged with the interests of the Empire as a whole, points to the probability that the organization of the kind of knowledge we have in view is likely to become requisite in new directions.

---

[1] See the Reports of the Committee of the Privy Council for Scientific and Industrial Research, 1915–16 (Cd. 8336), 1916–17 (Cd. 8718), and 1917–18 (Cd. 9144).

ALLOCATION OF FUNCTIONS BETWEEN DEPARTMENTS

In addition to the two problems of the constitution and procedure of the Cabinet, and the organization of enquiry and research, there is another which it is essential to solve for the smooth working of the executive as a whole. Upon what principle are the functions of Departments to be determined and allocated? There appear to be only two alternatives, which may be briefly described as distribution according to the persons or classes to be dealt with, and distribution according to the services to be performed. Under the former method each Minister who presides over a Department would be responsible to Parliament for those activities of the Government which affect the sectional interests of particular classes of persons, and there might be, for example, a Ministry for Paupers, a Ministry for Children, a Ministry for Insured Persons, or a Ministry for the Unemployed. Now the inevitable outcome of this method of organization is a tendency to Lilliputian administration. It is impossible that the specialized service which each Department has to render to the community can be of as high a standard when its work is at the same time limited to a particular class of persons and extended to every variety of provision for them, as when the Department concentrates itself on the provision of one particular service only, by whomsoever required, and looks beyond the interests of comparatively small classes.

The other method, and the one which we recommend for adoption, is that of defining the field of activity in the case of each Department according to the particular service which it renders to the community as a whole. Thus a Ministry of Education would be concerned predominantly with the provision of education wherever, and by whomsoever, needed. Such a Ministry would have to deal with persons in so far only as they were to be educated, and not with particular classes of persons defined on other principles. This method cannot, of course, be applied with absolute rigidity. The work of the Education Department, for example, may incidentally trench on the sphere of Health, as in the arrangements of school houses and care for the health of scholars. Such incidental overlapping is inevitable, and any difficulties to which it may give rise must in our opinion be met by systematic arrangements for the collaboration of Departments jointly interested in particular spheres of work. But notwithstanding such necessary qualifications, we think that much would be gained if the distribution of departmental duties were guided by a general principle, and we have come to the conclusion that distribu-

K   289

tion according to the nature of the service to be rendered to the community as a whole is the principle which is likely to lead to the minimum amount of confusion and overlapping. In this way such divisions of the business of Government as Health, Education, Finance, Research, Foreign Affairs, and Defence would each be under separate administration, the Cabinet being in a position of supreme executive direction, and Parliament holding the various Ministers directly responsible to it for the efficiency of the service with which they were respectively charged.

It is, moreover, only by distributing business between Departments on this principle that the acquisition of knowledge and the development of specialized capacity by those engaged in the several Departments can be encouraged to the full. These results are obviously most likely to be secured when the officers of a Department are continuously engaged in the study of questions which all relate to a single service, and when the efforts of the Department are definitely concentrated upon the development and improvement of the particular service which the Department exists to supervise.

It will be noticed that in certain cases the two principles of distribution which we have contrasted, namely, that of allocation according to the class of persons dealt with, and that of allocation according to the nature of the service rendered to the community, may lead to an identical concentration of functions. Thus, the great service of National Defence, which (whether given to one, or to two or to three Ministries) is essentially distinct from the function of the other Ministries, is also marked off by dealing, principally and specifically, with the large number of persons employed by the Government in all the various branches of the naval, military, and air services. In like manner, if the railways and canals should be nationalized, it would be necessary to make the administration of this great service of National Transport a separate Department, whether we had regard to the nature of the service thus rendered to the community, or to the dealings with so extensive a staff as would have to be employed. In short, there are, in relation to such nationalized services, two distinct forms of expert capacity which it is essential that the organization should develop. One of these is ability in the recruitment, promotion, co-ordination, and direction of a large body of persons of different grades and capacities, engaged in a common enterprise of a peculiar nature. It is this part of the work which tends to take up a large, and hitherto perhaps the greater, part of the time and thought of the Minister and his principal advisers. The other form of special ability in such nationalized occupations, certainly no less important, but of a different nature, is ability for the fulfilment of the technical requirements of the service which the Department has to render to the community. Thus, the Minister in charge of the Post Office is responsible to Parliament, both for the elaboration of a progressively increasing efficiency in the services which the Department undertakes for the community as a whole, such as the national systems of communication and remittance; and for the proper organization of a very large staff of employees.

We may conclude that where any great enterprise is nationalized – in the sense of being carried out, in the main, by persons in direct Government employment – as is the case with regard to National Defence and the Postal and Telegraph service, and as may possibly be the case with regard to railways and the coal supply, such an administration must form the sphere of a separate Ministry or Ministries.

It is with regard to other functions of Government – those that we may term services of administrative supervision or control – that the contrast between the principle of distribution of work among Departments according to the class of persons to be dealt with, and the principle of distribution according to the service to be rendered, becomes more acute.

Even if the principle of allocation by services which we suggest is fully applied, cases will continue to arise in which consultation or discussion will be required between Departments, and decisions will be sought from the Cabinet, as to the allocation of new, or the redistribution of existing duties. Each of the Departments may maintain that the duties in question partake mainly of the nature of the service entrusted to the Department's general supervision, and that the proper development of that service will therefore not be secured if the primary responsibility for these duties is placed elsewhere.

We are satisfied that the present existence of Departments designed to minister to particular classes of persons greatly increases the complexity of such problems by introducing cross-divisions into the main division by services which ought to prevail. We think that if the functions of Departments could be distributed among Ministries organized mainly on the other principle, it would be easier to determine the allocation to its appropriate Department of any particular function.

We suggest that, if this were done, all decisions to concentrate functions in particular Departments should, subject to the main principle of allocation by services, be governed by the extent to which particular functions conduce to the primary end of that Department's administration. This distinction between dominant and subordinate interests in a given piece of work cannot be absolute or irrevocable. It must be drawn for practical purposes, and the decisions which follow from it will rightly be reversed if in process of time a subordinate interest becomes, even temporarily, a dominant one.

The distinction cannot be absolute, because work which is of primary interest to one Department may well be within the province of that Department even when some portion of it is also undertaken as a secondary interest by Departments devoted to other ends. If, as we suggest, there should be one Ministry of Education, of Health, and of Finance, in which functions relating primarily to those ends should in each case be concentrated, there must at the same time be, within other Ministries, special branches devoted to educational, hygienic, or financial work as secondary interests of the Ministries within which they lie. Yet neither the Ministries of the primary interests nor the branches dealing with the secondary interests can operate with full effect unless they are in close and constant touch with each other. Sometimes this communication will need to be so close that there will have to be standing joint bodies of the Departments concerned. We refer in Part II of this Report to existing arrangements of this kind, and we think that there are many cases in which the introduction of a similar procedure would be found helpful. Sometimes regular or informal communication on specific questions will suffice. But contact of some kind is vital if the service in question is not to languish in Departments in which it is secondary, and if the Department in which it is primary is to exercise its full potentiality for making whatever contribution lies in its power to the general maintenance of the highest possible standard in all branches of the work upon which its main forces are concentrated.

22

Administrative Change*

D. N. CHESTER AND F. M. G. WILLSON

The machinery of central government in Britain has not been established from basic principles at any one time, but has grown and been modified in relation to a number of variable factors. On occasions, such as in the Report of the Machinery of Government Committee, there have been attempts to rationalize it or reform it in terms of certain principles, but recent history has demonstrated that it cannot be simply explained by applying a few generally accepted criteria. In this extract Professor F. M. G. Willson surveys a number of the factors that have effected administrative change in the half-century beginning in 1914.

If any Minister or senior civil servant were asked why the work of the central administration is arranged in its present form – why there are about thirty major and a host of minor departments, and why function X is the responsibility of department Y rather than of department Z – he would probably have no ready reply. If he were asked what principles governed these arrangements he would almost certainly suspect that the questioner had in mind two or three rules or laws whose application would make it possible to decide at any moment, clearly and without room for controversy, how many departments there should be and which department should undertake this or that new function, or which would reveal whether any particular arrangement of work was 'right'. Can there be, he might ask in turn, a set of rules so clear, so mechanical and so certain, applicable to a structure of government which is the result of centuries of growth and which is so liable to be affected by the needs and the public opinion of the moment?

Our study of the experience of the years between 1914 and 1964 has convinced us that scepticism of this kind is thoroughly justified. There is no simple or single formula by whose application all the

* From D. N. Chester and F. M. G. Willson, *The Organization of British Central Government 1914–1964*, London, Allen & Unwin, 1968 (2nd edition), pp. 390–413. Reprinted with permission of the publisher.

problems of administrative arrangement can be solved. The structure of central government and the distribution of functions among departments is the result in any one case of the interplay of several of a number of possible factors, all of which must be taken into account by anyone who attempts to find the best solution to any problem of administrative structure. At the same time it would be equally wrong to swing to the other extreme and to assume that there are no rules or guides to action. Indeed, as will appear from the subsequent analysis of the factors involved, there is a good deal of knowledge and experience available for those who have to make decisions in this field.

It is not possible to infer from a study of the period 1914–64 alone the factors underlying the present distribution of functions. In the first place, the main framework of departments already existed in 1914 – the result of a long period of development. Secondly, the historical narrative does not record all the factors which were taken into account in each administrative change: in most cases it only gives the immediate and particular causes. Nor is the narrative much concerned with functions which were added to existing duties without involving any structural change. Finally, there must be brought into the reckoning certain general considerations, particularly of a basic constitutional character. The subsequent analysis is not based exclusively, therefore, on our study of the last fifty years, though where possible examples from the narrative are given to illustrate the analysis.

The main factors influencing the distribution of functions will be analysed under two headings:

      (*a*) The Number of Ministers;
      (*b*) The Grouping of Functions.

THE NUMBER OF MINISTERS

In the British system the performance of any function of the central government must always be the responsibility of some Minister who is individually answerable to Parliament. The functions of government must, in fact, be distributed among a group of Ministers. A Minister may be responsible for several departments other than his main department – called hereafter his ministry – but this does not materially affect the constitutional position. A dominant consideration bearing on the distribution of functions is, therefore, the number of Ministers among whom functions can be distributed.

A variety of factors influences the upper and lower limits to the number of departmental Ministers at any one time. In British experience the most powerful pressure forcing an increase in the number has been the relentless growth in the functions and responsibilities of the central government, which in turn has resulted in some ministries becoming too large for the Ministers to control effectively.

Size, however, is not a simple concept. The size of a ministry cannot be measured by numbers employed, for this may not by any means indicate the pressure of work and responsibility on the Minister and his senior civil servants. If it did, the Post Office would be at least 200 times more difficult for a Minister to control than is the Treasury and some 30 times more than is the Board of Trade. The number of Under and Assistant Secretaries is perhaps a better guide, particularly if those holding positions of corresponding administrative responsibility in the Services and in certain scientific and professional fields are added in the case of the Service ministries and the Ministry of Aviation. Nor is it only a question of the number of powers and statutory responsibilities, though this is a surer guide than number of employees. For some functions may involve almost entirely routine and non-controversial action and seldom raise questions requiring the attention of the Minister or his senior advisers. The ideal size for a ministry is the size that throws up no more business than can flow smoothly across the desks of the Minister and his Permanent Secretary.[a] It is also worth noticing that

[a] Various expedients have been used when the load on either the Minister or the Permanent Secretary would be too heavy. The first is the device of the Minister of State. Such Ministers may relieve the Minister of a certain amount of work, particularly where the department has to be represented abroad a good deal or where, as in the case of the Secretary of State for Scotland, the Minister often has to be away from the scene of his main administrative responsibilities. An extra Parliamentary Secretary may also help in this direction. It is not suggested that in the absence of a Minister of State the ministry would have to be divided: but his presence should make a departmental Minister's life and responsibilities more tolerable. Another device of special value when the load on the Permanent Secretary would be too great is the use of two or more departments, each with its own permanent head, under the Minister. Thus the Chancellor of the Exchequer has responsibility for the Treasury, for the two large Revenue departments (Customs and Excise and Inland Revenue) and for a large number of other bodies – some sizeable like the Stationery Office, others small like the Public Works Loan Board and the National Debt Office. Here again the alternative may not be additional Ministers – indeed the satellite departments of this kind are usually engaged in work which raises few issues of policy. If that work was carried out by a special branch or branches of a ministry, it would add to the responsibilities of the ministry's senior officials. On the other hand, a separate Board or Office with its own senior staff, dealing directly with the Minister on

the same ministry with broadly the same functions may be a heavier responsibility and therefore from this point of view 'bigger' at one time than at another. Thus during a year of coal shortage and of overburdened electricity plant the task of the Minister of Fuel and Power was obviously much greater than in other years, even though his legal powers may not have changed.

It is also probably true to say that the more diverse the range of matters to be dealt with, the more difficult a department becomes and the larger the number of higher staff needed. The Foreign Office, which deals with almost every country in the world, and the Board of Trade, which deals with industries as diverse as cotton, films and furniture, present special problems to those at the top. Something of course depends on whether the internal organization of the department is good enough to prevent an undue load on the Minister and on whether the Minister and Permanent Secretary are prepared to delegate.

In passing it should be noted that any growth in the functions of government is likely to throw up problems of maintaining internal unity for some of the ministries. Not merely will each ministry become larger, but its functions are likely to become more diverse. On the other hand an increase in the number of departmental Ministers is likely to provide an opportunity to regroup functions with more regard for their affinities and homogeneity.

It is difficult to say at what point one should draw the line about the size of a ministry. It might be argued that the Treasury under Sir Stafford Cripps was too large – i.e. that at that time too many major and urgent decisions arose out of its functions – and that this hastened his death. It would probably be difficult to argue that the Ministry of Pensions and National Insurance had too much to do in the later 1950s, when the teething troubles of the arrangements introduced by the legislation of 1946 had been solved. But was the Ministry of Health too large in 1950? Or were the Foreign Office and the Board of Trade too big in 1964? Perhaps the only thing that can

such issues of policy as may arise, leaves the senior officers of the ministry free to concentrate on the main stream of the Minister's responsibilities. The motive for setting up such satellite departments is thus not to secure a measure of independence of the Minister, but the effect of creating them may in some instances be not unlike the effect of establishing the public boards and corporations mentioned later in this chapter. Finally, and very recently, there is the 'double-heading' of some departments with two 'Full' Ministers – even of Cabinet rank. It is possible that this practice has major constitutional implications, but it is as yet too early to judge whether the innovation is an effective and acceptable way of preventing or delaying the division of 'big' departments.

be said with any certainty is that sometimes in the life of a ministry there comes an increasing recognition that it has become so large that either it is no longer a candidate for new functions, or that it is time it lost some to another ministry. At this stage it may lose its appetite for adding any new function to its empire, particularly a really new function and not one which is just an extension of the powers available for carrying out an existing function. At a somewhat later stage the ministry may even contemplate without too much distress the prospect of losing part of its present empire.

On the whole, in view of the great increase in governmental activity during the last half-century, it is remarkable that the number of Ministers has been kept so low. If we count all members of the Cabinet and all Ministers outside the Cabinet who were regarded as being of 'Cabinet rank' or were in full charge of departments, there were 21 in 1914 and 27 in 1964 – only six more, though the total number of non-industrial civil servants increased from about 270,000 to 690,000; or more strikingly from about 40,000 to 340,000 if three big employing departments which have been in existence throughout (the Post Office and the Boards of Inland Revenue and of Customs and Excise) are excluded.

There must, therefore, be factors which offset the pressure for more Ministers. One such factor is that the greater the number of Ministers the greater the difficulty of securing inter-departmental co-ordination, notwithstanding the greater need for such co-ordination. The most important general factor, however, which limits the increase in the number of departmental Ministers, arises from the working of the Cabinet. Whether or not there can be said to be an optimum size of Cabinet, there is undoubtedly a size beyond which Prime Ministers will go only with considerable reluctance. When the number of Ministers reaches this point any increase may cause difficulties in the working of the Cabinet.

Up to October, 1964, the largest Cabinets in British history were Mr Asquith's in 1915–16, Mr Neville Chamberlain's in 1937–39, and Sir Alec Douglas-Home's in 1963–64: all of these reached a membership of twenty-three. Twenty to twenty-two was more usual in the inter-war period and between 1945 and 1960 the number of members never reached twenty. If, in addition to the Prime Minister, the inclusion of the Lord President and possibly one so-called 'non-departmental' Minister is accepted as common form, there could only be twenty departmental Ministers at the maximum – and only fifteen if much post-1945 experience counts – if they were all to have seats in the Cabinet. As Britain had fifteen departmental Ministers as long ago as 1889, clearly there must have been an increasing need to balance the advantages of creating new Ministers against the disadvantages of leaving more Ministers out of the Cabinet.

The use of Cabinet Committees and the work of the Cabinet Secretariat have made it easier to leave some Ministers out of the Cabinet, but there remain notable disadvantages in such a practice. Regular attendance at the Cabinet makes for greater administrative, political and personal cohesion. Ministers who are not members must inevitably feel of a lower status, the departments they manage may on occasion not get the decisions and attention they need from the Government as a whole, and the unity of the Administration may suffer. The fewer Ministers there are outside the Cabinet, therefore, the better. Other considerations point in the same direction. Politicians of ministerial calibre and experience are not unlimited, and the more powerful and able party leaders prefer departments with plenty of scope. The House of Commons dislikes having a very large number of 'placemen' among its Members, and it is politically and constitutionally impossible to have more than a small handful of Ministers in the House of Lords. Convention and considerations of expense also play some part.

There is, in short, a reluctance to establish new ministerial posts, and whenever the central government is charged with a new function there is a presumption in favour of adding it to the responsibilities of an existing Minister. In normal circumstances this accords with the manner in which the functions of government develop. Each year Parliament adds to the powers and responsibilities of the central government. But the great bulk of these additions consist of a multitude of smaller items, small at least in terms of the additional staff required to carry them out. The tasks which the Ministry of Housing and Local Government or the Board of Trade have to perform arise from literally hundreds of Acts extending for over a century. Probably no one of those powers or Acts would constitute in itself anything like sufficient reason for the establishment of a new ministry. Usually only the mass creation of new powers and functions in preparation for or during a war is sufficient to warrant this step, e.g. the establishment of the Ministries of Information and of Economic Warfare in 1939. In peace-time a new ministry is usually produced by a rearrangement of functions involving the transfer of powers from one or more existing ministries. This in itself constitutes a further important limit on any increase in the number of Ministers. For the powers that Ministers have they tend to hold and in any case the disruption caused to a ministry which loses part of its work and staff invites caution. If the transfer of a major function is suggested the effect on the remaining parts of the ministry must be seriously considered. Moreover, whether the function is major or minor it will have developed a network of links many of which will be broken if it is transferred. Transfers, like surgical operations, are only worth while if they achieve some important advantage.

It is also worth noticing two devices usually introduced for other reasons, which have, however, enabled public powers and functions to be increased without the equivalent pressure for further Ministers with claims to seats in the Cabinet. They are:

(i) The use of Boards, such as the National Coal Board, to manage the affairs of a large enterprise and be a large employer, leaving the Minister to concern himself with a much more limited range of matters concerning the industry. Had coal, electricity and gas been nationalized by transferring them not to public corporations but to a Minister, their everyday management might have been in total too great for a single Minister of Power.

(ii) The practice of placing politicians in charge of small departments but not giving them normal ministerial status. The Secretaries for Mines, for Overseas Trade, and for Technical Co-operation were in this position.[b]

Notwithstanding the pressure to restrict the number of departmental Ministers, a number of quite small ministries were established during our period, including the Dominions/Commonwealth Relations Office and the Ministries of Civil Aviation, of Materials,

[b] A device which has the effect of decreasing the number of Ministers with claims to seats in the Cabinet, but which involves an increase in the total number of Ministers, is that of appointing a Co-ordinating Minister with a seat in the Cabinet, leaving two or more ordinary departmental Ministers out of the Cabinet. Thus for almost twenty-five years before the merger of 1964, the existence of a separate Minister of Defence affected the status of the Ministers at the heads of the three Service departments. The appointment of a Secretary of State for the Co-ordination of Transport, Fuel and Power – one of the so-called 'Overlords' – by Mr Winston Churchill in 1951 had a similar effect on the position of the Minister Fuel and Power and the Minister of Transport.

The limit to this kind of arrangement is set by the fact that the departmental Minister still remains responsible to Parliament for the performance of the many duties conferred on him. Unless a clear distinction can be drawn between the responsibilities of the Co-ordinating Minister and of the other Ministers concerned – as was done in the case of the Minister of Defence and the Service Ministers – there is a serious danger of confusion both in Parliament and within Whitehall.

299

and of Town and Country Planning. In all these cases, therefore, there must have been exceptional forces pulling in the other direction. There was no need to have a separate Dominions Office in 1925 because of the burden of work on the Colonial Secretary – indeed the Dominions Office and the Colonial Office continued to have the same Minister until 1930. The Dominions Office was set up in order to take account of the independent status of the senior Commonwealth countries and to provide a channel of communication with them at once less paternal than that associated with the Colonial Office and more intimate than that associated with the Foreign Office. The Office has been continued under its new name as the Commonwealth's membership has extended because it appears to meet the peculiar needs of that strange and intangible community of nations. The Ministry of Materials was set up in 1951 when international economic conditions made the procurement of raw materials very difficult and when it appeared that those conditions would last for a considerable time. In fact an improvement set in almost as soon as the department was established and within three years it was abolished.

The Ministries of Civil Aviation and of Town and Country Planning represent a different idea. The initial stages of developing rapidly a new or enlarged function are capable of occupying the full time of a Minister and his senior advisers, but when the initial impetus has been given and the administrative machine is running smoothly the new ministry can be merged into some other ministry. Thus the Ministry of Civil Aviation, set up in 1945, had to deal with the relatively new and peculiarly difficult problem of putting Britain's civil aviation services on a sound and greatly extended basis immediately after a war in which civil flying had been almost completely subordinated to military needs. Not only did the domestic aspects of civil aviation demand close attention but its international aspects were equally important. As the new structure of Air Corporations and the machinery of international services settled down, the need for a separate ministry declined, and in 1953 it was deemed practicable to make one Minister responsible for all transport matters, including civil aviation.

If, therefore, we look at the administrative history of Britain since 1914 simply in terms of the number of departmental Ministers, the dominant theme is a struggle between two powerful forces. On the one hand, the continual increase in functions has created problems of size and heterogeneity which have generated pressure for the appointment of more Ministers. On the other hand, the needs of co-ordination and the advantages of government by a small and well-knit body of Ministers have been strong arguments against increasing the number of Ministers. The main pressure for an increase has been supplemented by the need, on occasion, to establish new ministries to handle functions which, in the view of the Cabinet, demanded special attention, or which well-organized interests or interests with a strong public appeal felt would not receive adequate attention unless they became the sole responsibility of particular Ministers. The main pressure against an increase was supplemented by such factors as the recurring shortage of politicians of front-rank ministerial calibre, the preference of prominent politicians for administrative responsibilities which gave them plenty of scope, parliamentary dislike of too many 'placemen', and the use of public boards and corporations instead of ministerial departments.

The precise number of departmental Ministers suitable at any particular time cannot be calculated from a consideration of the factors discussed – there is always room for difference of opinion. But such consideration would at least narrow the limits. It would not enable one to decide whether at the end of 1956 there should have been twenty-two or twenty-six departmental Ministers rather than twenty-four. It would, however, incline one to doubt whether fifteen or thirty departmental Ministers would have been equally desirable. The balance of the opposed factors decides the number of Ministers among whom the functions of government have to be distributed. We may now turn, therefore, to examine the factors which influence the grouping of functions under those Ministers.

THE GROUPING OF FUNCTIONS

General Criteria

It is clear from simple inspection that some functions are closely related whereas others have little or nothing in common. Housing, for example, has close affinities with sewerage and street cleansing, less with agriculture and fisheries, and little or none with foreign affairs. As one writer has put it, a first approximate answer to the question of which functions should be grouped together in one department can undoubtedly be found by seeking the closest affinity or the greatest measure of homogeneity.

'Each Government Department should have a reasonably homogeneous block of work, or one or two homogeneous blocks of work amounting *in toto* to enough, and not more than enough, to keep fully occupied the normal departmental hierarchy consisting of

Minister, Permanent Secretary, Deputy Secretary (or Secretaries), etc. . . . one should avoid (always provided there are not over-whelming common-sense reasons to the contrary) creating un-necessary heterogeneity either in assigning new functions or in switching existing ones.'[1]

It is easy for those familiar with the names of the British central departments to think of the total functions of government as distri-buting themselves naturally among a number of readily recognizable departments or boxes: agriculture, education, foreign affairs, health, home affairs, labour, trade, war and so on. That departments with similar names are to be found in other countries shows that thinking in these terms is at least a reasonable starting point. Yet these titles are not due to any one basis of classification. Foreign affairs and home affairs obviously are mutually exclusive, but agriculture is an industry and labour is a section of the population, and it is therefore by no means self-evident what should go into each of the boxes so labelled. Does agriculture exclude any activities concerned with agricultural labour, or does labour cover all workers except agricultural workers? Are there any alternative labels, i.e. any alternative methods of grouping functions? In other words, what criterion or criteria will result in the greatest measure of homogeneity?

Before dealing with these questions one overriding consideration needs to be stressed. In the British system of Cabinet Government ministerial responsibility is a fundamental constitutional principle. Some individual Minister is responsible to Parliament for the per-formance or non-performance of every power conferred on the central government. Therefore the distribution of functions between different Ministers must as far as possible be such as to make it clear who is responsible for any major issue of governmental policy. Any distribution which blurred the responsibility for any important field of government policy over two or three Ministers would be most unlikely to work satisfactorily as regards Parliament and the public and even as regards the working of the Cabinet system as a whole. It also follows that where a departmental Minister is responsible for an important field of policy he has a *prima facie* case for having within his department any minor or ancillary functions of govern-ment essential to the successful performance of that policy.

Four Alternative Methods
General experience indicates that there are four main ways in which

governmental powers and activities may be grouped for administrative purposes:

(i) By class of persons dealt with or clientele – e.g. children, pensioners, a particular industry, Local Authorities.
(ii) By major purpose – e.g. education, health, defence.
(iii) By area served – e.g. Scotland.
(iv) By kind of work or administrative process – e.g. legal, research, printing.

The distinction between 'clientele' and 'major purpose' goes back to Aristotle who, in his discussion of the distribution of functions in a Greek city state, said

'... we have also to consider whether to allocate duties on the basis of the subject to be handled, or on that of the class of persons concerned: e.g. should we have one officer for the whole subject of the maintenance of order, or a separate officer for the class of children and another for that of women?'[2]

The Haldane Committee spelt this out in a much-quoted passage. They defined the alternatives as

'... distribution according to the persons or classes to be dealt with, and distribution according to the services to be performed. Under the former method each Minister who presides over a Department would be responsible to Parliament for those activities of the Government which affect the sectional interests of particular classes of persons, and there might be, for example, a Ministry for Paupers, a Ministry for Children, a Ministry for Insured Persons, or a Ministry for the Unemployed. Now the inevitable outcome of this method of organization is a tendency to Lilliputian administration. It is impossible that the specialized service which each Department has to render to the community can be of as high a standard when its work is at the same time limited to a particular class of persons and extended to every variety of provision for them, as when the Department concentrates itself on the provision of the particular service only, by whomsoever required, and looks beyond the interests of comparatively small classes.

'The other method, and the one which we recommend for adoption, is that of defining the field of activity in the case of each Department according to the particular service which it renders to the community as a whole. Thus a Ministry of Education would be concerned predominantly with the provision of education wherever

303

and by whomseoever, needed. Such a Ministry would have to deal with persons in so far only as they were to be educated, and not with particular classes of persons defined on other principles.'[3]

Let us now look at these and the other two alternative methods of distributing functions.

Class of Person

It is difficult to see how any government could be organized wholly or even to any major extent on the basis of class of person dealt with: for in its extreme form it would mean having separate police forces and fire brigades, and separate educational and health services, etc., for each category of persons. And if the classes of people were not mutually exclusive the difficulties would be even greater. The classic British example found in Local Government of the use of this basis – *viz.*, the Boards of Guardians which existed between 1834 and 1929 for the relief and care of the poor – did not go very far. The local Poor Law was overwhelmingly a system of cash payments to and workhouses for the poor, and the medical and hospital attention provided specially for paupers was limited.

The criterion is worth discussing, however, for it underlines the contrast between services seen in terms of law and administration and services seen in terms of groups of citizens. In other words the same function can be viewed either as a job to be undertaken by officials, or as work of special concern to a particular section of the community. However much the stress is placed on distribution by service provided, the department concerned will find itself dealing regularly with certain individuals. This departmental clientele is likely to include not only the recipients of the service but also Local Authorities and associations concerned in the administration, their staffs, and a variety of other interested bodies. Experience shows that there is a tendency for this clientele to look to the department with whom it is in regular contact to provide other governmental services for it, and the department is also tempted in this direction. Thus, a new function is sometimes added to a department because it already has the closest contact of any existing department with the groups or bodies that are the concern of, or are concerned with, the new function. During the recent period when new building, raw materials and other matters were subject to governmental control and allocation, links of this kind led to the development of the idea that each department should act as the sponsor of, or as the advocate for, the interests of its particular clientele in securing the necessary supplies.

The danger in certain circumstances is that a department because of the direct pressure on its Minister or because of its desire for a quiet life, may so become the mouthpiece of its clientele as to find it increasingly difficult to take a general view of the public interest. It was sometimes alleged, for example, that the Minister of Agriculture was the mouthpiece of the farmers, and the amalgamation of his Ministry with the former Ministry of Food may in part have been due to the desire to ensure that the different demands of the consumers and the producers of food are reconciled in the one department. Even if functions are distributed without reference to clientele there will probably be a tendency in practice for each department dealing with a particular section of the public, whether as individuals or as associations, to try to satisfy that public. Sometimes, however, a department may be able to show that it cannot please one part of its clientele without offending another part – e.g. the Ministry of Housing and Local Government in relation to the boundaries of Counties and County Boroughs.

Purpose

The purposes of government may be defined at differing levels of generality. At the most general level they would include defence against external aggression, preservation of law and order, promotion of trade and industry, education of the population, promoting the well-being of the Commonwealth, safeguarding the public health, and providing security against want. At a lower level of generality they would include the provision and proper utilization of fuel and power supplies, development of agriculture, provision of adequate housing and roads, and the planning of town and country.

Distribution of functions by purpose at the most general level might lead to the establishment of some ten or twelve ministries. As some of these would be too large, the functions in respect of certain major objectives would have to be divided among two or more ministries. A less general approach might avoid this difficulty but run into another, because some of the purposes at this level might not justify the exclusive attention of separate departments. Apart from these limitations, however, British experience has shown distribution according to purpose to be an important criterion. It gives, on the whole, a greater unity of work at the policy level than any of the other criteria, and this is very important, as Parliament is mainly interested in policy and in seeing that ministerial responsibility is unequivocal.

The promotion of trade and industry provides a good example of the manner in which the component functions of a major purpose can be distributed if they are too numerous for one Minister. In and for some time before 1914 the powers of government with regard to trade and industry (excluding agriculture and fisheries, which were treated separately) were in the hands of one department – the Board of Trade. When those powers became too wide in range or too heavy for a single department, subdivision by industry was considered to be the solution. The different forms of transport and the fuel and power industries, by virtue of their size and their need for special consideration, have been separated. The building industry has also been made the responsibility of another department; in this case it was found convenient to use the department responsible for government building. For a time the Ministry of Supply, established primarily to provide the arms and equipment required by the Army, was responsible for government policy and control in respect of the engineering and metal industries because its work brought it into close contact with those industries. There has indeed been a tendency to place governmental responsibilities for any particular industry in the hands of the ministry which, as part of its other activities, already has close links with that industry. The Board of Trade has tended, therefore, to be left with those industries which are not large or complex enough to warrant a separate ministry, or for which no other Minister can be made conveniently responsible.[c]

There are some functions within the field of trade and industry not peculiar to a particular industry but common to all industries. To what extent should distribution by industry apply only to the former and totally exclude the latter? In Britain such general matters as control over the location of industry, registration and supervision of patents, promotion of exports, supervision of monopolies and restrictive practices, are the responsibility of the Board of Trade even though they concern industries which are the responsibility of other departments. If these general matters were split among the several departments the formulation and carrying out of a general governmental policy would be more difficult. Indeed it would probably need almost constant inter-departmental consultation, certainly more consultation than is caused by the present distinction between general and particular industrial responsibilities.

Let us take the field of labour or employment. How far should the distribution by industry apply here? Should all matters connected

[c] The reader should be reminded that the experience being reviewed ended in October, 1964, and that this survey takes no account of later changes involving the new Ministry of Technology and Department of Economic Affairs, etc.

with agricultural labour, with transport workers, or with coal miners, be the responsibility of the ministries concerned with those industries, leaving either no need for a Ministry of Labour or only for a smaller ministry confined to functions not easily subdivided according to industry? In Britain it has increasingly been assumed that unless there are strong reasons to the contrary, all the Government's powers in respect of labour should reside in the Ministry of Labour. This ministry is thus able to specialize in what is a difficult field for governmental action, and to be responsible for a general governmental policy. It is also put in a position to develop close relations with an important and well-organized section of the community – the Trade Unions. Moreover, the arrangement gives that section a single Minister to whom representations can be made on all matters affecting the unions, wages and conditions, and employment generally.

Area

A distribution on the basis of area[d] has obvious limitations in the case of a country or countries with a common Parliament and Government and a unified economic system. This has not, however, ruled out the possibility of recognizing in the sphere of administration, the differing conditions, partly political, partly legal, partly historical, that prevail in the countries making up Great Britain and Ireland. Arrangements of this kind are of course still operating in Northern Ireland, Scotland and to a small extent in Wales.

As regards the general principles as to which functions may properly be handled by an area Minister, it is clear that certain activities, e.g. defence, external affairs, finance and economic affairs, call for a unified approach, not least by reference to their international aspects; shipping and civil aviation are also international in scope. Moreover, as was recently pointed out by the Committee on Scottish Finance and Trade Statistics,[4] Scotland and England have a unified economic system with complete freedom of intercourse by rail, road, sea and air, and this is equally true of Wales. Consequently it has been the practice for government to deal with trade and industry primarily on the basis of Great Britain as a whole, though this principle is not now followed in the case of electricity. The Ministry

[d] We are not concerned with the regional organization of central departments or with the distribution of functions between central and local government. Nor do we take account here of the establishment of the Secretaryship of State for Wales and the Welsh Office by the incoming Labour Government in October 1964.

of Labour has also remained a Great Britain department with head-quarters in London where are also be to found the headquarters of many organizations such as Trade Unions which operate throughout Great Britain and with which the Ministry requires to keep in close touch. On the other hand in this case and in the case of other Great Britain departments with important Scottish and Welsh interests, e.g. the Board of Trade, it is customary to maintain strong organizations in Scotland and Wales under senior officers in order that those interests shall be duly safeguarded.

So far as Scotland is concerned, it has been possible to go further towards recognizing what the recent Royal Commission on Scottish Affairs[5] called 'a separate Scottish ethos, history, and tradition'. Thus in such matters as education, health, housing and police, both policy and administration have been placed by legislation or otherwise in the hands of a Scottish Minister and Scottish departments. The same has also happened to Scottish agriculture and fisheries.

It would be useless to attempt to make a strictly logical distinction between those activities which are properly capable of being distributed according to the area in which they are administered and those which are not. It can, however, be said that subject to the overriding authority of a common Parliament and Cabinet, and the exclusion from separate treatment of activities on which it is essential or highly convenient to have a common front, there have been continuing efforts over many years to recognize in administration the existence of special Scottish conditions as well as the insistent urge of the Scottish people to manage their own business. Administrative measures with similar aims have also been taken from time to time as regards Welsh affairs.

Kind of Work

There are two main interpretations of this criterion. First, there is what is known as the common service, which applies to services needed by all or most departments, e.g. provision of offices, stationery and equipment, printing, or legal advice. Should each department cater for its own needs or should the service be concentrated in a single department, or should there be some mixture of these two extremes? Examples of all three possibilities can be found in British Government, though usually some degree of concentration is favoured. The Stationery Office (for printing), the Ministry of Public Building and Works (for Government buildings, offices, furniture and a wide range of office needs and equipment) and the Central Office of Information (for general governmental publicity) are three examples of concentration which have produced separate departments. The Ministries of Munitions, Supply, and Aviation have, at various times, been responsible for providing differing proportions of the arms, equipment and other supplies needed by the fighting Services.

The advantages of the common service department are the pooling of expert knowledge, of which there may not be enough to go round, the concentration of a particular kind of work and, in some cases, the gains from large-scale purchases. The disadvantages are that the other departments lose control over what to them may be an important ingredient in the successful performance of their functions; that they may have to accept something which suits all departments on average rather than something designed or provided for their peculiar needs; and that another department is added to the number to be dealt with and co-ordinated.

The conduct of scientific research by the government raises issues only partly of the common service kind, for it is also a matter of providing the right environment. Instead of such research being treated as a normal governmental function, efforts have been made to give it a special status by creating special research authorities under the Privy Council. Where, however, research is vital to a department, e.g. as is research on weapons to defence ministries, it is kept within the department. In other cases the department has some liaison with the main research body in the field.

The second interpretation of this criterion concerns the suitability of a department for carrying out a function either because it has the relevant experience and expertise, or because the attitude or tradition required to operate the new function successfully is found in this particular department, or because the new service needs some administrative management – regional or local – already possessed by this department. In a sense this is no more than underlining the advantage of affinity whether it be by clientele, purpose or area. But it can be a more specific pointer than that. Thus it was presumably because the Office of Works had developed some expertise in the handling of government building that this common service department became a Ministry of Works and later a Ministry of Public Building and Works with responsibility for an important economic function – conducting the Government's relations with the building and civil engineering industries. Possession of the necessary administrative machinery has been an important factor on several occasions. A good example before the period of this study concerns the executive work of Old Age Pensions, which was entrusted to the Board of

Customs and Excise because the latter had a comprehensive network of outposts. More recently the merger of the Ministries of Pensions and of National Insurance was in part defended because the combined department would be able to offer war pensioners a better local counter service than the Ministry of Pensions could provide. Running the Post Office Savings Bank is a function which can hardly be said to be part of the postal, telephone or telegraph services, but it nevertheless fits conveniently into the Post Office organization. Sometimes a department with a wide network of local offices is used on an agency basis by another department – e.g. the Ministry of Labour acts as an agent for the Foreign Office in the issue and renewal of passports. The 'principal' department still retains responsibility for policy in these cases.

Other Criteria

Though at first glance the functions of government may appear to be composed of large, homogeneous and indivisible blocks of work readily recognizable as health, education, industry, defence and so on, closer inspection shows them to be made up of a mass of smaller items. When these are looked at in detail it is by no means always clear which function should be placed in which ministry even though the broad pattern of ministries is already well known and accepted.

If military administration, for example, is scrutinized closely it will be seen to involve a wide variety of tasks, even in peace time. Some of them are:

Recruitment
Settlement of pay and conditions
Clothing and provisioning
Training
Equipment
Research and development work on weapons
Medical care and attention
Housing
Transport
Payment of pensions to disabled soldiers or to dependants of soldiers killed in course of duty

In 1914 all these tasks were part of the total responsibility of the Secretary of State for War. In later times some have been handled by other Ministers. Thus from just before the Second World War

310

until the early 1960s national service was compulsory and was administered by the Ministry of Labour and National Service:[e] the provision of equipment and research and development on weapons were for many years the province of the Minister of Supply: and disablement pensions have been handled by the Minister of Pensions and his successors since 1916. Several other departments are concerned at various other points.

The word function may thus cover anything from the direction of the armed forces to the arrangement whereby conscientious objectors may appeal against their call-up. The question of which ministry handled the call-up of conscripts is probably more typical of the vast majority of decisions affecting the distribution of work between departments than is a question which involves the creation of a new department. Though the four general criteria are important tests, however small the activity of government under consideration, it is probably true that the less important a function is in itself the greater the choice of possible ministries for its home. In any case there will quite often be a choice of solutions. The hospitals for the military sick could be the responsibility of the Ministry of Defence or the Ministry of Health: the grants to universities could be made either by the Treasury (as before 1964) or by the Department of Education and Science (as from 1964): the Factory Inspectorate could be either in the Home Office or in the Ministry of Labour or in the Board of Trade or even split among the departments concerned with the various industries.

The Haldane Committee thought that further help on how functions should be related could be obtained from drawing a distinction between dominant and subordinate interests. They suggested that, subject to the main principle of allocation by service, all decisions to concentrate functions in particular departments should be governed by the extent to which particular functions conduce to the primary end of the department's administration.

Once the main framework of the departments has been settled, a test of this kind is sometimes of assistance. Thus having decided on other grounds that there should be Ministries of Education and of Health the question of which should be responsible for the School

[e] A national network of local offices was required: the Ministry of Labour had that network. Moreover, as the call-up was linked with such matters as exempted occupations and reinstatement into civilian occupations, it was administratively convenient to use the department which was concerned with placing labour in jobs, collecting and analysing employment statistics, etc. It should be noted, however, that the War Office still recruited those wishing to enter the Army other than under the compulsory call-up.

Medical Service can be subjected to this test. In this case, however, the answer is complicated by the fact that the service was originally established by the Board of Education and is more easily administered as part of the educational service because the inspection normally takes place on the school premises. Sometimes the dominant interest is a matter of opinion. Is control over the location of industry subordinate to the dominant purpose of securing full employment in formerly depressed areas, or to that of securing a properly planned community, i.e. part of town and country planning policy? Here again other factors may be more important – for example, the methods which the Government proposes to use to influence location. These methods may in some cases dictate the choice of a department which has the kind of relations with industrial concerns most likely to lead to successful persuasion. These are good examples of the difficulty that may arise in practice from using this test.

Some of the changes which have taken place in the distribution of functions have been due to the emergence of new primary purposes. Thus when in 1940 the Minister of Labour and National Service was charged with the difficult task of securing the best use of the nation's manpower, including the power of direction, he took the view that this aim made it necessary for him to take over the Factory Inspectorate. If he was to be responsible for the industries and firms in which individuals must work he must be able to assure himself that factory conditions, including such matters as canteens, were up to standard. In reply it could hardly be argued that this particular function was essential to the primary purpose of the Home Office, which is law and order.

Another example of the way in which the passage of time can render an existing pattern of distribution inappropriate is in the field of National Insurance. What is now National Insurance, a unified service under the control of a single Minister, first developed as a series of services in the hands of five Ministers. Perhaps it could not be argued in each of these five cases that the particular function was in a particular department because it conduced to that department's primary purpose, but undoubtedly there were close links in each case, e.g. workmen's compensation with the Factory Inspectorate (at the Home Office), health insurance with the health services, and unemployment insurance with the employment service. As soon, however, as the emphasis came to be placed on a comprehensive uniform scheme of national insurance the existing distribution appeared indefensible, and was indeed so administratively.

312

So far this discussion has proceeded on the assumption that the task is to find the closest affinity for the function or functions whose proper allocation is in question. There are, however, occasions when an 'obvious' affinity is deliberately avoided, and where some measure of heterogeneity appears to give the best result. Thus from 1919 to 1964 the University Grants Committee answered to the Chancellor of the Exchequer and not to the Minister of Education – the main reason being the desire of the universities to avoid the kind of approach and the measure of control which characterized the Ministry's relations with other branches of the educational system. Again, the Eve Committee on Crown Lands[6] recommended that the responsibility for Crown Lands should be that of a Minister without any special interest in land, rather than that of a Minister like the Minister of Agriculture. The classic case in our period has been the refusal of official opinion to be impressed by the Haldane arguments for a Ministry of Justice which began: 'If the principle to be adopted in distributing the business of Government is that of concentrating the various branches of each service as far as possible in the hands of a single authority, considerable changes will be requisite in the case of the administration of Justice.'[7] The orthodox view on this has been that we should be particularly chary of concentration of authority when dealing with the delicate relation between the executive and the judiciary.

It is sometimes suggested that political and personal considerations should play no part in questions of administrative organization. This view ignores the fact that government is essentially political, and that a democratic Government must take account of parliamentary and public opinion on all matters, including departmental arrangements. Long-term political considerations may rightly affect the structure of the central administration, as for instance in the setting up of Scottish departments for health, home affairs, etc. Shorter-term political considerations inevitably affect the timing of change, as they probably did when the Ministry of Health was divided into two departments in 1951. Occasionally, too, in allocating functions, regard is paid to the views on policy and to the personalities of the Minister who will become responsible for the work. Thus the allocation of planning to the Ministry of Works in the Second World War owed much to the presence there of a Minister, Lord Reith, who was known to be keenly interested in planning policy. His successor, Lord Portal, preferred to concentrate on other matters and in due course planning was taken away from the Ministry of Works and assigned to a separate department. Cases must also

313

arise from time to time in which the political strength or persuasiveness of a particular Minister in the Cabinet may prevent or delay administrative change or secure it against some opposition.

There are some obvious dangers if considerations of this kind play anything but a minor part in decisions affecting the structure of government. There is a limited case for them in the rare instance of a difficult task depending for its success entirely on the right man being put in the position to carry it out. The main danger is that though the allocation of a function to a particular ministry may be successful whilst the particular person is in charge, once he departs, which in the case of a Minister may be quite soon, the basic inappropriateness of the allocation may cause difficulties. In the long run, therefore, in deciding on the distribution of functions, primary consideration must be given to the administrative factors discussed in the earlier paragraphs of this chapter.

Just which criterion or combination of criteria will give the best result, or just which modifying factors must be taken into account, will depend on the circumstances of any case. In many instances it will be found that the considerations set out in this chapter are most effective when turned into a series of questions which should be answered before a decision is reached. What is the precise character of the function to be performed? Where is it to be performed, and for what purpose? What kind of work is involved: is it mainly regulatory, or stimulative, or managerial, routine or discretionary, highly specialized and technical or mainly clerical? With whom will the department concerned mainly have to deal? Does the new function need to be administered locally, and if so which department has the most appropriate local arrangements? Is the function likely to grow rapidly and if so will a particular department continue to have the capacity to be responsible for it? Has the clientele to be served any strong views? Which departments already have links with the function, or already do this kind of work, or have this type of staff or experience? And so on. It is the multiplicity of argument, the difficulty of settling the issue by appeal to one or more clear and uncontestable principles, that leaves room for disputes, for the exercise of judgment, and even, on occasion, for the interplay of personalities and of politics.

Nevertheless knowledge of the possible criteria, of the questions to be asked and of how similar issues have been dealt with in the past should be of the utmost assistance. This knowledge, wisely used, should reduce the possibility of a wrong allocation of functions because it should narrow the range of effective choice. This is the significance of the modern (1939–55) developments in the Treasury's Machinery of Government work. We turn, in conclusion, therefore, to consider briefly the overall experience and some aspects of the handling of administrative change.

THE HANDLING OF MACHINERY OF GOVERNMENT QUESTIONS

It is extremely difficult to pass any worthwhile judgment on the period and the changes surveyed in this book. Were all the changes justified, and if not, which proved to be failures? Should some of the changes have come earlier? Should other changes have been made? Nobody with a real knowledge of British government would claim that everything had been 'for the best of all possible worlds'. Nobody could possibly make that claim for any large-scale and complicated organization over fifty years. To express a judgment on more particular matters is even less easy. Should a Minister for the Coordination of Defence have been established earlier than 1937 and should he in any case have been a Minister of Defence on the present model? Was it only the problems of war that led to a Minister of Fuel and Power being appointed, or did the need for such a Minister exist in the 1930s? Were the various changes involving the Ministries of Health, Town and Country Planning, and Housing and Local Government during the period 1943–51 evidence of fumbling, or were they mainly inevitable and the correct responses to a changing situation? These and many other questions come to mind in reading the administrative history of the period. To answer them with any conviction would need far more evidence than is provided in this study. It would need an inquiry not merely into the reasons advanced for and against the changes but also into the consequent working of the machinery over a reasonable period. And if the judgment was to be fair it would have to take account of what was possible in the political climate of the day.

The sheer volume of change during the period must strike the reader. New departments were created, quite a few departments were abolished or amalgamated with others, and there were numerous transfers of functions between departments. It can hardly be charged, therefore, that British Government proved too rigid to meet the changing needs of the period. The Ministers of the Crown (Transfer of Functions) Act, 1946, greatly facilitated the continuous process of readjustment, especially in connection with comparatively minor changes. Between 1946 and October 1964, some 65 Orders were made under the Act. It is probable that had this procedure been available in the inter-war years some changes – especially minor changes which were crowded out of the legislative programme by more urgent matters – would have been accomplished earlier. There is thus less reason, nowadays, why the Machinery of Government should not keep pace with the changing demands on it.

Decisions affecting the distribution of functions fall into three main categories according to whether they concern:

(i) Entirely new functions, e.g. conscription, food rationing, or the control of monopolies.

(ii) Existing functions which need to be considered afresh due to some major event or change of policy or because there is something wrong – e.g. shipping during a war, the Ministry of Food after the end of rationing, or the Commissioners of Crown Lands after the Crichel Down case.

(iii) Existing functions, other than (ii), which for one reason or another are not working as they should.

Every new function immediately poses the question of which department should be responsible for its administration: the question cannot be avoided. Similarly a major change of emphasis or policy usually quickly brings to light any administrative problems. Experienced advice is very necessary when decisions in either of these cases have to be made. But with the third category, finding the right solution once the issue is posed may be very much the lighter part of the task compared with discovering which problems need consideration.

The arrangements for dealing with these Machinery of Government questions cannot be the same in all circumstances. As we have seen, the procedures adopted during the forties and fifties changed several times, reflecting variations in the intensity with which administrative adaptation was needed. But while it is impossible to suggest any single, permanent procedure, it does seem beyond dispute that the adaptation of the organization of government must be continuous and cannot be divorced from the normal administrative process. It is a governmental responsibility which should not be entrusted to intermittent public enquiry, though occasional parliamentary and 'outside' enquiries, and the use of non-civil service expertise, can certainly make valuable contributions.

When we consider the great strain imposed on the central administration during most of the period between 1914 and 1964, the story of the way in which the whole machinery developed and was adapted is impressive. Some problems remained unsolved, but the structure which had evolved over previous centuries was changed and extended with a fair degree of success to meet the conditions of the twentieth century. The process of adaptation became more conscious, and increasing attention was paid to what Lord Waverley called 'the broad organizational plan on which Ministers rely for the discharge of their executive responsibilities'.[8] We have seen that the beginning of wisdom in this context is the firm rejection of any belief in the possibility of defining a rigid and comprehensive framework of organization into which every function of government can be fitted for all time. But we are convinced that within the limits set by the essential need of flexibility the efficiency of administration can be enhanced by the constant study of the factors influencing the structure of government and by the application of such knowledge as can be distilled from that study. We hope that a little of that knowledge is contained in these pages.

REFERENCES

[1] L. Petch: 'The Study of the Structure of Government,' *O & M Bulletin*, Vol. 5, No. 6.

[2] *The Politics of Aristotle*, Bk. IV, Ch. xv. (Translated by Sir Ernest Barker.)

[3] Cd. 9230/1918, pp. 7–8.

[4] Cmd. 8609/1952.

[5] Cmd. 9212/1954.

[6] Cmd. 9483/1955.

[7] Cd. 9230/1918, p. 63.

[8] Sir John Anderson: 'The Machinery of Government,' *Public Administration*, Autumn 1946.

23

The Civil Service Department and its Tasks[*]

SIR WILLIAM ARMSTRONG

The Civil Service Department was established by the Government as a result of a recommendation of the Fulton Committee, and Sir William Armstrong, previously at the Treasury, became its Permanent Secretary and Head of the Home Civil Service. He quickly gained a reputation for openness, through his willingness to give public lectures, address university and other seminars and make himself available for television interviews. This article is a transcript of a talk he gave at a seminar for management consultants organized by the CSD in May 1970.

My object this morning is to give you as clear an account as I can of the tasks of the Civil Service Department, and how we are going about them.

As I expect many of you know, the Department came into existence a little over a year ago, on 1 November 1968. It was not an entirely new creation, but was formed by the transfer from the Chancellor of the Exchequer to the Prime Minister of the staff of the Treasury which up to then had formed what was called the 'Pay and Management Group' – just under 900 people. To them was added the staff of the Civil Service Commission. Up to that time the Civil Service Commission had been a wholly independent body; under the new arrangements the Commissioners continued to be wholly independent in matters of selection, but on what one might call recruitment policy and planning they and their staffs are part of the Civil Service Department. They brought some 700 people to be added to the new Department and with subsequent additions we now number some 2000 in all.

Our aims derive partly from what we inherited from the Treasury

* From Sir William Armstrong, 'The Civil Service Department and its Tasks' *O and M Bulletin*, Vol. 25, No. 2, May 1970, pp. 63–79. Reprinted with permission of the Controller, Her Majesty's Stationery Office.

and the Civil Service Commission, and partly from the report of the Fulton Committee on the Civil Service on whose recommendation we were set up. This gives us at the present time a twofold aim:

First, to 'manage' the Civil Service – i.e. to keep it running as a going concern.

Second, to carry out a programme of reforming the Civil Service, with the object of improving its efficiency, and its humanity – and humanity has both an internal and an external aspect; I mean both humanity as between the Civil Service as a whole and the public which it serves, and humanity as between the management of the Civil Service and the civil servants who are managed.

The second of these aims was, of course, included in a sense in the first, of managing the Service as a going concern; but the Fulton Report and all the thinking within and around the Civil Service that had been going on for some years before it, has demanded something more than the continuous improvement of efficiency that any decent management likes to claim – it involves a thoroughgoing root and branch examination of the tasks of the Civil Service and the way it is staffed and organized and controlled so as to carry them out, on a scale so large as to require it to be stated, as I have done, as a separate aim in itself.

CENTRAL GOVERNMENT

Before I describe in detail how we are interpreting these aims and how we have organized ourselves to carry them out, I must say something about the Department's field of activity – that is, about the central Government itself and the civil servants who work in it. This is, I am afraid, an intensely complicated affair and in order to help you follow my description I have prepared some visual aids. I hope that they will prove to be helpful rather than distracting. (*Diagram* 1, *see page* 320.)

The first thing to be noted about the central Government of this country is that it is a federation of departments. On this diagram I have included 22 major departments. By major I do not mean the 22 largest; the sizes range from the Ministry of Defence with nearly 263,000 civil servants to the Cabinet Office with nearly 600; and there are a good many departments larger than the Cabinet Office which I have left out. But the departments I have shown on the diagram are distinguished because they are all directly under the charge of a Minister, and all but two have a Permanent Secretary.

No department with a Minister or a Permanent Secretary has been omitted. Between them they cover a total of nearly 690,000 civil servants – about 95 per cent of the total. I have arranged them in a circle with three departments at the centre. These three between them provide for the central controlling functions of the Government as a whole. The three areas in which central control is exercised are policy, resource allocation and the management of the Civil Service – perhaps it would have been more familiar if I had used the

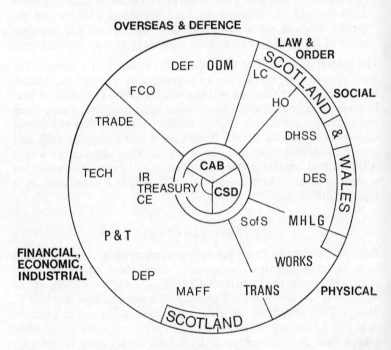

three words – policy, finance and personnel. I shall have more to say about them later.

Meanwhile, let us look at the departments ranged round the circle. You will see that I have divided the circle into five segments:

First, *overseas and defence.*

Second, *financial, economic, industrial.* I have tried to make the size of the segments roughly proportional to the number of departments in it, and you will see that on this criterion this particular segment is much the largest.

Third, *physical*. This includes the departments whose main concern is with the changes which the Government makes in the physical environment and its regulation of the changes which the rest of us make or seek to make.

Fourth, *social*. The social services for which the Government is directly or indirectly responsible.

The final segment I have called *law and order*.

In addition to these five segments I have marked off certain parts round the edge of the circle mainly in the law and order, social and physical fields but with a small area also in the financial, economic and industrial fields. These areas are meant to represent the field of activity of the special 'national' departments: the Scottish Office with its sub-departments and the more recently created Welsh Office.

You will notice that certain departments are shown as straddling the boundaries – that is, they are involved in more than one of the segments. The Treasury is shown both as one of the central departments and as in the financial economic and industrial sector. The Board of Trade is so near the border of the overseas and defence sector that it may be said to stray into it – and the same is true to some extent of the Treasury as well. The Ministry of Transport is put across the boundary of the financial, economic and industrial sector on the one hand and the physical sector on the other. Similarly, the Ministry of Housing and Local Government straddles the physical and social sectors, while the Home Office is partly in the social sector and partly in that labelled law and order. This reflects the fact that the departments with their functions are, so to speak, part of the real world, while the sectors which I have invented and in which I have tried to place them are merely my attempt to suggest some useful groupings. You may think this is a rather futile exercise; on the other hand you may think it the first beginnings of some rational restructuring of the machinery of Government. You may also think that you could produce a more rational structure by grouping the departments in different ways. The doubts and uncertainties about all this, however, do not simply mean that the whole thing is an academic exercise; it is highly relevant not only to the re-ordering of Government and the attempt to introduce a simplified control structure, but it is equally relevant to the kind of career pattern, skills and training needs of the civil servants in the various departments.

CENTRAL DEPARTMENTS

I now want to look more closely at the three central departments which I mentioned at the beginning. In order to illustrate this more clearly, I have produced yet another diagram. (*Diagram 2, see below*).

Here you must imagine that the circle of the first diagram has been

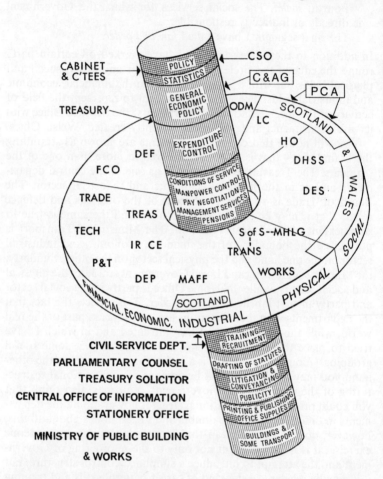

turned over on its side, so that I can show the central departments running as it were like a spine through the centre. This device enables me to bring into the picture a number of other central services as well as the three main ones I have mentioned. The broad idea of the diagram is that those I have shown at the top of the spine are part of the controlling apparatus of Government, while those I have shown at its lower end are more in the nature of central services.

Thus at the top of the upper end of the spine I have put the Cabinet Office. This does not mean, of course, that the civil servants who make up the Cabinet Office are in any sense in control of the policy of the Government. That is reserved for Ministers, who carry it out through the Cabinet and its committees. The job of the civil servants in the Cabinet Office is to provide the secretariat for these activities.

Next down the spine comes the Treasury and the control of expenditure. Here again, the function of those civil servants who are concerned in the Treasury with the control of expenditure is not to control it themselves – or even to put the Chancellor of the Exchequer in a position to control it. Their function is to provide a system which enables the Cabinet as a whole to control it and to choose priorities for the allocation of expenditure within the determined total. It is noteworthy, however, that whereas the Cabinet secretariat are responsible to the Cabinet as a whole, and in particular to the Prime Minister, the people in the Treasury concerned with this control of expenditure function are brigaded with their other colleagues under the Chancellor of the Exchequer. Thereby hangs a tale which is of considerable interest, but which is so long that it would have to form the subject of a quite separate lecture.

Next, the Civil Service Department. You will see that I have put it both above and below the main ring – that is to indicate that the Civil Service Department has both certain controlling functions and certain servicing functions. As I am sure you are aware, it is not always easy to tell where service ends and control begins – and this is so in our case. I will take you through our various functions in a moment; in the meantime I simply draw attention to the fact that my diagram effectively conceals part of the functions of the Civil Service Department. That is in one sense the accidental result of the way I have chosen to set up the diagram, but you might perhaps say that hidden from view are our functions in relation to honours and security.

Before returning to the Civil Service Department in detail, let me just draw attention to some of the other central services which are separately organized. I have space only to show the main ones:

The legal services, including advice on all kinds of legal matters including litigation, conveyancing, etc., and the drafting of statutes and subordinate legislation. These services are centralized for many but not all departments.

The printing and publishing services of the Stationery Office and the publicity services of the Central Office of Information.

The supply services, which at the present time are split between the Stationery Office, who supply office machinery and other office supplies except for furniture, furnishings, cars, etc., which are supplied by the Ministry of Public Building and Works, who occupy the next and far and away the largest space on this part of the diagram signifying their responsibility for government buildings of all kinds.

You will observe that all these central services are in some sense semi-independent – a bit 'hived off' as it were – except the Ministry of Public Buildings and Works, who appear in two places in my diagram, first up on the circle in respect of its functions as the sponsoring department for the construction industry, and secondly down there on the spine in respect of its functions as the provider and maintainer of buildings for government. The reason why this should be so is itself an interesting topic, but to pursue it would take me too far afield.

Before I leave this diagram I should refer to an aspect which I have not included because I thought it would complicate the picture quite intolerably. If the general pattern of the diagram is to put what one might call operational activities in the horizontal plane and services in the vertical, then there ought to be another vertical spine running through the Ministry of Technology, so as to represent the services which that Ministry provides to the Ministry of Defence, in the procurement of weapons systems, mainly aerospace and electronic fields. In this case also, like that of the Ministry of Public Building and Works, we have a combination of service function and a more obviously Ministerial one in a single department.

I should just like to emphasize again the federal character of the Government. I think the picture I have drawn would be nearer the truth if the horizontal plane were shown not as a solid wheel with the departments as it were riding on it, but as a series of planets circling round the central spine. The departments are to a very great extent independent entities and in a very real sense masters of their own affairs. It is this on the policy level that produces the situation which puts not the Prime Minister but the Cabinet in charge of affairs – which makes our system different, so far as the organization of the central executive of the country is concerned, from the system of the United States of America. This has, of course, important consequences for the role of the Civil Service Department in the management of the Civil Service. The employers of civil servants are not ourselves in the Civil Service Department; they are the individual departments themselves. The ultimate bosses of civil servants are their own Ministers and Permanent Secretaries; although I am called Head of the Civil Service I have no authority whatever over

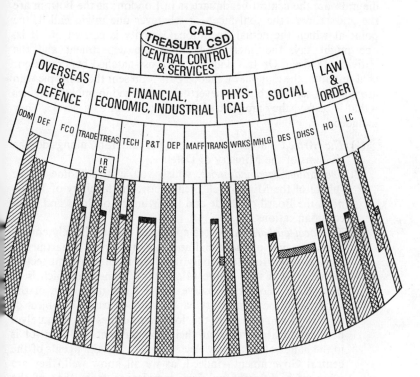

individual civil servants in any department other than my own, and contrary to the belief of many there is no appeal to me from the decisions of other Permanent Secretaries. On the other hand, we are responsible to Parliament for the salary bills and the general administrative expenses of departments in the same way that the Treasury is for their expenditure on programmes.

OPERATING DEPARTMENTS

I fear that before I can come to the advertised subject of my talk, I must inflict on you one more diagram. (*Diagram 3, see above.*)

Now you must imagine that I have opened out the circle and produced a kind of Mercator's projection of the machinery of Government. My interest for the moment is no longer in the central departments, but in the operating departments and their connections with the field of activity in which they operate. At the top of the diagram are the central headquarters in London; at the bottom are the grass roots – the coal face – or whatever one might call it, the point at which the actual operational activity is carried on. It is, one might say, the interface between the department and the individual citizen. On this diagram the cross-hatched bars represent civil servants; the diagonally shaded bars represent those people who are not civil servants but are nevertheless engaged in public activities – that is to say, they are part of the public sector as a whole. They include:

(1) *The Armed Forces* – shown on the diagram alongside the civilians of the Ministry of Defence.

(2) *The nationalized industries*, which you will see come in the sphere of the Ministry of Technology, the Ministry of Transport, the Board of Trade and the Ministry of Posts and Tele-communications.

(3) *The local authorities*, whose sphere of activity largely corresponds to that of the social and law and order departments, though they are also heavily involved in the physical sector, including that part of the Ministry of Transport which is in that sector. You will observe that I have given each of the solid black local authority bars a stippled cap. The object of that is to indicate that the local authorities are themselves political institutions; that their management and control is in the hands of separately elected bodies, not the agents of the central Government – indeed, as we all know well, they are often of a different political complexion from that of the Government itself.

(4) Finally, the *National Health Service* – an organization which is neither local authority, nor a public corporation nor Civil Service, but something else again.

Several interesting points emerge from this diagram. First, it gives a rough indication of the comparative size of departments – at any rate it shows which are the largest and why that is so. I would have liked to draw the diagram so as to make the cross-hatched bars proportional to the number of civil servants which they represent; but that would have produced something almost impossible to follow, because just over 40 per cent of the total area would have been taken up with the civil servants in the Ministry of Defence. Thus, although the diagram perhaps sufficiently indicates that it is far and away the largest of the departments, it cannot possibly show how much larger it is.

Next in order of size come the Department of Health and Social Security with 70,000 civil servants and the Board of Inland Revenue with 67,000 – almost exactly a quarter the size of the Ministry of Defence.

What puts these departments in a class by themselves is that their activities run right down to the interface with the individual citizen. They have large networks of local offices all over the country and count the number of their clients in tens of millions. It is obvious that the managerial problems of these departments, and the kind of civil servants they need, must be quite different from those at the other end of the scale like the Ministry of Posts and Telecommunications whose sole function is the oversight of the Post Office Corporation, the two broadcasting authorities and frequency regulation. Equally small are those parts of the Board of Trade, the Ministry of Technology and the Ministry of Transport, whose function is to supervise the main nationalized industries. What makes those departments relatively large – the Ministry of Technology with just over 38,000 people, the Board of Trade with just under 17,000 people and the Ministry of Transport with 8300 – are their other activities – for example, the procurement functions of the Ministry of Technology, the Board of Trade's civil aviation work, which includes responsibility for air traffic control, and the Ministry of Transport's responsibility for the construction of motorways. Departments of intermediate size are typically those which deal with local authorities; good examples are the Ministry of Housing and Local Government with over 4500 people, and the Department of Education and Science with 3300. The Home Office comes into this category to some extent, but is in fact much larger – at 24,000 people – because it also has direct responsibility for the prison service.

My main object in showing you this diagram is to illustrate not only the wide variety of the individual tasks which civil servants have to perform and the variety of skills required, but the widely differing management situations. The control of what one might call a single-purpose organization such as Inland Revenue or Social Security is very large, but presents a relatively homogeneous set of problems. This is quite different from the situation of departments like the Ministry of Technology which combine direct responsibilities for procurement with what I have been calling supervision of nationalized industries and other functions which are comprehended in the blessed word 'sponsorship' for some parts of private industry.

This immensely varied situation so far as the work is concerned is reflected when one comes to look at the disposition of the various kinds of civil servant. The facts here are endless and I can only give you a few of the more striking examples.

First, in the large administrative departments, like Inland Revenue and the Department of Health and Social Security, the overwhelming majority of civil servants are of the kind we call clerical and executive – that is to say, they are primarily people who left school either at 15 or 18 and who are now the operators, supervisors and middle managers of these immense processes. When one turns to the more specialized kinds of civil servant, the following is typical of the situation in very many fields:

75 per cent of all the scientists in the Civil Service are in two departments – the Ministries of Defence and Technology;

90 per cent of the civil engineers in the service are in two departments – the Ministry of Public Building and Works and the Ministry of Transport;

77 per cent of the mechanical and electrical engineers are in two departments – the Ministry of Public Building and Works and the Ministry of Defence;

81 per cent of all the accountants in the Civil Service are in three departments – the Ministry of Technology, the Board of Trade and the Ministry of Defence.

This then is the environment in which we in the Civil Service Department have to carry out our two aims – of managing the Civil Service as a going concern, and carrying out our great programme of reform. How are we going about it? For the purposes of exposition it is convenient to group our activities under three heads:

first, those which concern the actual jobs which civil servants have to do;

second, those which concern the people who do the jobs;

third, those questions which arise from the situation of people in jobs – the special problems which come from the existence of a large career service.

Of course, the distinctions are to some extent arbitrary and artificial;

when one is considering the jobs one must always remember that they have to be done by people; and conversely, when considering people one always has to remember that they come under one's eye only because they are there to do jobs. Nevertheless, the distinction has its uses and we follow it to a considerable extent.

JOBS

What are we doing under the heading of jobs? First of all we are looking at a wide variety of questions of organization. As you will have gathered from the earlier part of this talk, there are a lot of questions to look at. Are the functions of the respective departments properly allocated or could the Government as a whole be helped to be more efficient by a different division of responsibilities? Does the grouping which I suggested in my diagrams suggest a means of improving the mechanism for the control of policy, personnel and finance? Would it be better if in these groups, or perhaps some improved variant of them, there were one Minister who was acknowledged to be in charge of the broad objectives of the group as a whole so that a much smaller number of Ministers meeting together could, as a Cabinet, in some sense represent the whole activities of central government? Is it right to retain the essentially federal concept of government or should the powers of the centre – that is, effectively of the Prime Minister – be increased? Is the division between the functions of Ministerial departments and other institutions in the public sector the best that can be devised – bearing in mind that the division occurs in different places in different spheres of activity and that in some cases, but in some cases only, a new and separate political level of decision-making is introduced?

These are questions which would require a whole lecture to discuss and I have time for only one point about them. I think it would be quite wrong to view these problems solely as a question of finding the most efficient form of organization, on the assumption that what is wanted is a managerial system comparable to that found in a large private enterprise or group of such enterprises, or for that matter in a place like the Inland Revenue. In the field in which we operate, political considerations can never be excluded; the disposition of managerial authority is also the disposition of political power; and these institutions reflect not simply the desire to produce an efficient Government machine, but also the need to keep it under democratic control. The balance between these two points of view will differ in differing fields of activity and at different times in

329

history, and I know of no general formula which will unfailingly point to a correct solution in every case.

We then come to the activities of particular departments and their organization and internal control. Here the story is very much influenced by the cardinal fact that departments are to a very large extent independent, particularly so in this field of management and organization. Again, the sheer variety of the different departmental situations makes it clear that no tidy uniform solution is likely to be practicable. As you know, for many years now the Treasury O and M service has been advising departments on their organization, their work methods and, in recent years, on management systems and techniques. The situation now is that the larger departments have their own inhouse O and M and management services, which work in co-operation with our own, while we provide a sort of halfway house service for the smaller departments. All of us, as you know, make a good deal of use of the services of management consultants. In this whole area it is evident that over the years a very great deal of progress has been made – but it is equally evident that there is still enormous scope for improvement. We have a large programme of enquiries, experiments, management reviews going on in every department, while at the same time we have mounted an enquiry, in which management consultants are taking part, into the efficiency and the future organization of our management services themselves.

Finally, in this area, we get down to the individual jobs themselves – the tasks into which the various work processes are divided. Here we are not only conducting a very large enquiry into work levels and job gradings but are also investigating the possibilities of job enrichment – the restructuring of whole activities so as to introduce a sense of managerial responsibility at lower levels in the organizations, to give people more challenging and satisfying work and to find adequate measures of performance.

All of this is, as you will see, closely related to the question of efficiency and in particular to the size of the Civil Service. We have now no doubt at all that by improving our work systems, processes and division of work, we can increase productivity and reduce the numbers of civil servants required for any given task. On the other hand, it must be remembered that the heads of departments, unlike the heads of private enterprise, do not control either the number or the nature of the tasks that have to be performed by their staff; and there are limits to what improved work systems can do for the size of the Service as a whole, if at the same time, the tasks continue to increase in number and complexity. In this work we are being greatly assisted not only by management consultants, but also by the efforts of a team of businessmen under the leadership of Sir Robert Bellinger, who investigate particular areas of Civil Service activity, in company with our own and the department's management services people so as to identify the jobs which are obsolete, the processes which are unnecessarily complicated and the ways in which they can be eliminated or reduced. Here again, however, I must remind you of the differences between the situation in private enterprise and that in the Civil Service. Again, we come up against the political factor – the fact that what we do must be subject to democratic control. This has in the past led to a much more elaborate system of checking, recording, etc., so that our activities can if necessary be put under parliamentary or other public scrutiny; and this alone accounts for a great deal of the additional staff and additional elaboration that we go in for. This means, therefore, that in addition to identifying the possibilities of more streamlining we also have the task of persuading Parliament and public opinion generally that no worthwhile element of democratic control will be lost.

PEOPLE

As I said at the outset, all these activities, which are primarily related to securing efficiency on the job, must of course be looked at with the people in mind. At the same time there is another whole range of our activities primarily concerned with people as such. These can be summarized fairly simply, though each heading involves a very considerable activity in itself. You are very well aware of them and I can merely list them as follows:

(a) recruitment and selection;
(b) training, both initially and at subsequent stages in a man's career;
(c) career development, including the development of management potential;
(d) the settlement of conditions of service – a field which for us in addition to covering the normal questions of discipline, deployment, etc., includes also the regulation of political activities and the requirements of security;
(e) superannuation, including the arrangements for compensation in the event of premature retirement.

Under each of these headings we are mounting a considerable effort, both to improve our existing processes and procedures as part of our reponsibility for the ongoing service in its present state, and for analysing and diagnosing the more fundamental changes which we expect to bring in as part of our process of reform. Thus in the field of recruitment we have already modified our procedures and after a review by management consultants have changed the organization of the Civil Service Commission so as to speed up the processes. At the same time, we are near the end of a great enquiry into the future needs of the Service for recruits of different kinds and the effect that that will have on our whole recruitment processes.

Here again the political factor comes in. The Civil Service Commission was originally set up as an independent body, in order to ensure that there could be no political patronage or other malign influence in the selection of civil servants. That is as important today as it was a hundred years ago, but at the same time we have to secure that the impartiality in selection does not mean remoteness from departmental needs or is unduly restrictive on the freedom and authority of management. This is part of a great dilemma which I would not like to claim we have fully solved but is one on which we are actively working.

In the field of training, the broad story is similar; on the one hand we have greatly expanded our central training and have taken the first steps to the setting-up of the Civil Service College; simultaneously we are working out the training needs which will become apparent when our major reforms have gone through. For the next year or two we shall be concentrating primarily on extending training in management to very large numbers of civil servants who have hitherto not had it – both the non-graduate executives who provide the bulk of junior and middle management in our great administrative processes, and the specialists and professionals of all kinds who have felt themselves excluded from managerial posts up to now and whom we are anxious to equip and use in positions of greater managerial authority.

This I regard as one of the most important sides of our work, both because I believe that over the Service as a whole there is much underused talent, which by suitable training and career management can be brought into use, and because I am sure that the training activities of the Centre for Administrative Studies, which was started in 1963 and is now to be absorbed into the Civil Service College, has been and must continue to be a tremendous engine for change. In the Centre we had young people teaching young people new techniques, new outlooks, new possibilities; we must retain this in the College and make absolutely certain that it does not, over the years, become simply the guardian of a tradition.

In the remaining areas of this enormous field of personnel management the broad story is the same; we are hard at it improving our current procedures in ways where the need for change is obvious, while at the same time working out what the more fundamental changes will be when we put the whole reform package together. In all of this, of course, we have to have constant regard to what is being done in the field of organization and job systems which I described earlier.

PEOPLE IN JOBS

Now I come to the range of activities which I referred to as my third category – that of people in jobs. Under this heading I put our activities in the field of what we call structure, and our closely associated activities for the pay of civil servants. As is now widely known, civil servants are divided into different classes. The reasons for this have nothing whatever to do with social class, although unfortunately in one respect (that is the position of the administrative class) the system came to have social overtones; and in any event it developed undesirable rigidities. But the starting point was sensible enough. Firstly, the large generalist classes were divided according to the different outputs of the educational system. The clerical classes which traditionally drew their people from those who left school immediately after the compulsory age, the executive classes who drew on those who left at 18 or so, after 'A' levels, and the administrative and other classes which called for graduates. This was a practical method of recruitment for a particular level of jobs and did not in any way mean that the classes remained exclusive. For example, around 40 per cent of the present administrative class started off in other classes.

This, however, is by no means the whole of the story; as Fulton discovered to his evident horror and astonishment, there are some 1500 different classes in the Civil Service. Before one dismisses this with a laugh as the kind of absurdity that bureaucrats left to themselves produce, it is worth considering how it came about. The most obvious reason is the wide variety of different occupations, skills and services which go to make up what we call the Civil Service. It was (and for that matter, is) sensible enough to recruit your statisticians or engineers or driving examiners or draughtsmen, as such, with the rates of pay appropriate to the market for people with such qualifications and with gradings appropriate to the organization of the work they are to do. Some of the classes are very small precisely because only a few specialists of particular kinds in some fields are needed.

Again, there is nothing wrong with devising rates of pay for them appropriate to the market, and the fact that they are called a class may be rather bureaucratic in terminology, but is merely a way of recognizing different qualifications and specializations.

Another big influence has been the one I have mentioned many times already: the independent position of departments. To get recognition that a particular kind of activity required people of a particular sort, who should be organized into a class with its own pay and grading structure, was one of the ways in which departments secured managerial freedom – both to pay at levels appropriate to the specialization, and not be tied to the rates for the generalist classes, and to develop their own patterns of career structure in isolation from the rest. There are areas where some system of this kind seems almost inevitable, where the work is highly specialized and concentrated in one department; there are equally many areas where it seems to have worked very well, especially where the classes are large and the different types of work are sufficient to provide a satisfactory career within the class.

The trouble is that over a period of time this process developed too many fine distinctions and therefore a bewildering proliferation of classes which even from a pay point of view are unnecessarily complicated and inhibiting to efficient management. Still more important perhaps is that classes which were developed originally for the purpose of specialized recruitment and appropriate pay came to acquire, partly under staff pressures, some of the characteristics of private estates, with fences which sometimes inhibited management from making the best use of the men available, and above all prevented appropriate career development across the Service as a whole. The lack of mobility is particularly damaging in the small classes or in classes which are contracting because of changes in the pattern of work. Furthermore, those in the specialist classes have felt that the generalists, who because of their very lack of specialism have been able to move from one job to another as circumstances have changed, have had an unfair advantage.

In the event the Fulton Committee recommended the abolition of all classes and the substitution of a single uniform grading structure over the Service as a whole, to be brought into being by a gigantic process of job evaluation. The Government accepted the objectives of

334

the Fulton recommendations and we are now engaged on the process of investigating to what extent a practicable system can be devised.

All of this is closely bound up with another major issue – to what extent should we increase the amount of specialization within the areas which have formerly been the domain of the generalists? Here one may go back to my original picture of the machinery of government; for one possible type of specialization would be in the groups into which the main functions of Government are divided. Fulton did not envisage as many as five groups; in fact he picked out only two – the economic and financial on the one hand, and the social on the other. However, he realized that further work needed to be done on this and this is what we are doing. There is, however, another dimension of specialization, which is brought out more clearly in Volume 2 of the Fulton Report than in the main report itself. This is in the functional areas of management – such things as personnel management, financial control, management information, etc. In these fields we have for the most part used generalists in the past; we are now investigating the extent to which it would be more efficient to encourage people to specialize. All of this, as you will see, has a great bearing not only on the question of the abolition of classes, but also on our concepts of the kind of career that individual civil servants can look forward to.

CONSULTATION

As I have said, there is a pattern running through it, of keeping the Service going on the one hand and thinking out the lines of reform on the other. In some fields we have marked this by having separate groups of people on the two functions; thus in the fields of recruitment and superannuation we have established separate forward planning groups alongside those who are keeping the present schemes going; and in the field of grading again we have the review team separate from those who are dealing with current questions. In other fields where it seems to us that the reforms are likely to be of a more evolutionary nature, growing out of the present system, we have not made so sharp a division.

All this, of course, requires a considerable effort of management and co-ordination, for which we have developed the normal central services for monitoring progress, planning the forward programme and so on.

This then is the broad outline of our current activities. In all of it, we can never forget the federal nature of the Government and another fact which up to now I have not mentioned – that civil servants are unionized to an extent far greater than is commonly realized. Of the half-million or so white-collar civil servants, over 95 per cent are members of a trade union; and the staff movement, through the Whitley Council system, has a long history of sturdy independence of mind combined with a remarkable willingness to co-operate with management in seeking solutions to problems which will be in the interests of the staff and public alike. They are, of course, deeply concerned with the reform programme, and virtually all our activities are geared to consultation, and eventual negotiation, with them. This means that the apparatus for considering what shape the reforms should take, and for implementing them, is inevitably complicated. On the one hand we have to have an elaborate system of consultation with departments; on the other an equally elaborate system of discussion, persuasion, consultation and negotiation with the unions. All of this we are doing, as far as practicable, in public; we have adopted the practice of publishing our findings as we go along and we already have a growing pile of reports, statements, proposals, which are made available not only throughout the Service but also to the public at large. We are now working up to a further statement which we expect will contain the first outline of some of the major elements in the reform, which we expect to make available to the staff associations early in the new year, for the purposes of discussion within their various executives, so that they can bring it to their annual conferences next May.

These two great areas – departmental managements on the one hand and the staff associations on the other – are perhaps the most important, but certainly not the only parts of our environment to which we look for criticism, guidance and help. Two other important parts are the universities, with whom we are concerned both as sources of recruits, facilities for training and repositories of knowledge and wisdom on many parts of our affairs; and industry, including in particular the management consultants, who have been particularly helpful in putting at our disposal the knowledge they have gained of similar problems in private enterprise.

STAFFING OF THE CSD

Finally, I should just like to say one word about our own policy in staffing the Civil Service Department. As I have explained, this was not a new creation out in a green field but was formed from the existing Pay and Management side of the Treasury, together with the staff of the Civil Service Commission. Both of these organizations contained large numbers of highly intelligent, imaginative and devoted people, who were simply waiting for the chance to show what they could contribute to the reform of the Service. But my own experiences on the other side of the Treasury had convinced me of one very important thing. Both the Treasury and the Civil Service Department, as relatively small central brains trusts, suffer from the disadvantage that, in their day-to-day work, they are not personally experiencing the kind of problems which daily confront the large administrative and managerial departments which it is their task to serve or control. This situation, which is of course quite inevitable, can lead to very great difficulty if those in the central departments come to think that they can rely entirely on what is reported to them by the operational departments. Useful though all this is, it is in my opinion no substitute for personal experience. There is also the imperative need to bring to bear on the problem the innocent eye of the outsider – the man who is able to tell us that, in spite of our imperial bearing, we do not in fact have any clothes on. In our first year we have of necessity been expanding and we have therefore had an opportunity to change the character of our personnel. In the year we have had nearly a hundred new entrants to the Department at the middle and senior levels – an increase of about 40 per cent. They have come from every one of the departments shown on my diagram except the Lord Chancellor's Office – and I wouldn't be surprised if we get someone from there before long. They are bringing to us experience which we could not possibly claim for ourselves. They are also of many different kinds; we now have 25 scientists, 13 engineers, 3 economists, 6 accountants and auditors as well as many others. At the same time we have brought in 23 people from outside the Civil Service altogether, including 8 from universities and 10 from private industry, including 5 from management consultants. In this way we are hoping to match our new tasks with new men.

337

24

Natural Justice and Administrative Decisions*

The Committee on Ministers' Powers, under the chairmanship of Lord Donoughmore, was set up in 1929 as a result of growing public concern focused in such books as C. K. Allen's Law in the Making *(Oxford University Press, 1927) and Lord Hewart's* The New Despotism *(Benn, 1929), to consider powers exercised as a result of delegated legislation and judicial or quasi-judicial decision. In this extract from its report, one of the classics in British administrative law, the Committee is primarily concerned with examining the process of administrative decision making from the judicial point of view.*

THE DIFFERENCE BETWEEN JUDICIAL AND QUASI-JUDICIAL DECISIONS

The word 'quasi', when prefixed to a legal term, generally means that the thing, which is described by the word, has some of the legal attributes denoted and connoted by the legal term, but that it has not all of them. For instance, if a transaction is described as a quasi-contract it means that the transaction has some of the attributes of a contract but not all. Perhaps the best translation of the word 'quasi', as thus used by lawyers, is 'not exactly', A 'quasi-judicial' decision is thus one which has some of the attributes of a judicial decision, but not all. In order, therefore, to define the term 'quasi-judicial decision', as it is used in our terms of reference, we must discover which of the attributes of a true judicial decision are included and which are excluded.

A true judicial decision presupposes an existing dispute between two or more parties, and then involves four requisites:

    (1) the presentation (not necessarily orally) of their case by the

* From *Report of the Committee on Ministers' Powers*, HMSO, Cmd. 4060, 1932, pp. 73–82.

338

parties to the dispute; (2) if the dispute between them is a question of fact, the ascertainment of the fact by means of evidence adduced by the parties to the dispute and often with the assistance of argument by or on behalf of the parties on the evidence; (3) if the dispute between them is a question of law, the submission of legal argument by the parties; and (4) a decision which disposes of the whole matter by a finding upon the facts in dispute and an application of the law of the land to the facts so found, including where required a ruling upon any disputed question of law.

A quasi-judicial decision equally presupposes an existing dispute between two or more parties and involves (1) and (2), but does not necessarily involve (3), and never involves (4). The place of (4) is in fact taken by administrative action, the character of which is determined by the Minister's free choice.

For example, suppose a statute empowers a Minister to take action if certain facts are proved, and in that event gives him an absolute discretion whether or not he will take action.[1] In such a case he must consider the representations of the parties and ascertain the facts – to that extent the decision contains a judicial element. But, the facts once ascertained, his decision does not depend on any legal or statutory direction, for *ex hypothesi* he is left free within his statutory powers to take such administrative[2] action as he may think fit: that is to say the matter is not finally disposed of by the process of (4). Whereas it is of the essence of a judicial decision that the matter is finally disposed of by that process and nothing remains to be done except the execution of the judgment, a step which the law of the land compels automatically, in the case of the quasi-judicial decision the finality of (4) is absent; another and a different kind of step has to be taken; the Minister – who for this purpose personifies the whole administrative Department of State – has to make up his mind whether he will or will not take administrative action and if so what action. His ultimate decision is 'quasi-judicial', and not judicial, because it is governed, not by a statutory direction to him to apply

[1] e.g. s. 91 of the Road Traffic Act, 1930 (20 & 21 Geo. 5, c. 43), under which the Minister of Transport is directed to consider the report of the person appointed by him to hold a public enquiry, the responsibility for deciding the question of fact and considering the arguments of the parties being left by the Section upon the Minister's own shoulders. See R. *v.* The Minister of Transport. *Ex parte* Southend Carriers, Ltd. *The Times*, 18 December, 1931.

[2] Usually the administrative action imports an executive decision: sometimes it partakes of a legislative character – as for instance when the Minister makes an order 'approving' a town planning scheme – but the distinction for the purposes of this Section of our Report need not be laboured.

the law of the land to the facts and act accordingly, but by a statutory permission to use his discretion after he has ascertained the facts and to be guided by considerations of public policy. This option would not be open to him if he were exercising a purely judicial function.

It is obvious that if all four of the above-named requisites to a decision are present, if, for instance, a Minister, having ascertained the facts, is obliged by the statute to decide solely in accordance with the law, the decision is judicial. The fact that it is not reached by a court so-called, but by a Minister acting under statutory powers and under specialized procedure, will not make the decision any the less judicial.

For example the Unemployment Insurance Acts, 1920[1] to 1930,[2] require all 'employed persons' aged sixteen and upwards, of either sex, whether British subjects or aliens, to be insured against un-employment, unless engaged in an 'excepted employment' or unless, although engaged in an 'insurable employment', they are 'exempt persons'. The Acts provide that if any question arises whether any employment or class of employment is such employment as to make the person engaged therein an employed person within the meaning of the Act, the question shall be decided by the Minister of Labour unless he elects to refer it for decision to the High Court. In such a case the decision is clearly judicial whether it is given by the Minister or by the Court. Neither the Minister nor the Court has any discretion in the matter. The question to be decided turns entirely on the application of the law as laid down in the Acts to the facts of the particular case. The judicial character of the Minister's decision, when he gives the decision himself, is recognized and illustrated by the provision in the Acts that any person aggrieved by the decision of the Minister may appeal from that decision to the High Court and by the further provision that the Minister shall have regard to the decisions given by the Umpire by whom such questions were determined under the earlier Unemployment Insurance legislation.

NATURAL JUSTICE

In the above analysis we have tried to explain the essential characteristics of a judicial decision in the full sense of the phrase; and we have expressed the view that the quasi-judicial decision imports only some, and not all, of those characteristics; or, putting the same point

[1] 10 & 11 Geo. 5, c. 30.
[2] 20 & 21 Geo. 5, c. 16.

in another form, that the Minister at some stage in his mental operations before his action takes final shape passes from the judge into the administrator. But whether the function be judicial or quasi-judicial, its exercise presupposes the existence of a dispute and parties to the dispute, and it is this feature which separates the judicial and quasi-judicial function on the one hand from the administrative on the other. As we have already pointed out, a judicial element is involved in quasi-judicial as well as in judicial functions; and it has been truly said that, however much a Minister in exercising such functions may depart from the usual forms of legal procedure or from the common law rules of evidence he ought not to depart from or offend against 'natural justice'. That phrase is perhaps more often used than understood, and we therefore venture to say what we understand by it.

Before doing so, however, it may be well to call attention to two cases – *Buchanan* v. *Rucker*[1] and *Schibsby* v. *Westenholz*[2] – which show that the conception of 'natural justice' must be regarded as belonging to the field of moral and social principles and not as having passed into the category of substantive law, so as necessarily to make every act obnoxious to its canons a transgression of a legal rule recognized and enforced as such by our Courts. In the former case Lord Ellenborough declared at *nisi prius*[3] that it was 'contrary to the first principles of reason and justice that either in civil or criminal proceedings a man should be condemned before he was heard' and that 'the practice of the Law Courts of Tobago to summon a defendant who was out of the jurisdiction and never had been within by nailing the writ on the door of the Court-house was *mala praxis*'[4] and could not be sanctioned. In the latter case these observations were considered by the Court of King's Bench. The judgment of the

[1] (1807) 1 Camp. 66.　　[2] (1870) L.R. 6 Q.B. 155.

[3] Note on the meaning of the Latin expressions '*nisi prius*' and '*in banco*'. Lord Ellenborough was Chief Justice of the Court of King's Bench. When he was trying cases with a jury at the Guildhall, he was said to be sitting at *Nisi Prius*, because the writ for summoning the jury commanded the Sheriff of Middlesex to bring the jurors to the Court of King's Bench at Westminster on a certain day 'unless before that day' (*Nisi Prius*) the Judges came to the Guildhall, as in practice they invariably did. The issue of fact having been determined by the jury at *Nisi Prius*, the Chief Justice reported the verdict of the jury to the Court of King's Bench, which pronounced judgment. But before judgment was pronounced all rulings on points of law given by the Chief Justice at the trial at *Nisi Prius* were subject to review by himself and the four other Judges of the Court, sitting *in banco*, i.e., in Bench or full Court. See Ralph Sutton's *Personal Action at Common Law*, c. 7. (Butterworth, 1929.)

[4] '*Mala praxis*'. This hybrid Latin and Greek phrase may be translated 'bad practice'.

Court (Mr Justice Blackburn, Mr Justice Mellor, Mr Justice Lush and Mr Justice Hannen) was delivered by Mr Justice Blackburn. Their Lordships stated that 'Lord Ellenborough's expressions were used in the hurry of *nisi prius*,[1] and that when the case came before him *in banco*[1] in *Buchanan* v. *Rucker*[2] he entirely abandoned what (with all deference to so great an authority) they could not regard as more than declamation'. But although 'natural justice' does not fall within those definite and well-recognized rules of law which English Courts of Law enforce, we think it is beyond doubt that there are certain canons of judicial conduct to which all tribunals and persons who have to give judicial or quasi-judicial decisions ought to conform. The principles on which they rest are we think implicit in the rule of law. Their observance is demanded by our national sense of justice; and it is, we think, the desire to secure safeguards for their observance, more than any other factor, which has inspired the criticisms levelled against the Executive and against Parliament for entrusting judicial or quasi-judicial functions to the Executive.

(i) The first and most fundamental principle of natural justice is that a man may not be a judge in his own cause. It is on this ground that a decision of a bench of magistrates may be quashed by the King's Bench Division of the High Court of Justice, in the exercise of its supervisory jurisdiction, on the ground of bias, if a single magistrate on the bench had any interest in the question at issue.

In *Dimes* v. *Grand Junction Canal* (*Proprietors of*) (1852) 3 H.L.C. 759, the House of Lords, after consulting the Judges, decided that the decree of the Lord Chancellor, affirming the order of the Vice-Chancellor, granting relief to a company in which the Lord Chancellor had an interest as a shareholder to the amount of several thousand pounds, which was unknown to the defendant in the suit, was void-able on that account and must therefore be set aside. In the course of his speech Lord Campbell said:

> 'No one can suppose that Lord Cottenham could be, in the remotest degree, influenced by the interest that he had in this concern; but, my Lords, it is of the last importance that the maxim that no man is to be a judge in his own cause should be held sacred. And that is not to be confined to a cause in which he is a party, but applies to a cause in which he has an interest. Since I have had the honour to be Chief Justice of the Court of Queen's Bench, we have again and again set aside proceedings in inferior tribunals because an individual who had an interest in a cause took

[1] See footnote 3 on page 341.   [2] (1808) 9 East 192.

part in the decision. And it will have a most salutary influence on these tribunals when it is known that this High Court of last resort, in a case in which the Lord Chancellor of England had an interest, considered that his decision was on that account a decision not according to law, and was set aside. This will be a lesson to all inferior tribunals to take care not only that in their decrees they are not influenced by their personal interest, but to avoid the appearance of labouring under such an influence.'

In that case the Lord Chancellor's disqualification was pecuniary interest. It goes without saying that in no case in which a Minister has a pecuniary or any other similar personal interest in a decision, e.g. as the owner – whether in his own right or as a trustee – of property which may be affected, should he exercise either judicial or quasi-judicial functions. Such cases may be presumed to be rare, and we do not think it necessary for us to make any special recommendations about them.

But disqualifying interest is not confined to pecuniary interest. In *Reg* v. *Rand* (1866) L.R. 1 Q.B. 230 the Court of Queen's Bench laid it down that wherever there was a real likelihood that the judge would, from kindred or any other cause, have a bias in favour of one of the parties, it would be very wrong in him to act. In *Rex* v. *Sunderland Justices* (1901) 2 K.B. 357 this rule was applied by the Court of Appeal in the case of certain borough justices, who were also members of the Borough Council and adjudicated in a matter arising out of a proposal which they had actively supported in the Council, although their pecuniary interest as trustees for the ratepayers was held insufficient in itself to raise the presumption of bias. 'It is hardly necessary to point out,' said the Master of the Rolls, 'how very important it is that persons who have to exercise judicial functions with regard to any matter should not lay themselves open to any suggestion of bias on their part.'

Indeed we think it is clear that bias from strong and sincere conviction as to public policy may operate as a more serious disqualification than pecuniary interest. No honest man acting in a judicial capacity allows himself to be influenced by pecuniary interest: if anything, the danger is likely to be that through fear of yielding to motives of self-interest he may unconsciously do an injustice to the party with which his pecuniary interest may appear to others to identify him. But the bias to which a public-spirited man is subjected if he adjudicates in any case in which he is interested on public grounds is more subtle and less easy for him to detect and resist.

We are here considering questions of public policy and from the public point of view it is important to remember that the principle underlying all the decisions in regard to disqualification by reason of bias is that the mind of the judge ought to be free to decide on purely judicial grounds and should not be directly or indirectly influenced by, or exposed to the influence of, either motives of self-interest or opinions about policy or any other considerations not relevant to the issue.

We are of opinion that in considering the assignment of judicial functions to Ministers Parliament should keep clearly in view the maxim that no man is to be judge in a cause in which he has an interest. We think that in any case in which the Minister's Department would naturally approach the issue to be determined with a desire that the decision should go one way rather than another, the Minister should be regarded as having an interest in the cause. Parliament would do well in such a case to provide that the Minister himself should not be the judge, but that the case should be decided by an independent tribunal.

It is unfair to impose on a practical administrator the duty of adjudicating in any matter in which it could fairly be argued that his impartiality would be in inverse ratio to his strength and ability as a Minister. An easy-going and cynical Minister, rather bored with his office and sceptical of the value of his Department, would find it far easier to apply a judicial mind to purely judicial problems connected with the Department's administration than a Minister whose head and heart were in his work. It is for these reasons and not because we entertain the slightest suspicion of the good faith or the intellectual honesty of Ministers and their advisers that we are of opinion that Parliament should be chary of imposing on Ministers the ungrateful task of giving judicial decisions in matters in which their very zeal for the public service can scarcely fail to bias them unconsciously.

We desire to make it plain that we are recommending a general principle as a future safeguard: we do not wish to imply that the principle, though it has perhaps not been clearly envisaged, is in fact violated in any existing statutes, and we have been unable to find evidence to support the view held by some critics that it occurs extensively. An interesting example of the way in which Parliament has observed the principle will be found in old age pension legislation: under Sections 7 and 8 of the Old Age Pensions Act 1908[1] the Minister of Health is the central pension authority for determining appeals, although the Commissioners of Customs and Excise, who

[1] 8 Edw. 7, c. 40.

344

are responsible to the Treasury, i.e. in practice to the Chancellor of the Exchequer, are the Department responsible for the administration of pensions.

The application of the principle which we have just enunciated to quasi-judicial decision is not so easy, since a quasi-judicial decision ultimately turns upon administrative policy for which an executive Minister should normally be responsible. We think, however, that before Parliament entrusts a Minister with the power and duty of giving quasi-judicial decisions as part of a legislative scheme, Parliament ought to consider whether the nature of his interest as Minister in the carrying out of the functions to be entrusted to him by the statute may be such as to disqualify him from acting with the requisite impartiality. The comparative importance of the issues involved in the decision will, of course, be a relevant factor. Where it appears that the policy of the Department might be substantially better served by a decision one way rather than another, the first principle of natural justice will come into play, and the Minister should not be called upon to perform the incongruous task of dealing with the judicial part of the quasi-judicial decision as an impartial judge, when *ex hypothesi* he and his Department want the decision to be one way rather than another. We recognize that this kind of case may be rare, but it is a real possibility. In such a case the judicial functions which must be performed before the ultimate decision is given and on which that decision must be based should be entrusted by Parliament to an independent Tribunal whose decision on any judicial issues should be binding on the Minister when in his discretion he completes the quasi-judicial decision by administrative action.

(ii) The second principle of natural justice is one which has two aspects, both of which are as applicable to quasi-judicial as to judicial decisions. No party ought to be condemned unheard; and if his right to be heard is to be a reality, he must know in good time the case which he has to meet. But on neither branch of this principle can any particular procedure (i) by which the party is informed of the case which he has to meet, or (ii) by which his evidence and argument are 'heard', be regarded as fundamental. That a Minister or a Ministerial Tribunal does not conform to the procedure of the Courts in either respect imports no disregard of natural justice. There is, for instance, no natural right to an oral hearing.

(iii) It may well be argued that there is a third principle of natural justice, namely, that a party is entitled to know the reason for the decision, be it judicial or quasi-judicial. Our opinion is that there are some cases when the refusal to give grounds for a decision may be plainly unfair; and this may be so, even when the decision is final and no further proceedings are open to the disappointed party by way of appeal or otherwise. But it cannot be disputed that when further proceedings are open to a disappointed party, it is contrary to natural justice that the silence of the Minister or the Ministerial Tribunal should deprive him of his opportunity. And we think it beyond all doubt that there is from the angle of broad political expediency a real advantage in communicating the grounds of the decision to the parties concerned and, if of general interest, to the public. We deal with this question more fully later in our Report.

(iv) Some judges have discerned a fourth principle of natural justice, which other judges have declined to admit, *viz.*: that when Parliament has provided for what amounts to an oral hearing by the method of a 'public enquiry', local or otherwise, held before an inspector appointed for the purpose by the Minister, as a means of guidance to the Minister in his decision – whether judicial or quasi-judicial – it is contrary to natural justice that the inspector's report upon the enquiry should not be made available to the parties so heard. Such an enquiry is plainly intended by Parliament to be the means by which all the main relevant facts are to be ascertained, and the main arguments of the parties affected are to be heard. Those parties are justly entitled, it is said, to know what facts are found by the inspector and how he sums up the arguments he has heard, so that they may know what material is put before the Minister for his decision.

Whether a refusal of such publication to the parties is contrary to natural justice may possibly be open to some doubt; but it is plain that important considerations of public policy are involved, and we need not pause to survey the border land between high public policy and natural justice in order to discover the theoretical boundary. We revert to this question at greater length later in our Report.

ADMINISTRATIVE DECISIONS TO BE DISTINGUISHED

Decisions which are purely administrative stand on a wholly different footing from quasi-judicial as well as from judicial decisions and must be distinguished accordingly. Indeed the very word 'decision' has a different meaning in the one sphere of activity and the other. When a person resolves to act in a particular way, the mental step may be described as a 'decision'. Again, when a judge determines an issue of fact upon conflicting evidence, or a question of law upon forensic argument, he gives a 'decision'. But the two mental acts differ. In the case of the administrative decision, there is no legal obligation upon the person charged with the duty of reaching the decision to consider and weigh submissions and arguments, or to collate any evidence, or to solve any issue. The grounds upon which he acts, and the means which he takes to inform himself before acting, are left entirely to his discretion. We may illustrate our meaning by two examples of such a 'decision'; (1) the decision of the Admiralty to place a Departmental contract for stores – an act of a purely 'business' character; (2) the decision of the Home Secretary to grant naturalization to a particular alien, a matter upon which Parliament has given him an absolute discretion.[1]

But even a large number of administrative decisions may and do involve, in greater or less degree, at some stage in the procedure which eventuates in executive action, certain of the attributes of a judicial decision. Indeed generally speaking a quasi-judicial decision is only an administrative decision, some stage or some element of which possesses judicial characteristics. And it is doubtless because so many administrative acts have this character that our terms of reference have specially included quasi-judicial decisions.

The intermingling of the two elements in one composite 'decision' is well illustrated by the type of case where the judicial element looms large in proportion to the administrative, although the final act is administrative. Instances we have in mind are the decisions of licensing authorities constituted under an Act of Parliament with an obligation to grant licences to fit and proper persons in accordance with the intentions and under the conditions of the Acts; as for example the Licensing Justices in their annual meeting under the Licensing Acts, 1910[2] and 1921:[3] The Traffic Commissioners under Part IV of the Road Traffic Act, 1930;[4] or the Minister of Transport himself on appeal from the Commissioners under Section 81 of that Act. The ultimate decision is administrative and not judicial in each case – whether given by a justice, a commissioner, or the Minister. But evidence has to be considered and weighed; arguments on fact and possibly law have to be heard, and conclusions reached; irrelevant and improper considerations have to be excluded; and the body hearing the application must be disinterested and free from bias. And it is only after they have taken all the above preliminary steps judicially that they pass into pure administration and in the exercise of

[1] The British Nationality and Status of Aliens Act, 1914 (4 & 5 Geo. 5, c. 17), s. 2, ss. (3).
[2] 10 Edw. 7 & 1 Geo. 5, c. 24, s. 10.
[3] 11 & 12 Geo. 5, c. 42, s. 12.
[4] 20 & 21 Geo. 5, c. 43.

administrative discretion on grounds of public policy choose to grant or withhold a licence.[1]

[1] Lord Halsbury's exposition of the duty of justices to exercise their discretion to grant or not to grant a licence judicially in *Sharp* v. *Wakefield* [1891] A.C. 173 at 178–182, may be consulted by those who wish to pursue the analysis further.

25

Openness, Fairness and Impartiality*

The Franks Committee on Administrative Tribunals and Enquiries was set up because there was considerable public concern at the administrative behaviour revealed by the public inquiry into the Crichel Down case. Before the Committee examined the working of administrative tribunals it considered the wider issue of the relationship between the individual and authority and how disputes arose. This extract is taken from the introductory paragraphs of the report where the wider issues and general principles are discussed.

Disputes between the Individual and Authority
How do disputes between the individual and authority arise in this country at the present time? In general the starting point is the enactment of legislation by Parliament. Many statutes apply detailed schemes to the whole or to large classes of the community (for example national insurance) or lay on a Minister and other authorities a general duty to provide a service (for example education or health). Such legislation is rarely sufficient in itself to achieve all its objects, and a series of decisions by administrative bodies, such as Government Departments and local authorities, is often required. For example, in a national insurance scheme decisions have to be given on claims to benefit, and in providing an educational service decisions have to be taken on the siting of new schools. Many of these decisions affect the rights of individual citizens, who may then object.

Once objection has been raised, a further decision becomes inevitable. This further decision is of a different kind: whether to confirm, cancel or vary the original decision. In reaching it account must be taken not only of the original decision but also of the objection.

---

* From *Report of the Committee on Administrative Tribunals and Enquiries*, HMSO, Cmnd. 218, 1957, pp. 2–7.

The Resolution of these Disputes

These further decisions are made in various ways. Some are made in courts of law and therefore by the procedure of a court of law. For example, an order made by a local authority for the demolition of an insanitary house may be appealed against to the County Court. Frequently the statutes lay down that these further decisions are to be made by a special tribunal or a Minister. For example, a contested claim to national insurance benefit has to be determined by a special tribunal, and the decision whether or not to confirm an opposed scheme for the compulsory acquisition of land by a local authority must be made by the Minister concerned. In these cases the procedure to be followed in dealing with objections to the first decision and in arriving at the further decision is laid down in the statute or in regulations made thereunder.

But over most of the field of public administration no formal procedure is provided for objecting or deciding on objections. For example, when foreign currency or a scarce commodity such as petrol or coal is rationed or allocated, there is no other body to which an individual applicant can appeal if the responsible administrative authority decides to allow him less than he has requested. Of course the aggrieved individual can always complain to the appropriate administrative authority, to his Member of Parliament, to a representative organization or to the press. But there is no formal procedure on which he can insist.

There are therefore two broad distinctions to be made among these further decisions which we have been discussing. The first is between those decisions which follow a statutory procedure and those which do not. The second distinction is within the group of decisions subject to a statutory procedure. Some of these decisions are taken in the ordinary courts and some are taken by tribunals or by Ministers after a special procedure.

THE TWO PARTS OF THE TERMS OF REFERENCE

It is noteworthy that Parliament, having decided that the decisions with which we are concerned should not be remitted to the ordinary courts, should also have decided that they should not be left to be reached in the normal course of administration. Parliament has considered it essential to lay down special procedures for them.

Good Administration

This must have been to promote good administration. Administration must not only be efficient in the sense that the objectives of policy are securely attained without delay. It must also satisfy the general body of citizens that it is proceeding with reasonable regard to the balance between the public interest which it promotes and the private interest which it disturbs. Parliament has, we infer, intended in relation to the subject-matter of our terms of reference that the further decisions or, as they may rightly be termed in this context, adjudications must be acceptable as having been properly made.

It is natural that Parliament should have taken this view of what constitutes good administration. In this country government rests fundamentally upon the consent of the governed. The general acceptability of these adjudications is one of the vital elements in sustaining that consent.

Openness, Fairness and Impartiality

When we regard our subject in this light, it is clear that there are certain general and closely linked characteristics which should mark these special procedures. We call these characteristics openness, fairness and impartiality.

Here we need only give brief examples of their application. Take openness. If these procedures were wholly secret, the basis of confidence and acceptability would be lacking. Next take fairness. If the objector were not allowed to state his case, there would be nothing to stop oppression. Thirdly, there is impartiality. How can the citizen be satisfied unless he feels that those who decide his case come to their decision with open minds?

To assert that openness, fairness and impartiality are essential characteristics of our subject-matter is not to say that they must be present in the same way and to the same extent in all its parts. Difference in the nature of the issue for adjudication may give good reason for difference in the degree to which the three general characteristics should be developed and applied. Again, the method by which a Minister arrives at a decision after a hearing or enquiry cannot be the same as that by which a tribunal arrives at a decision. This difference is brought out later in the Report. For the moment it is sufficient to point out that when Parliament sets up a tribunal to decide cases, the adjudication is placed outside the Department concerned. The members of the tribunal are neutral and impartial in relation to the policy of the Minister, except in so far as that policy is contained in the rules which the tribunal has been set up to apply. But the Minister, deciding in the cases under the second part of our terms of reference, is committed to a policy which he has been charged

351

by Parliament to carry out. In this sense he is not, and cannot be, impartial.

The Allocation of Decisions to Tribunals and Ministers

At this stage another question naturally arises. On what principle has it been decided that some adjudications should be made by tribunals and some by Ministers? If from a study of the history of the subject we could discover such a principle, we should have a criterion which would be a guide for any future allocation of these decisions between tribunals and Ministers.

The search for this principle has usually involved the application of one or both of two notions, each with its antithesis. Both notions are famous and have long histories. They are the notion of what is judicial, its antithesis being what is administrative, and the notion of what is according to the rule of law, its antithesis being what is arbitrary.

What is judicial has been worked out and given expression by generations of judges. Its distinction from what is administrative recalls great constitutional victories and marks the essential difference in the nature of the decisions of the judiciary and of the executive.

The rule of law stands for the view that decisions should be made by the application of known principles or laws. In general such decisions will be predictable, and the citizen will know where he is. On the other hand there is what is arbitrary. A decision may be made without principle, without any rules. It is therefore unpredictable, the antithesis of a decision taken in accordance with the rule of law.

Nothing that we say diminishes the importance of these pairs of antitheses. But it must be confessed that neither pair yields a valid principle on which one can decide whether the duty of making a certain decision should be laid upon a tribunal or upon a Minister or whether the existing allocation of decisions between tribunals and Ministers is appropriate. But even if there is no such principle and we cannot explain the facts, we can at least start with them. An empirical approach may be the most useful.

Starting with the facts, we observe that the methods of adjudication by tribunals are in general not the same as those of adjudication by Ministers. All or nearly all tribunals apply rules. No ministerial decision of the kind denoted by the second part of our terms of reference is reached in this way. Many matters remitted to tribunals and Ministers appear to have, as it were, a natural affinity with one or other method of adjudication. Sometimes the policy of the legislation can be embodied in a system of detailed regulations. Particular decision cannot, single case by single case, alter the Minister's policy. Where this is so, it is natural to entrust the decisions to a tribunal, if not to the courts. On the other hand it is sometimes desirable to preserve flexibility of decision in the pursuance of public policy. Then a wise expediency is the proper basis of right adjudication, and the decision must be left with a Minister.

But in other instances there seems to be no such natural affinity. For example, there seems to be no natural affinity which makes it clearly appropriate for appeals in goods vehicle licence cases to be decided by the Transport Tribunal when appeals in a number of road passenger cases are decided by the Minister.

We shall therefore respect this factual difference between tribunals and Ministers and deal separately with the two parts of the subject. When considering tribunals we shall see how far the three characteristics of openness, fairness and impartiality can be developed and applied in general and how far their development and application must be adapted to the circumstances of particular tribunals. We shall then proceed to the decisions of Ministers after a hearing or enquiry and consider how far the difference in method of adjudication requires a different development and application of the three characteristics.

26

The Chalkpit Case*

In 1957 the owners of land in Essex applied to the Saffron Walden Rural District Council for permission to develop their land by digging chalk. The Council refused the application, so the owners appealed to the Minister of Housing and Local Government who sent an inspector to hold an enquiry. Although the inspector did not report in favour of the owners, the Minister allowed their appeal and gave permission for the chalkpit to be worked. Subsequently, adjoining landowners appealed to the High Court to set aside the Minister's decision on the ground that the Minister had relied on advice which he asked for and received from experts in the Ministry of Agriculture after the local enquiry had been closed; but the High Court held that only persons who had some legal right in the land under dispute could apply to the High Court – it was not enough to own adjoining *land. Later, the complaint was considered by the Council on Tribunals which reported on it to the Lord Chancellor. This extract from an editorial in* Public Law *comments on part of that report, with special reference to the general principles that guided the Council's examination. See also J. A. G. Griffith, 'The Council and the Chalkpit',* Public Administration, *Vol. 39, pp. 369–74.*

On 30 March 1962, the Council on Tribunals made a report to the Lord Chancellor in connection with statutory enquiries. The report read:

'1. On 24 February, 1961, the Saffron Walden Planning Appeal (the *Chalkpit* case) was the subject of a special report by the Council under section 1 (1) (c) of the Tribunals and Enquiries Act, 1958. Since then the matter has been debated in both Houses of Parliament.

2. In the opinion of the Council a question of special importance arose out of this case and in their statement of 24 May, 1961, the Council indicated their intention to make a report on the whole

* From *Public Law*, 1962, pp. 125–9. Reprinted with permission of Stevens & Sons Ltd.

problem of handling new factual evidence after an enquiry, and the application of the principles laid down in the report of the Franks Committee.

3. In examining this problem the Council have been guided by the following general principles:

(*a*) If the public is to have confidence in the procedure laid down by Parliament, it must be made clear that enquiries are not just an incident in the administrative process. The true nature and purpose of these procedures are described in paragraphs 262–277 of the Franks Report.

(*b*) The public regards an enquiry as a requirement by Parliament that before the final decision is reached, local feeling and local facts must be taken into account by the Minister. Most enquiries fulfil this purpose: but complaint understandably arises where a Minister rejects the recommendations of an inspector[1] who has both heard the evidence and seen the site –

(i) if the rejection is based on Ministerial policy which could and should have been made clear before the enquiry, or,

(ii) if the Minister takes advice after the enquiry from persons who neither heard the evidence nor saw the site, but yet controverted the inspector's findings as to the facts of the local situation.

(*c*) As recommended by the Franks Committee in paragraphs 286–290 of their Report, every effort should be made to make clear Ministerial policy before the enquiry.

(*d*) Proper respect should be paid to an inspector's findings of fact and recommendations about the particular case in its local aspects; otherwise parties will naturally feel that they have wasted their time and money in appearing at the enquiry.

4. The number of cases where the inspector's recommendation is rejected by the Minister is in any case small. It therefore appeared to the Council that the most satisfactory general rule might be for the Minister to refer back to the parties for their comments in every case in which he proposed to differ from the inspector's recommendations and, on the request of any party whose comment he rejected, to reopen the enquiry except where the reasons for his disagreement with the inspector's recommendation were founded upon a conflict between the recommendation and general Ministerial policy.

5. After a full exchange of views with government departments the Council have, however, come to the conclusion that the right solution can be found in two rules:

(1) Where the Minister proposes to disagree with the inspector's

[1] Reporter in Scotland.

recommendation either because of some factor not considered at the enquiry or because he differs from a finding of fact made by the inspector, he will notify the parties to the appeal of his disagreement and the reasons for it and afford them an opportunity for making comments and representations in writing before finally making his decision.

(2) Where the Minister proposes to depart from the inspector's recommendation because of (a) fresh evidence on a question of fact, or (b) fresh expert evidence (including expert advice), or (c) the introduction of a fresh issue, the enquiry should (if any of the parties so desire) be reopened and the new evidence or issue should be produced at the reopened enquiry.

6. The Council believe that a solution on these lines can be put into effect without delay and they recommend that in due course the proposed rules should be embodied in the rules of procedure for statutory enquiries'.

The first 'general principle' referred to by the Council is perhaps a little too vague for guidance. There are many beholders of statutory enquiries and what they see will vary according to their interest. The private citizens directly involved, their neighbours, public authorities, the inspector, the civil servant reading the report and contemplating his own decisions, a Member of Parliament, the Minister, the Lord Chancellor – persons and bodies so diverse in interest and function can hardly be expected to agree about the 'nature and purpose' of an enquiry. And the search for 'truth' is not likely to be successful.

The Franks Committee, in the paragraphs referred to, adopted a method of exposition which stated 'at their extremes' two strongly opposed views which they called 'the administrative' and the 'judicial'. The Committee, predictably, rejected both these conceptions and preferred instead to address themselves to 'the task of finding a reasonable balance between the conflicting interests'. Whether this formulation helps to solve the problems of procedure and substance which enquiries throw up is doubtful. The restatement of a difficulty in an apparently objective and practical tone of voice may lower the temperature of controversy but does not necessarily do more. But certainly the Franks Committee in those paragraphs wisely did not commit themselves to a definition of truth about the nature or purpose of the procedures involving an enquiry.

Nor does it advance the matter to declare that enquiries are 'not just an incident in the administrative process'. To an objector or appellant they are his forum. But to the local authority involved and to the Minister they are a part of an administrative process and the use of loaded words like 'just' or 'incident' cannot alter this.

The second 'general principle' has its own difficulties. 'Complaint' arises, 'understandably' or not, where a Minister rejects the recommendations of an inspector on any grounds. Several of the civil servants who gave evidence to the Franks Committee foresaw this danger which flows from the publication of the inspector's report. If an objector or appellant persuades one civil servant, face to face, of the rightness or justice or expediency of his case, of course he will complain if another civil servant, for whatever reasons, refuses in private to accept the inspector's recommendations. This is the central dilemma from which there is no escape. It does not follow that the inspector's report should not be published. But there is this price to be paid.

The third 'general principle' reopens an old argument. For the recommendations of the Franks Committee were, on this point, not adopted by the Government. The Committee were thinking, if their illustrations are a guide, mainly of planning appeals when they urged that statements of Ministerial policy should be made available before enquiries. But before such statements are made, policy must be fairly explicit. The Committee said: 'We also recognize that policy is, by its very nature, evolutionary and that a Minister's policy in relation to some aspect of compulsory acquisition or planning may change after the enquiry.' This is ambiguous. Is 'and' disjunctive or conjunctive? For the fact is surely, so far as planning decisions are concerned, not only that the policy may change because of and during the course of a particular appeal, but, much more importantly, that planning policy emerges and is ascertainable as an agglomeration of individual decisions. The absence of *a priori* policy is the sickness at the heart of town and country planning today. General propositions seem, according to the Ministry, to be necessarily induced from decisions, not deduced from a positive view of the future development of industrial location, the road and rail transport system, the relief of over-spill and the preservation of the rural countryside. We may agree with the Council that 'every effort should be made to make clear Ministerial policy before an enquiry'. But it is necessary first to have a policy which is obscured.

The fourth 'general principle' adds nothing. Of course 'proper respect' should be paid to an inspector's findings of fact and recommendations. And of course every civil servant thinks he is paying proper respect. If a civil servant were told he had not paid proper respect, the only line the argument could follow would be 'I did,'

'You didn't,' 'Yes, I did,' 'No, you didn't.' Which, while it may show a healthy appreciation of the true nature of political controversy does not lead naturally and of itself to a constructive synthesized conclusion.

As will be seen from the Council's report, they first thought that the Minister should reopen the enquiry where he differed from his inspector's recommendations unless the disagreement stemmed from the Minister's general policy. It is a little difficult to see how this could arise if the Minister's policy were stated before the enquiry and, presumably, adhered to by the inspector. But perhaps the Council were assuming that their earlier recommendation about policy statements would not be accepted (a fair bet) or were thinking of the case where the policy changed in the course of the enquiry.

In any event, the Council abandoned this argument after the exchange of views with government departments and arrived at the two rules set out above. The first rule is not clear in one important respect. What is meant by saying that the Minister will give an opportunity for further written representations when his disagreement with the inspector is based on 'some factor' not considered at the enquiry? Does this assume a Ministerial statement of policy before the enquiry or not? In either case, does it include policy? Does it include any unconsidered factor? Or does it mean 'fact' not policy? The second rule seems to be drawn widely enough to cover the *Chalkpit* case. There the Minister took evidence or advice or something from another Ministry. Does the Council mean to include evidence or advice given to the Minister by those within his own department? And does evidence or advice or a fresh issue include any questions of policy?

The objector or appellant needs to know what he is up against and needs to be persuaded that his views have been accurately put to the Minister. The first need relates not only to policy in a grand sense but also to 'the line' which the Ministry tend to take on the sort of case being considered. We suggest that the Ministry should take a provisional but official view, on the papers put to them by the parties; and should say that because of considerations A, B & C, they incline to the opinion that the decision should be X; and that if their final decision is to be not X but Y, then they will need to be persuaded that A or B or C or all of them should not be determinants in this case. That provisional view should be published before the enquiry and should be both general in the grand policy sense and as particular as possible a description of 'the line' for this sort of case. Then the enquiry would be focused on the relevant issues. The second need can best be met by adopting another of the recommendations of the Franks Committee not adopted by the Government: that the parties should see the factual part of the inspector's report (including his summary of their views) before the decision is made so that they may have an opportunity of saying that that part is inaccurate.

There still remains the possibility that the Minister might wish to take into account facts, evidence or advice emerging after the close of the enquiry. We believe that the decision must be left to the Minister whether he ought to invite written representations or to reopen the enquiry or to do neither. Someone has to exercise judgment on whether the new information justifies the reintroduction of the parties. Phrases like 'new factual evidence' or 'expert opinion on matters of fact' or 'expert assistance in the evaluation of technical evidence' (to quote the Franks Committee) cannot be precise and so cannot be used to distinguish those matters which should let in the parties again from those which should not. The ultimate conclusion is one which the Minister has to reach: whether to confirm or not, whether to allow the appeal or not. Procedural requirements can be laid down to try to ensure that the parties are heard in their cause. But only the Minister can decide whether later developments justify the reopening of issues or the opening of new issues. It is an unpalatable truth that although the gentlemen in Whitehall may not know best, yet they have to take decisions.

27

The Crichel Down Case*

D. N. CHESTER

The Crichel Down case is significant in British public administration for a number of reasons: although it was not the first (or last) time public attention has been focused on a particular case, civil servants had never before been subject to an enquiry where they had publicly to explain their actions. Consequently, students of administration were enabled to see how a number of doctrines and processes worked out on a particular occasion; and in particular the case seems to have acted as a watershed in the history of ministerial responsibility, because the doctrine has had to be reinterpreted and there has since been a tendency to move more and more in the direction of civil servants being held accountable in a management sense (culminating, perhaps, in the Fulton Committee recommendation for accountable management).

The chief *dramatis personae* were a piece of land some 725 acres in extent in the County of Dorset known as Crichel Down; the Minister of Agriculture (Sir Thomas Dugdale, Bt, M.P.); Lieutenant-Commander Marten – a local landowner who desired to purchase the land and reunite it with the family property of which some 15 years or so earlier 328 acres of it had been part; Mr C. G. Eastwood, Commissioner of Crown Lands and until a short time before this a senior official in the Colonial Office; Mr C. H. M. Wilcox, an Under Secretary at the Ministry of Agriculture and Fisheries; Mr H. A. R. Thomson, a partner in a firm of estate agents, who was acting as an agent for the Crown Lands Commission; the two Parliamentary Secretaries to the Ministry (Lord Carrington and Mr G. R. H. Nugent); and the M.P. for the area (Mr R. Crouch). The cast also included sundry officials at various levels of the Ministry or of public bodies closely associated with that Department.

Act I concerns what happened to the piece of land after it was

* From D. N. Chester, 'The Crichel Down Case', *Public Administration*, 1954, Vol. XXXII, pp. 389–401. Reprinted with permission of the author and the editor of *Public Administration*.

compulsorily acquired in 1937 by the Air Ministry for use as a bombing range. How it passed into the hands of the Ministry of Agriculture in 1949 (a Ministry which would not have been able to acquire it compulsorily for their purpose). It tells of the decisions that were made and how they were made about the use to which the land should be put; of how various farmers were officially promised a chance to bid for the tenancy and of how it came about that this promise was not honoured; and of how Lieutenant-Commander Marten, not being satisfied that his offer to acquire the land was being properly considered, with the help of his M.P. took the matter up with the Minister; and of the subsequent agitation which finally led the Minister to ask Sir Andrew Clark, Q.C., to enquire into the procedure adopted and report.

Act II starts with Sir Andrew's seven-day public enquiry held in Blandford, Dorset, at which almost everybody concerned (except the Minister) gave evidence. Some of the more exciting parts of the testimony were reported in all the leading newspapers and so whetted everybody's appetite for the Report (submitted to the Minister in May and published[1] a month later) and possibly stimulated a public desire for heads to fall.

The third Act sees the initial statement by the Minister in the House of Commons on the day that the Report was published (15 June, 1954). To the horror of the onlooker who knows that something dramatic is required, Sir Thomas Dugdale plays down the whole affair. The enquiry, he says, has achieved his main purpose because it has found no trace of bribery or corruption; he takes full responsibility for the actions of any officials criticized in the Report and announces that after hearing further explanations from those concerned he has formed a less unfavourable view of many of their actions. On the 20 July, on that most harmless of House of Commons' motions, 'That this House do now adjourn', the Minister makes a further statement at the end of which he announces his resignation. Next day the two Parliamentary Secretaries submit their resignations, but withdraw them at the request of the Prime Minister. The position of the five officials chiefly concerned is considered by a Committee presided over by Sir John Woods (formerly Permanent Secretary to the Board of Trade), which recommends[2] that Mr Eastwood be

[1] Public Enquiry ordered by the Minister of Agriculture into the disposal of land at Crichel Down. Cmd. 9176.

[2] Report of a Committee appointed by the Prime Minister to consider whether certain Civil Servants should be transferred to other duties (Cmd. 9220). On 1 November, 1954, Mr Eastwood was replaced as Permanent Commissioner by

transferred to other duties (as 'his usefulness as a public servant would be impaired if he were to remain in his present post'), and that no further action be taken in respect of the other four – in two cases because the officials have already been transferred to other work which differs in character and needs from that of the posts in which they had been criticized. Lieutenant-Commander Marten has his costs reimbursed by the Government and is given the opportunity to purchase Crichel Down subject to the existing tenancy. Curtain.

SIGNIFICANCE OF THE CASE

The affair aroused considerable public interest. Some of this was no doubt the kind that responds to any *cause célèbre* – from murder to the strange goings on of a film star. Some of it was party political, for government versus private ownership of land is always a lively issue. Both the main parties, however, found themselves rather schizophrenic in their comments – the Conservatives because it was their Minister (and a popular one) and their Government that were being criticized, and the Labour Party because, while wanting to criticize the Government, they were not happy at supporting a large landowner in criticism of the management of publicly owned land. Some of the comments on the Report and its findings were not very well informed or were blatantly partisan. Anyhow the Crichel Down affair was a complicated matter. Sir Andrew Clark's very concise factual narrative required 24 pages and his conclusions a further five pages. It is difficult, indeed almost impossible, to summarize them briefly. The whole Report and the Minister's two statements in the House must be read by all who wish to make any accurate comments. But when the discussion has been trimmed of all personalities, excitement, emotion and political controversy, something still remains. Crichel Down is likely to prove an influential event in the development of the British Civil Service. Already the case has had important repercussions on the atmosphere and method of working of the Service.[1] Also it has caused a reconsideration if not a redefinition of the relations of the civil servant with his Minister and with the public.

Sir Osmond Cleverly (who had retired from the post in 1952) and resumed duties in the Colonial Office.

[1] Among the particular repercussions must be mentioned a 'thorough examination' of the organization and methods adopted within the Ministry and the Agricultural Lands Commission for managing transactions in agricultural land, and an enquiry by a Committee under the Chairmanship of Sir Malcolm Trustram Eve into the present administration of Crown Lands.

The significant feature of the Crichel Down case is that it brought into question, not a Department as a vague corporate body, nor a Minister as the political head of a Department from which he receives anonymous advice, but the actions of individual civil servants. These individuals had to give evidence and be examined in public and their files and correspondence were open to Sir Andrew Clark. The six volumes of evidence and much correspondence were available to Members in the Library of the House of Commons. The whole of the administrative process and the parts played by a dozen or more civil servants were subjected to minute scrutiny. Thus the public were able to read about how the report of the Agricultural Land Commission on Crichel Down to the Ministry was prepared by a recently recruited junior official to the Commission and was incorrect at many points; they heard of the letters that passed between Mr Eastwood and Mr Wilcox and of the attitude these officials appeared to adopt to the public and so on. This is the first occasion possibly since the Sadler-Morant dispute of 1903 (a comparatively minor affair) on which the whole of the administrative paraphernalia has been so treated and made public, the share of named civil servants in that process analysed and appraised and their names and actions discussed and criticized in public.

It is legitimate to ask how this serious departure from tradition came about. It is not the first time that Ministers, Departments (even the Ministry of Agriculture) and civil servants have been in error. The Reports of the House of Commons' Committee on Public Accounts always contain a few examples. Thus the Third Report for the Session 1953/4 published in September 1954 (H.C. 231), contained several examples. The Commissioners of Crown Lands, 'in order to facilitate Government policy ... were induced to pay £112,000 for an asset which, to them, was worth approximately £32,000'; the Ministry of Food might lose as much as £650,000 through accepting delivery of orange juice not in accordance with their specification; and the Ministry of Health permitted the Regional Hospital Boards to buy some 14 houses which then lay unused for two years. These and similar errors that come to light from time to time, though criticized by the Public Accounts Committee, are virtually ignored by the House of Commons. But even the Public Accounts Committee, though it examines leading departmental officials and publishes its proceedings, does not set out to ascribe praise or blame to individuals and only occasionally names an official in its critical comments.

The reason why officials are not named or criticized in public is, of course, the strongly held doctrine of Ministerial responsibility. The great mass of governmental powers are bestowed by Parliament, not on the Cabinet or on Departments, but on the Minister of this or the Minister of that. In the case of the prerogative powers and of Departments of an apparently corporate character (e.g. the Board of Admiralty) the convention is quite clear and well accepted that some individual Minister is responsible. Thus some Minister is responsible for every act of the Government. Civil servants, and for that matter Parliamentary Secretaries, act by virtue of powers conferred on their Minister and each Minister is responsible to Parliament for the action or lack of action of every official employed in his Department. Thus if departmental errors come to light or somebody is dissatisfied with departmental action or decision, criticism in Parliament and in the Press must be directed at the Minister in charge of the Department concerned. The Minister himself, of course, may not be satisfied with the action of one or other of his officials, but his remedy is to take disciplinary or other measures inside his Department. He cannot publicly disown responsibility for his agents. All this is orthodox British constitutional doctrine and in the end it appears to have been vindicated by Sir Thomas Dugdale's resignation. But, unfortunately for the doctrine, though the Minister's resignation took the sting out of the attack, it came too late to prevent the names and actions of individual civil servants being the subject of public discussion and criticism. Ministerial responsibility was for a time in danger of being blurred and perhaps even a little in question.

It is not at all clear why the Minister ordered a public enquiry into the actions of his officials. In his statement on the day the Clark Report was published, he said the enquiry had achieved his main purpose, which was to deal with rumours and suggestions of bribery and corruption. But, as Mr Clement Davies pointed out in the full debate, if bribery and corruption were the main issue, why were they not mentioned in the terms of reference? Moreover there exists an accepted procedure for dealing with charges of this kind under the Tribunals of Enquiry (Evidence) Act, 1921, as is shown by the Stanley case of 1948.

The terms of reference are indeed somewhat strange and it would be interesting to know how they came to be drafted. They were:

'To enquire into the procedure adopted (a) in reaching the decision that land at Crichel Down should be sold to the Commissioners of Crown Lands; (b) in the selection of a tenant by them; and the circumstances in which those decisions were made, but

364

excluding from the enquiry all questions of governmental policy and, in particular, any question of whether preferential treatment should have been given to any applicant on the ground of previous ownership or occupation of the land.'

Thus the major point of policy at issue – who should have got the land – was definitely excluded and attention instead focused purely on the administrative process. These terms of reference and the choice of Sir Andrew Clark could only have been made in the expectation of a thorough public enquiry into the actions of all the officials concerned. It may be, of course, that the Minister and his advisers underestimated the extent of the mess. It would appear from the evidence that the Minister and one or two of the top officials of the Ministry of Agriculture were not in possession of all the facts. Possibly they thought that an enquiry would prove Lieutenant-Commander Marten's criticisms to be unfounded. In any case it is difficult to understand why the Minister did not first order an internal enquiry. The answer, in part, to the last point is, of course, that he did, but that this got caught up in the same inefficiency and atmosphere that pervaded the whole case. Only an internal enquiry by somebody with Sir Andrew Clark's independence and burning desire to get at the truth would really have helped the Minister.

FAILURE OF THE POLITICAL PROCESS

In many ways it is remarkable that nothing like this has happened before, certainly since the great increase in the scope and character of governmental powers. At one time Ministers were concerned largely with a few big issues of public policy. In so far as their Departments had to make decisions in individual cases, these could be made in most instances on lines clearly prescribed by law or in accordance with general policy decisions of the Minister, and the others were unlikely to be so numerous that the Minister and his chief advisers could not give them their personal attention and reach decisions with a full understanding of the facts. Wartime powers and recent legislation have required Departments to make hundreds of thousands of discretionary decisions in individual cases – should this or that piece of land be acquired compulsorily? should X be given a licence to build or to obtain this or that amount of steel or timber? It is clear, even to the uninitiated, that no Minister can handle personally more than the smallest fraction of these cases and, indeed, that whatever the wording of the departmental letter or order the decisions are, in fact, often taken by officials quite low down in the departmental hierarchy. Some of these decisions must have meant a great deal to the individual members of the public concerned – the difference between prosperity or poverty in some instances. It is remarkable that only a few minor cases of bribery or corruption have occurred: it is equally remarkable that we had to wait until Crichel Down before the decision-making process was publicly examined in an individual case.

There are various explanations. Under wartime conditions most people suffer in some way or other and individuals who complain about the apparent unfairness of a particular official act done in the general interest do not get much popular support. In some instances Departments, appreciating the difficulties inherent in making masses of discretionary decisions, have adopted simply applied and easily understood rules, e.g. allocating materials according to a percentage of consumption in a base year, or they have used Trade or other Associations as a kind of buffer between them and the public. Where possible guidance is given to the decision-makers in the form of broad principles laid down by the Minister or with his explicit approval, e.g. that priority should be given to this rather than to that kind of application. For the rest, individual or general discontent with a Department eventually falls to be handled by the Minister. It may be that a dissatisfied individual raises a matter with his M.P. (as did Lieutenant-Commander Marten), who then asks the Minister concerned to 'investigate' and explain, usually in a letter, the reasons for his Department's action. Or if numerous complaints arise representations may be made to the Minister through a Trade Association, Local Authority Association or other form of group interest. The way in which the Minister handles the grumbles and complaints determines, in the long run, the effectiveness of departmental administration and the attitude of the officials all down the line who have to make decisions. If there is a steady and unsatisfied grumbling at the Department's decisions, some day it will be bound to erupt in public. If a number of individuals feel strongly enough to take up matters with their M.P.s, one of them may well be a Lieutenant-Commander Marten. One of a Minister's chief functions, therefore, is to adjust the administrative process to public feeling. He must be sensitive to what the public will or won't stand. He must sense when a case is likely to cause real trouble or when a policy is gradually losing public support. And as he cannot handle everything in his Department, it behoves those senior civil servants nearest to the Minister also to have sensitive political antennae.

Primarily Crichel Down was a failure of political sensitivity. It would appear that the Minister of Agriculture continued, with little or no change, the policy of his predecessor notwithstanding that the Conservative Government had come into power avowedly to handle government controls rather differently and with much greater regard for individual interests. It would also appear that the Ministry continued to work very much under the wartime atmosphere, even though public opinion was changing against this and other Departments were adjusting their administration accordingly. This general surmise appears to be borne out by the handling of the Marten complaints. The matter was taken up at the political level as early as June 1952 – the Minister and both the Parliamentary Secretaries handled the case on more than one occasion and it was also examined by several top Administrative Class officials. Yet in March 1953 an Under Secretary at the Ministry, knowing that this piece of land was politically 'hot', took part in a decision not to implement a promise which had just come to light that various applicants should have a chance to bid for the land. Moreover, although the case was still 'political', those concerned (Ministers and officials) went ahead without apparently making any attempt to deal with the criticisms and doubts which were now becoming more public. In some part this reflects the 'tough' attitude of the Ministry and also perhaps the almost inevitable attempt to tire out the complainant (for what would happen to the administrative process if everybody who complained had to be fully satisfied?). Mr Wilcox wrote, as late as the 20 August 1953, 'Commander Marten it is thought will continue to make himself as much of a nuisance as he can both to you [i.e. Eastwood] and to us so long as he thinks there is any chance of getting either of us to change our minds.' The matter was still before those at the political level and it would appear almost certain that the decision on the 11 September, 1953, to lease the land to Mr Tozer and disregard the criticism of Marten and others was taken if not by the Minister at least with his knowledge. After that things moved quickly and as a result of public agitation in the area, and possibly for other reasons, the Minister decided in October that a Public Enquiry should be held. Thus for 16 or so months this particular case was under the nose of the Minister or his Parliamentary Secretaries and senior officials. Had the political antennae been functioning properly it is difficult to see how one month Marten could have been sent away dissatisfied and the next granted a Public Enquiry.

FAILURE OF THE ADMINISTRATIVE PROCESS

Unfortunately for the Civil Service, Crichel Down cannot be written off purely as a failure in the political process. Its public consequences might have been avoided if the political sense had been more acute or if Lieutenant-Commander Marten had been less determined. But Enquiry or no Enquiry, Crichel Down revealed failures in the Civil Service process. For one thing there was undoubtedly a fair amount of sheer inefficiency. At no time does any one person ever seem to have been in full possession of the facts of the case. The information on one or more of the files was inadequate or inaccurate.[1] A large part, though by no means all, of this was due to the unusual number of Departments, and satellites of the Ministry having a finger in the pie. One of the basic documents in the case, a report supplied by the Agricultural Land Commission to the Ministry following the first raising of the matter by Mr Robert Crouch, M.P., was found at the Enquiry to have been prepared by a recent junior recruit to the Commission's staff and to be inaccurate at several points. Section 88 of the Agriculture Act, 1947, required an Order to be made when the land was transferred from the Air Ministry to the Ministry of Agriculture, but none was made. No wonder that the Home Secretary could say that 'The Service, as a service, is as shocked by the errors brought to light as anyone else' (530 H.C. 1292, 20 July 1954).

The evidence of inefficiency was, however, not the important aspect of the case except in so far as it raised the question of whether the inefficiency was such as to cause the Minister to make a wrong decision on inaccurate information.[2] Mistakes can occur in the best organizations, and with a large number of employees there are bound to be failures from time to time. Moreover the Land Commission had only been established a few years. What really shook people was the conduct of certain civil servants, including two at a very high level.

The outstanding example of this was the failure to honour the promise made to a number of farmers that they should be given the opportunity to bid for the land. At first this breach was due to the file containing the applications not being known to the new Land Service Officer. In March 1953, however, the Officer found the file

---

[1] The case confirms the old view that reliable filing and registry systems are essential.

[2] 'Although there were certain inaccuracies and deficiences in the information given me, when I took my decision, I had the main facts before me, and my advisers were certainly not guilty of wilfully misleading me,' Sir Thomas Dugdale. 530 H.C. Deb. 1190–1. 20 July 1954.

and notified Mr H. A. R. Thomson, who then notified Mr C. G. Eastwood. Thomson added that as it was rather late in the day and as he had gone rather far with Mr Tozer (the eventual tenant), he hoped the matter would go through. Eastwood, instead of enquiring whether the matter could still be handled by publicly advertised competitive tender (which in fairness it must be said was not the custom of the Crown Lands Commission), wrote to Thomson asking him to get a list of the possible applicants so as to judge whether any were likely to have been serious competitors, 'and we can then decide, in conjunction with the Ministry of Agriculture, what if anything we need do, at least to appear to implement the promises made to them'. Eastwood sent a copy of this letter and the correspondence leading up to it to Mr C. H. M. Wilcox, an Under Secretary at the Ministry of Agriculture. Wilcox replied on the 25 March 1953, as follows:

'It is of course a pity that Middleton [the Land Service Officer concerned] did not let Thomson have earlier information about the promises given to various farmers on behalf of the A.L.C. that they would be given an opportunity of tendering if it were being let by the Agricultural Land Commission.

'Clearly if you buy a property then you are in no way bound by these promises,[1] and I appreciate it may be too late for Thomson to go back on anything he may have arranged provisionally with Tozer but I am very glad that you asked Thomson to get hold of the list of names from Middleton so that we can consider whether there is anything that could be done with a view at any rate to appear to be implementing any past promises. I imagine that you and Thomson for your part will be anxious to avoid doing anything that may leave a bad taste in the mouths of any of the disappointed applicants, which might, e.g. prejudice your chance of getting them as tenants for other of your properties on your Bryanston Estate at some future date.'

The comments of Sir Andrew Clark were:

'When Crown Lands first learnt of the previous applications there would have been no difficulty whatever in then advertising

---

[1] It should be noticed that the Minister of Agriculture is *ex officio* one of the three members of the Crown Lands Commission, the other two being the Secretary of State for Scotland (*ex officio*) and the Permanent Commissioner. The Commissioners never meet as a body and their business is conducted by the Permanent Commissioner, who refers at his discretion matters of major policy to the Minister.

the tenancy for public tender and so keeping faith with the applicants. When Mr Wilcox received Mr Eastwood's letter showing that Crown Lands did not intend to do this, the matter should at once have been referred to the Minister for his directions. Mr Wilcox was guilty of a grave error of judgment in taking upon himself to tell Crown Lands that they would not be expected to implement any promises the Lands Service had made. His ready acceptance of Mr Eastwood's improper suggestion that something might be done to mislead the applicants was equally improper, and had he not thought that there might be some such way out of the difficulty it is very unlikely that he would have been so ready to tell Mr Eastwood that Crown Lands could ignore the previous applicants.'

There was also more than a suggestion in the findings and the conclusions of the Report that on occasion certain information had been withheld from the next party in the decision-making process so as to make a hoped-for decision more likely. Some of this was, no doubt, a reflection of the general inefficiency and inexperience. Also Sir Andrew Clark stated that Eastwood, Wilcox and Thomson (not a civil servant it should be remembered) and, to a lesser degree, certain junior officials had evinced an attitude of hostility towards Lieutenant-Commander Marten, 'engendered solely by a feeling of irritation that any member of the public should have the temerity to oppose or even question the acts or decisions of officials. . . .' This is perhaps stronger language than the evidence warrants. But the Woods Committee took the point very seriously when they stated:

'There is no defined set of rules by which the confidence of the public in the administration of Government Departments can be secured and held. Incorruptibility and efficiency are two obvious requirements. In the present case corruption has not been in question; inefficiency has. Beyond that it is difficult to particularize. But the present case seems to us to emphasize one further factor which may be less self-evident but which we regard as of the highest importance. In present times the interests of the private citizen are affected to a great extent by the actions of Civil Servants. It is the more necessary that the Civil Servant should bear constantly in mind that the citizen has a right to expect, not only that his affairs will be dealt with effectively and expeditiously, but also that his personal feelings, no less than his rights as an individual, will be sympathetically and fairly considered. We think that the admitted shortcomings in this respect are the main cause of such loss of public confidence as has resulted from the present case.'

Since then this paragraph has been called to the attention of all civil servants in a letter from the Permanent Secretary to the Treasury. The letter from Sir Edward Bridges says:

'The circumstances that led up to this report have brought forcibly to their Lordships' attention, as to that of the country as a whole, the need for constant vigilance to ensure respect for the rights and feelings of individual members of the community who may be affected by the work of Departments. The confidence of the public in the administration of Government Departments depends upon this vigilance.

'My Lords consider that this most important consideration could not be better expressed than in the words of paragraph 3 of the report: [already reproduced above].

'My Lords strongly endorse this view and direct that the attention of all grades of the service should be drawn to it.'

The necessities of war, the pressure of official business and above all the political atmosphere of the time have, without doubt, all tended to subordinate the individual to what are considered to be the necessities of the State. So much power is exercised by individual civil servants at all levels these days that the Crichel Down affair will have done good if it succeeds in emphasizing the importance of the individual in the administrative process.

It is worth noting that notwithstanding the strong party feeling aroused by the case there was no suggestion in the Report or in Parliament that any of the officials concerned had been influenced by party political motives. Sir Richard Acland and one or two other Labour Members were prepared to attack Sir Andrew Clark because he had been a Conservative candidate and had expressed strong anti-socialist views at the election. Those who advocate complete freedom for all civil servants to take part in party political activities may well ponder over what the Labour (Conservative) Members would have said if one of the officials criticized had been known as an active Conservative (Labour) Party worker.

IMPLICATIONS FOR DOCTRINE OF MINISTERIAL RESPONSIBILITY

What are likely to be the long-term effects? Clearly there has been a shock to public confidence. This may show itself in a greater readiness to question decisions made in Whitehall and to ask whether they are based on full and accurate information. No doubt this will lead

371

Ministers and civil servants to be particularly careful and to avoid any appearance of riding rough-shod over anybody. And in due course, providing there are no further shocks, the wound will heal and confidence should be restored.

One feature, however, may have more lasting effects. The Crichel Down Enquiry opened up to ordinary human gaze the decision-making process of Whitehall. In place of the Minister or the Ministry, powerful yet vague, and symbol of the public interest, there was revealed a number of officials – some obviously not well-informed, acting like ordinary human beings, sometimes differing amongst themselves, but in the end reaching a decision which then had the full power of the Cabinet and its House of Commons majority behind it. Had the Report dealt at all adequately with the Minister's actions and responsibility for the affair, the actions of the officials would have been seen in better perspective. But their contribution to the decision and their processes of thought and action would still have been laid bare.

In the modern State, when a small number of politicians share with a large number of permanent officials the task of making numerous decisions affecting intimately the lives of masses of citizens, the question is bound to arise from time to time whether it is fair to place the whole responsibility on the politician and whether this is adequate protection for the citizen. Thus, in the case of a local enquiry, e.g. under the Town and Country Planning Acts, there have been many attempts to secure publication of the report of the Inspector holding the enquiry largely in order to throw light on the Minister's decision and to see upon what facts and recommendations he made that decision. This demand has always been resisted on the ground that the decision was that of the Minister and that there is no more justification for revealing the report of the Inspector than the minutes and advice of any of the other officials in his Ministry.

Those who want to bring the part played by individual officials more into the open and even subject them to public blame use several arguments. They point out that a large number of cases are decided without reference to the Minister, sometimes by an official quite low in the hierarchy, and ask why then should the Minister suffer for something which has not been near his desk? Moreover, they argue, asking for the resignation of the Minister is too powerful a weapon for everyday use. Would it not be more appropriate to be able to take direct action against the particular official who did what they consider to be the wrong thing? This is particularly so if the official has either disobeyed instructions or acted in a way which the Minister

372

would not have approved had he known about it beforehand. Why should a Minister have to suffer for any acts of his staff done contrary to his views? The Crichel Down Report has provided ammunition for this school of thought. Though the case was due primarily to a failure of the political process, there was sufficient muddle and error on the part of officials to cause a demand for some form of action against them. The Minister's attempt to excuse them in his first statement only added fuel to the flames. Even *The Times*, after stating quite clearly the constitutional doctrine and the dangers of departing from it, was moved to say that 'there will remain considerable disquiet at the apparent immunity of civil servants from public control'.

Sir Thomas Dugdale's decision to resign was a brave and welcome reinforcement of the doctrine of Ministerial responsibility. It is very rare for Ministers to resign or even to allow public enquiry into the actions of their Departments. There was, for example, no resignation over the ground nuts muddle even though a particular Minister was intimately involved. But in the long run it is difficult to see how the resignation of the Minister can be the solution in the everyday case of official error. If, however, the Minister is not to resign, the demand for some action against the official concerned is likely to be the greater, particularly if there are reasons for believing that that decision was contrary to the Minister's views or that the Minister took it on the basis of incorrect information or advice.

In replying to the general debate on the 20 July, the Home Secretary (not, as might have been expected, the Chancellor of the Exchequer) enlarged upon the doctrine of Ministerial responsibility to meet those critics who thought that the doctrine rendered civil servants effectively responsible to no one. After pointing out that all civil servants hold their office 'at pleasure' and can be dismissed at any time by the Minister concerned, Sir David Maxwell Fyfe went on to enumerate four different categories of cases in which there may be Parliamentary criticism of a department and for which he said different considerations applied. They were:

1. Where a civil servant carries out an explicit order by a Minister, the Minister must protect the civil servant concerned.

2. Where a civil servant acts properly in accordance with the policy laid down by the Minister, the Minister must equally protect and defend him.

3. Where a civil servant 'makes a mistake or causes some delay, but not on an important issue of policy and not where a claim to individual rights is seriously involved, the Minister acknowledges

the mistake and he accepts the responsibility, although he is not personally involved. He states he will take corrective action in the Department'. (Col. 1290).

4. '. . . where action has been taken by a civil servant of which the Minister disapproves and has no prior knowledge, and the conduct of the official is reprehensible, then there is no obligation on the part of the Minister to endorse what he believes to be wrong, or to defend what are clearly shown to be errors of his officers. The Minister is not bound to approve of action of which he did not know, or of which he disapproves. But, of course, he remains constitutionally responsible to Parliament for the fact that something has gone wrong, and he alone can tell Parliament what has occurred and render an account of his stewardship'. (Cols 1290–91.)

It is interesting to see Mr Herbert Morrison's views on the subject. Mr Morrison spoke just before the Home Secretary and on this particular issue he said:

'There can be no question whatever that Ministers are responsible for everything that their officers do, but if civil servants make errors or commit failures the House has a right to be assured that the Minister has dealt with the errors or failures adequately and properly, or that he will do so. That is a duty that falls on Ministers as well, and it would be wrong for a Minister automatically to defend every act of his officers or servants merely because they belong to his Department. Therefore, the House has to be satisfied that he is dealing with the matter adequately.' (Col. 1278.)

In his book *Government and Parliament*, published in April 1954, Mr Morrison has more to say on this point:

'If a mistake is made in a Government Department the Minister is responsible even if he knew nothing about it until, for example, a letter of complaint is received from an M.P., or there is criticism in the Press, or a Question is put down for answer in the House; even if he has no real personal responsibility whatever, the Minister is still held responsible. He will no doubt criticize whoever is responsible in the Department in mild terms if it is a small mistake and in strong terms if it is a bad one, but publicly he must accept responsibility as if the act were his own. It is, however, legitimate for him to explain that something went wrong, in the Department, that he accepts responsibility and apologizes for it, and that he

has taken steps to see that such a thing will not happen again.'
(Pp. 320–1.)

Later he says:

'Somebody must be held responsible to Parliament and the
public. It has to be the Minister, for it is he, and neither Parliament
nor the public, who has official control over his civil servants. One
of the fundamentals of our system of government is that some
Minister of the Crown is responsible to Parliament, and through
Parliament to the public, for every act of the Executive. This is a
corner-stone of our system of parliamentary government. There
may, however, be an occasion on which so serious a mistake has
been made that the Minister must explain the circumstances and
processes which resulted in the mistake, particularly if it involves
an issue of civil liberty or individual rights. Now and again the
House demands to know the name of the officer responsible for
the occurrence. The proper answer of the Minister is that if the
House wants anybody's head it must be his head as the responsible
Minister, and that it must leave him to deal with the officer
concerned in the Department.

'There is a circumstance in which I think a considerable degree
of frankness is warranted. If a Minister has given a specific order
within the Department on a matter of public interest and his
instructions have not been carried out, then, if he is challenged in
Parliament and if he is so minded, he has a perfect right to reveal
the facts and to assure the House that he has taken suitable action.
Even so he must still take the responsibility. It is, I think, legitimate
in such a case that disregard of an instruction should be made
known, even if it involves some humiliation for the officer concerned and his colleagues knowing that he was the one who disobeyed; for the Civil Service should at all times know that the
lawful orders of Ministers must be carried out. However, such a
situation is rare, though I did experience one and told the House
about it.

'In all these matters it is well for the Minister to be forthcoming
in Parliament. Unless the matter is exceptionally serious nothing is
lost by an admission of error. The House of Commons is generous
to a Minister who has told the truth, admitted a mistake, and
apologized; but it will come down hard on a Minister who takes
the line that he will defend himself and his Department whether
they are right or wrong or who shuffles about evasively rather

than admit that a blunder or an innocent mistake has been made.'
(Pp. 323–4.)

What does all this add up to? In the first place it confirms the
doctrine of Ministerial responsibility. Civil servants, whatever their
official actions, are not responsible to Parliament, but to a Minister.
It is the Minister who is responsible to Parliament and it is he who
must satisfy the majority in the House of Commons that he has
handled a particular policy or case properly. It is for the Minister,
therefore, so to direct, control and discipline his staff that his policy
and views prevail. But the fact that the Minister is responsible for
everything done, or not done, by his Department does not render the
civil servant immune from disciplinary action or dismissal by the
Minister nor even from public admonition by him in extremely
serious cases, nor does it prevent the Minister from admitting to
Parliament that his Department is in error and reversing or modifying
the decision cricitized.

On the whole the House of Commons and the Press behaved with
a high regard for the constitutional doctrine. In the general debate
the resignation of the Minister and the recommendations of the
Woods Report rather took the wind out of the sails of those who
might have asked for official heads to fall. Even so there appeared
to be general concern at the danger of individual civil servants being
the subject of Parliamentary and public discussion. But it would be
useless to deny that Crichel Down has raised doubts in people's
minds about the public responsibility of officials. Some must have
been left with the impression that the Minister had come off pretty
badly, but that little or nothing had happened to the civil servants involved. The Home Secretary's attempt to restate the doctrine of
Ministerial and official responsibility was hardly made on the spur of
the moment and shows that the Government felt that something
more was necessary than a reiteration of the simple doctrine that a
Minister is responsible for all the actions of his officials.

This restatement and Mr Morrison's recent writing take account of
the fact that a Minister can deal personally with only a small part of
the decisions made by his Department. They would appear to open
up the possibility of a distinction being drawn between actions for
which the Minister is responsible both to Parliament and also personally, and those for which he still remains responsible in the Parliamentary sense, but which, it is known, are the fault of some official.
As things stand at present, however, the latter class is likely to be
very rare. A Minister appreciates that he often gains personal credit

for the actions of anonymous officials and that he must take the rough with the smooth. More important, he appreciates that his political future will not be improved by appearing to be weak and having ineffective control over his Department. Any Minister who tried to avoid criticism by blaming his officials would soon lose his Parliamentary reputation and be felt to be an unsure Cabinet colleague.

PART III

BRITISH ADMINISTRATIVE STYLE
IN PERSPECTIVE

And what should they know of England
who only England know? Kipling.

It is the poet of jingoism who asks. In that spirit, we aim to present in this section some pieces by (with two exceptions) Englishmen who have made the effort to stand outside their own system, and see it alongside others, if not quite as others see it.

There are two extremes in approaches to comparative public administration. The first seeks the 'global overview', a typology of systems by which to label all the countries of the world. There is a long line of such typologies, from Aristotle onwards: Fred W. Riggs represents one modern approach, dividing administrative systems into 'fused' or traditional, 'diffracted' or modern, and 'prismatic' for systems which show some characteristics of each – mainly from the 'third world', although readers of his early essay on 'Agraria and Industria – Toward a Typology of Comparative Administration' may find with interest that the oldest industrial nation in the world (Great Britain) undoubtedly retains many agrarian characteristics. (Riggs, in William J. Siffin *ed.*, *Toward the Comparative Study of Public Administration*, Indiana University Press, Bloomington, 1957; and F. W. Riggs, *Administration in Developing Countries – The Theory of Prismatic Society*, Houghton Mifflin Company, Boston, 1964.)

At the other extreme, there are the very detailed studies of particular administrative measures as they operate in a large number of different countries, undertaken by the International Institute of Administrative Sciences; three to date are those on foot and mouth disease control, on river pollution management, and on workmen's compensation for industrial injury.[1] Little of general significance is deducible from such studies; though they may make us think about things we otherwise take for granted about our own system, at the same time they indicate the sheer impossibility of either exploring the entire world of public administration in this amount of detail, or making any sense of it if one did. For making sense, for 'understanding', a reduction or abstraction of principles is necessary; the creation of a logical hierarchy of viewpoints, like the series of photographs of the same scene you can take from the same spot through camera lenses of decreasing focal length, from 'telephoto'

[1] Cases in Comparative Administration, International Association of Legal Science and International Institute of Administrative Sciences, Brussels, 1965: André Heilbronner, *Prevention of Cattle Diseases with special reference to foot-and-mouth disease*; Joseph Litwin, *Control of River Pollution by Industry*; G. Spielmeyer, *Ascertaining Entitlement to Compensation for an Industrial Injury*.

to 'wide-angle'. Less and less can one inspect detail, but more and more can one locate the objects in their setting.

If the IIAS studies are 'close-ups', and Riggs is 'panorama', there is no place for either in the present book of readings – partly because Englishmen take well to neither. But all the gamut of normal vision lies between; the familiar middle-range treatments of legislatures, civil services, and judicial systems of the classic comparative government texts – which often did not so much compare as present side by side for the reader to draw what conclusions he would. In European comparative public administration, however, there appeared only in 1957 the first full-scale work of this kind, which is not yet superseded or even challenged; not by an Englishman, but by Poul Meyer, a Dane. Since the book is long out of print we break a rule and include an extract which illuminates the present theme. Two years later came another pioneering book, *The Profession of Government* by Brian Chapman, which, too, is still standard; then in 1963 Chapman published his highly polemical pamphlet *British Government Observed*, which vividly conveys the climate of radical discontent with the British administrative system pervading much academic and other journalism in the late fifties and early sixties, contributing to the appointment of a long series of Royal Commissions and Committees, from Mallaby to Crowther. To some extent, that critical mood depended upon the spread of knowledge of other systems, and to represent both that mood and approach we have selected an extract from *Modern Capitalism* by Andrew Shonfield.

There is a genre of comparative studies which approaches the present theme very closely, through 'national character'. The ancient exponents included Aristotle and Hippocrates; among later writers, Montesquieu and de Tocqueville, Salvador de Madariaga, George Mikes. Of English writers, Bagehot can assuredly stand comparison with de Tocqueville; Graham Wallas was the forerunner of more than one later school of social and political psychology; and for shrewd analysis of national character, George Orwell surely has few peers.

The good name of national character studies was gravely besmirched, and indeed for a time eclipsed, by nationalistic perversions like Gobineau's Nordic myth and the taint of racism. It is still perhaps an open question whether respectability has returned in their rebirth as 'cross cultural comparison', exemplified in Almond and Verba's *The Civil Culture, Political Attitudes and Democracy in Five Nations* (Princeton, 1963). From the older tradition, we include extracts from Shils' classic study of government secrecy, and Graham

Wallas' essay on English, French and American 'types of thought', which is full of insights.

Some differences between British practice and that of its continental neighbours may seem to be more in style than in effect; others show deep divergence of basic approach. To explore these ideas we end with an extract from Sisson on the relationship between the politician and the top official, and the important article by Mitchell which, as well as giving a historical perspective on the legal setting of British administration, provides an inkling of what it is like under a very different system.

It must be left to the user of this book to determine for himself what are the characteristics of the national style of British public administration, and to judge also how this is changing over time. London in the 1960s was the 'swinging city', and many old standards went crashing down; some of the iconoclasm can perhaps be detected in some official reports of the time. The decade ended with the publication of two rather different official papers, which may be thought to mark a new trend in British administrative style. These were the White Paper, *Information and the Public Interest* (Cmnd. 4089), June 1969, and the Report of the Skeffington Committee on Public Participation under the title *People and Planning* in July 1969. Each promised a move away from 'administration behind closed doors', towards publicity and participation. Earlier release of Cabinet papers (after thirty years instead of fifty), and easier access to official papers by research workers, are further indications. Implementing 'Fulton' in the civil service, and some version of 'Maud' in local government, will engender changes of attitude, of assumption, and possibly of style, not all of which will be easily predictable beforehand, and which may combine to produce a set of characteristics and patterns of behaviour in the British public administrator of the late 1970s that are recognizably different from what is presented in these pages.

28

Proliferation of Departments, Terminology of Departmentalization, and History of Regionalism*

POUL MEYER

One of the best, but least readily available, European studies of comparative administration was written in 1956 by the Danish scholar Poul Meyer, His survey covered the basic problem areas of organization in the public service, including truly comparative analysis of administrative terminology, rationality and efficiency, methods of dividing work, administrative authority and decentralization. The extracts reproduced here have been selected because they reflect the approach of the whole book and also use a certain amount of British material in discussing problems which have considerably teased the minds of British public administration experts, particularly in recent years.

The counterpart of cumulation, and the forms of organization where not even an internal work division takes place, is *proliferation*. This term means structural innovations which are necessary because of the emergence of new tasks, or the growth of old tasks, which – due to the increasing amount of work in the organization under whose control the tasks originally were – must be segregated from the old organization and transferred to a new one.

Of course, the new agency need not be new in the proper sense of the word; what generally happens is that an organizational unit receives another structural placing, e.g. a bureau under a government department is raised to the status of an independent agency, or to a departmental status. The members of the staff who have hitherto worked in the office will, naturally, continue their work in the new

* From Poul Meyer, *Administrative Organization: A Comparative Study of the Organization of Public Administration*, London, Stevens, 1957; pp. 108–12, 194–6, 217–25. Copenhagen, NYT Nordisk Forlag Arnold Busck, 1957. Reprinted with permission of the author and NYT Nordisk Forlag Arnold Busck.

agency, or, strictly speaking, they remain where they are and a series of promotions take place.

Of all the administrative phenomena, proliferation is the easiest to illustrate. Here are a few examples: The British Board of Trade, in the early part of the seventeenth century (under the name of Committee of Trade) was segregated from the Privy Council as a special Committee. In the course of time, a long series of tasks have been segregated by proliferation from the Board of Trade, and from the Board stem the Ministry of Agriculture (1889), the Ministry of Labour (1917), the Ministry of Transport (1919), the Ministry of Food (1939), the Ministry of Fuel and Power (1942), and (partly) the Ministry of Supply. In 1789, the federal American administration started its activity with three departments, *viz.* the Departments of State, War, and Treasury; in 1949 the Hoover Commission ascertained that there were 12 federal departments, besides 40 other agencies which report direct to the President, most of them established by proliferation. At present (January 1956) 62 agencies report direct to the President.

In most European countries, government administration sprang from the Royal Chancellery, or the Royal Household. Subsequently the members of the King's personal staff or of his council were entrusted with offices and thus transformed into officials of the State. The various European chancelleries, which, before the democratic era, most frequently consisted of advisory departments (collegia), underwent an enormous development. Here is an example: Before a free constitution was adopted in Denmark in the year 1849, the Royal Danish administration was transformed into a ministerial system. Seven ministries were established, including a Ministry of the Interior, and from this Ministry, in the course of time, the following have been segregated: the Ministry of Labour (1894), the Ministry of Agriculture (1896), the Ministry of Commerce (1908), the Ministry of Social Affairs (1924), and other government departments. Many similar examples from other countries could be quoted.

Proliferation can be carried through at all levels of the administrative hierarchy. At the lower levels a structural innovation as the outcome of proliferation may either be an independent phenomenon which is confined to the particular part of the organizational system, or a reflex of a similar development at a higher level. The establishment of special hierarchies with their own central, regional and local organizations are examples of the latter.

Lack of co-ordination, or a cumbersome and protracted disintegrated co-ordination, may be the result if proliferation is carried to excess. The more consistent the administrative hierarchy is, the easier

N   385

it is to proliferate the organizations at the lower levels on a functional basis. Excessive proliferation at the top, i.e. the establishment of too many new ministries, government departments and other central organizations with direct report to the supreme executive power, may lead to an inefficient top management, because the inter-ministerial and inter-departmental co-ordination is very sensitive and requires an enormous number of meetings in 'joint committees' and top level negotiations before any action can be taken. *Paul H. Appleby* in his survey of Indian public administration asserts that much of the inefficiency which the Indian government has to fight against, is due to such exaggerated proliferation.[1]

The designation 'work division' indicates that a certain type of work is distributed among a number of persons or organizational units. This description is valid as regards the functional division in the proper sense of the word, i.e. that the general objective is divided into subsidiary objectives standing in means-end relation with it; but in other cases no actual *division* is taking place, but there is a *collection* of a series of already existing functions under a common management, namely in an organizational unit.

That we, in certain cases, are concerned with a collection and not a division, is shown distinctly by the organizational type which is commonly termed the federal, or *holding-company type*, i.e. collections of unitary organizations, without any tangible single over-all goal. Each of the units has its own socially defined goal, which is independent of the goals of the others, and they have no operating services in common. The U.S. Department of Health, Education and Welfare is an example hereof. One of its divisions is the Social Security Administration entrusted with the following functions: Old-Age and Survivors Insurance, Public Assistance, Child Welfare, Employment Security, and the operations of the Federal Credit Unions.

It is not easy to quote examples of this organizational type in British and continental European administrations, which are marked by a long departmental tradition. In these countries, the corresponding type of organization is an outcome of the cumulation phenomenon, as understood by *Georges Langrod*, i.e. as an incomplete segregation of new or growing tasks. From Britain the Board of Trade may be mentioned again. As previously mentioned, several new departments have, in the course of time, been segregated from the Board by proliferation, but the Board still retains its rather

[1] Paul H. Appleby: *Report of a Survey. Public Administration in India.* New Delhi, 1953, pp. 10 and 19.

composite character, and includes divisions with so widely different functions as the Patent Office and the Bankruptcy Department. As examples from continental Europe, we should first mention the Ministries of the Interior, which in most countries constitute the original nucleus of the central administration, and which, in its turn, has sprung from the Royal administration. It is a general rule in these countries that cases which do not come under any other Minister are placed under the Ministry of the Interior, which consequently, becomes a very heterogeneous organization.

Other forms of holding-company organizations are those under which a number of partly autonomous units are gathered under a certain supervision. As examples of organizations, to some extent partaking of this character, may be mentioned the boards of the nationalized British industries, which in some measure are subordinate to the minister concerned, and the Swedish central government agencies, which enjoy a rather considerable independence but which to a certain extent are subject to the general direction of the King in Council – which in fact means the minister concerned.

Such holding-company organizations, or departments characterized by cumulation, present a number of special problems. In the unitary organization the various social tasks solved by the organization in its various divisions, can be compared in the way that coordination can be facilitated, and the varied importance in terms of money and work, allocated to the individual tasks, can be considered in a rational manner. This possibility is absent in the holding-company organization. It is impossible to make a rational comparison between the work which in a European Ministry of the Interior is carried out in the section concerned with public health and that carried out in the section concerned with local government. But, as regards the possibility of centralizing the auxiliary services there is no difference between the two forms of organization.

Organizational units are created when the division of work is institutionalized. If functionalism is carried out in the theoretically correct manner, the smallest organizational unit corresponds to one of the indivisible subsidiary objectives into which the general objective can be divided. As already mentioned, a correct application of the functional principle of division is very difficult in practice, and it is only encountered very rarely. When speaking about organizational units we must therefore adhere to the structural concept, i.e. any organization which constitutes a group of people working under a single chief.

Each item of the common terminology recommended by the

Hoover Commission for use in U.S. Government (*viz.*, *departments* or *agencies*, divided into *services* or *bureaus* which are subdivided into *divisions*, *branches* and *sections*) is the designation of an organizational unit. *Office* is proposed as the designation for a staff unit. The larger organization is thus partly an organizational unit itself, and partly the embodiment of a number of less comprehensive organizational units. In other words, the concept is highly relative, its meaning depends on the angle from which it is approached.

The question of the most expedient distribution of the tasks among a series of government departments has in our days been treated in Great Britain by the Haldane Committee (1918), and in the U.S.A. by the Hoover Commission (1949). The Haldane Committee stressed the importance of an undefined functional principle as the basis for the departmental division of work. Speaking of this committee *W. J. M. Mackenzie* says that it 'was composed of persons exceptional in ability, in experience and in good will, but we can see after thirty years that their conclusions were largely wrong, or at least irrelevant'. History will pass a similar verdict on any commission if it has failed to understand that general viewpoints are only of very little value in reorganization work and that progress can be achieved only by periodical painstaking analyses of the actual conditions and of the relevant value elements. Only on such a basis can the interests be weighed against each other, and only if each situation is considered on its own merits. . . .

TERMINOLOGY OF DEPARTMENTALIZATION

By departmentalization is understood the process by which the supreme levels of administration are organized. According to *Webster's* dictionary a department is a subordinate division of something *having a considerable extent*. In the field of administration the department is the major unit of the organization dealing with a substantial field of administration.[1]

In U.S.A. the term department is used to describe all principal divisions, whether in the Union, the states, the cities, the counties, or in business administration. In Britain the term is used in the same way, although especially of government departments. In Norway and Sweden the term is exclusively used to describe the ministries; in Denmark exclusively to describe the primary divisions of the

[1] *White*, pp. 76 ff, Schuyler C. Wallace, *Federal Departmentalization*, N.Y., 1941.

ministries. In France *les départements*, as already mentioned, are the main regions of the state administration, cf. the military departments of the U.S.A. The supreme French government administration is performed by the ministries (*les ministères*), the divisions of which – corresponding to the Danish departments – are the directorates (*les directions*).

Students wishing to make comparative studies in the field of public administration should be aware of this variety in nomenclature. Therefore some further details should be given. As mentioned above, the supreme division of the federal administration of the U.S.A. as well as in the states of the Union, is the division into departments. Admittedly, the department is also the technical term for the British ministries, but the word does not appear in the name of any ministry; on the contrary, when the term department is used, it usually denotes an organization below the ministerial level, e.g. the *Industries and Manufactures Department* (a subdivision of the Board of Trade). The principal divisions of the ministries are often known as departments. Thus a British Ministry may be composed of a number of departments which actually are sub-departments, since the department is the technical term for the ministry as such. Sometimes the term division is used as the name of the primary division of a ministry, and the Home Office is divided into a number of hierarchically equal divisions, some of which are called *departments*, and some of which are called *divisions*. British terminology does not apply any special term for a group of departments (or divisions) under the leadership of a single official – usually a Deputy Secretary. By way of example, the British Ministry of Agriculture is divided into three 'Groups' of departments each under a Deputy Secretary, and the 'Groups' are divided into 'Sub-Groups' each under an Under Secretary. The head of the department is an Assistant Secretary.

The older British ministries are often called 'offices', for example the Home Office and the Foreign Office, while the newer ministries are called ministries, for example the Ministry of Supply, the Ministry of Housing and Local Government, and many others.

The secondary levels of the U.S. Departments present a rather heterogeneous nomenclature which calls for further examination before a comparison can be made. As already mentioned, the Hoover Commission recommended that the primary division of a department should be called *Service* or *Bureau*. As only a comparatively small number of government departments are established in the U.S.A., several bureaux of the federal departments may be functionally compared to European ministries. A number of bureaux are sometimes

389

grouped under an *Administration*, or *Service*, for example the frequently mentioned Agricultural Research Service. However, it must be remembered that a number of offices which according to American terminology are staff offices, are inserted between the Bureau and the Secretary, or between the Administration (Service) and the Secretary, and these staff offices actually perform a good deal of the higher administrative supervisory and co-ordinating work which in Europe is performed by the supreme units of the ministerial hierarchy.

The ministries of the federal government of the Dominion of Canada are often divided into a small number of Services corresponding to the U.S. Services, and each under a civil servant who is frequently called *director*. The directors report to the Deputy Minister (Permanent Secretary) who is the chief of all the civil servants of the ministry. The Deputy Minister reports direct to the politically appointed Minister.

In France the directorates (*les directions*, or, *directions générales*) constitute the first level in the internal hierarchy, whereas the Minister's Cabinet lies between the directorates and the minister, and the *Chef de Cabinet* corresponds to the British Permanent Secretary. The Minister's Cabinet is concerned with current administration and is a proper level in the hierarchy, not only a personal office like the office of the British minister, or a connecting staff unit like the American Secretary's Office. The French directorates are in their turn divided into sub-directorates which are divided into bureaux. The bureau is the smallest organizational unit of a French ministry, and also of the German, Danish, Norwegian, and Swedish ministries. In the U.S.A. the smaller units are called divisions, branches, and sections. Occasionally the same terminology is used in Britain. . . .

THE HISTORY OF REGIONALISM

By regionalism we mean an administrative system under which a centralized organization divides the area over which its authority extends, and places an official or local organization, both of which are subject to the hierarchical authority of the central administration, at the head of each area.

Historically, regionalism has developed in direct proportion to the political and administrative centralization, and it is a typical instrument for implementing this centralization. Regionalism, accordingly, arises simultaneously with the growing central power, usually the expansion of the power of the Crown over an area that had hitherto consisted of a number of autonomous areas.

When the Babylonian central rule had been created on the ruins of the Sumerian city states, *Hammurabi* (2083–2041 B.C.E.) developed a complicated regional hierarchy of officials, particulars of which are known from the letters which the great king sent to his local officials. When dealing with feudal systems, however, it is frequently difficult to decide in our time, whether an ancient system of officials was a manifestation of the regional development of a centralized organization, or whether it was a manifestation of a decentralization with local feudal princes. When *Darius I* (522–486 B.C.E.) united Persia he appointed local *satraps* as his officials in the provinces. These *satraps*, however, were very independent and, in certain cases, could declare war without the king's consent.

Wherever a central royal power has arisen and conquered former autonomous areas, the central power has developed on a regional basis; from the Far East comes the example of *Shih Huang Ti* (256–206 B.C.E.), the Great Chinese Emperor of the Ch'in dynasty, who divided China into 36 provinces governed by the imperial officials.

In the Northern Countries, the central royal power did not begin to assert itself as a definite central power until the twelfth century. The first local officials appointed by the Danish kings were the men whom the kings entrusted with the work of managing their estates in the hundred (*herredet*). This manager of the king's estate (in old Danish *kunungs bryti*) in the course of time took over the work of collecting all royal revenues in his area, and during the Middle Ages became the king's general representative in the hundred. During the rule of the nobility, these regional offices developed certain feudal features, but they were always subject to the central power, and during the period of absolute monarchy (1660–1849) the officials were the personal representatives of the kings. The system was adopted by the new democracy, and the regional officers became subordinate to the general central administration, although they are still, formally, the personal representatives of the king.

Denmark is divided into 22 regions (*amter*), each with a prefect (*amtmand*) as the chief. A development along similar lines has taken place in Norway, where there are 20 regions (*fylker*), each with a prefect (*fylkesman*), and in Sweden, where there are 24 regions (*län*), each with a prefect (*konungens befallningshavande*, i.e. the king's officer.)

When the Roman Empire was at its zenith, it was a strongly centralized organization extending over most of the then civilized world. This enormous empire, however, could be kept together only by means of a consistent regionalism. This development was simply the continuation of a principle which had been applied right back to

391

the time when Italy proper was being organized. When the *municipes* and *coloniae* were swallowed up by the *civitas Romana*, their existence as self-governing *civitates* came to an end and they were governed by *praefecti* sent out from Rome. The Roman provinces were originally partly under the Senate and partly under the Emperor. In either case, however, they were ruled by regional officers under the Senate and the Emperor respectively. Their designations varied considerably. It was only after the reforms introduced by *Diocletian* (284–305 C.E.) that a uniform organization of the empire was implemented, after which it appeared as the most perfect hierarchy ever seen, with the emperor at the apex of the pyramid and possessing unlimited authority.

The empire was divided into four areas, each with its pretorian prefect, who was immediately subordinate to the emperor (*praefectus praetorio galliarum, italiae, illyrici et orientes*). Each of these areas was divided into a number of *dioceses*, e.g. Gaul, Britain, and Spain. The *vicarius* was the head of a *diocesis* and he was thus immediately subordinate to the prefect. Each *diocesis* was divided into a number of provinces, whose governors were known by rather varying designations. Gaul, for example, was divided into four provinces: Gallia Narbonensis, Gallia Aquitania, Gallia Lugdunensis and Belgica. It is characteristic of the connections between regionalization and centralization that the 300–400 self-governing areas which *Caesar* found in Gaul (like their Italian prototype, they were called *civitates*) formed the basis for the division of Gaul into 64 administrative districts introduced by *Augustus*.[1]

Similarly, the Egyptian *nomes* were undoubtedly originally self-governing areas, headed by *nomarchs*; later, however, royal officials were appointed, who in the Ptolemaic era were known as *strategoi*. During this period the Egyptian administration, incidentally, constituted a consistent hierarchy, with the king at the top of a widely ramified regional organization. The individual *nomus* was divided into *toparchies* and *kōmais*.

From the above it will be seen that the modern European prefectorial system has had several historical models, although the direct inspiration was the system of prefects introduced by *Napoleon* in France. In the course of the Middle Ages the central rule had been dissolved by feudalism in France. To counteract the local feudal lords, the French king placed his *intendants* in each region. They exercised the royal power in the region and were chosen from among the king's

[1] For the history of Roman administration, see Joachim Marquardt: *Römische Staatsverwaltung* I, Leipzig 1873.

councillors. The system was confirmed by the *Code Michaud* of 1629. It was strongly attacked by *de Tocqueville*, who claimed in his book '*De l'Ancien Régime*', that France was ruled by the 30 intendants, on whose conduct the well-being of the country was dependent. This formed the foundation of the French absolute monarchy.[1]

The absolute monarchy meant the downfall of the intendants, and as far back as 1789 the French *départements* – each headed by a prefect – were set up as the regions for the centralized rule. Simultaneously, the *communes* were established to replace all existing units on the lowest level. During the reign of Napoleon I the prefects were the personal representatives of the Emperor, and they have since been the regional representatives of the central administration. As sub-divisions of the *départements*, the *arrondissements* were subsequently established, headed by the sub-prefects. As the leader of the commune, the *maire* is at the same time representative of the central rule and of the local self-government.

Napoleon's administrative reforms exercised great influence on developments in the other European countries. In 1815, for example, the Prussian administration was organized on a regional basis, and a hierarchy was set up on similar lines to those in France. Prussia was divided into ten provinces, each with its *Oberpräsident*; and each Prussian province was subdivided into a number of administrative areas (*Regierungsbezirke*) each headed by a *Regierungspräsident*. The *Bezirk* is divided into *Kreise*, each head by a *Landrat*, and the smallest unit is the *Gemeinde* (the parish). As the agency for the central administration, the whole of this system constituted a compact hierarchy.[2]

The German federal state (the Weimar Republic) had only very few actual regional federal agencies (*reicheigene Verwaltungsorganen*); but made use of the administrative agencies of the individual states (*Länder*). The individual states within the German federation in most cases carried out the administration of the federal legislation, just as the case is in the present West German Federal State.[3] In Eastern Germany (*Die Deutsche Demokratische Republik*) the individual

[1] For the history of French administration, see Paul Viollet: *Histoire des institutions politiques et administratives de la France*, I–III, Paris 1890–1903.

[2] For the history of German administration, see Ernst Forsthoff: *Lehrbuch des Verwaltungsrechts* I, München u. Berlin, 5te Aufl. 1952 § 2, and the works referred to on p. 14. For a brief survey of the German administration, see Fr. Giese, E. Neuwien und E. Cohn: *Deutsches Verwaltungsrecht*, Berlin und Wien, 1930, pp. 46 ff.

[3] Otto Bachof: *German Administrative Law*, in *The International and Comparative Law Journal*, 1953, p. 376.

states have been entirely deprived of any governmental power, regardless of the fact that article 1 in the East German Constitution of 7 October 1949 lays down that the states shall carry into effect the decisions passed by the federal republic. Under an act of 23 July 1952, on further democratization of the state agencies, a special regional system of agencies has been set up, which are immediately under the control of the republic. The whole territory has been divided into a number of *Kreise* which are united in groups known as *Bezirke*. *Kreis* as well as *Bezirk* in Eastern Germany are, then, exclusively agencies of the central administration of the federal republic.[1]

As already mentioned, the French administrative reforms exerted some influence on the Scandinavian administrative systems so that the original royal organization in these countries was transformed into a prefectorial system on the French and German pattern. In all the Northern countries the parish (in Denmark: *sognekommunen*), which is the basic unit of self-government in the rural districts, also carries out certain functions for the central administration, and in this respect must be regarded as its local representative. The parishes therefore are subject to the hierarchical authority of the central administration as far as these functions are concerned. In Denmark and Norway there is one further regional tier between the prefects and the parishes, *viz.* a special local state official (*politimester*) who is the ordinary representative of the central administration in a subdivision of the country (*amt, fylke*). In these countries the prefect (*amtmand, fylkesman*) is considered the *regional* representative of the government while the *politimester* is considered the *local* representative of the government.

This development in continental Europe had no influence on developments in Britan or in the U.S.A. In Britain, a general regional system came into existence during and after World War II; but such regions are still unknown in the U.S.A. In Britain, the sheriffs were the king's officers for local business, from the Conquest to the Tudors. The Tudors created Lords Lieutenants of counties to take over the military responsibilities of the sheriffs; they put the taxation in the hands of special officials and transferred the supervision of local administration to the Justices of the Peace, chosen from among the local gentry. Whereas the sheriffs had been chosen by the Exchequer, the Justices of the Peace were appointed by the Lord Chancellor; they fixed and levied rates on the parishes and saw to the maintenance of local services.

[1] *Unrecht als System. Dokumente* . . . Teil II, 1952–54. Published by Bundesministerium für gesamtdeutsche Fragen, Bonn 1955.

The Justices of the Peace were superseded by the County Councils in 1888, and since then their duties have been of a purely judicial character.[1] It is obvious that the absence of a powerful royal organization could not help but strengthen British local self-government, and this led to so strong a decentralization that *Lorenz von Stein*, in the previous century, could say with some justification – yet with no little exaggeration – that conditions in England were bordering on an entire 'lack of government' (*Regierungslosigkeit*).[2]

While a general regional development of the central administration has recently taken place in Britain, nothing corresponding to the European prefectorial system is found in the U.S.A., either in the federal administration or in the individual states. In all countries, including those where the prefectorial system has been introduced, regional organizations of a *special* character have been introduced, however.

A number of government departments have their own regional organizations which, geographically and functionally, are independent of the general prefectorial system of the country. The Danish Workers' Protection Act of 1954 may be mentioned here. This act has set up a number of districts which have no relation to the division of the country into counties (*amter*). Each of these special districts is headed by a supervisor, and the decisions made in the various districts may be brought before an attached organization, *viz.* the Labour Directorate whose decisions may be appealed to the Minister of Labour. Similar systems are in use in several countries, and thus a series of parallel hierarchies are established in addition to the general prefectorial system.

Special hierarchies of this kind are the precursors of regionalization in countries, such as the U.S.A. and Britain, where there is no prefectorial system. Regional organizations established by federal departments are not new phenomena in the U.S.A. In the course of time many departments have created regions of their own, exclusively to serve the purposes of the departments concerned, and in some larger cities too, the central administration has set up its field organization on a regional basis. Among numerous examples it may be mentioned that the U.S. Social Security Administration has representatives attached to the 9 regional offices of the Department

---

[1] Among the many works on English administrative history should be mentioned: T. F. Tout: *Chapters in Administrative History of Medieval England*, I–V, 1920–1930, D. L. Kerr: *The Constitutional History of Modern Britain, 1485–1937*, London, 1938, and Sir John Craig: *A History of Red Tape*, London, 1955.

[2] Lorenz v. Stein: *Die Verwaltungslehre* I[2], 2. Aufl. 1869, p. 156.

of Health, Education and Welfare. In addition 534 district offices, and 6 area offices established throughout continental U.S.A. and the territories, handle most of the work under the Old Age and Survivors Insurance programmes. The U.S. Department of Agriculture has several regional systems, each with its special task; there are, for example, seven Agricultural Equipment Committee Areas, covering the whole of continental U.S.A. Approximately 90 per cent of the employees in national service operate from about 2,000 federal field offices outside Washington D.C., not counting the civilian employees stationed overseas.

In Britain the development of the administrative regions began only recently, but then it made rapid strides. It is only during the twentieth century that the British Civil Service has widely extended its operations beyond the boundaries of Whitehall. The first factory inspectors appointed under the Factory Act of 1833 divided the country between them; in 1894 the country was divided into regions for the purpose of agricultural statistics; in various earlier periods such ministries as the Post Office and the Customs and Inland Revenue Department had their local districts for specific administrative purposes. It was the introduction of national wide social services, however, operating through local offices throughout the country, that led to the pattern of departmental regionalism in Britain.

During World War II Britain was divided into a number of regions and, in a form modified for peacetime purposes, this system has been continued. The regional organization is made up of 11 regions, including Scotland and Wales, which have a special status and are not termed regions. The regions are the executive arms of the central departments responsible, in general, for all executive work which has to be carried out in the field. They are multi-purpose executive organizations; but it is not their immediate purpose to bring the powers of central administration closer to the sphere of local governments such as was the purpose of British wartime Civil Defence System. The ministries which have applied regionalism to a wide extent are among those which have least to do with local government affairs; for example the Post Office and the Ministries of Labour and of National Insurance.

So far, we have assumed that the regional organizations serve solely as connecting links between the government departments and their field agents. In numerous cases, however, the central administration carries out work in the field, but has no agencies of its own to perform such work. By way of example, we may refer to the observations on p. 393 above on the federal German administration which is performed mainly by the administrative organizations of the individual states or the local governments on behalf of the federation. Similarly, in practically all countries we find examples of central administration applying agencies which do not generally belong to the central administrative hierarchy and which, more particularly, have not been established by this hierarchy. The most widespread arrangement is the co-operation between the central administration and local governments. As a stock example may be mentioned the French *maire* who is elected by the *conseil municipal* but none the less is the last link in the prefectorial system of the state, and consequently subject to the hierarchical authority of the government in so far as the performance of state functions are concerned. In all the Northern countries an increasing number of tasks are imposed on local governments – tasks which have to be discharged on behalf of the central administration and under its supervision. During World War II, many British local government officials were employed by the central departments as their agents and were consequently acting in a dual capacity: as local government officials and as agents of the state. Furthermore the American County Agent is at the same time a county, state, and federal officer. He has, however, no real administrative powers.

This intermingling of centralized and decentralized organizations will tend to further the centralization at the expense of local self-government.

What has been called geographical distribution of government functions[1] has nothing to do with regionalism. The term can be used when a national institution, i.e. an institution with the whole country as its field of operation, is situated in another part of the country than the other central government organizations which will normally be situated in the capital.

A special form of regionalism occurs in an administration whose local area is determined by the existence of special public tasks within the area concerned. In the U.S.A. this form has become particularly important because several large tasks, especially the exploitation of water power, the irrigation of arid lands, and soil conservation, extend over areas which stretch across the borders of the states, e.g. the Tennessee Valley Authority, the organization of the Colorado River Compact, soil conservation in the 'dust bowl' (the prairies of Kansas, Nebraska, Oklahoma, and other states). This form of

[1] Kjeld Philip: *Intergovernmental Fiscal Relations*, Copenhagen 1954, pp. 20 f.

organization, admittedly, raises partly the same problems as regionalism in the sense we have already discussed in that the authority of these regional organizations is partly based on the delegation of authority from the national government; but they take up special positions in that they usually possess a considerable measure of administrative independence.

29

Britain in the Postwar World*

ANDREW SHONFIELD

In Modern Capitalism *Andrew Shonfield was mainly concerned with presenting a somewhat personal survey of the change in the capitalist system in the West since the 1930s. His general conclusion was that although there have been great differences in the responses of individual countries to the new situation – ranging from France, which enthusiastically adopted centralized economic planning, to Germany, which equally forthrightly rejected it – there are clear traces of a common pattern of behaviour in West European society, and to a lesser extent in North America. In his final chapter, from which these extracts are mainly taken, he discussed the political consequences of the continuing reinforcement of public power in modern capitalist society. It should be noted that whilst the facts given about institutions, particularly in the early part of this reading, are accurate for their period, later events have resulted in many changes; it is also interesting to see how much, since 1964, the psychological attitude to secrecy has changed and there is now a more open policy towards civil servants publicly speaking about their work (though many civil servants still have remnants of the old attitude). See also Brian Chapman,* British Government Observed, Allen & Unwin, 1963; *Hugh Thomas (Ed.)* The Establishment, Anthony Blond Ltd., 1959: *The Administrators; the Reform of the Civil Service,* The Fabian Society, 1964.

The change in the mood of Government in the early 1960s bore all the signs of one of those sudden ideological waves which periodically seem to sweep through Whitehall. The excesses of market worship in the 1950s had been of a similar type. But now the doctrine of the 'invisible hand', which was supposed to look after the needs and desires of the community better than the community knew how to do the job for itself by any conscious effort, was entirely out of favour.

* From Andrew Shonfield, *Modern Capitalism, the changing balance of public and private power*, RIIA and Oxford University Press, 1965, pp. 102–7, 391–9, 404–5, 411–14. Reprinted with permission of the RIIA and the publisher.

The Tories declared themselves for 'planning'. But it was not a simple return to the techniques developed by the Labour Government of the 1940s, for whom planning was essentially the short-term management of the economy in conditions of scarcity. The new approach of the 1960s was based on the long view. It was a rebellion against the technique of administration by short-term expedient which had been given an extended run over the previous decade.

It is impossible to attach a precise date to the change. The establishment of the central planning organization, the NEDC, is perhaps the most striking manifestation of the new spirit. However, it should be noted that the minister officially responsible for the decision on NEDC, Mr Selwyn Lloyd, was himself very much an old-time Chancellor of the Exchequer. Indeed, he was at the time when he gave his approval to the planning organization, during the first half of 1962, in the middle of the traditional exercise of deflating the British economy in an effort to improve the balance of payments. As usual, industrial investment was the chief sufferer, so that the country's capacity for sustained growth was once again squeezed for the sake of strictly short-term ends. In fact the idea of a central economic planning body, analogous to the French system, had been under discussion for some time before this. There is little doubt that the impulse to embark on this experiment derived very largely from the Prime Minister himself. Mr Macmillan's part in the dramatic reversal of policies in the early 1960s was a decisive one. His personal contribution was only occasionally played out in full public view, as in the sudden upheaval in his Cabinet in the summer of 1962, when almost overnight one-third of the senior ministers in the Government lost their offices. This led to the dropping of some very old hands, including Mr Selwyn Lloyd himself, who were deeply imbued with the Tory spirit of the 1950s – essentially the spirit of economic non-intervention – and also gave enhanced power to a number of younger ministers with a technocratic bent and a radical spirit, brought in to run departments concerned with the problems of long-term national planning. The most important of these were in housing and other forms of construction and in education.

Equally important, though much less in the public eye, was the internal reorganization of the key government department concerned with economic policy, the Treasury. This, too, occurred in the second half of 1962. The date was a coincidence; the reform was largely the work of the civil service itself, and the process had been set in motion some time before. There had been criticisms of the efficacy of Treasury control over the spending of other government departments by the Select Committee on Estimates in 1957–8, and this was followed by the appointment of a special committee under Lord Plowden, consisting of five people from inside the civil service and three outsiders, to examine the whole question. Its report, published in 1961 as a White Paper,[1] set out the principles which guided the Treasury changes in the following year. There were two major deficiencies which it identified in the existing system. First, decisions about government expenditure were taken in an *ad hoc* spirit, and no serious attempt was made to place them in the framework of long-term trends, either of likely public needs or of the future resources available to meet them. Secondly, there was no adequate machinery for bringing the competing demands of the different departments of government together in a single coherent picture, so that decisions could be readily made by the Cabinet about the orders of priority in public spending.

The 1962 reorganization of the Treasury was designed to increase the range of administrative control by the government in these two dimensions. First, all decisions which involved the spending of public funds were to be subjected systematically to the techniques of forecasting several years ahead. Secondly, these decisions were to be looked at in relation to other immediately desirable forms of expenditure competing for public money. Since almost any government decision of any significance is bound to involve some spending of money, this pointed to a considerable reinforcement of centralized control throughout the public sector.

The new system involved some profound changes in the traditional organization of the Treasury. Because of the crucial position of this department in the whole apparatus of government, the rest of the civil service machine was caught up willy-nilly in the reorganization. The old Treasury system bore some resemblance to a royal court at the centre of a medieval kingdom, dealing with a lot of very independent barons. The convention was that each baron was allotted to a particular court official, who looked after all his needs and handed out orders or rebukes as they were required. What the baron finds after the reorganization is that the court chamberlains have disappeared and that he has to cope with a lot of specialists, each with his own limited function – as if, for all the world, the place had been

---

[1] *Control of Public Expenditure*, Cmnd. 1432. The original Plowden Report was a confidential document submitted to the Chancellor of the Exchequer. But the version which was eventually published, according to R. W. B. Clarke, Second Secretary at the Treasury, 'covered most of the essentials' (lecture to Royal Inst. of Public Administration, 19 Nov. 1962).

turned into the headquarters of an army. This functional division of authority at the centre has other consequences for visitors from the outside. Some of those who were barely on speaking terms are now forced to rub shoulders with one another, and even to adapt themselves to each other's needs.

The effect of the new arrangement in Whitehall was, intentionally, to allow scope for more independent initiative in the government departments subject to ultimate Treasury control. There was no longer the single official overlord appointed to keep a supervisory eye on all the activities of any one ministry. But the new relationship was also intended to be more demanding; that was because the rearrangement of functions at the Treasury itself was designed to bring a wider range of different criteria to bear on the making of economic policy. Most important, a deliberate effort was made to escape from the old exclusive obsession with money; after the reform, one of the three main sections into which the Treasury was divided had the specific task of looking at government operations in terms of their effect on the real resources of the nation. This was the National Economy Group.[1] By contrast, the Finance Group is concerned exclusively with money. Its task is to look after the management of all money flows affected by government policy, both inside the country and as they impinge on the external balance of payments. Thirdly, there is the Public Sector Group, which looks after the expenditure of all public funds by government departments and agencies. Here again, those responsible for the reorganization made it clear that their intention was to go beyond the purely monetary aspect of securing efficiency in departmental spending activities. Getting 'value for money' was to be measured not only in terms of financial income and outgo at the Exchequer, but also by the effect which it had on the growth of the economy as a whole.[2]

Clearly the significant novelty in the new set-up was the National Economy Group.[3] The ideas about long-term economic trends (now based on standard five-year forecasts), as well as about the long-range effects of public policy on particular issues such as monopoly and restrictive practices, the supply of skilled manpower, impediments

[1] Subsequently transferred to the Department of Economic Affairs. This account of the Treasury deals only with its management of economic and financial policy. There is another portion of the Treasury, under a separate Permanent Secretary, which looks after the management and pay of the civil service.

[2] Clarke, lecture to R.I.P.A., 1962.

[3] When the Labour Government set up the Department of Economic Affairs in the autumn of 1964, with the task of supervising long-range economic policy, the National Economy Group became the central core of the new ministry.

to productivity, industrial costs and prices, were supposed to be developed in this wing of the Treasury. It could be regarded as an embryo planning department.[1] But in practice everything depended on how effectively the influence of the new Group would be brought to bear on the other two – both more solidly grounded in the older conventional work of the Treasury, and commanded by officials (Second Secretaries) of greater seniority than the head of the National Economy Group. The interesting feature of the Treasury experiment was the establishment *within* the administration of a professional agency, packed with the best economists on the staff of the Treasury, whose specific task was to press the long-term viewpoint in the formulation of economic policy. It had the advantage, not possessed by NEDC, of operating on the inside of the administrative machine. The French, as will be seen in the next chapter, have always assumed that planners have to be insiders. So much of modern planning depends on making the multiple arms of governmental power move in unison. But of course over the rest of the field of planning, where private enterprise is ultimately responsible for the decisions, the Treasury is not equipped to do the work of either the Commissariat du Plan or the NEDC. It is still very far from being a Ministry of Planning.[2]

So far as can be judged, the establishment of the NEDC and the Treasury reorganization were the outcome of quite separate initiatives. Indeed, in some ways they were competing initiatives. At any rate the Treasury seems to have been concerned to shift the main

[1] A senior Treasury official, who was closely concerned in the reorganization, described the function of the National Economy Group as follows: 'This group will in a sense co-ordinate and orientate the direction of the large-scale administrative operations of the Finance and Public Sector Groups' (Clarke, ibid.). It is not certain how far the original impulse which found its expression in the National Economy Group was effective in converting the Treasury to the practice of long-range economic planning. According to Mr Robert Neild, there was no fundamental change of method. The Treasury, he stated, 'now looks at estimates of spending five years ahead and not just one year ahead. But this is a financial exercise which consists of adding up all the bits of departments and nationalized industries and scaling them down to fit some percentage of the national income. It is not an exercise in planning, in which long-run objectives are surveyed, alternatives are costed, and choices presented to ministers' (*Listener*, 27 Aug. 1964). All that can be said with assurance is that the administrative structure which *could* accommodate systematic planning of the type described in the last sentence was established in 1962.

[2] The Labour Government of 1964 again separated the function of liaison with private industry, which was left with NEDC, from the new Department of Economic Affairs. The Department meanwhile took over the 'pure' planning staff and functions of NEDC.

focus of its administrative energies from the traditional one of 'saving candle-ends' to the task of reshaping its policies, especially those which impinged on industry, in line with the requirements of long-term economic growth. Behind the new administrative thinking of the early 1960s there were two discoveries about the enhanced power of public authority which are central to modern economic planning in a capitalist context. Both are exceedingly obvious once they have been understood. But there was apparently a deep spiritual resistance to their recognition among postwar politicians and officials in the Anglo-American world. The resistance was stronger in the United States than in Britain, and continues. But in Britain it was strong enough to divert the attention of government from many of the crucial issues of contemporary economic and social policy during the 1950s.

The first discovery was that the volume of economic activity now controlled by the public authorities was exceedingly large, and exerted an overwhelming influence on particular sectors of the economy. Of course, the British Government had understood for a long time that it controlled the resources necessary to even out the short-term market forces which had been responsible for the violent alternation of boom and slump in the past. The advance in economic management during the 1960s was to begin to mobilize the mass of government power and influence in the pursuit of more ambitious objectives. Central and local government together employed 3 million people who earned 15 per cent of all wages and salaries. The public sector as a whole was responsible for over 40 per cent of all fixed investment and for as much as 50 per cent of the building work done in the country. In terms of strategic control this gave the Government outright possession of the 'commanding heights of the economy' – about which the socialists continued to talk wistfully as if they were a remote target for some ultimate assault. The lesson which the British Government learnt belatedly in the early 1960s, and which the French had absorbed much earlier, is that mere occupation of this terrain by public officials instead of private businessmen does not of itself make any difference to the result. A sustained and elaborate effort has to be made if this great mass of public power is to function in any kind of unison.

The second important discovery of the 1960s was that the character of this public economic power is of a kind which tends to produce its effects over long time periods. In the years immediately following the war, when the Keynesian techniques of short-term economic management were being given their first trial run, there was a tendency to exaggerate the day-to-day influence which the state could exert on the course of events through its control over public investment. But after a while it became clear that fiscal measures, in a society where the share of taxation in the national product had greatly increased,[1] provided a more powerful and quick-acting regulator of the economy, especially if they were combined with efficient management of the supply of credit. The central bank, working with the Chancellor of the Exchequer, especially after he was equipped with the power to vary certain consumer taxes by up to 10 per cent between his annual budgets,[2] made a formidable team. By contrast the big decisions about public investment cannot be easily shifted or changed in response to short-term fluctuations in the state of business or the balance of payments. This is partly because the objectives on which public capital is expended tend to be long-range ones. A decision to expand a social service like education or health requires first of all that teacher training colleges or medical schools are established; then the teaching capacity of these institutions has to be built up; and only after the lapse of some years can the extra schools and hospitals be manned and brought into full operation. Long-range forecasting is of the essence of the social investment that is characteristic of our times.[3]

British Theory of Executive Authority

There are two separate problems of democratic control which need to be distinguished. One is how to ensure that the elected representatives play a meaningful role in the business of government. The other is how to secure the protection of the individual citizen against the arbitrary exercise of an ever more extensive public power.

The British case, as suggested earlier, serves especially well to illustrate the nature of the difficulties that have to be overcome in order to achieve these two objectives in the context of the new con-

[1] In 1962 total public expenditure, including interest paid on the national debt, was equivalent to 44 per cent of GNP. The ratio had varied but never fallen below 40 percent at any time in the previous decade (see Cmnd. 2235, 1963).

[2] This was the so-called 'regulator' which was introduced in 1961. Initially it was a crudely designed and rather rigid instrument, which required *all* consumer taxes to be raised or lowered by an equal amount, if the Chancellor of the Exchequer decided that he wanted a quick change between budgets. Subsequently he was given more room for manoeuvre and was allowed to discriminate in the tax increases or decreases to be applied to different classes of goods.

[3] That is not to say that there is no scope for short-term adjustments in social investment projects as part of business cycle policy. . . . But to be successful this requires much more subtle and elaborate advance planning than the first generation of Keynesian policy-makers in Britain, the men responsible for framing the 1944 White Paper on Full Employment Policy, understood.

405

ditions that have emerged in Western society since the Second World War. The essential issue is how to expose the active and ubiquitous government which we face today to more effective pressure from public opinion and from the courts. The growth of public power demands the reinforcement of both. In Britain the parliamentarians treat it as an axiom that the country ought to have a strong executive. The rules of the game allow the government to be endlessly teased but not to be seriously incommoded in the conduct of its ordinary work. The British tend to see it as one of the chief defects of the French parliamentary system that the lack of restraint of the contending parties under the Third and Fourth Republics weakened the executive to the point of exhaustion. The criticism that can be levelled at the performance of the British parliament today is that it continues to be excessively preoccupied with the problem of allowing the executive to be strong, at a time when the latter's strength has in fact become overwhelming.

The point can best be made by way of examples. We have already mentioned the need to induce parliament to organize itself into a system of specialist committees. The members of the existing Standing Committees do not stay for long enough with any particular segment of government to become expert in it. Moreover, even if their work were differently organized, they would hardly have the opportunity to educate themselves since the committees have no research staff. Why do not the M.P.s insist on being properly serviced? The answer which is suggested by the experience of another committee, an unusually successful one by British standards, the Select Committee on Nationalized Industries,[1] is that the M.P.s themselves have no desire for the kind of help which experts can give them. They are generalists – and proud of it. When this Select Committee took a look at its own varied work of supervision in 1958–9 and considered proposals that have been made for improving it, or simply for easing the burden, by calling in some outside specialist assistance, it unerringly found strong reasons why it could better do without. The most illuminating commentary on its underlying attitude is provided by the reasons which it gave against employing a high-power investigating officer with the status of a senior civil servant:[2] this, it objected, might seem to point towards a 'grand

[1] It was established in 1955 and has issued a number of influential reports on the conduct of individual nationalized undertakings (see Bernard Crick, *Reform of Parliament*, London, Wiedenfeld, 1964, App. D).

[2] Someone corresponding to the Comptroller and Auditor General employed by the Public Accounts Committee.

inquisition' of the nationalized industries. Why not? one might ask. To someone fed on the British parliamentary tradition the answer is clear. Such a relationship between parliament and any operating agency would involve an obnoxious degree of tutelage by the legislature over the executive power.[1] The only case in which parliament feels it right to intervene in this way, with expert facilities for investigation at its disposal, is in its control over the spending of public money exercised by the Public Accounts Committee. But this is because parliament is supposed to be expert in only one thing, and that is in securing the proper expenditure of the money which it votes for public purposes.

For the rest, the executive must be permitted to get on with its own work as it sees fit, subject only to the need to answer queries from M.P.s put at Question Time every afternoon in the House of Commons. That this system of questioning does not begin to meet the problem posed by the huge extension of the apparatus and range of modern government is sufficiently shown by the fact that the duration of Question Time – something under an hour – is no longer than it was in the early years of this century.[2] The same attitude is apparent in the permissive approach towards delegated legislation – the purest expression of modern executive power. The theory is that parliament is given the opportunity to consider all executive orders, made in the form of Statutory Instruments, before they become law. They are published and circulated to members of parliament forty days in advance, and during that period are examined by the Scrutiny Committee of the House of Commons, whose task it is to draw attention to any anomalies. But in practice parliamentary control

[1] Thus, for example, Michael Ryle, a Senior Clerk of the House of Commons, after making a series of radical proposals to reform and strengthen the committee system of parliament, produced the following argument against experts: 'The members' own standing would be significantly weakened if they came to rely on their own expert advisers on the American model. And it would probably destroy the necessary good relations with the departments if responsible civil service experts were, in effect, to be examined by non-responsible, unofficial experts. The committees should therefore obtain their expert advice from those giving evidence' ('Greater Committee Scope for M.P.s', *The Times*, 17 April 1963).

[2] D. N. Chester and N. Bowring, *Questions in Parliament* (London, OUP, 1962), quoted by Crick, *Reform of Parliament*, p. 48. At the same time parliament is getting through fewer oral questions during the period (see *Second Report from the Select Committee on Procedure*, HMSO 1965). This is because more supplementary questions are being asked. The result was that in early 1952 there were questions which were waiting up to three months for an answer. *The Economist* (13 March 1965) remarked that 'many of the subjects . . . are out of date by the time they are reached'.

over the content of such delegated legislation is far less complete than it sounds. First of all, a large number of Statutory Instruments escape the procedure of being laid before parliament altogether; the proportion was estimated in the mid-1950s to be as high as 50 per cent.[1] This is the result of legislative laziness, the failure of the legislature in drafting the original enabling Acts. The interesting point, however, is that no one seems to object when the executive exploits the opportunity thus presented to it to extend its law-making powers independently of parliament.

Secondly, the scope of the Scrutiny Committee is subject to strict limitations. It may not comment on the merits of any piece of delegated legislation put before it, even to the extent of giving its view on whether it is in fact a proper use of the power delegated to the executive. Its task is solely to draw the attention of the House of Commons to any Statutory Instruments which raise doubts on certain stated grounds. Among these grounds, it is true, is that the proposed law makes 'unusual or unexpected use of powers'[2] that have been delegated. But the Committee cannot explain its doubts; it can only point dumbly. When Sir Gilbert Campion, as Clerk of the House of Commons, suggested in the mid-1940s that the Scrutiny Committee's functions might be stretched to allow it to report 'on the merits of a Statutory Instrument, as an exercise in the powers delegated', the Government rejected the idea out of hand. The whole operation would, it alleged, become an intolerable burden on busy ministers. It 'would mean that ministers would have to attend before the Select Committee to defend the policy embodied in subordinate legislation'. But in fact Campion's proposal had nothing to do with policy; its purpose, as A. H. Hanson has pointed out, was to allow parliament to make an assessment of the actual use of 'that discretion which parliament . . . intended the Minister to exercise'.[3] No doubt it was this which made the Government of the day shy away from the proposal like a frightened horse. For, as Campion went on to argue, the people who would naturally be called upon to explain the intended use of the discretionary powers embodied in any particular Statutory Instrument would not be ministers, but the officials responsible for the actual drafting of the order. If the officials were

[1] J. E. Kersell, *Parliamentary Supervision of Delegated Legislation* (London, Stevens, 1960), p. 19, who quotes the estimate of Sir Cecil Carr, Counsel to the Speaker of the House of Commons, 1943–55.

[2] Ibid., p. 50 ff.

[3] The Select Committee on Statutory Instruments: 'Further Note', *Public Administration*, Autumn 1951, quoted by Kersell, p. 50.

competent to make the orders, he argued, they 'would be competent to explain their purpose and the reasons for making them'.[1]

Thus the real threat in this proposal for reform was to the myth of total ministerial responsibility. There seemed to be a danger that parliament was about to extend its finger and touch, ever so lightly, some part of the actual business of public administration. However, all that was necessary was for the Government to draw attention to the peril and parliament desisted. Why this extraordinary self-restraint? No doubt, the answer is that parliament, having evolved over a long period a technique for securing government which is strong enough to be efficient and yet malleable enough to be changed without disturbance, is very wary of anything which might upset the system. The anonymous civil servant, separated from parliamentary contact by an opaque screen, has come to be regarded as an essential element in this arrangement; he must be politically 'sterilized', to use the somewhat contemptuous term applied to him by one French commentator,[2] in order to make possible those marvellous friction-less changes in the political composition of British government. This element in the machinery is, in fact, of comparatively recent origin. Britain was later than other European nations in developing a professional civil service; it dates only from the second half of the nineteenth century. But having decided, somewhat belatedly, on the need for a non-political body of officials, the British proceeded to make their divorce from the world of politics more complete than it is anywhere else.

To this end the old notion of the separation of powers contained in the Act of Settlement of 1701 was revived.[3] We have seen that the practical significance of the doctrine of separation from the early eighteenth century onwards was, in Britain, the independence of the judiciary. Walter Bagehot in *The English Constitution* makes amusing play over the misunderstanding of the Founding Fathers of the American Constitution, who thought they were copying the English

[1] Kersell, *Parliamentary Supervision*, p. 51.

[2] Charles Fourrier, *Liberté d'opinion du fonctionnaire* (Paris, Pichon & Durand-Auzias, 1957). Titre II, in particular pp. 100 ff.

[3] The official handbook for the civil servant refers to the Act explicitly in connexion with its prohibition on members of the House of Commons from holding an 'office of profit' under the Crown. It says: 'This prohibition was later modified, and Ministers and holders of certain other "offices of profit" under the Crown are now allowed to sit in the House; but as a general rule civil servants are still excluded, and if a Member of Parliament should become a civil servant his seat in Parliament will automatically become vacant' (*A Handbook for the New Civil Servant*, 11th edn, 1964, p. 34).

model, but in fact 'were contriving a contrast to it'.[1] The Americans most carefully separated the legislature from the executive, whereas the characteristic feature of the English system is 'the fusion of the executive power with the legislative power'.[2] Writing as he was in the 1860s, Bagehot did not foresee the growth of an administrative branch of government endowed with an initiative of its own over a wide area of activity and effectively removed from parliamentary scrutiny. This is not quite the separation of powers, as the eighteenth-century theorists envisaged it. The civil servant is in the last resort subject to the orders of his minister who in turn depends on the support of parliament. But in practice, the fiction that all the actions of a department are the personal responsibility of its minister and that therefore parliament cannot carry its enquiries beyond the confines of a dialogue with the minister, means that there is a considerable, and constantly growing, range of administrative activity which escapes effective legislative oversight.

The people with the strongest interest in preserving this system are the civil servants themselves. They may be 'sterilized' in terms of overt party politics; but this is regarded as a small price to pay for being almost entirely protected from the rude gaze of outsiders, and even more from their questions about what they are doing in the exercise of immense power. Any attempt by the press to identify the particular civil servant responsible for certain actions is especially resented.[3] Meanwhile the minister often enjoys the over-lifesize role which the civil servants are anxious to help him to perform – being not merely the head but the personification of a portion of the apparatus of state.

It hardly needs to be said that the minister himself, working under the personal pressure which the conditions of modern government impose on such a person, cannot be expected to do the job of over-sight on parliament's behalf. In any case, as Bagehot shrewdly remarks, an especially important task of parliament when it questions the doings of the executive – more important than its legislative activity – is its 'informing function'.[4] It enables the public to learn

[1] Fontana Library Edition, 1963, p. 219.   [2] Ibid., p. 81.

[3] In the early 1960s there were the beginnings of an attempt, in such books as *The Treasury under the Tories* by Samuel Brittan (Penguin, 1964) and *Anatomy of Britain* by Anthony Sampson (Hodder & Stoughton, 1962), to break down the myth of ministerial responsibility in its extreme form which treated civil servants as a species of *un*person. The pained reaction to the naming of officials held to have influenced certain decisions suggested that they would fight hard to retain their cocoon of anonymity.

[4] *English Constitution*, p. 53. Bagehot lists as the most important function of

what the issues are and what considerations have been, or ought to have been, taken into account in shaping the actions of the government. The minister in private conversation with his civil servants cannot do that.

The 'Informing Function' of the Bureaucracy

Indeed, the senior civil servants, who are in fact taking an active hand in the making of the nation's policy, whatever the theory may say to the contrary, might reasonably be expected to regard it as part of their duty to contribute personally to this 'informing function', even if parliament happened to be more efficient than it is as an intermediary between them and the public. In order to do so usefully they would, of course, have to be given some freedom to express opinions of their own, without committing the minister in charge of their department to their conclusions. This is readily done in other countries, notably in France, where officials of any intellectual distinction tend to see it as part of their business – unmistakably a pleasurable part – to bring the underlying issues in their administrative work to the attention of the public. Some of them are prolific writers of books and articles. Their subjects, moreover, are often right on top of some issue of popular controversy. It is recognized, of course, that they cannot engage in such an argument at the level of unrestrained popular polemic, without damaging their professional reputations for impartiality. As Fourrier puts it, a civil servant must always appear '*serein*' and therefore in his public utterances must show '*réserve*'.[1] But this is a matter of individual self-discipline; parliament that of maintaining an effective executive in being. The 'informing function' comes next.

[1] *Liberté d'opinion*, III–II–Chs II and III. There is only one exception to the rule of political freedom of expression, within the limits of 'réserve', and that applies to the Prefects and Sub-Prefects (p. 311). They are held to be in an especially close political relationship with the government of the day, through the Minister of the Interior who is their chief. Roger Gréoire, in the standard work on the subject, *La fonction publique* (Paris, Colin, 1954), mentions two specific regulations governing the publications of French civil servants on political matters. They are not supposed to make damaging statements about their superiors in the service and 'in certain cases' must avoid making 'a direct attack against the authority of the state' (p. 298). These limitations both clearly come under the general rule of 'réserve'. All the evidence is that they are liberally interpreted by the Conseil d'État, which is the ultimate arbiter of civil servants' behaviour. That is not to say that a French official who expresses views which are unpopular with the politician in charge of his department suffers no disadvantages whatever. He will very likely not be the first person to be considered when there is an opportunity for promotion, in which the minister has a say. But he cannot be demoted or dismissed for the views which he expresses; the Conseil d'État, with its highly developed sense of professional solidarity, has quite sufficient power to protect him in case of need.

411

there is no system of internal censorship for members of the civil service. They are not required either to obtain permission before they write something for publication or to submit the text to official scrutiny by someone else in the service before publication. British civil servants in all but the very lowest grades must do both.

Thus in recent years there have been books on French price control policy by the civil servant who was for many years in charge of the Price Control Office, and on the government's economic planning by a senior official of the Commissariat du Plan. . . .[1] They are typical products of a certain highbrow journalism, what the French call, with a touch of self-deprecating affectation, *haute vulgarisation*, in which high French officials engage on a wide range of topics and with undisguised gusto. No one doubts that they benefit by exposing their ideas to public comment and criticism by book reviewers and others. It is also assumed to be a help to the administrator in the conduct of his work, if the public has been given an insight into what the problems of administration really are. Admittedly the French approach to the whole question of freedom of expression has a certain doctrinaire quality. The right of the civil servant to publish, it is argued, is guaranteed to him by the Declaration of the Rights of Man; it is built into the constitution.[2] Indeed, it is regarded as the duty of the authorities positively to help an official who wishes to take part in a political election – for example by granting him paid leave during the election campaign.[3]

No doubt the instinctive British reaction to all this would be to say: 'Well, just look at the result. The French may enjoy throwing off all these irksome restraints; but once they have done so, the only way in which they seem to be able to give themselves an effective government is by setting up an authoritarian régime under a strong man, preferably a general.' Without attempting to judge the merit of the accusation, it is at least possible to reply that even within the limita-

[1] See L. Franck, *Les Prix* (Paris, Presses Universitaires, 1964), p. 50, and H. Bernard Cazes, La Planification en France et le *Quatrième Plan* (Paris, L'Épargne, 1962), p. 84.

[2] See Fourier, *Liberté d'opinion*, p. 304.

[3] See Grégoire, *Fonction publique*, p. 339, who remarks that the provisions of a 'recent circular' on the subject seem to be generously interpreted, so that not only the officials who are actual candidates, but also those who merely wish to take an active part in the campaign in support of someone else are able to claim election leave. If elected to parliament, a French official is treated as being on secondment and has full rights of reinstatement at the end of the parliamentary term. He can even get some extra pay out of the government while seconded; if his parliamentary salary is less than the official salary he was receiving beforehand, the difference is made up (ibid., p. 341).

tions of the Fifth Republic there is a more frank and informed debate on certain matters of public policy, for example the choices implicit in the national economic plan, and a more effective scrutiny of the actions of the bureaucracy, including most notably its delegated legislation, by the Conseil d'État than by the parliament in Britain.

The French way is only one of various possible methods of putting the essential work of a modern administration on public view. The Americans have another technique. A much larger segment at the top of their bureaucracy is filled by political appointments. It is to be observed that most of the men who occupy these posts, which in other countries would be occupied by civil servants, are not politicians in the ordinary sense, but men of administrative experience or ability who are politically committed.[1] Once in office, it is their business to be articulate. Further down the scale of the American bureaucracy, among the 'career officers', there is still considerable scope for the public expression of opinion. The rule is that all civil servants may speak without submitting their speeches in advance, even though it is known that the speech will be published, but that anything written specifically for publication is subject to certain restrictions. Officials working in the two most sensitive areas of public policy, in the State Department and the Department of Defense, must submit everything that they write for preliminary vetting; indeed, there is a well understood though informal rule – informal because Congress might object to the restriction if it were made explicit – that even the spoken words of officers of these departments are, wherever this is feasible, subject to advance censorship. But over the wide range of economic and social affairs, the rule is that only articles or books which set out to discuss some aspect of government policy, rather than do so incidentally in connexion with a more general argument, have to be submitted for official approval before being published. Plainly with several hundreds of articulate political appointees in the field, the scope for journalism by the 'career' men is, in any case, limited.

The Independent Official
One question which is raised by the argument in the preceding sections is the degree of personal independence which is appropriate to

[1] The French achieve something not altogether dissimilar by the device of the *cabinet* of the minister. This is composed of civil servants and others chosen by the minister because of their political affiliations with him. Admittedly the *cabinet* does not have the same formal position of commanding authority in the French system as political appointees have in the American system; but it can at times exercise an influence which is as powerful as theirs.

officials of states of the Western capitalist type. The British adopt an extreme theoretical position which is symbolized in the legal doctrine that a civil servant holds his post 'at pleasure' of the Crown and can be summarily dismissed without redress. The reality is quite different, and the civil servant is thought of in Britain as being a more than usually permanent fixture in his job.[1] Nevertheless the notion that he is in an essentially military relationship with his employer, the Crown – a good servant who obeys orders to the best of his ability but has suppressed any independent will of his own – has bitten deep into British institutions.

This whole approach is, as we have observed on several occasions, sharply at variance with French ideas on the role of the public servant. In France the characteristic quality ascribed to the great official in his 'independence'. This is not intended to describe a quality of mind which is indifferent to political considerations: to be 'independent' does not mean to be exclusively devoted to the autonomy of individual conscience, regardless of how its behests impinge on others. On the contrary, it goes with an active readiness to compromise, if this will serve to achieve the expression of some real consensus among colleagues engaged in the joint exercise of power. That is the spirit which animates the members of the Conseil d'État. It is the opposite of that displayed by French parliamentarians, who have tended to treat the floor of the chamber as a forum for professional displays of political intransigence – and have in consequence divorced parliament from an effective role in the business of government.

The 'independent' official is, above all, a person who is loyal to certain professional standards. Being in a position of trust, he must actively resist the pressures of mere convenience, whether private or public; there is no excuse for failure to press an honest personal judgment. Loyalty to the professional service of the state is not supposed to swamp the individual personality; rather, the service is seen as providing the opportunity for an especially noble expression of the private *persona* in a public context.[2] The notion is complex and

[1] See L. Blair, 'The Civil Servant – Political Reality and Legal Myth', *Public Law* 1958. However, as Professor W. Friedmann says, 'the problem of dismissability at will remains . . . of practical importance in times of public nervousness and preoccupation with security and loyalty considerations' (*Law in a Changing Society*, abridged edn, London, Penguin, 1964, p. 299).

[2] It is interesting to observe that the notion of the independent public official in France goes back to the *ancien régime*, before the Revolution. W. R. Brock remarks that in the eighteenth century, by contrast with the absolute obedience exacted from the civil servants of the Prussian and Austrian imperial regimes, 'an

sometimes confused,[1] it certainly lacks the logic of the English doctrine of the civil servant. It has, however, proved its usefulness in practice – and not in France only. To obtain a clearer view of its significance, it is worth looking at its further elaboration in another context, where it has produced some striking results.

The apotheosis of independent officialdom in the postwar world is the European Commission set up in Brussels by the European Economic Community. In the course of grappling, rather effectively, with some of the most complicated administrative problems of economic policy, it has evolved methods which have a relevance to the national, as well as international, institutions of contemporary Western society....

Discretionary Power versus Judicial Authority

The second of the two major questions which we distinguished earlier – the first being the problem of democratic participation in modern government – is how to protect the individual against the growing range and penetrating power of public authority. The collective provision of so much more welfare and the progressive effort to relate it more subtly to varied individual needs, coupled with the central control over many more decisions which in one way or another affect private initiatives, whether in business or in personal life, argue the need for new techniques of judicial supervision. In this section of the argument I shall again use the British case as a reference point, because here too its institutions have in the past, especially during the formative period of Western capitalism in the eighteenth and nineteenth centuries, proved especially effective in defence of the individual against the exercise of arbitrary public power. Of late, however, their success in this regard has been less in evidence.

In a sense the trouble with the British courts is the same as that which we observed earlier in parliament: there is too much concern with the problem of providing the executive with the conditions that it deems to be necessary for the efficient conduct of its work. This may

intendant could and did resist and criticize the central Government' (*New Cambridge Modern History*, Vol. vii, *1713–63*, p. 159).

[1] The French, for instance, seem to have difficulty in running a genuinely independent public corporation, like the BBC. Here the sharp British distinction between those who are 'servants' of the minister in a department, with no independent initiative of their own, and those public officials (e.g. in the BBC) who are not covered by the doctrine of total ministerial responsibility helps to secure more genuine independence for the latter than the French have been able to achieve.

seem a surprising conclusion about the courts in Britain, in view of the tough way in which they insist on the letter of the law regardless of administrative convenience. But it may be precisely because they are so tough about the letter that they feel themselves to be obliged to be pretty lax on occasion about the spirit. The criticism applies particularly to cases where justice would seem to require analysis of the *intentions* of the legislators, in addition to the actual words used by the drafters of the law, and those where the exercise of administrative *discretion* is involved.

It is in the treatment of the latter that the executive in Britain can rely on the courts to give it vast benefit of the doubt. The point is best illustrated by the statement of the Lord Chief Justice in a recent case involving some campaigners for nuclear disarmament, who tried to organize a demonstration on an airfield in 1962. Some of the demonstrators were sentenced to imprisonment and appealed. Lord Parker, in dismissing the appeal, said that there were certain matters into which the courts could not enquire because they concerned the exercise of powers left to 'the unfettered control of the Crown'. The defending counsel had previously argued that evidence of harm to the national interest should be produced and that it surely could not be right that 'all the Crown had to do was to call a government official of some kind to say "that act is in fact prejudicial because I am the only person who knows" '.[1] But Lord Parker pointed to 'the general power of Ministers whether in war or peace to claim Crown privilege'. He added: 'A similar principle underlies the power of the executive . . . to requisition or to do other acts where in its discretion that is considered necessary in the national interest.'[2]

The principle that the courts do not inquire into the reasons which lead officials to exercise administrative discretion granted to them by law is well established. As C. J. Hamson put it in his comment on the judgment in the case of *Liversidge* v. *Anderson* (1942), concerning a man who claimed that he had been wrongly imprisoned under a wartime detention order: 'The detention order accordingly was valid by reason of the mere statement of the Home Secretary that the Home Secretary believed himself to have reasonable cause to believe that the appellant ought to be locked up'.[3] Some judges have been increasingly irked by the petty way in which the executive's right to refuse to give reasons is exercised. In a case in 1964 involving a dispute between the British Railways Board and a group of hotels

[1] *The Times*, Law Report, 3 April 1962.
[2] *All England Law Reports*, 15 May 1962, p. 320.
[3] *Executive Discretion and Judicial Control* (London, Stevens, 1954), p. 13, n. 7.

(the *Grosvenor Hotel* case), in the course of which the Minister of Transport, responsible for the Board, refused to produce a document that was held to be relevant, claiming Crown privilege, one of the judges commented that he 'detected a desire in the official mind to push ever forward the frontiers of secrecy' – a process which he regarded 'with distaste'.[1] Another judge in the same case went further. He said that when Crown privilege was unreasonably claimed in matters like this, 'the Court ought to have the power to override the Executive'. In his view,

'. . . it was incredible that the public service should not function properly unless commonplace communications between one civil servant and another were privileged from production. . . . Industry seemed to have got along very well without privilege for communications even at the highest level. The law had already given the Executive complete protection in respect of high level communications and communications made under a statutory duty.'[2]

The rebellion of these High Court judges is not an isolated incident. The three judges, led by Lord Denning, Master of the Rolls, who had presided over the *Grosvenor Hotel* case, repeated their strictures on the arbitrary exercise of administrative discretion by government officials in another department, the Ministry of Housing and Local Government, in December 1964. Again, it was a question of producing official documents, which were relevant to a dispute with some borough councils, for examination by the court; this was refused without other explanation than that it was 'necessary for the proper functioning of the public service to withhold from production' documents in this class.[3] This statement was covered in the usual way by the signature of the minister, and, it was claimed, his say-so was sufficient to settle the matter. Lord Denning asserted, on the contrary, that when a minister put a blanket of secrecy over a whole class of documents 'he *must* justify his objection with reasons. He should describe the nature of the class and the reason why the document should not be disclosed, so that the Court itself could see whether the claim was well taken or not'.[4]

[1] Lord Justice Harman, *The Times, Law Report*, 30 July 1964. The case was about the refusal by the Railways Board to renew the lease of the Grosvenor Hotel (at Victoria Station) on a site which the Board owned.
[2] Lord Justice Salmon (ibid.).
[3] The case involved the reorganization of local government and the objections of Wednesbury Borough Council and four other local authorities in the Midlands to the decision of the Ministry. They claimed that the inquiry held by the Ministry had not been properly conducted and was therefore invalid.   [4] Ibid.

He admitted that the blanket statement of refusal by a minister had been accepted as 'common form' before the *Grosvenor Hotel* case, and indicated that the court would in future try to control the unrestrained – and unexplained – use of ministerial discretion. However, so far the challenge to the executive is no more than a promise, for in both cases – the Grosvenor Hotel and the borough councils – Lord Denning and his fellow judges ruled that the official documents which had been demanded by the litigants against the Government were not, in fact, necessary for the court's decision. The match between judicial authority and discretionary power has, therefore, for the present, been postponed.[1]

How did it happen that the frontiers of British justice had been allowed to retreat as far as this? The chief cause lies in what Mitchell has called the conception of 'the Minister-judge' in parliament, who must answer for all administrative acts done on his responsibility and 'against whom the Common Law can do nothing'. He describes the further process as follows:

'From that fact, coupled with the dependent fact of the anonymity of the civil service, flowed the judicial answers that the individual was not entitled to know or see the individual official who decided (this being, it was considered, immaterial, since the Minister was responsible) and that decisions need not be reasoned. The last was an acceptance of administrative practice which was itself dependent upon the doctrine of ministerial responsibility. The decision, it was thought, should, if need be, be justified in Parliament but not elsewhere'.[2]

The story is a telling example of the way in which a useful piece of mythology – the absolute sovereignty of parliament and the total subordination of servants of the Crown – may actively impede progress if people insist on remaining loyal to it when circumstances, and the problems to be solved, have changed. There is no mystery about what is lacking: it is a system of administrative law which will allow acts of official discretion to be judged by an independent tribunal. But there is no means of accommodating such a reform without pulling the doctrine of ministerial responsibility up by the roots. The result of not making the wrench is a profound distortion at the centre of the administrative system. 'The civil servant in

[1] Lord Denning's view of the proper role of the courts in this matter is not by any means uniformly accepted by the rest of the British judiciary.

[2] 'The Causes and Effects of the Absence of a System of Public Law in the United Kingdom', *Public Law*, Summer 1965, p. 102.

England', C. J. Hamson says,[1] 'necessarily suffers a gross professional deformation, not by reason of any naturally inherent vice but mainly by reason of the condition in which he operates – namely, as the bearer collectively within the community of a power which is as great as it is arbitrary'. It is a comfort that civilized administrative habits and a strong tradition of fair play limit the actual employment of this arbitrary power. But it might also be argued that the cultivated reticence of the British civil servant, the restraint on his initiative, and the damper on verbal expression, which he accepts as the price for being left undisturbed in the twilight zone between parliament and the people whom he administers, endow Britain with a less effective form of public power than the natural talent of the nation is capable of providing.

[1] *Executive Discretion*, p. 19.

30

Types of Thought*

GRAHAM WALLAS

In The Art of Thought, *Graham Wallas considered further the problem how far the knowledge accumulated by modern psychology can be made useful for the improvement of the thought-processes of a working thinker. His book is mainly based on his reflections after many years as teacher and administrator, combined with accounts of their thought processes by a number of writers. In this chapter he argues that certain ways of using the mind are characteristic of nations, professions and other human groups. Some of these are the unconscious results of environment; others have been consciously invented; and others are due to a combination of invention and environment. Whereas the French and English nations have acquired different mental habits and ideals which they indicate respectively by the word 'logic' and the phrase 'muddling through', the 'pioneer' habit of mind is perhaps more prevalent in America than any other single type.*

In the last two chapters I have discussed certain mental habits and expedients which may be deliberately acquired by individual thinkers for the purpose of increasing the fertility and energy of their thoughts. In this chapter, I shall discuss a few of those mental habits which are characteristic of nations, or professions, or other groups of men.

Some of these mental habits were in their origin half-conscious results of the conditions under which men earn their livelihood. No one, for instance, consciously invented the legal type of thought (with its tendency to treat words as identical with things), or the military, or clerical, or bureaucratic, or academic type; nor need one search for an inventor to explain why the Bradford type of thought is different from the Exeter type, or why a Roumanian peasant thinks differently from a Viennese merchant. On the other hand, a type of thought

* From Graham Wallas, *The Art of Thought*, London, Jonathan Cape, 1926, pp. 171–203. Copyright 1926 by Harcourt, Brace Jovanovich Inc., New York; renewed 1954 by May Graham Wallas. Reprinted with permission of the publishers on behalf of the Estate of Graham Wallas.

sometimes follows a pattern that was first created by the conscious effort of a single thinker, Anaxagoras, or Aquinas, or Descartes, or Hegel, and was afterwards spread by teaching and imitation. The prevalence of a type of thought is often due to a combination of conscious invention and the less-conscious influence of circumstances. Someone invents a new type of thought, and, either at the time or later, a new fact appears in a national or group environment which makes the new type widely acceptable. In that way, types of thought, like the words and word-meanings by which they are often indicated, may be invented and neglected or superseded in one country, and be afterwards enthusiastically adopted in another country whose environment suits them better. One can see why Rousseauism, for instance, as interpreted by Jefferson, 'caught on' in America after the Declaration of Independence; or why a crude 'Darwinismus' spread in Germany as the German Empire began to extend beyond Europe; or why, in the same decade, the Hegelian dialectic fitted the needs of troubled Oxford religious thinkers. The type of thought painfully worked out by Locke and his friends from 1670 to 1690 went to France in 1729 to justify the liberal opposition to Louis XV: Bentham's *a priori* deduction of social machinery from primitive instinct suited the conditions of the South and Central American colonies after their separation from Spain: Herbert Spencer's *Synthetic Philosophy* suited Japan after her sudden adoption of western applied science. Sometimes, though with much hesitation, one may ascribe the spread of a particular type of thought to innate racial factors – the victory, for instance, of Mohammedanism over Christianity among the stronger African tribes, and possibly the greater success of Buddhism in the eastern than in the western half of the Eurasian continent.

In examining such types of thought we have constantly to remember that there never exists a body of people all of whom are equally possessed of any type-quality. In interpreting nineteenth-century English political history, we may usefully speak of Conservative or Liberal types of thought as dominant at this or that moment, and yet we must never forget, not only that a Liberal or Conservative Government may be supported by a bare majority, or even a minority of the voters, but that every Liberal or Conservative voter or minister differs from every other, and that no one can ever be truthfully described as being politically a Liberal or Conservative and nothing else. In the same way, we may fairly speak of a national English or a French type of political thought, and yet remember that the fact behind our statement may be that a way of thinking which is characteristic of 60 per cent of active French politicians is only equally characteristic of 40 per cent of active English politicians. This warning is specially needful when international friction arises from the prevalence of different types of thought among different nations; but the international policy of a modern nation at any given moment is for its neighbours a unity, and Englishmen and Frenchmen have therefore to recognize and try to understand the types of thought actually prevalent in the two countries without exaggerating either the universality or the permanence of the type in each case.

A type of thought characteristic, in that sense, of English politicians (though, owing to differences of political, educational, and religious history, not equally characteristic of Scotland and Wales), is often indicated by the English use of the expression 'muddling through', as a term of approval. That use went out of fashion, for obvious reasons, during the war; but, now that the English people intensely desire a return to peace and the ways of peace, it is reappearing. Canon Barnes (now Bishop of Birmingham) wrote, for instance, in 1922, while discussing certain educational proposals, that: 'Administrative difficulties we are rapidly solving by our national genius for "muddling through". In more respectful and more accurate language, we are finding the path to success by experiment, and we remain indifferent as to whether a logically perfect scheme will result.'[1] Lord Selborne, in 1924, spoke of 'the glorious incapacity for clear thought which is one of the distinguishing marks of our race. It is the cause of our greatest difficulties and has been the secret of some of our greatest successes.'[2] Mr Lytton Strachey, in his *Queen Victoria* (pp. 150 and 152), declared that 'Lord Palmerston was English through and through', and explained this by saying that 'he lived by instinct – by a quick eye and a strong hand, a dexterous management of every crisis as it arose, a half-unconscious sense of the vital elements in a situation'. And Mr Austen Chamberlain was cheered by his party in Parliament when he said (24 March, 1925), 'I profoundly distrust logic when applied to politics, and all English history justifies me.'

On the other hand, French writers who have concerned themselves with the comparison between French and English mental habits, emphasize the 'classic', or 'logical' or 'mathematical' character of typical French thinking. Taine, when writing as an opponent of that type of thought, declared that the French Revolution was the work of 'the classic spirit' and defined it as follows: 'to follow out in every

[1] 'The Problem of Religious Education,' Canon Barnes (a paper read to the Association of University Women Teachers, 5 Jan. 1922).

[2] *Church Times*, 20 June, 1924.

enquiry, with complete confidence, and without either reserve or precaution, the method of mathematics; to abstract, define, and isolate certain very simple and very general ideas; and then, without reference to experience, to compare and combine them, and from the artificial synthesis so created to deduce by pure logic all the consequences which it involves. This is the characteristic method of the classic spirit' (*L'Ancien Régime*, 1876, p. 262). And in his *Notes on England* (1872), p. 306, Taine says that 'the interior of an English head may not unaptly be likened to one of Murray's hand-books, which contains many facts but few ideas'.[1] E. Boutmy (*Psychologie politique du peuple anglais* (1901), p. 27) quotes a sentence of the French writer Royer-Collard, 'I despise a fact', and compares it with a saying of Edmund Burke about abstract ideas, 'I hate the very sound of them.' A. Fouillée, in his *Psychologie du peuple français* (1898), goes into greater detail while describing the French type of thought: 'The strong point of our intelligence lies less in apprehending real things than in discovering connections between possible or necessary things. In other words, ours is a logical and combining imagination, which delights in that which has been called the abstract pattern of life' (p. 185), and, speaking of French political thought, he says, 'We believe that we can carry out principles merely by proclaiming them, and that if we change our constitution by a stroke of the pen we thereby transform our laws and customs' (p. 204).

It is possible, but, I believe, wholly misleading, to explain the difference indicated in these quotations in terms of racial biology. Although the greater part of England and the greater part of France contain almost exactly the same racial admixture, writers have invented a 'Latin race', which is biologically less 'sentimental' and 'more passionate', or less 'phlegmatic' and more 'restless' than the equally imaginary 'Anglo-Saxon race'. Or one can ascribe the difference wholly to education; one can represent the typical French politician as having received a thorough training in logic and the use of language, and the typical English politician as a golf-playing barbarian; or, on the other hand, one can ascribe the difference to the training in 'character' of the English 'public schools' as compared to the 'intellectualism' of French education. I myself believe that the difference which exists, and which (owing in part to the difficulty of observing our own mental habits) it is so hard either to describe or to explain, is mainly due to a difference of intellectual tradition, transmitted partly by education, and partly by political catchwords and legal institutions, and strengthened by differences in

[1] See also Rignano, *The Psychology of Reasoning*, p. 276.

the political and international history of the two countries. I do not know of any evidence that this particular difference of intellectual tradition was noticed before the French Revolution. Voltaire's *Letters on the English* (1730) for instance, and Montesquieu's *Esprit des Lois* (1748) imply that the English, rather than the French, are the consistent followers of logic. But, in any case, the Revolution, and the twenty years of 'war against armed ideas' which followed the Revolution, fixed and emphasized the acceptance of Reason as the republican ideal in France, and opposition to Reason, in the French sense, as the ideal of the English governing class. It is, perhaps, unfortunate that we have never invented a single easily-personified word for our own idea in this respect. It would be difficult for the leaders of the most successful English Revolution to set up, in imitation of the French 'Goddess of Reason', a temple in London to 'Our national Genius for Muddling Through', or to 'Our Glorious Incapacity for Clear Thought'.

This difference can, however, be stated in terms of the analysis of the thought-process which I have been attempting in this book. We can say that English tradition has produced a greater emphasis on the less-conscious stage of Intimation and Illumination, and that French tradition has produced a greater emphasis on the more-conscious stages of Preparation and Verification. I have already quoted Mr Lytton Strachey's statement that Lord Palmerston lived politically by 'a half-unconscious sense of the vital elements in a situation'. One gets a still better illustration of what I mean in the exchange of letters towards the end of 1885 between Lord Spencer and Sir Henry Campbell-Bannerman (who, though Scotch, was in many ways a typical Englishman) after Gladstone had begun to show himself a Home Ruler on the Irish question. Lord Spencer (13 December 1885) said that he himself was 'uneasy at the drift of my thoughts and inclination'. Sir Henry Campbell-Bannerman answered: 'I confess that I find my opinions moving about like a quicksand. . . . It is a great comfort and relief to me to hear that you are so much bothered and complexed. It shows that my disease is in the air and is not peculiar to myself.'[1] M. Fouillée might have taken this as a typical instance of English thinking, and might have compared this apparently passive waiting upon the drift of one's thoughts with the rigorous application of definite political principles to a new problem at which M. Clemenceau would have aimed in the same circumstances.

Our English habit of thought leads us easily to change our minds

[1] *Life of Sir Henry Campbell-Bannerman*, by J. A. Spender, Vol. I, pp. 90–1.

when we find that we *feel* differently about a situation. I have been told that, during one of Lord Salisbury's attempts to reach an Anglo-German understanding, a young official from the German Colonial Office was placed temporarily in the African section of our Colonial Office, and that he was astonished at the 'illogical' character of our dealings with the native tribes. A native chief would give us every possible justification for sending a punitive expedition against him, and we would not do so unless we somehow felt that it was at the moment worth while; and a young French official might have made the same observation. Both national habits involve, of course, their own special dangers. In war, for instance, our national ideal of 'muddling through' is not only apt to make our intellectual methods slow under circumstances where speed is essential, but also may lead, and has led British generals to avoid the severe effort of collecting and arranging all available knowledge and of testing all hypotheses by the most rigorous rules of consistency. English experience, again, shows that statesmen who accept our ideal of intellectual and emotional expectancy, should be very careful before committing their country to binding engagements with other countries. They may find themselves promising something this year because they feel inclined to do so, and next year putting aside their promise if their feeling has changed. The fact, for instance, that in 1917, during the stress of the war, we promised equal treatment of Hindoos and Whites in Africa, and that in 1923, when the stress was over, we refused, for reasons that then seemed good, to carry our our promise in the Crown Colony of Kenya, may prove a very serious element in the future relations of Great Britain and India. The typically English statesman is especially likely to exasperate the other parties to a contract if he permits himself to indulge in a glow of moral self-satisfaction over a change of policy which not only expresses his new feelings, but also clearly corresponds to the economic interests of his nation. On the other hand, the 'muddling through' type of thought, with its allowance for sub-conscious mental changes, makes it easy for us to adapt our policy to new facts in our environment. We can under the new conditions either consciously recognize in ourselves new emotional factors, such as pity, or hope, or doubt, or, even if these factors remain below the level of full consciousness, can allow them to influence our half-conscious decisions.

In the working of Parliamentary government – the system by which a Cabinet, overburdened with detailed information, is dependent on the vague feelings and impressions of facts which produce votes in the House of Commons, and on the still vaguer feelings and impressions of the electorate – our 'muddling through' tradition, with its frank motto of 'wait and see', has enabled us to avoid certain dangers which have destroyed the whole system of Parliamentary government in some other countries. The British House of Commons, for instance, while discussing the machinery of representation, is able to give weight in a somewhat inarticulate way to the psychological processes by which political opinions are formed, as well as to the mathematical processes by which votes are recorded and compared. The great French mathematician, M. Henri Poincaré, to whose vivid account of the psychological processes of mathematical discovery I have already referred, once wrote a preface to a book on Proportional Representation by G. Lachapelle (1913). Henri Poincaré there said that the electors should recognize 'that they are voting not for persons but for ideas. . . . It will be, under the proposed system, to the interest of the political parties to place on their electoral lists the names of no candidates who do not give pledges against changing their minds (*que des candidats qui leur présentent des garanties contre les palinodies*). It will be to the interest of the elected members to remain loyal to the party which has secured their election, and whose support will be necessary for their re-election'. M. H. Poincaré even carried his logical consistency to the point of proposing that it should be made illegal for any elector to vote for candidates drawn from more than one party list.[1] There are in the British House of Commons a not inconsiderable number of members who in this respect have what I have called the French habit of mind, and it will be interesting to observe whether, in the presence of admitted defects in our existing voting arrangements and the difficulty of inventing new remedies, they will in the end secure a majority for a scheme of Proportional Representation based on multi-membered constituencies, and securing, as it seems to me, mathematical precision in the counting of votes by ignoring the psychological conditions of wise voting.

In all countries political direction is largely in the hands of lawyers, and the difference between the English and French political habits of mind may be connected with the difference between the conditions which produced English and French law. English Common Law, with its defects and virtues, has been avowedly built up by the decisions of judges, who in deciding particular cases seldom asked themselves what was the origin of the impulses which in fact played a part in their decisions. A French lawyer is encouraged to believe,

---

[1] *La Répresentation Proportionelle*, by G. Lachapelle, 1913; Preface by H. Poincaré, pp. v, vi, xi.

even against his daily experience, that he is following a completely logical Civil Code, in the application of which personal feeling and impulse can play no part at all.

In literature, the habit of energetic intellectual opportunism, though it has led to much confused and ineffective work, helped us, even before we adopted it as a political ideal, to produce Shakespeare and Fielding, just as the same habit helped the French to produce Montaigne and Rabelais before they adopted the 'classic spirit' as their literary ideal. And we have done rather more than our share of the world's work in those scientific discoveries which require a readiness to depart from established dogma and established forms of proof. Darwin, whose methods Huxley once compared with those of 'a miraculous dog', and Harvey, and Faraday, were in this respect typical Englishmen.

As I write, the divergence between the French and English types of political thought is increased by the European situation. The French secured our signature to the Treaty of Versailles, and are made anxious by signs that we are tending towards a 'palinodie' on some of the clauses in that Treaty. As long as M. Raymond Poincaré (who seemed to us as typical a Frenchman as Palmerston was a typical Englishman) was in power, he gave us a series of Sunday sermons on the duty of consistency and sincerity, combined with the perfectly logical argument of building hangars for an enormous air-fleet as near as possible to London. The English find it less easy to formulate, even to themselves, their own less conscious and less logical position as regards the Treaty of Versailles. We want to keep our promises, but feel vaguely that the Treaty was based upon a false view of the facts and was largely inspired by emotions of which we are now ashamed. Those French statesmen who argue that all discussion must start from the French interpretation of the letter of the Treaty, seem to us to be deliberately inhibiting in themselves the 'still small voice' which might prove to be the 'Intimation' of new doubts or new humanitarian motives; and we try to express our meaning by saying that the French have carried over the 'war mind' into peace. We are afraid that if we treat, as M. R. Poincaré did, any doubt as to the wisdom of a single phrase in the Treaty, or any pity for the future of any European people outside the circle of France and her present allies, not as a psychological factor in a problem of human conduct, but as a blunder introduced into a legal or mathematical proof, we shall crystallize the passions of November 1918 into the unchanging premises of a series of 'practical syllogisms', which can only end in the destruction of European civilization. Meanwhile the years run on, and the simple logic of the Treaty of Versailles is being reinforced by the equally simple logic of the French *Realpolitiken* who control the *Comité des Forges*, of the ecclesiastics who calculate the number of square miles of ex-Russian or ex-German territory which can be kept by force under the control of the Catholic Church, and of the peasant holders of French *Rente*. Even in September 1925, when France and England made their great attempt, at the Assembly of the League of Nations, to arrive at an understanding which should lead to permanent European peace, M. Painlevé and Mr Chamberlain found it necessary to explain to the whole world that their disagreements in the past had been caused by this difference of national mental habits, M. Painlevé said (Official Report of the Proceedings, 7 Sept. 1925): 'It is to these differences of mental outlook that the resistance to the Protocol [of 1924] is mainly due. The Protocol's universality, the severe and unbending logic of its obligations, were framed to please the Latin mentality, which delights in starting from abstract principles and passing from generalities to details. The Anglo-Saxon mentality, on the other hand, prefers to proceed from individual concrete cases to generalizations.' Mr Chamberlain replied (ibid., 10 Sept. 1925) by describing the 'Anglo-Saxon mind'. . . . 'We are prone to eschew the general, we are fearful of these logical conclusions pushed to the extreme, because, in fact, human nature being what it is, logic plays but a small part in our everyday life. We are actuated by tradition, by affection, by prejudice, by moments of emotion and sentiment. In the face of any great problem we are seldom really guided by the stern logic of the philosopher or the historian who, removed from all the turmoil of daily life, works in the studious calm of his surroundings.'

It is, of course, true that, for the moment, this sharp opposition between the 'illogical' position of the typical English politician, with its tendency towards a lazy neglect of the logical consequences of his own past acts and words, and the 'logic' of the typical French politician, which seems to require him to suppress all but the simplest and most selfish of his own motives, is in large part due to the difference in the military and economic position of the two nations. But the contrast is also, I believe, due, in part, to a mere clumsy accident of tradition; and I find myself hoping that some day an art of thought may prevail – perhaps after the horrors of a new Thirty Years' War – in which the psychological truths implied in both types of thinking may be recognized and combined, and the errors of both may in some measure be avoided. If the psychologists ever create such an art, it may be that, a century hence, in gratitude for escape from some world disaster which had seemed to be 'logically' inevitable, a statue will be set up in New York or Paris or Pekin, not to the Goddess of Reason, but to 'Psyche', the goddess who presides over the wise direction of the whole thinking organism. And then, even those 'philosophers and historians', whose professional mental habits Mr Chamberlain described with no appearance of irony, may cease, in the 'studious calm' of their libraries, to ignore most of the conditions of their problem.

Sometimes I hope that an art of thought which makes full use of every factor in the human organism may first be developed in America. When I try to imagine my ideal of a twentieth-century intellectual worker I find myself remembering certain Americans I have known, of whom, omitting those who are still alive, I will first name the late Professor William James. These men attained a high simplicity of mind, an accessibility to the feelings of kindness and humour, an amused humility in watching their own mental processes, an absence of the rigidity either of class or profession or nation, which may some day indicate to mankind many of the most important means for guiding human life by human thought. Would any man of learning who was not a modern American have been likely to write, as James wrote after opening (in 1885) the first psychological laboratory at Harvard, 'I try to spend two hours a day in a laboratory for psychophysics which I started last year, but of which I fear the *fruits* will be slow in ripening, as my experimental aptitude is but small. But I am convinced that one must guard in some such way against the growing tendency to subjectivism in one's thinking as life goes on.'[1]

In one of the letters, again, of W. H. Page, there is a passage which certainly would not have been written by Lord Curzon, or Kameneff, or Mussolini, or Raymond Poincaré. 'One day I said to Anderson. . . . Of course nobody is infallible, least of all we. Is it possible we are mistaken ? . . . May there not be some important element in the problem that we do not see ? Summon and nurse every doubt that you can possibly muster up of the correctness of our view, put yourself on the defensive, recall every mood you may have had of the slightest hesitation, and tell me tomorrow of every possible weak place there may be in our judgment and conclusions.'[2] No intellectual method is infallible, and Mr Page's own final conclusions may have been right or wrong. But here at least one has a type of thought more hopeful, I believe, than either the mere passive waiting on

[1] *Letters of William James*, Vol. I, p. 249, to Carl Stumpf, 1 Jan., 1886.
[2] *Life and Letters of W. H. Page* (1922), Vol. I, p. 386.

psychological events which often characterizes the English habit of 'muddling through', or the mechanical logic of M. R. Poincaré.

It would not, however, be easy to argue either that William James' and W. H. Page's type of thought represents the intellectual habit of a sufficient number of Americans to be called the American national type, or that a clearly recognizable and generally accepted national intellectual type is to be found in America. America is the oldest of the great existing democracies, and, though American journalists often complain of the political inertia of their fellow-citizens, a larger proportion of the American population than perhaps of any other civilized nation are able to influence the political, social and religious decisions of their communities. The many millions of men and women whose thought helps to create American opinion are the descendants of emigrants from every part of Europe. Each stock brought its own habits and ideals, and those habits and ideals have not yet been fused even in the enormous melting-pot of American written and spoken discussion. The mental outlook of Jefferson's Declaration of Independence seems to a foreign observer of America mainly to survive in much public oratory, and in the widespread impatience of legal coercion which sometimes clashes oddly with Andrew Jackson's doctrine of the unlimited coercive right of a voting majority. American politics, again, are largely influenced by the vigour and gusto with which the Roman Catholic Irish-Americans make use of the machinery of democracy, but the Catholic tradition seems to have contributed less in America than elsewhere to any general stream of national thought.[1] Perhaps the type of thought which could, at present, make the strongest claim to be dominant in the United States is that which Americans call the 'pioneer mind'. This type represents a combination between the Evangelical Protestant tradition, which sees life on this world as infinitely unimportant when compared with the rewards and punishments of another world, and the intellectual habits arising from the facts of daily life among the pioneer farmers who on the westward-moving frontier tamed the forests and prairies by a toil that would have been unendurable unless their minds had been set on distant results rather than present enjoyment.

Among the descriptions of the pioneer mind that I have met with the best is that given by Dr Frank Crane (whose short daily editorials

[1] Curiously few widely read novelists, poets, dramatists or historians in America seem either to be Roman Catholics or to have been influenced by Roman Catholic thought. Of philosophers who are read outside the Catholic fence I can only think of Mr Santayana as showing (though not himself a Catholic) the influence of the Catholic tradition.

are said to be read by five million Americans) in the American
magazine *Current Opinion* for June 1922. It is called, with a reference
to Mr Sinclair Lewis' novel, *The Little Church on Main Street*. It is, in
form, a hymn of triumph on the adoption of the Prohibition Amendment to the Constitution, but it contains a description of the forces
that carried the Amendment which raises wider issues. Dr Crane
points out that 'the Press, Society, the Intellectuals, the Church, the
Politicians, including the political parties and the Labour organizations . . . ignored or ridiculed' the prohibition movement. What
carried that movement to success was Main Street and its little
church. 'The United States may not have a homogeneous population, but it has the most homogeneous spirit of any nation in
the world'. – 'The people of the United States are essentially pioneers,
and the children of pioneers. They have the conscience of pioneers.'
– 'Here is the grim remnant of Puritanism, the deposit from the
evangelical wave of the eighteenth century. Here is that deep feeling
that man is first of all a moral creature, with a context in eternity, and
that every question is primarily a moral question . . . that a human
being is first of all an immortal soul, and that nothing shall be
allowed to persist which imperils that soul.' – 'The United States is
bourgeois to the backbone . . . and what makes the United States
bourgeois is that its people are almost entirely engaged in business.
That is to say, they are all occupied in trying to accomplish something. The keyword to America is Achievement, the keyword to Europe
is Enjoyment. The American conceives of life in terms of doing some
task . . . the European conceives himself as born to enjoy life, and
he only works enough to enable himself to have the means for this
enjoyment. That is why the United States is enormously efficient.'

No pioneer-minded American is, of course, exactly like any other
pioneer-minded American, and no American exists whose habits of
thought are wholly and exclusively of the pioneer type; but the test of
successive elections has shown how powerful that type still is. To a
foreign observer, however, the pioneer type seems likely to lose much
of its power in the near future. Mr Bryan saw, for instance, that
everything which weakens the doctrine of the infallibility of the Bible
weakens the pioneer type, of which he was the most conspicuous
example, and he therefore devoted the last years of his life to the
Fundamentalist agitation. But every intelligent boy or girl who reads
the first chapters of Wells' *Outline of History*, or a few extracts from
a translation of the Babylonian text of the Deluge story in the Gil-
gamish Epic, or sees a photograph of the Neanderthal and Piltdown
skulls, is in danger of being lost to the Fundamentalist cause; and

with Fundamentalism may go the old clear conviction of the utter insignificance of this life when compared with the life after death. Every change, again, in the direction of further industrialization either in American town life or American agriculture tends to weaken the pioneer type of thought. The man who sees daily before him his own newly reclaimed farm, which his sons and grandsons will inherit, may be content that in his own life he 'never is, but always to be blest'. The trade-unionist miner, or factory hand, or engine-driver, or the clerk or schoolmaster serving at a fixed salary some hugh public or private corporation, is certain, sooner or later, to ask for a measure of blessedness here and now.

To me it also seems likely that the dissolution of the pioneer type of thought in the United States may be greatly quickened by the spread of knowledge as to human psychology. There are at this moment some thousands of professors and instructors of psychology in the American universities and colleges. Almost every one of the half-million school teachers in the United States has received lectures on psychology, and soon almost every entrant to schools and colleges will have been submitted to psychological tests. There must also be a thousand or two of those practising Freudian psycho-analysists, who in America, as elsewhere, are exposed to the combined intellectual dangers of a rigid sect and of a lucrative profession. American newspapers and magazines use, therefore, technical psychological terms such as 'reaction', 'complex', 'sublimation', 'intelligence quotient', etc., with a confidence, which would not be felt in Europe, that the ordinary reader will understand them.

All this knowledge of psychology has, it is true, had little effect at present upon general American habits of thought, except in reviving the barren metaphysical controversy of free-will and determinism. But knowledge is a very active yeast when once it has started to spread in dough of the right temperature; and at any moment the psychological ferment may begin to act in America. One indication of the way in which this may happen is the success of Mr Sinclair Lewis' later novel *Babbitt*. Babbitt is a man of natural mental and aesthetic sensitiveness, who has started as a real-estate agent in a great city with the uncriticized intellectual traditions of the pioneer. He accepts as the purpose of his life 'achievement' in Dr Crane's sense, which means to him the making of as much money as possible for other people to spend; though the social good resulting from his achievement in taking away business from other 'realtors' is not so clear as that which resulted from his grandfather's achievement in breaking up his acres of prairie. But Babbitt, like his pioneer ancestors, is tormented by vague impulses tending towards something other than 'achievement'. There are occasional stirrings in him towards what Dr Crane calls 'enjoyment'. One danger of the pioneer tradition has always been that it looks on all impulses towards 'enjoyments' which are not 'achievements' as being equally 'temptations'; a man is 'tempted' alike to get drunk, or go after light women, or play poker, or to take a walk which will not earn money, or go to a theatre, or read a novel, or sit day-dreaming by a lake-side. Flesh is weak; one surrenders from time to time to temptation, and because all surrenders are sinful it was the cruder and more urgent temptations which on the western frontier two generations ago were most likely to win. In a modern commercial city the more subtle forms of enjoyment are apt to seem even more distant and unreal, and Babbitt's vague impulses push him, unwilling and unhappy and bewildered, to drink and women and repentance.

And since action and thought are part of the same primitive psychological cycle, Babbitt's impulses also push him towards opinions which are inconsistent with full devotion to the pioneer ideal of 'achievement'. He feels uncomfortable stirrings after talking to the friend who has weakened in his devotion to pecuniary success and who has followed the strange gods of liberalism and intellectual enjoyment. But Babbitt's discomfort soon passes away, and we leave him still loyal to the pioneer mind and only occasionally envious of his son who has finally abandoned it. Babbitt in the novel is helpless because he does not know what is happening to him. But a Babbitt who has read *Babbitt*, and has there recognized his own type, may be affected as powerfully as a friend of mine was when he recognized himself as Broadbent in Mr Shaw's *John Bull's Other Island*, and went straight out of the theatre to write a letter resigning his parliamentary candidature. He may learn to distinguish between his longing for poetry or for some type of thought more penetrating than his party slogan, and his longing for 'hooch' or for the widow in the 'Cavendish Apartments'. He may learn how to wait expectantly till his vague 'Intimations' develop into clear thought and clear decisions.

The spread of psychological knowledge may even create, here and there, exceptions to the naïve way in which the pioneer mind when translated to the city thinks and feels about competitive games. Games in American are apt to be, in Dr Crane's terms, matters of 'achievement' and not of 'enjoyment', and American 'tremendous efficiency' is fast imposing that habit of mind on the rest of the world. I went a few years ago to a great 'sports shop' in London under orders to buy a board on which ping-pong could be played. I asked the shop-assistant what was the standard size, and was told, 'I am sorry to say, sir, that there is now no standard size. Ping-pong has ceased to be a game, and has become a pastime.' Some boy Babbitt, ten years hence, in Cincinnati may sit waiting until the 'still small voice' that whispers the question why football or even baseball may not sometimes be a pastime makes its meaning clear, and his doubts may penetrate across the Atlantic to the football districts of Lancashire and Yorkshire.

But the most important effect of the spread of psychology in America may ultimately be found in its influence on the accepted standard of intellectual energy. At present the causes seem largely accidental which bring about in this or that American art or science the highest degree of creative energy. When first, for instance, I visited America in 1896, contemporary American architecture seemed to show a singular slackness in artistic creation. It was, in Mr Drinkwater's phrase, the work of 'chisels governed by no heat of the brain'; and tended to result in the style which builders call 'Carpenter's Gothic'. Since 1896, at successive visits, I have seen American architecture become the supreme creative world-force in the art of building. One is told that the change started when Mr Charles McKim went to Paris about 1870 to study. But the essential secret which he and other young architects learnt in Paris was not, apparently, how to draw certain forms, but how to evoke in themselves certain intense activities of the imagination. Henry James, in his admirable life of William Wetmore Story, has described the mental habits of the American painters and sculptors forty or fifty years earlier than my first visit to the States, the men whose works are now being edged out of the Metropolitan Museum of Fine Art in New York, and the poets who are now dropping into the less conspicuous parts of the school anthologies. They went to Rome, bought velvet jackets, worked endless hours, were good friends and good men. But somehow they never learnt how to make that elusive effort of the whole being by which the energy necessary for great art may be produced.

Sometimes, by a divine accident, an American thinker has learnt the 'stroke' which enables him to bring his whole force upon some form of creative work, not from watching other creators in Paris or elsewhere, but by himself and for himself. Some American psychologist ought to make a careful study of the psychological process which turned the Walter Whitman of 1846, the writer of intolerable edifying verse and more intolerable edifying novels, into the Walt Whitman who wrote 'When lilacs last in the dooryard bloomed.' Walt Whitman would perhaps have said that he 'let himself go free'. But what was that 'self', and how was it that what seemed in memory like a relaxation of tension was really an 'energy of the soul', an activity of the whole being whose intensity would have been unimaginable to the Whitman of 1846?

Mr Van Wyck Brooks has written, in his *Ordeal of Mark Twain*, an extraordinarily illuminating study of the mental history of a man whose inborn creative genius was even greater than that of Walt Whitman. Mark Twain, once or twice in his life, owing to some accident of subject or matter or memory, 'let himself go', and wrote *Tom Sawyer* or *Huckleberry Finn*, or *Life on the Mississippi*. The rest of his work consists either of fun which will be remembered only as fun, or of serious writing (such as his *What is Man?*) which is already forgotten. While doing that work Mark Twain, like Babbitt in his real-estate office, had moments and even years of vaguely agonizing discontent; but he never attained the great artist's control over his purpose and his powers, because he never had a reliable working knowledge of the mental 'stroke' necessary for the initiation of that control. Mr Brooks gives many reasons for this; Mark Twain's acceptance, for instance, of false social and economic standards in his personal life, and the intellectual and social timidity of his Boston patrons. To me one of the main causes of so great a loss to mankind is the fact that Mark Twain not only never permanently understood the kind of energy which great art requires, but also bedevilled his mind by a crudely determinist metaphysic, which, because it forced him to deny that Free Will in the old theological sense existed, forced him also to believe that no artist could or ought consciously to bring his will to bear upon the methods or purposes of his work. 'The influences,' he says, 'create [man's] preferences, his aversions, his politics, his tastes, his morals, his religion. He creates none of these things for himself.' His mental machine goes 'racing from subject to subject – a drifting panorama of ever-changing, ever-dissolving views, manufactured by my mind without any help from me.' 'Man originates nothing, not even a thought. . . . Shakespeare could not create. He was a machine, and machines do not create.'[1]

Meanwhile, I have noticed, in my successive visits to America since 1896, how, with small help from the psychologists, the secret of creative energy has spread to painting and sculpture, to dramatic production, to the writing of history, and to certain of the natural sciences; and many other new accessions of creative energy must

[1] *What is Man?* quoted by Brooks, pp. 263 and 259.

have occurred of which I am ignorant. But the coming of the great period of intellectual and artistic production in America for which I hope, still seems to me to require, not only a wider and more accurate understanding of the nature of intellectual energy than is at present common in America, but also an increase of American sympathy with intellectual effort in its severest and most disinterested forms. From time to time, in the history of mankind, individual creative artists and thinkers have carried through their life work in an atmosphere of almost universal contempt. But great periods of creation have generally been accompanied by a considerable measure of understanding and sympathy for the creator's work among those who will benefit from it; and it has been one of the main hindrances to human progress that the pioneer type of mind hates and despises and yet fears the creative type. Aristophanes, in *The Clouds*, interprets for us the feelings with which the free-born farmers who crowded into the theatre of Dionysus from the valleys near Athens thought of Socrates. Everything about Socrates, his detachment from their interests and prejudices, his indifference to the solid satisfactions of good clothes and proper food and regular hours, the perpetual suspicion that he was laughing at them, all went to strengthen their fear that the freedom and intensity of his thought might destroy the whole structure of society and the state. Exactly the same feelings may now, I am told, be found among the Australian followers of Mr William Hughes, the South African followers of General Hertzog, and those peasants of Central Europe whose political tendencies have been called the 'Green International', and whose type Mr Belloc desires to establish as the governing force of the world.

In America the pioneer, whether he is a farmer from Nebraska or Indiana or Tennessee, or a simple-minded devotee of finance in Wall Street, or the New York Union Club, or the Chicago Wheat Pit, or the Rotarian brotherhood, reveals his type by employing the word 'highbrow' as a term of contempt. Plato and Dante, Spinoza and Descartes, Locke and Darwin and Bentham, would if they were now living Americans all be 'highbrows' to the pioneer mind. My American friends assure me that it will be neither a short nor an easy task to change this attitude. Change, when it comes, will be the slow result of many causes. Already, if a man makes much money (or enables others to make much money) by his ideas, he may be as absent-minded and ironical as he likes, and not even Senator Lusk at Albany will call him a 'highbrow'. If, again, the fame of an American creator is sufficiently world-wide to reach the American newspapers from abroad, he is not likely to be called a highbrow. If Einstein had been born an American, and had succeeded in finding opportunities both of doing his work and of making it known, no American would now call him a highbrow. When the great American music composers of the future are acclaimed in the opera-houses of Berlin and Milan, no one in Nebraska will call them highbrows. No one even now, apart from the fact that he has made money from his plays, calls Mr Eugene O'Neill a highbrow.

The one justification of the contempt of the American pioneer type for the highbrow, is the existence of fraudulent or self-deceiving imitators of the creative type. My American friends tell me that in America, with its colossal system of book-education, there are more young men and women than elsewhere who are attracted by the idea of intellectual creation without either possessing the necessary natural powers, or acquiring the secret of stimulating and maintaining the necessary intensity of energy. Even in Ancient Greece there were, as the proverb said, many who carried the thyrsus and few who were inspired by the god. A recognition that an art of thought exists with standards of its own may diminish this proportion in America, both by helping the young genius to discover the kind of effort he is called on to make, and by helping his neighbours to distinguish between the real artist and the false. Progress in American intellectual creation may also be quickened by an extension of the conception of morality so as to include not only family, sexual, dietary, and business conduct, but also the conduct of the intellect. Dr Crane tells us that to the pioneer mind 'every question is primarily a moral question'. Anyone who has been in the habit of reading American newspapers and hearing American speeches, both before and during and after the war, will have noticed that the habit of thinking of every problem as primarily one of choice between right and wrong prevails in America much more largely than in any other country except perhaps China. At present the idea of morality is associated in America with the Christian religious tradition, and Mr Bryan in his Fundamentalist preaching seemed to me to be using the prestige of that tradition to inculcate every method of thinking which is most likely to prevent human beings from discovering truth or creating beauty. Sometimes the conscious idea, or the half-conscious 'censorship', of morality aims in America at the purely negative virtue of so preventing oneself from thinking freely, as to maintain certain social conventions. Eighteen years ago William James complained that 'We all know persons who are models of excellence, but who belong to the extreme philistine type of mind. So deadly is their intellectual respectability that we can't converse about certain subjects at all, can't let our minds play over them, can't even mention them in their presence. I have numbered amongst my dearest friends, persons thus inhibited intellectually with whom I would gladly have been able to talk freely about certain interests of mine, certain authors, say, as Bernard Shaw, Chesterton, Edward Carpenter, H. G. Wells, but it wouldn't do, it made them too uncomfortable, they wouldn't play. I had to be silent. An intellect thus tied down by literality and decorum makes on one the same sort of an impression that an able-bodied man would who should habituate himself to do his work with only one of his fingers, locking up the rest of his organism and leaving it unused.'[1] Fifty years hence words with the connotation of moral judgment, 'integrity', 'open-mindedness', 'courage', 'patience', 'thoroughness', 'humility', and the like, may have come to be widely used in America of those methods which the leaders of American thought shall have shown to be most efficient in the employment of the mind. Already there is a hint of moral judgment in Mr W. H. Page's statement, during his difficult relations as ambassador with Mr Bryan as Secretary of State, that 'a certain orderliness of mind and conduct seems essential for safety in this short life'.[2]

Perhaps, however, the main hope for the future of American creative thought lies in an extension of the American sense of need. We do not despise the intellectual creator who gives us something that we ourselves really desire; and to an increasing extent the desires of the great average population of America may turn towards values that cannot be expressed in terms of money. No one now makes money by looking at the glorious marble buildings in Washington, or the hall of the Union Railway Station in New York, or the painted corridors of the Boston Free Library, or the pictures and statues and biological collections that attract scores of thousands of eager visitors to the Metropolitan Museums of Fine Art and Science. And fifty years hence the great-grandsons of the American pioneers may feel not only moral sympathy but spontaneous gratitude for that kind of effort by which alone the weak and imperfect human brain can add to its scanty store of knowledge and beauty.

[1] W. James, *Selected Papers on Philosophy* (Everyman Series), p. 57.
[2] *Life*, Vol. II, p. 10.

31

The Torment of Secrecy[*]

EDWARD SHILS

*British institutions and processes of public administration are, by
convention, surrounded by a curtain of secrecy which is drawn aside
only very occasionally in extraordinary political situations or at public
enquiries, such as those instituted under the Tribunals of Enquiry
(Evidence) Act, or departmental enquiries such as that into the Crichel
Down affair. There is a desire for more openness, often sought by
academics and occasionally also by politicians (see, for example, Peter
Shore,* Entitled to Know, *MacGibbon & Kee, 1966). This reflective
extract on the British situation is taken from Edward Shils' book on
the background and consequences of American security policies.*

THE BRITISH PATTERN: THE BULWARK OF PRIVACY

The equilibrium of publicity, privacy, and secrecy in Great Britain
is more stable and its deviations from the normal state are smaller
than they are in the United States. Like America, Great Britain is a
modern, large-scale society with a politicized population, a tradition
of institutional pluralism, a system of representative institutions and
great freedom of enquiry, discussion and reporting. Like America, it
also has a sensational popular press which goes to the limits in the
infringement of privacy – limits which are narrower in Great Britain
than in the United States. It also produces demagogues of great
oratorical gifts, capable of arousing political passions and, as in the
United States, they seldom attain the highest positions of authority.
Yet this tells us very little about Great Britain because the differences
are considerable. Despite occasional outbursts of acrimony and gross
abuse, British political life is strikingly quiet and confined. Modern
publicity is hemmed about by a general well-respected privacy.
Secrecy is acknowledged and kept in its place.

[*] From Edward Shils, *The Torment of Secrecy*, London, Heinemann, 1956, pp.
47–57. New York, The Free Press, 1956. Reprinted with permission of The
Macmillan Company. © The Free Press, a Corporation, 1956.

Although democratic and pluralistic, British society is not populist. Great Britain is a hierarchical country. Even when it is distrusted, the Government, instead of being looked down upon, as it often is in the United States, is, as such, the object of deference because the Government is still suffused with the symbolism of a monarchical and aristocratic society. The British Government, of course, is no longer aristocratic. Only the House of Lords remains, although in a greatly diminished form, as an instrument and symbol of aristocratic prerogative. The members of the Government come from all classes, primarily from the middle and upper-middle classes, but they participate in a set of institutions which has about it the aura of aristocracy and it enjoys therefore the deference which was given to that aristocracy. It enjoys the deference which is aroused in the breast of Englishmen by the symbols of hierarchy which find their highest expression in the Monarchy. Although the British Government is as democratic as any in the world, the institutions through which the Government operates still enjoy the respect which their aristocratic incumbents once aroused and which connection with the Crown still confers.

British participation in political life is somewhat greater than participation in the United States, but it does not express populist sentiments. The mass of the politically interested citizenry does not regard itself as better than its rulers. In contrast with the United States, the mandatory conception of the legislator does not find much support in Britain outside a small and radical section of the Labour Party. The ordinary citizen does not regard his own judgment as better than, or even as good as, his leaders.

Walter Bagehot said many years ago that the English Constitution worked because the English were a deferential people. England has undergone many changes since Bagehot wrote; the peerage has been brought down, the Court is no longer so prominent and the great London houses have descended from their glory. The distribution of opportunity is far more equalitarian now than it was in 1867, and organizations supported by the working classes share in the power to an extent which seemed impossible at that time. But in the distribution of deference, Britain remains a hierarchical society.

The acceptance of hierarchy in British society permits the Government to retain its secrets, with little challenge or resentment. The citizenry and all but the most aggressively alienated members of the elite do not regard it as within their prerogative to unmask the secrets of the Government, except under very stringent and urgent conditions. For the same reason, the populace is ordinarily confident that their rulers can be counted upon to keep secret that which has to be kept secret.

The deferential attitude of the working and middle classes is matched by the uncommunicativeness of the upper-middle classes and of those who govern. The secrets of the governing classes of Britain are kept within the class and even within more restricted circles. The British ruling class is unequalled in secretiveness and taciturnity. Perhaps no ruling class in the Western world, certainly no ruling class in any democratic society, is as close-mouthed as the British ruling class. No ruling class discloses as little of its confidential proceedings as does the British. The televising of a cabinet meeting, such as happened recently in the United States, was profoundly shocking to British political circles.[1] The broadcast of the proceedings of a Parliamentary Committee or a Royal Commission would not be tolerated in Great Britain. Even the wireless discussion of issues about to come before Parliament is regarded as an intrusion into the autonomous sphere of the House of Commons. Even the most central public bodies are regarded as having an appropriate privacy which must be respected.

In contrast with the United States, where government documents are made available to historians without long delay, in Britain governmental papers which are not published at the time as part of government policy, are opened to scholarly inspection only after a very long lapse of time and even then with restrictions. Government officials, Cabinet ministers and their biographers always tread with discretion in personal and political matters. Again the contrast with America is very great. The memoirs of American political figures, although not always entirely written by themselves, disclose far more of the inner workings of party, government, and department than is the case in Britain. Only on very rare occasions does a British public figure, in his autobiography, make personal remarks disclosing his opinion of his fellow politicians or officials. There is practically no book in the modern literature of British political autobiography comparable to the late Harold Ickes' recent autobiographical works in which rivals are excoriated and enemies denounced in a language of extraordinary harshness. It is not that British politicians do not have animosities and mean thoughts of their colleagues and opponents. They have them in ample measure, but the rules of privacy forbid their public expression, beyond a narrow circle of equals.

---

[1] The dominance of public events in British political life by television engineers and camera men as has happened on various occasions in the United States, is quite inconceivable.

What is spoken in privacy is expected to be retained in privacy and to be withheld from the populace.[1] When journalists are confided in, it is with the expectation that the confidence will be respected. 'Government by leaks' in Great Britain is extremely infrequent. It is not a technique of warfare of one department against another or of one official against another.

The traditional sense of the privacy of executive deliberations characteristic of the ruling classes of Great Britain has imposed itself on the rest of the society and has established a barrier beyond which publicity may not justifiably penetrate. Nowhere is this more evident than in the conduct of the British press, through which the impulse towards publicity is expressed.

The press in Great Britain, with all its vulgarity and all its curiosity about the great, keeps its place. For all the criticism of the Government of the day, the press maintains its distance and seldom pries into the affairs of the bureaucracy. Certainly it never comes anywhere near the practice of the American press in such matters. Sensational though much of the press is, it seeks sensations of unveiled privacy in the main elsewhere than in the disclosure of the vices of government. Muckraking in the American style is not one of the features of the British press, even the most sensational type. The exposures of governmental misdeeds featured in the British press are largely those uncovered by the Opposition or by some meticulously conscientious member of the Government. It is only then that political scandal-mongering is rendered legitimate.

The awe of the press before the majesty of Government is expressed also in the silence of the press about cases under trial in the courts. Whereas in the United States, the newspaper treatment of trials may involve editorial comments on the issues and parties, interviews with some of the principals and even analysis of the jurors and their deliberations, in Great Britain the newspapers must acquiesce in the exclusion of these areas from the scope of their professional virtuosity.

The British journalist, in his dealings with the government, handles himself as if he were an inferior of the person clothed with the majesty of office. His esteem for his own profession does not permit him to look on judges, members of Parliament and civil servants as if they were dependent upon him for publicity which he had in his power to give or withhold. Politicians in Great Britain like publicity, but their conception of what is possible and permissible

[1] The journalist who discloses what is said behind the wall of privacy breaks the rules. He arouses the resentment of those on the 'inside' and the curiosity of those on the 'outside', but in both circles he is known to be doing the unusual thing.

usually falls within fairly narrow limits. The press conference plays a far smaller part in Whitehall and Westminster than it does in Washington. The balance of power between Government and the press favours the Government in Great Britain and the press in the United States.

In this manner, publicity in Great Britain is held in check. The Governments of Great Britain are not secretive in the way of an absolutist regime. Parliamentary debates are more fully reported than are Congressional debates in the United States and they are more widely discussed. A continuous flow of White Papers, Royal Commission Reports, Select Committee Reports, etc., throws light on the action and intentions of the Government. In the main, journalists are content to leave it at that. The secrets of the Government are not only protected by an Official Secrets Act and the strong silencing sense of corporate obligation on the part of ministers and civil servants; they are sustained too by the journalists' restraint in the presence of Governmental secrecy.

The professionals of publicity, political and journalistic, not being quite so fascinated by the secrets of the Government, do not feel their integrity and status dependent on the unravelling of secrets. Accordingly, they do not, like some American populist publicists and politicians, act as if salvation depended on secrecy as well as publicity. Very few strong complaints were made in Britain in 1948 that the Government's newly stated policy for keeping 'security risks' out of sensitive positions was not sufficiently stringent. The defection of Maclean and Burgess, scarcely more than the misdeeds of Fuchs, Nunn May and Pontecorvo did not rouse a great outcry in Britain for far more stringent restraints on those entrusted with secrets.[1] There was practically no demand for stricter measures against civil servants; the recent decision of the Government to increase the number of sensitive positions from which Communists would be excluded was not the product of popular pressure, in the House of Commons or in the press or in any organizations. Miss Rebecca West's suggestion that scientists have a special disposition towards treason found a louder echo in the United States than in Great Britain.

Secrecy is less fascinating in Great Britain because privacy is better maintained and publicity less rampant. The balance produced by the moderation of the demand for publicity, respect for the integrity of secrets and insensitivity to the magic of secrecy rests then on

[1] It is possible that the slackness of British security which allowed Burgess and Maclean to escape notice so long arose from the mutual confidence of the different sectors of the ruling classes.

443

hierarchy, deference and self-containment. Self-containment is a part of the pluralism of British society.

By pluralism we mean the firm attachment and simultaneous and intermittent loyalty to a plurality of corporate and primordial bodies; to family, profession, professional association, regiment, church, chapel, club, and football team, political party, friends, and nation. Pluralism entails the more or less simultaneous exercise of attachments to these diverse objects and the maintenance of a balance among them so that none is continuously predominant. It is not rootlessness. On the contrary, it depends on solid bonds, on the enjoyment of traditions and the belief in the supra-individual character of the institution and of the members' obligations to them. But it does not permit such a degree of absorption into any one of the groups that members would be blind to the claims and values of the others.

It is the reverse of specialization of interest and concentration of loyalty. In Great Britain, politics, ideally and in practice, is not permitted to claim all of an individual's attention. Naturally, the politician will usually prize political activity above most others, but he will feel compelled to show an interest in other fields of activity as well and to show himself to be a well-rounded human being. The scientist is expected not to allow science to rule out every other interest or concern. The situation is the same in other professions. The multiplicity of interest which this standard maintains in each individual means that passions are less frequently absorbed by single objects. In consequence, fanaticism appears less frequently in British ruling circles in the twentieth century than it does in many other modern countries. The reality of the propertied and leisured classes, devoting themselves in an amateur way to politics, sports and philanthropy scarcely exists any longer in Great Britain, but the tradition which it set going, however, is still a force among men whose condition in life is very different.

The tradition of the amateur, with its aversion to specialization, is a major constituent in the internal solidarity of the British ruling classes, regardless of their class of origin. It promotes amicable relations within the elite and amicable dispositions and a ready empathy with one another. Mutual trust reduces the fear of secretiveness and the need for publicity. In such a situation there is less fear on the part of sensitive persons that secrets are being kept from them. The feeling of affinity which members of the elite in Great Britain have towards one another, the feeling of proximity and of understanding which they have for one another despite all disagreements and antagonisms, restrains the tendency to fear hidden secrets. It increases the acceptability of secrecy within the elite since it symbolizes an acknowledgment of equality. By increasing the solidarity of the elite it increases the capacity to keep secrets within the group and reduces the disposition to 'leak' secrets in order to show 'outsiders' that one is 'on the inside'. The internal solidarity and mutual confidence of the elite is accompanied by a greater insensitivity to the sentiments of those outside.

The respect for one's 'betters' and the mutual trust within the ruling classes are infused with a general disposition towards a lack of interest in the private affairs of the next man. In all classes of the population in England, men can live close to one another and even be friends for a long time while remaining quite ignorant of each other's affairs and past. This ignorance is partly a function of indifference, partly of tact and the belief that the other's affairs are his own business.

There is less active curiosity in England on the part of one individual about another. There is less probing, there is less quick empathy, and less readiness to imagine oneself into the state of mind of another person. The general lack of social understanding, the ignorance of the social structure of Great Britain which one finds in so many sections of the British population – the blindness about British society which one finds in the educated classes – means that alongside of the broad sense of unity, which reduces anxiety, there is also a lower level of mutual, imaginative penetration and less of an impulse to penetrate into the interior life of other persons.

This does not mean that there is not gossip, often of a very malicious sort, or that there is not pathological curiosity, a considerable market for literature about the private life of the royal family, or a considerable audience for scandal from the divorce courts. England has all of these. But they all exist within the matrix of a quite striking acceptance of the legitimacy of the privacy of one's fellow man. The person who keeps to himself in Britain will be less criticized than he would be in America. This difference in the sense of privacy contributes to the maintenance of the equilibrium by offering resistance to pressures for publicity and for the search for salvation in the opposite of publicity, namely, the concentration of secrecy.

Through the spirit of privacy, the deferential attitude towards government is reinforced. If anybody in Britain would have grounds to feel that the ruling group was secretive, it would be the lower and middle classes who are so excluded from 'inside' knowledge. Much more is withheld in Britain than in America from the scrutiny of the

445

public. Yet the ruling classes in Great Britain are respected, and they are entitled, in the eyes of the mass of the population (lower-middle class and working class, rural and urban) to possess their secrets as long as they are not obviously harming anyone. Thus the circle is turned, and an equilibrium of secrecy, privacy, and publicity kept stable.

Although the British and the official spokesmen of their corporate institutions are much afflicted with national conceit, on the whole they are less preoccupied with the symbols of nation and of national unity than some of the more vociferous Americans. Those who are so preoccupied get less of a hearing and are less influential. On ceremonial occasions, the national symbols are less frequently invoked and less intensely invoked in Great Britain than in America. In the United States a trade or professional association, being addressed at a conference, is more likely to learn about the threat of Communism and the needs of national defence. In Great Britain this is less likely to be so. The fact of nationality lies less continuously and less restlessly on the minds of the British upper and upper-middle classes. It is not that there are not in all political positions in Great Britain, hyper-patriots who refer everything they discuss to a British standard and find it wanting. There are many Englishmen, especially since the war, who have Britain on their minds over all else. But they do not, on the surface at least, seem to be defending themselves from external attack. British jingoism does not seem to be in such need of the internal homogeneity of society as its American counterpart. American hyper-patriotism seems always to call for loyalty, maximal loyalty, while British national conceit is capable of being unworried by the internal heterogeneity of British society. The British phenomenon is directed towards foreigners; the American towards other Americans as well as foreigners.

Feeling less exposed to attack from hidden enemies allied to external enemies, there is less need for publicity to root them out and to uncover their secrets. Less preoccupied with secrets and indeed accepting a mild type of secrecy as a normal mode of life, there is more confidence that such secrets as are deemed necessary will not be stolen or disclosed with harmful intentions. Just as the British are less perceptive of crises than the Americans and more apt to deny their existence, while the Americans tend to overemphasize them, so British security measures tend towards an overconfident and gentlemanly laxity and inefficiency, while American security measures tend towards excessive and unncessary rigidity and comprehensiveness.

The two patterns which we have just described have much in common. It would be impossible for two large-scale, highly industrialized, highly democratic liberal countries to exist at opposite poles. In each of the countries there is normally an equilibrium of publicity, privacy, and secrecy. Each of the countries has, however, a somewhat different weighting of the elements. In America it is publicity, in Britain privacy, and even a matter-of-fact, unemotional, unmagical secrecy which weigh a lot more heavily than the other elements in the culture. In America, for the balance to be maintained, there must be a perpetual struggle to keep publicity and a nervous worry about secrets, good and bad, from inundating individual and corporate privacy. In Britain the equilibrium requires a constant alertness lest the privacy of the upper stratum in government and culture proves too great a bulwark against publicity.

The specifically British disequilibrium, which is restricted in range, is the preponderance of privacy and traditional government secretiveness over publicity. The specifically American disequilibrium is the preponderance of publicity and its attendant stress on salvationary secrecy over privacy.

32

The Politician as Intruder*

C. H. SISSON

The relationship of politics and administration, or of the politician and the administrator, has for long been the subject of speculation in Britain. It could not be the subject of serious study and analysis with official approval for that would have contravened the conventions of political neutrality by civil servants (but see the chapter on this subject in Richard A. Chapman, The Higher Civil Service in Britain, *Constable, 1970). However, a number of writers have used their civil service experience to discuss the situation as they saw it within the limitations of convention, and among these one of the best is C. H. Sisson, whose book on the permanent administration in Whitehall is, in fact, one of the few British attempts at comparative public administration.*

It is possible for the political and administrative authorities in this country to act as effectively as a single power for the very reason that there is so sharp a differentiation of function between them, because, in short, there are no administrative *authorities* but only administrative instruments used by the political power. This differentiation is by no means to be taken for granted. It is least marked in those régimes which have a tradition of the Civil Servant as governor, and it is precisely in the case of such officials as the *préfet* that the danger of their being at cross-purposes with the political power is most feared. An English authority on the prefectoral system, speaking of 'the events of 1940 and 1944', says that they 'confirm, if that was necessary, that the Prefect's place in the administration of the country is of such importance that a real change in political direction must be accompanied by a profound modification in the composition of the corps. This, to the French, appears reasonable'.[1] Both 1940

---

* From C. H. Sisson, *The Spirit of British Administration, and some European comparisons*, London, Faber & Faber, 2nd edition, 1966, pp. 109–18. New York, Praeger Publishers, Inc. Reprinted with permission of the publishers.

[1] Brian Chapman, *The Prefects and Provincial France* (1955), p. 157.

and 1944 were years of revolution and it is natural that, at such times, the governing politician should be alarmed about what the governing official might get up to. Although the possible dichotomy of the political and administrative powers, resulting from the imperfect differentiation of their functions, gives most cause for anxiety in times of violent change, the anxiety is not confined to such times and is indeed endemic in the system. Hence, of course, the special insecurity of tenure of such officials as the *préfet*. Chapman's comment, which is illuminating, is no doubt intended to have a wide application:

'The selfless administrator,' he goes on, 'without clear or profound convictions is of little use either to a Government or to a society when called upon to deal with matters so fundamental as the control of education, police and industrial conflict'.[1]

This comes very near to equating 'clear and profound convictions' with the specific differences of opinion which are the stock-in-trade of politicians; an administrator might reply that there are national terms of reference, the common ground of parties, which may be held to not less firmly than the items of a party programme, though admittedly they are less clearly seen in a country which has undergone frequent changes of régime than in one which has been more fortunate. The British, anyhow, do not pay their officials to 'control education' nor to exercise their own opinions in the conflicts, industrial or other, that are played out upon the national stage. And it may be added that, in these matters, it is far from certain that the play of opinion is more effective than a long patience.

The British system rests on the obedience of the official or, if all systems may be said to do the same, one may fairly characterize our own as exhibiting a remarkable degree of mutual confidence as between politicians and officials. It is not suggested that French Ministers do not, in general, trust the officials in their Ministries to carry out the policies imposed on them from on high, but it is probably true that the relative instability of French governments gives high officials in that country a somewhat strong sense that the government rests on them and a consequent predisposition to nurse their private policies. It is hard for an outsider to judge such matters. A certain distrust of 'the selfless administrator' is, however, openly written into the administrative system of France, as into that of a number of other countries. The French Ministry is, in effect, divided into two interacting parts, a large neutral part and a small part of high political voltage. The neutral, stable element is made up of the *bureaux*, divided up, much like a British Ministry, into what in

[1] Ibid., p. 157.

France are called *directions* and *sous-directions*. The political part is made up of the Minister's *cabinet*, and one might say that that institution is there to ensure that the permanent structure of the Ministry is sufficiently responsive to his direction. Up to 1940, there were really several *cabinets*: an office which received and registered correspondence and shared it out among the *bureaux*; sometimes a technical office made up of specialists; and finally the private secretaries doing a mixture of political work and routine office work.[1] The *cabinet* consists of people of the Minister's own choosing. Their number is fixed by law,[2] and, if the law does not prescribe their functions it is at least at pains to give each of them a general description. There is a *directeur* and a *chef du cabinet*; there are assistant *chefs*, a chief private secretary, and two people who in some sort act as specialist advisers – normally nine people in all. The appointment is a formal one, announced in the *Journal Officiel*. The members of the *cabinet* may be ordinary officials, but the law lays down only the minima of qualifications, or rather of disqualifications, namely that they must be people who have not been deprived of their civil rights and that their military service papers must be in order, and anyone may be chosen. They are, collectively, the dynamite with which the Minister, in the course of his peregrinations, enters a new establishment. But more gently, one might say that they are supposed to form a link between the Minister and the permanent administration. The scheme must be supposed to have some advantages in the contexts in which it is used, but it is probably better administratively not to interpose a body of trusties between the Minister and his Ministry. A Minister commands loyalty by virtue of his office, but it is difficult to believe that a band of wandering hangers-on does not arouse something more like suspicion and jealousy, and make the ground more fertile for intrigue. However that may be, the system inevitably creates a class of officials who follow the personal fortunes of Ministers in a way which is unknown in this country and which can hardly contribute to the smooth working of the administration. There are certain safeguards in the law.[3] Public officials called upon to serve in a Minister's *cabinet* may be promoted only in accordance with the rules governing promotion in the class to which they belong, but the situation is not without possibilities and the placing of ex-members of Ministers' *cabinets* in the prefectoral corps does not pass without jealous notice from their colleagues.

[1] Louis Rolland, *Précis de Droit administratif* (1957), p. 163.
[2] Décret du 28 juillet 1948 (Code administratif).
[3] Décret du 13 juillet 1911 (Code administratif).

The British administration enjoys an extraordinary degree of freedom from political intrusion, and there is no doubt that this freedom greatly facilitates the responsiveness of the administration to the purposes of cabinet government. The British administrator is able to be genuinely indifferent to the political colour of the government he serves because politicians accept constitutional limitation of their field of influence in a manner which is by no means to be taken for granted in countries outside Britain. The forbearance of British politicians is systematic, resting on the critical force of the opposition and on public opinion. It gives us, in contrast with what might fairly be described as the general system in Europe – or indeed in the world at large – permanent heads of Ministries who owe nothing to political connections and whose status is such that they can as a matter of course, without reference to political connections and subject only to Treasury concurrence which prevents more than a limited amount of departmental idiosyncrasy, determine the *personnel*, or as the scarcely less inelegant usage of Whitehall has it, the establishments policies of their Ministries.

The German Civil Service of the Bismarckian Empire, which in some respects must have been exceedingly unlike the present Service in Whitehall, is said to have enjoyed an independence of political influence in its internal workings somewhat similar to that we still enjoy. Such independence is possible only under the shadow of a strong political *régime*. Theodor Eschenburg says of the old German service that it was 'socially one-sided, but it operated as a unity and in accordance with firm standards of quality. The much exaggerated class consciousness of this service corresponded to a high professional ethos and standard of performance. Neither political nor economic groups had influence on its establishments, not even the agrarian organizations'.[1] One has not to wander long in the corridors of Bonn to discover that things are not like that now. It is a long time since they have been exactly like that. Eschenburg puts the beginning of the modern patronage of office in 1921, when the political parties began to press for a quota of posts as a means, though it would seem an inadequate one, of securing a bureaucracy sensible of the needs of the new times. Hitler hated the bureaucracy and tried to secure its dominance by *one* party, partly by planting or promoting sympathizers, partly by employing agents, sometimes among the messengers and drivers, who could keep an eye on their nominal masters. If the new politicians suspect the Civil Service, they are not in a particularly good tradition in doing so, nor in a particularly demo-

[1] Theodor Eschenburg, *Herrschaft der Verbände?* (1955), p. 12.

cratic one. And if the personnel has changed, so that one could say that something a little different was being suspected by each of the three régimes, the changes as between consecutive régimes have affected only a small, though admittedly important, proportion of officials. A modern state has need of its bureaucracy and is hardly more likely to lose the lot in a revulsion of public feeling than it is to lose the whole of its hospital or newspaper staffs.

The German official[1] is still, in his way, a proud creature. His preserve (as distinct from that of other employees or workers in the state service) in general includes all those administrative and executive posts which carry with them a bit of the authority of the state or of a public corporation, as well as all those more modest positions of trust, such as those of the postman, the railway-driver and the signalman, in which public safety is involved. The generic name for the tasks carrying with them a morsel of public authority is 'hoheits-rechtliche'[2] activities. The etymology of the word 'hoheitsrechtliche' is no doubt significant: 'Hoheit', 'Highness', 'Hoheitsrecht' 'royal prerogative'. The official is the successor of all those advisers and executants who flourished around the German courts of former times. This touch of what was once magic is probably, in these times, more damaging than helpful to the official's reputation with politicians and public. And yet if in one sense the politician may be said to distrust the officials and perhaps tends to be a little too desperately anxious to prove that he is commanding and not taking advice, in another sense there tends to be, from our point of view and indeed from that of some German critics, an insufficient gap between officials and politicians. No single feature of the arrangement is, to an Englishman, more striking than the fact that the *Staatssekretär* (the equivalent of the Permanent Secretary) can and does deputize for his Minister in the House. When he does so he may get into trouble either for not putting forcefully enough all his Minister might have

[1] There are three categories of state servant in Germany; the *Beamte*, or official proper, with whom we are here concerned; the *Arbeiter*, or worker, who corresponds, though not exactly, with the 'industrial' Civil Servant in Britain; and the intermediate class of *Angestellte* or employee. There is some overlapping of function as between *Beamte* and *Angestellte*; see von Rosen-von Hoewel, *Allgemeines Verwaltungsrecht* (1957, Schaeffers Grundriss des Recht und der Wirtschaft, 29 Band, I Teil), p. 37.

[2] According to the definition given by the German High Court, a *hoheitsrechtlich* activity is one involving the issue, by or on behalf of the state or a public corporation, of a duly authorized order or prohibition. *See* the official collection of decisions of the High Court (*Reichsgericht*), Vol. 93, p. 258. I am indebted to Professor Menger, of the Hochschule für Verwaltungswissenschaften Speyer, for this note.

said or for taking upon himself more than becomes a mere official, or both.

The *Staatssekretär* is of course a political official, nominated by or at any rate pleasing to his Minister. So are the *Ministerialdirektors*, his lieutenants, who may be regarded as the equivalent of our Under Secretaries. It is not to be supposed, however, that political influence on establishments policy ends there. It is of course impossible for an outsider, and perhaps not always easy for an insider, to say exactly how far it does go and what is involved in it. One cannot fail, however, to notice a certain uneasiness in German officials on this point; either urging that the extent of political influence has been much exaggerated or openly regretting that it is there. The influence is not only that of the parties directly but of other outside bodies which, generally, make their influence felt through the politicians. One instance, taken from Eschenburg who offers a varied selection, will show not merely outside influences at work considerably below the level of those appointments admitted to be political but working in a manner which we should regard as the grossest interference with a question of conscience. The case is one of a candidate for promotion to a rank below the rank of our 'principal'. He was a Roman Catholic, married to a Protestant, and he had allowed his children Protestant baptism, in defiance, of course, of the Roman rule for mixed marriages. The Minister was also a Roman Catholic and, it was expressly said, could not answer for such a promotion. It is as if, in England, an Anglican Cabinet Minister should stop the promotion of an Anglican on his staff who had married a Roman Catholic and given way to the Roman rule that the children should be baptized into her branch of the Church. The considerations involved in an appointment or a promotion would, happily, rarely be of this intimate character. More often it takes the form of looking for a candidate with the right combination of connections, political, confessional, and other. There is no doubt that the confessional question is a very live one, and the situation is dominated by an inextricable mixture of politics and religion which can be paralleled, in what were once the British Isles, only in Ireland. To listen to an impassioned sermon, in a packed cathedral, telling the congregation that they were '*das Volk Christi, das Reich Christi*', with the Pope at the head, is involuntarily to recall that one had heard those words '*Volk*' and '*Reich*' resounding with an equal but different passion on ground not very remote some twenty years before, and to reflect that a priest is not precluded, even during an exposition which is textually orthodox, from invoking evil spirits.

The examples given by Eschenburg of the interests of outside groups being brought to bear on establishments include cases involving the peasants' group and the refugees. Eschenburg points out that the importance attributed to groups in 1945 was virtually inevitable owing to the disarray of the political parties, and he says: 'Even today there are Ministries where the key positions – not always marked as such – are occupied by high officials who in the bottom of their hearts think of themselves more as commissars of their interest groups than as the advocate of the state. The view that certain Ministries in Federation and *Länder* are state-organized and maintained strong points in the service of the interest-groups, is fairly widely held.'[1] In a more exuberant mood Eschenburg declared that every organization would like if possible to have its own Ministry – 'the doctors a health ministry, the middle class block a Ministry for the middle classes' and so on. 'All that is missing from the claims to date is a Ministry of Midwives.'[2] Claims of this nature are not unknown in other democratic countries, and are perhaps not to be avoided in the modern mass state, for which Eschenburg also has the names the 'group state' and, more comprehensively, '*der Gefälligkeitsstaat*'[3] the state that tries to please. One can, however, usefully distinguish between claims for the setting up of special ministries and other bodies, which are public acts and can therefore be the subject of public discussion, and the more private business of interfering with appointments and promotions inside the ministries. The latter is a truly sinister phenomenon of which this country has happily almost no experience, though there is something of the sort in the claims that are made that certain posts should be reserved for Scotsmen, Welshmen, or women.

The working of political and (through the political) of other pressures on recruitment and promotion is limited, so far as federal officials are concerned, by the operation of a government order,[4] and it would be misleading to suggest that the outside pressures play more than a subordinate – though it is by no means a negligible part – in establishments policy. The rules laid down are applicable to all officials including those of the rank of *Ministerialdirektor* (Under Secretary) and above, which in the German system are the properly political offices whose holders have not the same security of

[1] Eschenburg: H.d.V? p. 16.
[2] Theodor Eschenburg, *Bemerkungen zur deutschen Bürokratie* (1955), p. 12.
[3] Eschenburg: B.z.d.B., p. 18.
[4] *Verordnung über die Laufbahnen der Bundesbeamten* (*Bundeslaufbahnverordnung* – BLV) – Bundesgesetzblatt, 8 August 1956.

tenure as the rest. The rules are, as is inevitable with such things, limiting rather than determining. That is to say, they lay down certain general minimal qualifications for recruitment and promotion, but cannot determine *who* is recruited or promoted. They are comparable to the conditions of eligibility for a Civil Service competition, and the choice in the hands of the particular ministry is, broadly speaking, as wide as that which, with us, is, in the matter of recruitment, open to the Civil Service Commission, though the shortage of qualified candidates has in fact meant that the freedom of choice is, at the recruitment stage, very restricted. In the matter of promotion, the British establishment officer has no regulations of any kind to guide or restrict him, though, for all but the higher posts, there are agreements with the staff which effectively govern procedure, though they leave the choice open to the authorities as in Germany.

There is little doubt, however, that the choice is not exercised in Germany in quite the same way as in England. Leaving aside the procedural differences which affect the middle and lower grades only, and leaving aside the question of political influence, the German official lays greater stress than we should do on specialist knowledge, and the career of the typical administrator is made in a narrower field than is the case with us. People tend to specialize and to be promoted within the speciality. The high official faced with an awkward question feels for a specialist as Goering felt for his revolver when he heard the word 'culture'. The passion for specialization, so characteristic of the Germans and betraying their desperate hope for certainty and their basic wobbling, may increase the size but certainly cannot increase the homogeneity of the service or the facility of communications within it.

The service has, of course, already a basis for homogeneity in the academic training of the entrants. We have seen that the general administrative cadre is, in accordance with the general European pattern, an affair of lawyers, though with some who have done something less than the full course, in addition to those who have done the full course of legal studies leading up to the second state examination and others who have pursued some other supposedly utilitarian studies such as economics. There will also be a smaller number without university training. The academic training is never quite forgotten as it cheerfully is in England. It is recalled when people are moved from one job to another and is a factor in limiting movement. We are free of this sort of thing in our general Civil Service classes, but not outside them, where a man of fifty may still be classified as a chemist on the basis of a not very good degree he took thirty years before.

The pride in their legal training and in their specialization strengthens among German officials an *esprit de corps* which tends towards exclusiveness. It might be said that the official feels himself not only separated from the people but from his Ministers, neither of whom, he likes to think, can really appreciate the complicated laws he weaves for them. It might be said that in a blundering way the injection of political influence is an attempt to put this right. It is a blundering way, however, for it increases distrust and so makes the service a less sensitive instrument of the popular will. Only a service where there is no fear or favour, or so little as not to matter, can respond in a ready and integrated fashion to governmental control and the feeling of the country. Such steadiness is not to be found in the Germany that has known 1919, 1933 and 1945, and a bureaucracy is, after all, a secondary thing, sick or well as the country is sick or well. As to popular feeling, the German bureaucrat probably never had any antennae.

Changes of political habit in Germany would be needed if the defects of her bureaucracy were to be remedied. 'It is notable', to quote Eschenburg again, 'that the Opposition in Germany frequently restricts itself to control of the direction of policy. . . . A pre-condition of public control is not only that it succeeds in forensic criticism, but that it finds an echo in public opinion.'[1] Eschenburg is not the first German to regard his country (somewhat mistakenly one may think) as a kind of England *manqué*.

[1] Eschenburg: B.z.d.B., p. 25.

33

Public Law in the United Kingdom[*]

J. D. B. MITCHELL

Because the legal system in Britain is fundamentally one of common law, administrative law does not exist in the way it does in a number of other countries. Indeed, it exists only in the sense of a term applied somewhat vaguely to the law that is made by, as well as the law that controls, the administrative authorities of the government – it is neither codified nor recognized by lawyers as one of the parts of law. Such public law as exists, and the consequence of it in terms of the administrative sub-system, is the subject of this article by the Professor of Constitutional Law in the University of Edinburgh. (See also H. W. R. Wade, Administrative Law, *Oxford University Press, 3rd edition, 1971, and J. A. G. Griffith and H. Street*, Administrative Law, *Pitman, 4th edition, 1967.)*

The task of a constitutional critic is not simple. Detachment is perhaps more difficult for him to attain than it is for the scientist. His material is more difficult to measure, and often provokes emotions within himself, since he has a personal relationship with it in a way which it is almost impossible for the scientist to have with his materials. So the lawyer may too easily fall into an uncritical acceptance of the virtues of another system, or too readily dismiss that system with the spoken or unspoken thought – 'That would not work with us.' With equal ease he may see nothing but the virtues or nothing but the faults of his own system. He is too close to it.

[*] From J. D. B. Mitchell, 'The Causes and Effects of the Absence of a System of Public Law in the United Kingdom', *Public Law*, 1965, pp. 95–118. Reprinted with permission of Stevens & Sons Ltd.

The basic text of this article was prepared for publication in *Études et Documents* (The Conseil d'État). The Editor of that journal has kindly allowed the publication of an English version. In the text that follows, the generality and relative lack of annotation dictated by the original form has been preserved, and, save where alteration was required by the different place of publication, the text remains close to the original and references have largely remained at the stage at which the original text was settled.

Anyone who, from outside France, contributes to *Études et Documents* becomes acutely conscious of these dangers, and that awareness is perhaps heightened when he writes from the United Kingdom. Natural and proper admiration for the Conseil d'État is coupled with an acute awareness of certain deficiencies of his own system of law in a modern age in which we, like all others, have become a much governed nation. If what follows is critical of the state of public law in the United Kingdom, let it be said at the outset that much could be said of present and enduring virtues in other aspects of our constitutional structure. Of those virtues or believed virtues much has been said, perhaps indeed too much, for many of our present difficulties may be attributable to past virtues of a system, praise of which has led us to be too reluctant to change or adapt it. Nevertheless at the outset it should be emphasized that virtue exists.

Within small compass it is intended to assess the present state of public law with us and to examine the causes which have produced that state. General constitutional devices intended to control governments in a political sense (wherein many of the virtues are to be found) are therefore beyond the scope of this article, except in so far as they may incidentally affect detailed rules. Attention must also be drawn to the title of the article. It is concerned with a system of public law. Inevitably public law exists in some form wherever the machinery of government operates. The necessities of government have a way of making themselves felt, whether one likes it or not. The proud declaration of section 2 of the Crown Proceedings Act, 1947, that 'the Crown shall be subject to all those liabilities in tort to which, if it were a private person of full age and capacity, it would be subject' is inevitably made 'subject to the provisions of this Act' and those other provisions are those wherein the necessities of government appear, and perhaps appear too strongly. The argument is then about the fact that public law is too often regarded as a series of unfortunate exceptions to the desirable generality or universality of the rules of private law, and is not seen as a rational system with its own justification, and perhaps its own philosophy.

There was certainly at one stage an embryo system of administrative law, which perhaps developed too early or too quickly for its health. Both in England and in Scotland the Privy Council exercised a jurisdiction over the administration, in ways which could have produced, by the process of evolution, a genuine administrative jurisdiction. In exercise of its supervisory powers, the Privy Council of Scotland is to be found requiring the Town Council of Edinburgh to hear each month complaints against its officers and to redress injuries[1] or hearing a complaint that the magistrates of Linlithgow were 'slack, negligent and remiss', and imposing a supervisory officer.[2] Abuse of power was checked, notably in relation to matters which could affect liberty such as the right of quartering soldiers or deportation,[3] and public officers who were failing to perform duties, such as that of maintaining roads or bridges, were corrected and threatened with severe penalties should the default continue.[4] The Exchequer was also exercising (though feebly) an administrative tutelage over local authorities.[5] In England the Privy Council exercised both aspects of an administrative jurisdiction, protecting officials from suits in the ordinary courts, and protecting individuals from abuse of power.[6] Even in so far as such bodies were concerned simply with the efficient administration of justice, it is easy to visualize the possibility of the development of that supervision into a more general supervision and control of administrative activity as the latter activity developed. Such an evolution was, however, frustrated. In both countries the jurisdiction of the Council and of conciliar courts, whatever virtues they had had at one time in protecting citizens from corruption and oppression, tended themselves to become the instruments of oppression. Indeed the neglect of the magistrates of Edinburgh referred to above was a neglect in the enforcement of oppressive laws. The Court of Star Chamber was abolished in 1641 and with the revolution of 1688 other conciliar courts were abolished in England. In Scotland the Privy Council lingered on, but after the Union of 1707 its abolition came in 1708 (an abolition which had been foreshadowed in the Acts of Union) and its amalgamation with the Privy Council of England (now without this supervisory jurisdiction) resulted from the same Act. The end of the Privy Council in Scotland caused little grief to those who remembered its character in its latter years before the revolution of 1688, by which time it often acted not as a bulwark against the oppressive use of power but as an accomplice in illegality.

The characteristics of these special courts were not, of course,

[1] Fountainhall, *Decisions*, Vol. I, p. 301. In the same volume at p. 234 we find John Forbes sued before the Privy Council for oppression in collecting the excise and fined 900 merks.

[2] Ibid., p. 208.

[3] See *Register of the Privy Council of Scotland* (3rd Series), Vol. II, pp. 4–6, or at pp. 512–13 for examples, or see Vol. VIII, pp. 3 and 6, for an order to release one improperly detained by the magistrates of the Canongate.

[4] Ibid., Vol. III, p. 466.

[5] *Conn* v. *Magistrates of Renfrew* (1906) 8 F. 905 at p. 911.

[6] Holdsworth, *History of English Law*, Vol. IV, pp. 87–8.

peculiar to them; they were shared by like institutions elsewhere and, as Dicey perceived, there was in them the germ of something which could have evolved into an institution akin to the Conseil d'État.[1] Nor were the abuses of such bodies peculiar to our history. The peculiarity, and, perhaps, the tragedy is to be found in the time and setting in which the crisis in relation to such courts occurred. It is one of our pieces of good fortune as well as one of our misfortunes that we had our overt revolutions early. The whole revolutionary process which can be generally designated by the phrase the 'revolution of 1688', happened early enough for it to be achieved with little bloodshed, and on the whole with little obvious upheaval in society. These things are all to the good. On the other hand that process happened at a time which, in retrospect, was unfortunate both as to the then current climate of thought of lawyers and as to the scope of governmental activity and the nature of constitutional machinery.

The abolition of the conciliar courts in the revolution of 1688 meant the unchallenged dominance of the ordinary courts, the courts of common law, in both jurisdictions, and in those courts there was the dominance of the concept of private property. It has been said that 'unlike the conciliar courts, the common law courts were only concerned with the fulfilment of legal obligations, and not with the execution of policy. In controlling governmental acts they were necessarily limited to considering the letter of the law'.[2] This concern with property rights certainly had its merits. It aided greatly in cases such as *Ashby* v. *White*[3] where the right to vote was treated as a property right, or in the great case of *Entick* v. *Carrington*,[4] wherein the defence of private property against invasion by agents of the government lay at the heart of the dispute. On the other hand its disadvantages became apparent once, for example, local government was no longer based essentially on a grant or charter to a borough (which clearly had a proprietary aspect) but was based on a system of authorities created by a legislative scheme. Not merely was thought confined within the ideas of property (of which more must be said) but available remedies were, on the whole, limited to those appropriate to property rights, or to those which were appropriate to the hierarchical control by a superior court of an inferior court. Thus

[1] For a discussion and defence of Dicey's views, see Prof. Lawson, 'Dicey Revisited' (1959), Vol. VII: *Political Studies*, pp. 112–20.

[2] Keir, *Constitutional History*, p. 234. The emphasis of Locke, in his justification of the revolution, upon the fact that government has no other end but the protection of property (*Second Treatise on Civil Government*, Chap. VIII, § 94) should be noted.

[3] (1703) 2 Ld. Raym. 398.   [4] (1765) 19 St.Tr. 1029.

limited, remedies became inappropriate to the control of administrative activity. So even where, as in Scotland, it was accepted that the supreme civil court should assume the jurisdiction formerly exercised by the Privy Council,[1] the exercise of jurisdiction was bound to be confined by reason of the available techniques even if it had not also been limited by other circumstances. The full consequences or even the existence of these limitations were not immediately apparent; rather did the immediate advantages (demonstrated in cases such as those which have been mentioned) catch and hold attention so that the attitude of lawyers tended to harden. The disadvantages only became apparent when the nature of governmental activity had changed and once the rudimentary constitutional machinery of 1688 had evolved.

There was inherent in the ideas of the revolutionary settlement a double control of governmental activity; control of legality in the courts and political control in Parliament. The broad limits of each form of control (but particularly of the first) were established in relation to the central government at a time when governmental activity in an internal sense was limited. Issues were either those of foreign affairs or, in relation to home affairs, were issues of policy of the most general order; issues of administration were rare. By the time that such issues had in the late nineteenth century become frequent and important to individuals, there had evolved what appeared to be an effective system of parliamentary control. That system was held in respect, a respect which grew as Parliament itself became more democratic, as a result of the process starting with the great Reform Act of 1832. This dependence upon parliamentary controls can be seen operating in the steady suppression of public boards in favour of administration through machinery of government cast in the mould of a department headed by a Minister who was himself subjected to parliamentary control through the doctrine of ministerial responsibility. It can also be seen in the steady rise in the popularity of Parliamentary Questions, a rise which reflects both this reliance on parliamentary controls, and the need for a mechanism for dealing with individual grievances.[2] While it may be true that individual grievances are now not normally raised as Questions in the first

---

[1] See Lord Kames, *Historical Law Tracts*, p. 228: 'The Court of Session has, with reluctance, been obliged to listen to complaints of various kinds that belonged properly to the Privy Council while it had a being.'

[2] See Chester and Bowring, *Questions in Parliament*, and Howarth, *Questions in the House*. In modern times the device of a question is supplemented by the letter to the Minister from a Member on behalf of one of his constituents. From 1870 to 1900 the number of questions in a Session rose from 1200 to over 5000.

instance, but are first raised in correspondence with the Minister, the Question is the unspoken threat which adds weight to the latter. Belief in the efficacy of Questions grew among the public and among members, and indeed their value does not, in many ways, need argument. As a means of securing redress in an ordinary case of maladministration in its simpler forms, the Question could be admirable. The disadvantages are of two sorts. There is first the remedy which may result. The answer, even when it is followed by a rectification of an administrative error, lacks the quality of a judgment in two respects. It lacks the enduring and formative quality of a judgment which enters into a system of jurisprudence, and it lacks the ability of a judgment to decree compensation. Very often the mere rectification of an error without compensation is today an inadequate remedy. In the second place, the disadvantages spring paradoxically enough from the forum wherein questions are asked. When one speaks of a Parliamentary Question, one thinks above all of the House of Commons. That House is, above all, a political House, and it is right that it should be so. Yet the forum for political debate may often not be the appropriate place to argue a question of maladministration. The question is not a political one in the true modern sense of the word 'political'. Moreover, the reliance upon parliamentary controls has its effect (which is possibly disadvantageous) on the structure of government. It necessarily imposes, since Parliament is in one place, a high degree of centralization upon the machinery of the national government, even in relation to administration. The forms of parliamentary control, even if they do not require it, make it highly desirable that the answer can be found speedily in the Minister's department in London.

Clearly, however, at the time when the modern administrative state was emerging, not merely were these disadvantages not apparent, but even their existence might reasonably not be suspected. For the moment it appeared that parliamentary controls could be adequate. This situation had, and continues to have, its effect on the law, as well as on the practice of the administration in ways which are relevant to the present theme. The respect for, and belief in, the efficacy of parliamentary controls moved courts to assume an attitude of restraint in the exercise of their admitted powers of control, which otherwise they might not have assumed. The point may be made by three sentences from the opinions in *Liversidge* v. *Anderson*.[1] The majority of the House of Lords clearly accepted the finality of the certificate of the Secretary of State and in the majority opinions the

[1] [1942] A.C. 206.

parliamentary background stands out. Lord Maugham, in coming to that conclusion, emphasized that the Secretary of State was 'a member of the Government answerable to Parliament', and that 'he would be answerable to Parliament in carrying out his duties'. Lord Macmillan equally emphasized that the Secretary was a high officer of State 'answerable to Parliament for his conduct in office'. Lord Wright emphasised the same point, adding, 'the safeguard of British liberty is in the good sense of the people and in the system of representative and responsible government'. It was Lord Atkin, who, in his dissent, emphasized the continuing role of courts and who clearly was not so satisfied of the perfection of parliamentary control. So too, in *Duncan* v. *Cammell Laird Co.*[1] the acceptance of the finality of ministerial certificates was undoubtedly helped by the emphasis upon the fact that the Minister was the 'political head of the department' and as such subject to the doctrine of ministerial responsibility. The insistence on the continuing role of courts came only with *Glasgow Corporation* v. *Central Land Board*[2] as a result of an insistence on the need for justice. Subsequent events (which will be discussed later) have demonstrated the need for that insistence, and also the fact that the House of Lords was over-optimistic in its reliance on parliamentary control.[3] It should not be thought that Scotland was unaffected by the other line of thought. Lord President Normand in *Pollock School* v. *Glasgow Town Clerk*[4] says, 'I am of opinion that the question whether the supply of houses is a purpose within Regulation 51 (1) is a political question and thus the exercise by the competent authority of a discretion in deciding it may be controlled by Parliament but cannot be reviewed in a court of law.' This attitude affected not only the decision of such large matters but even questions such as that of a right to a pension. Lord Sorn, speaking in the context of a claim to a naval pension, said,[5] 'In execution of its delegated power the Crown is answerable to Parliament, but I doubt if it becomes answerable to the subject.' That is to say that the subject might enforce the duty (which admittedly existed in some form) by parliamentary or political pressures, but not in a court of law.

These are modern cases illustrating the hardening of principle, but the same deference can be seen in the formative years. In *Institute of Patent Agents* v. *Lockwood*,[6] the source of the modern cases on

---

[1] [1942] A.C. 624. See too Lord Greene M.R. in *Point of Ayr Collieries Ltd.* v. *Lloyd George* [1943] 2 All E.R. 546 at p. 547.

[2] 1956 S.C. (H.L.) 1.

[3] See the *Grosvenor Hotel Case* [1964] Ch. 464, discussed below.

[4] 1946 S.C. 373.   [5] 1950 S.C. 448 at p. 451.   [6] [1894] A.C. 347.

delegated legislation, Lord Herschell opened the critical passage of his judgment with the assertion 'it must be remembered that it' [*scil.*: a wide discretionary power of legislating] 'is committed to a public department, and a public department largely under the control of Parliament itself'. This point was one of the main foundations for his argument limiting judicial control. It was coupled with the point that the rules made by the department were to be laid before Parliament and hence it was said Parliament had 'full control'. This second point illustrates another aspect of deference to Parliament, which in origin may have been justified but, as things have developed, is certainly no longer so. There is here the refusal of courts to examine the realities of parliamentary life, and hence their inevitable tendency to build the law upon the fictions rather than the realities of that life. Clearly, the pressures arising from the increase of legislation which is inescapable in a modern society have meant a diminution in parliamentary scrutiny of primary legislation and a still greater diminution in the scrutiny of delegated legislation. Yet the law, and the operation of courts, is based on the theory of 'full control' implying, as that phrase does, full scrutiny. In the same way at the time when a Minister became more and more a judge of disputes, whether between inferior public authorities or between citizens and public authorities and the legal rules governing this situation were being settled, the same influences were felt. In *Local Government Board* v. *Arlidge*[1] the key to the decision may reasonably be said to be found in two sentences: 'My Lords', said Lord Shaw of Dunfermline, 'how can the judiciary be blind to the well-known facts applicable not only to the Constitution but to the working of such branches of the executive. The department is represented in Parliament by its responsible head'. From that fact, coupled with the dependent fact of the anonymity of the civil service, flowed the judicial answers that the individual was not entitled to know or see the individual official who decided (this being, it was considered, immaterial, since the Minister was responsible) and that decisions need not be reasoned. The last was an acceptance of administrative practice which was itself dependent upon the doctrine of ministerial responsibility. The decision, it was thought, should, if need be, be justified in Parliament but not elsewhere. Once the pattern of judicial activity had been set in this mould the shape of the more recent decisions became predictable.

It is necessary at this point to link the two elements already emphasized in relation to the revolution of 1688. The concern with private law ideas and techniques might by itself alone have stimulated this

[1] [1915] A.C. 120.

464

reliance upon parliamentary controls. Private law operates between parties who exist in the same plane, and are thus equal. Rights are in issue. In public law properly conceived there is an inequality; private right is in conflict with public interest in a quite different way.[1] The mechanisms appropriate to striking a balance in the one condition will of necessity be inappropriate or inefficient in the other. Therefore, relief in the second state of affairs would tend to be sought by other means. Yet, to an extent, the two causes, the legal and the parliamentary background coinciding as they did, increased the effect which either alone might have had. Each cause increased the effect of the other. That point is made by contrasting the vast evolution of private law in the nineteenth century which was necessary to absorb the industrial revolution (an evolutionary process which, to some extent, at least, continues in the field of private law) with the failure of lawyers to produce a similar evolution in the field of public law even when the needs for such an evolution had become apparent.[2] Instead, such evolution as there was came in the area of parliamentary techniques, an evolution which, it seems, was perhaps accelerated by the failure of the courts. The latter failure was also attributable to the remedies at the disposal of the courts. When it is said that administrative issues did not arise at the critical formative period, that is true of the central government. It was not true in relation to local government, in relation to which the disappearance of the conciliar courts had also meant the disappearance or weakening of central controls. In relation to the counties, wherein (in England) local government was largely conducted through the justices in quarter sessions, a degree of supervision by the courts could exist, but through mechanisms, in particular the prerogative writs or orders, which were appropriate to the control *en cassation* of an inferior court. The subsequent reforms of these remedies were reforms which contemplated exclusively their operation in the field of judicial proceedings properly so called, and had the effect as time went on of severely limiting judicial control in the field of administration just when the need for that control was growing. The supervision of the superior court could only be effectively invoked when the lower 'court' had stated reasons and those reasons were in error. Normally, because of procedural reforms, reasons were not stated.[3] This necessity for a 'speaking record' was particularly important

---

[1] Compare the development of ideas in Sandevoir, *Études sur le Recours de Pleine Juridiction.*

[2] British jurisprudence remains essentially a philosophy of private law.

[3] *R.* v. *Northumberland Compensation Tribunal, ex parte Shaw* [1952] 1 Q.B. 338.

since here again the lawyers and Parliament combined to the same end – silence. If the Minister were to answer in Parliament the decision was often not a 'reasoned' one. To give reasons could be to give hostages to fortune. Thus the process of administration tended to be a closed rather than an open one.

These procedural matters had a special significance in England, but had not, in strict theory, the same importance in Scotland. There there was a more general basis for judicial control. Perhaps this arose because of the circumstances commented on by Lord Kames, perhaps also because in Scotland Parliament was until recently felt to be more remote than was the case in England. The Court of Session, it was said, must be open to anyone who complains of a wrong done by an inferior body,[1] and, more clearly than the English courts, it could insist that decisions should be taken in such a form as would facilitate review by the courts.[2] Nevertheless, the scope of such review in Scotland tended not to be greatly different from that in England. The fact that the House of Lords was the ultimate court of appeal in both jurisdictions had an obvious effect,[3] and the same attitude towards Parliament was operative, as the cases cited above demonstrate. Indeed, the Scottish cases show clearly the effects of the evolution discussed. In 1843 in *Pryde* v. *Heritors of Ceres*,[4] in which the court was asked to review the rates of payment for poor relief, the court accepted jurisdiction, although it was conscious of the difficulty and the delicacy of the task. The greatest difficulty envisaged was that of ascertaining the facts necessary for a decision, but it *was* assumed that relief from the decision of a statutory board must be found in the courts. Three things should, however, be noted. The heritors were a local body; secondly, in 1843 no simple means of parliamentary redress was apparent; thirdly, the matter was finally regarded as fit for decision in a court as a pecuniary claim; it was not regarded as a political matter. In contrast, the *Pollok School* case indicates a very marked change of attitude. The full effect of the use of the parliamentary arena for seeking redress has had its consequences in broadening the scope of what can be comprised within the term 'political'. Essentially the issues in *Pryde's* case were social, yet at that time a court would deal with them. A century later the interpretation of words, normally a lawyer's province, was treated in

[1] *Jeffray* v. *Angus*, 1909 S.C. 400.

[2] *Robb* v. *School Board of Logiealmond* (1875) 2 R. 698.

[3] Though *Magistrates of Ayr* v. *Lord Advocate*, 1950 S.C. 102 shows a departure from the English pattern set in such cases as *Franklin* v. *Minister of Town and Country Planning* [1948] A.C. 87, see Mitchell, 'The Scope of Judicial Review in Scotland' [1959] *Juridical Review* 197.   [4] (1843) 5 D. 552.

a similar context as quite outside the competence of a court. The forum for redress had had the effect of changing the classification of problems. Moreover, the decline, if one should not say the decay, of local government had accentuated that change. Increasingly all matters of principle involve the central government, and it is the central government which is represented in Parliament and amenable to challenge there. Hence, granted the constitutional background, in this way also the range of matters with which courts will feel a reluctance, and often an overwhelming reluctance to concern themselves, has increased greatly. One could almost say that the philosophical questions about what is a 'political question' and what is a 'justiciable issue' have become the burning questions which lawyers must debate before it is too late.[1] Put in lawyers' terms it could be said very briefly that we have no system of public law because reliance upon parliamentary redress (a reliance fostered both by the growth of Parliament and the reticence of the courts), has made development of such a system impossible.

Before turning to some of the more detailed consequences in law which flow from the causes which have produced that general result, one may perhaps, though the dangers are obvious, emphasize the significance of this general constitutional background by contrasting it with that in France. There a revolution similar in basic principle to our own was delayed for a century. As a result it was more violent and the disturbance of political life was deeper and longer lasting. Yet, occurring when and how it did, there could be born or reborn in that revolution an institution, the Conseil d'État, which could develop those beneficent functions of a Privy Council which our history condemned to frustration. The troubled history of parliamentary evolution in France enabled, and perhaps encouraged, the development of those functions in the nineteenth century whereas the different parliamentary history with us had the opposite effect. No doubt the law of 3 March 1849 (which decisively affirmed the character of the Conseil d'État as a court), is important in that history, but, to a stranger, much more significant is a reaffirmation of the same principle in the law of 24 May 1872, Article 9, which indicated more fully the scope of the jurisdiction, followed as it was by the decision in *Blanco*,[2] which opened the door to wide extensions of the work of

---

[1] Clearly we are not alone in the Anglo-Saxon world in this. The issue is sharply posed in *Baker* v. *Carr*, 369 U.S. 186 (1961), and in the later cases in the same line the debate continues.

[2] 1873 D. III 20. The evolution of ideas is admirably described in Sandevoir, *Études sur le Recours de Pleine Juridiction.*

the Conseil. The reaffirmation of the existence of an administrative jurisdiction and the reformulation of its basic principles came at the time when the modern state was already starting to have effect (the facts of *Blanco*, in that it could be said in modern times to involve a nationalized industry, alone show that). The jurisdiction could develop to keep pace with the development of that state, having not merely this philosophic basis, but also having behind it already a long history. Even if much of that history was in the quiet field of contract, that quietness had its advantages for the future. If with us the conciliar courts could have been quieter and duller their history might have been longer.

To return to the other side of the Channel, one must first note the ways in which the modern state drew itself to the attention of lawyers. Even that most far-seeing man Maitland, lecturing in 1888, while he emphasized the possible importance of contract in suits against the Crown, could also write: 'The Queen and her officers are no longer in the habit of seizing land upon all manner of pretences; there are few pretences available.'[1] He did not clearly foresee compulsory purchase for schools, hospitals, electricity installations and all the other 'pretences' available to a modern state which must exist but which may be abused. Beyond the field of contract he was content that the plea 'act of state' was excluded and for the rest to leave matters on the basis of private law. At the critical stage attention was fixed upon two matters, delegated legislation and administrative tribunals. The prominence of *Lockwood's* case and *Arlidge's* case in the history of English administrative law is significant, as is the contrast between them and *Blanco*. One consequence of this was the tendency to regard 'administrative law' as confined to these two issues. Dicey's article 'The Development of Administrative Law in England',[2] does not go beyond these bounds; the first book entitled *Administrative Law* in this country – that of Dr Port – was similarly confined, and the tendency to think in these restrictive terms was fortified by the two great inquiries: the Committee on Ministers' Powers and the Committee on Tribunals and Inquiries,[3] which concerned themselves exclusively with these matters, and were themselves the centres of debate, focusing interest upon their own subject-matter.

[1] Maitland, *Constitutional History*, p. 483.

[2] (1915) 31 L.Q.R. 148. It may be noted that in that article (at p. 152) Dicey criticized the reliance on the doctrine of ministerial responsibility in *Arlidge's* case.

[3] The Reports were respectively published in 1932 as Cmd. 4060 and 1957 as Cmnd. 218.

The emergence of these two issues, delegated legislation and administrative tribunals, as the central ones, is clear, yet needs further explanation. It is only a partial explanation to say that it was in this context, and most clearly in relation to inquiries, that the problem of reconciling judicial and parliamentary controls of administrative action became apparent and demanded solution. A fuller explanation is to be found in the technicalities of remedies which have already been mentioned. Especially in England the prerogative writs or orders were available, inefficient though they might be. Through them, in these contexts some relief could be sought. Elsewhere it was difficult to find a starting point. What was sought in *Arlidge's* case was a writ of certiorari. Yet this circumstance had further consequences. The availability and effectiveness of these remedies depended largely upon procedural matters. Hence the tendency has been for courts to be concerned not with substantive merits but with procedural defects involved in the matter in question which may or may not have had any real significance. What is attacked is not the substance or the merits of a decision, but the procedure by which it has been reached. It is certain that procedural rectitude can have advantages. In the Middle Ages insistence upon procedure was one means of securing regularity of administration. Too close a concern with procedure is probably only appropriate to an early stage of development, and in this context this concern with procedural questions has had a series of disadvantageous consequences.[1] First, and perhaps most importantly, it has the effect of producing technicality rather than generality in the law, a technicality which may sometimes do injustice to the individual, sometimes to the administration. The incidence of injustice is random. In order to come within the scope of certiorari a function had to be classified as judicial or quasi-judicial, terms which have never been satisfactorily defined.[2] As a result, since they are not classified as quasi-judicial, decisions may surprisingly escape judicial control. The cases wherein the courts refuse to intervene in 'disciplinary' proceedings are perhaps the outstanding examples.[3] Technicality is increased by the fact that

[1] Many of which can be exemplified by *Johnson & Co.* v. *Minister of Health* [1947] W.N. 251; [1947] 2 All E.R. 395, and could be prophesied from *Errington* v. *Minister of Health* [1935] 1 K.B. 249.

[2] See de Smith, *Judicial Review of Administrative Action*, Chap 2. Rightly the author remarks that in this area of law 'an aptitude for verbal gymnastics is obviously an advantage'. It may be doubted if a body of law which demands that aptitude so strongly is the best that can be devised in this field.

[3] *Ex p. Fry* [1954] 1 W.L.R. 730; see, too, *R.* v. *Metropolitan Police Commissioner* [1953] 1 W.L.R. 1150.

while stages in the process of taking one decision may be classed as quasi-judicial, so that certain minimum standards of conduct are required during those stages, the later stages which are classed as administrative escape this requirement.[1] This can mean, then, that the whole decision is not subjected to review even on procedural grounds, and while the subleties of distinguishing between stages may appeal to the lawyer, the result of these subtleties is likely to be a feeling of dissatisfaction in the mind of the citizen, to whose eyes the decision is a decision – an indivisible whole. Technicality and concern for procedure may have other results. It may mean that an order is upset when in substance it is recognized as correct, and when in fact it is recognized that no injustice has been done. Thus in one case a misdescription in the area of land subjected to an order under schemes for regulating agriculture was sufficient to upset the order, even though it was clear that everyone knew what farm and what land was under discussion, and even though the misdescription was slight, referring to narrow strips at the edge of the farm in question, which could not affect the decision in question.[2] So also, although it appears that in substance a decision was right, and had been properly arrived at, an error in drafting the formulation of the decision may result in its overthrow.[3] In these cases it is the reasonable needs of the administration which are unreasonably impeded. In other cases, such as those of the type of *Errington's* case, it may be that the individual is left with a strong conviction that although certain procedural rules have been rigidly followed, substantial justice has not been done. Both of these types of consequences can be serious, and it is probable that too little thought has been given to the first type – the neglect of the needs of government, in the efficiency of which we too have an interest.

This neglect of a fundamental consideration of the nature and purposes of judicial review which flows from the concern with procedure is itself responsible for a second disadvantageous consequence, which has a double aspect. There grew, almost accidentally,

[1] The process of division is apparent in *Errington's* case above, wherein the Minister was in some sense deciding between a local authority and an individual. The difficulties of course came to a head in *Franklin* v. *Minister of Town and Country Planning* [1948] A.C. 67. Rare exceptions to the generality of what is said above, such as *Hoggard* v. *Worsbrough U.D.C.* [1962] 2. Q.B. 93, exist but they do not substantially affect the validity of the statement.

[2] *R.* v. *Agricultural Land Tribunal, ex p. Benney* [1955] 2 Q.B. 140. The whole history of the litigation starting at [1955] 1 All E.R. 123 indicates the degree of technicality which may exist.

[3] *R.* v. *Minister of Housing, ex p. Chichester R.D.C.* [1960] 1 W.L.R. 587.

a belief that if procedural safeguards could be strengthened, if more administrative decisions could be taken in a form which could be called quasi-judicial, then all would be well. That belief was fostered by the circumstance that it came to be thought that if the method of reaching a decision could not be described by the magic words 'quasi-judicial' (which had the effect of the incantation of 'abracadabra', opening the cave of judicial review), then rules of fair-dealing, such as the *audi alteram partem* rule, were excluded or inapplicable. Clearly these two things are related, the first (the belief in procedural safeguards) being prompted by the second. The second may be illustrated (apart from *Ex p. Fry*, already mentioned) by *Nakkuda Ali* v. *Jayaratne*.[1] That the Controller of Textiles, exercising his power to grant or revoke licences to trade in textiles, could be said by the Judicial Committee of the Privy Council to be 'taking executive action to withdraw a privilege' had the effect that he was under no obligation to regulate his action by any analogy to judicial rules. Hence, in the absence of any provision in the particular regulations there was no obligation upon him to serve notice on the trader or hear him before revoking the licence. Because the act was executive or administrative it was unencumbered by procedural rules, and in a system of judicial review so concerned with procedure, the serious consequences to an individual of such an attitude are sufficiently obvious. It is equally obvious that pressure would therefore arise to change the mode in which decisions were taken to avoid these consequences, even though procedural complications in the process of taking decisions may well render the process of government slow and cumbersome, when a modern age demands speed with safety. It is not always remembered that governments are expected to do something, or that in the end of the day complex procedures may not be the best protection for individuals. Nevertheless, evidence of these pressures is to be seen in the report of the Committee on Tribunals and Enquiries, and in the consequential Tribunals and Enquiries Act, 1958; both of which are essentially concerned with trimming the mode of taking decisions to fit an inadequate system of law rather than being concerned with that law itself. Indeed, the scope and terms of reference of the Committee are in themselves sufficient evidence of a belief that the vital issue was conceived to be a procedural one rather than being one of the whole nature of administrative law. The Report and the Act were limited by the circum-

[1] [1951] A.C. 66. Although criticized in *Ridge* v. *Baldwin* [1964] A.C. 40, it is by no means certain that this unhappy case is dead; *cf. Vidyodoya University of Ceylon* v. *Silva* [1964] 1 W.L.R. 77.

471

stances of their origin and it has already become apparent that an awareness of the limitations of the reforms brought about by the Act is growing. The fact that that awareness often takes the form of pressure for other administrative palliatives, such as the appointment of an Ombudsman, is in part a result of the limited concepts of the role of public law induced by these procedural considerations. Thus blinkered, we cannot see the real scope of administrative law.

That this reliance on remedies which, as they have developed, focus attention on procedure has inhibited the courts in fulfilling their traditional role in a modern society can be demonstrated even by resort to internal sources.

In England the sudden growth in the popularity of an action for a declaration instead of, and in substitution for, applications for certiorari is one mark of this, for the former action is free of some of the limitations of the latter.[1] Indeed, it has been claimed to be a perfectly general remedy available where one party 'has a real interest to raise, and the other to oppose'.[2] It may, however, be doubted whether it can break free from the shackles of thought created by the older forms of action, and in any event it is a remedy without result. The action produces in the end of the day simply a declaration of rights. It cannot of itself be productive of redress, let alone compensation. Even our concepts of what is a real interest are fragmentary, rudimentary and underdeveloped. In Scotland, as has been said above, remedies were more general. The standard form of action is one for reduction, which is available wherever there exists a document or decision which can be quashed, where in effect there is something on which the order can act. The problem of classification of an act does not arise in an acute form, for the same remedy can be used whether it be administrative or judicial. In *M'Donald* v. *Lanarkshire Fire Brigade Joint Committee*[3] another fireman had been disciplined, and he too appealed to the courts, but this time with success. 'The irregularity of the proceedings and the unlawfulness of the penalty are sufficient grounds of action', said Lord Guthrie. He had had *Ex p. Fry* pressed upon him in argument (which is one sign of how decisions in one jurisdiction may affect those in the other), but he avoided following that decision. Although he did, in fact, class the proceedings of the Fire Brigade Authority as judicial

[1] See *Vine* v. *National Dock Labour Board* [1957] A.C. 488 and Zamir, *The Declaratory Judgment.*

[2] Lord Denning, *Pyx Granite Co.* v. *Ministry of Housing, etc.* [1958] 1 Q.B. 554 at p. 571.

[3] 1959 S.C. 141.

or quasi-judicial, this classification was not, it seems, fundamental to the decision; the bare grounds quoted above sufficed, as indeed they should. The case illustrates not merely that varying decisions can be reached on what are essentially similar facts, but it also perhaps demonstrates how different might have been the state of our administrative law had it been possible to maintain a generality of approach, particularly in the dominant jurisdiction of England.

One further result may here be noted. Since the most familiar field of operation of the courts was in relation to quasi-judicial decisions, the law in relation to the control of administrative acts has a hesitant or tentative air. Certainly there are to be found broad declarations of principle. There is the much-quoted dictum of Lord Greene. 'The court is entitled to investigate the action of the local authority with a view to seeing whether they have taken into account matters which they ought not to take into account, or conversely have . . . neglected to take into account matters which they should have taken into account'.[1] The practical application of such declarations is, however, much more limited than these terms suggest. In that case Lord Greene was speaking of a local authority, and in respect of such authorities there is certainly a much greater readiness to examine their actions, though even in relation to such authorities it is likely that the courts in this century are much less ready to examine decisions in depth than was formerly the case. In relation to activities of the central government, it is even more true that a like reluctance has increased very greatly. The reasons for it are clear; once a court is concerned with questions other than those of *ultra vires* in a narrow sense, but is being asked to concern itself with the motive or propriety of an act, all those secondary influences of the development of the system of parliamentary control which have been noticed become operative. So, where the court was asked to declare unreasonable part of a town planning scheme confirmed by a Minister, Lord Greene himself said,[2] 'The common law does not control Parliament, and if Parliament confers on a Minister a power to make regulations, how can the court enquire into these regulations beyond ascertaining whether they are within the power?' adding, when cases dealing with local authorities were pressed upon him, 'We are dealing with a totally different class of subject-matter and one in which the ultimate arbiter

---

[1] *Associated Provincial Picture Theatres Ltd.* v. *Wednesbury Corporation* [1948] 1 K.B. 223 at pp. 223–4.
[2] *Taylor* v. *Brighton Borough Council* [1947] K.B. 736; see too *Sparks* v. *Edward Ash Ltd.* [1943] K.B. 223. The steady fusion, in fact, of central and local government obviously increases the importance of this tendency.

is the Minister himself.' Thus, it is parliamentary influences which have ensured the perpetuation of the concept of the Minister-judge.

The full significance of such phrases is realized when enquiry as to the scope of any power is considered in the light of statements such as those in the *Pollok School* case referred to above. The definitions critical to the determination of that scope may be determined by a Minister, not the court. These difficulties become abundantly apparent when questions of motive become important. In *Earl Fitzwilliam's Wentworth Estates* v. *Minister of Town and Country Planning*[1] the majority in the Court of Appeal, and all judges in the House of Lords, were of the opinion that once a proper motive could be established, then the existence of other motives which might not be proper was irrelevant. Denning L.J. vigorously dissented: he regarded the other purpose as dominant and therefore the order was bad. In a short space it is necessary to express the decision in sharply contrasting colours, though there are, of course, subtleties of shading which can be found by a careful reading of the judgments. Even so, the case indicates the difficulties which face courts, as at present organized, when they attempt to probe in depth. Partly the difficulties spring from the fact that the traditional forms of judicial review, which have already been discussed, have encouraged an attitude of mind which is not inclined to such probing. Partly they spring from the fact that the techniques available to the courts, being those appropriate to ordinary civil litigation between private parties of roughly equal status and interests, are not appropriate to this form of litigation when one party may be in a dominant position in relation to essential information. The second of these propositions is more easily understood when the basic concepts upon which the equivalent rules have been built in France are considered.

In France the preponderant character of the administration has been recognized and compensated for. So, in the most critical area of *détournement de pouvoir* the private citizen is required only to raise such a case as will raise sufficient suspicion to merit investigation, and to counterbalance the dominant position of the administration the Conseil d'État has inverted the normal burden of proof putting upon the administration the burden of proving innocence[2] and has supplemented this general attitude by derivative rules such as that in *Barel*[3]

[1] [1952] A.C. 362; [1951] 2 K.B. 284.

[2] See Auby and Drago, *Traité de Contentieux Administratif*, Vol. III, p. 322 ff.

[3] C.E. 28 May, 1954; 1954 R.D.P. 509. Note Waline, and see in particular the *conclusions* of M. Letourneur at p. 522 for the admirable deft approach to the administration which combines understanding, firmness and a deep concern for

whereby the silence of the administration is construed against it. Again, because of the recognition of the peculiarity of the public service, it has been possible to evolve rules of considerable subtlety and effectiveness on the control of motives[1] which have the effect of striking a proper balance between the interests of the administration and those of the individual. All these rules are, however, dependent on a deliberate effort to achieve rules appropriate to a public-law situation. The contrast is sufficiently indicated by the rule in *Duncan* v. *Cammell Laird Ltd.*[2] and its subsequent developments. The leave granted to a Minister to reformulate a claim to privilege[3] indicates at the same time a concern for formalism and an attitude radically different from that of the Conseil. Even when protests are made against undue formalism,[4] in the sense that a particular set of words should not be regarded as automatically and necessarily sufficient justification for a claim by a Minister to withhold documents, it does not appear, on an examination of the judgments, that any real power of the courts to press their own enquiries is contemplated, or perhaps is possible under the existing system. The impression remains that '*vox et praeterea nihil*' may yet prove to be an appropriate summary simply because the courts will be unable without a major reorientation to achieve the necessary subtlety of procedure and of rules. Without such a power the element of ritual or formalism which will make such a claim unchallengeable will remain even though the formula used may be an expanded one, as compared with the formula currently in use.

This same line of cases may be used to illustrate one further difficulty which springs from the peculiar history of the role of courts in relation to the administration with us. Already it has been noted that judicial review, the control by a court, is dominated by the concept of a judicial or quasi-judicial decision. The concern in the Tribunals and Enquiries Act, 1958, s. 12, was to ensure that reasons, if required, should be given in decisions falling within that category,

administrative morality. The extension of this line of cases in the *conclusions* of M. Braibant in *Poncin*, C.E. 17 June, 1964; 1964 R.D.P. 811 should be noted.

[1] Auby and Drago, *Traité de Contentieux Administratif*, Vol. III, p. 49 f. where a similar approach is demonstrated.

[2] [1942] A.C. 624.

[3] 1963] 3 All E.R. 426; [1964] 1 All E.R. 92 (C.A.). The sense of inadequacy of these decisions was enhanced by reading them in the library of the Palais Royal.

[4] *Merricks* v. *Nott-Bower* [1964] 1 All E.R. 717 and *Re Grosvenor Hotel (No. 2)* [1964] 3 All E.R. 354.

or where a decision was taken by a Minister in cases where a preliminary enquiry could be required by law. Clearly it is as important, or perhaps more important that reasons should also be given for administrative decision especially when the preliminary stages in reaching the decision have not been in public. It is curious, and perhaps significant that section 12 does not impose any obligation to give reasons where any enquiry which precedes the decision is not one which could be compelled by law. The difficulty arising both from the absence of an obligation to state reasons in a fully significant way and from the reticence of the court once it is outside the familiar territory of the quasi-judicial, is apparent from the cases just discussed. In effect the tragedy is that the peculiar evolution of judicial review by artificially segregating one group of decisions from another has prevented the courts from creating and applying any general concept of administrative morality. The artificiality can be said to exist because in essence the decisions in either group have normally the same nature, and the process by which the decision is now reached is the result of historical accidents. The tragedy (perhaps the word is not too strong) is there because this question of administrative morality is a fundamental and general one; the mechanisms of the law have prevented the question being approached in the way that is necessary even though the question is, at times, seen to exist.[1] The approach must be as general as the problem and not as particular a one as the available remedies dictated.

The possibility of achieving a generality of principle has hitherto been denied by one other major consideration. Increasingly the services of government are becoming unified, because problems have become national. Neither education nor the relief of the poor can any longer be regarded as local issues. The nation as a whole has an interest in the quality of education in each part of the country. Increasingly there is talk of regional planning, in the interest not merely of the particular region but of the country as a whole. Thus economic and other forces compel a unification of services (which need not mean centralization) but the theory of our law conflicts with these facts. The 'administration' does not exist. Instead the law contemplates two things: 'the Crown' – which is very broadly the central government, and other public authorities – largely local authorities with public corporations existing in an uncanny half-world. To the

[1] The Franks Report says at § 405 'We wish to emphasize that nothing can make up for a wrong approach to administrative activity by the administrative servants'. Because of the circumstances discussed consideration of the enforcement of this necessary morality was not open to the committee.

ordinary citizen it does not matter whether or not the public authority with whom he deals is or is not regarded in law as 'the Crown'. To him it is simply 'the government' or the administration. In law this classification matters a great deal. It affects profoundly the remedies which are available, since section 21 of the Crown Proceedings Act makes inapplicable certain remedies otherwise available; it affects also, as has been noted above, the way in which courts regard the activities of public authorities, since courts are much less ready to scrutinize closely the sections of the Crown. These things may matter a great deal in particular cases,[1] but they probably matter even more since they also are responsible for impeding the formation of general ideas.

Certain rights, because they are associated with the Crown, are called prerogatives, and because of this appellation and association they tend to be regarded as peculiar to the Crown. This has a double psychological effect. The rules are not clearly seen as being rules peculiar to government in general and in a practical sense: instead, they have, through the word 'Crown' with its overtones of feudalism, a mystic air of being related to monarchy (an air perhaps all the more dangerous when monarchy has become innocuous but the rules are in truth applicable to a government with much greater power than a monarch ever had). This unrealism has the effect that the rules are allowed to operate when in some sense the Crown is involved even though that operation is to the detriment of the government and community. In the notable instance, the immunity which properly the Crown, in the sense of government, has from taxation, was allowed to operate even where the effect of its operation was exclusively to benefit a private individual at the expense of the government, because there was involved an official, the Custodian of Enemy Property, who could be regarded as a servant of the Crown.[2] Thus on the one hand the terminology tends to prevent, or at least to impede, the application of realism and common sense to rules affecting the central government. Equally the rules tend to have a universal effect in relation to that government, because it is 'the Crown', and so it is impossible to achieve those subtleties of application dependent on the character of the governmental act in question which are clearly necessary if a proper balance between the needs of government and the rights of individuals is to be struck. Because the rules are too

[1] In *Nottingham* (*No. 1*) *Area Hospital Management Committee* v. *Owen* [1958] 1 Q.B. 50 the quick effective and necessary remedy was excluded for like reasons.

[2] *Bank voor Handel en Scheepvaart N.V.* v. *Administrator of Hungarian Property* [1954] A.C. 584.

absolute they are inappropriate to the varied activities of a modern government which acts in many characters.[1] On the other hand, because of terminology such as 'prerogative' or 'Crown', rules which are in truth general are not seen to be so. Local authorities as much as the central government perform governmental functions, yet this characteristic is only with difficulty recognized because terminology has obscured thought. The rule in the *Amphitrite*,[2] that the Crown cannot fetter its future executive action, is normally seen as distinct. The cases in which local authorities are faced by the same problem are regarded as somehow being different.[3] Similarly in relation to local authorities the consequences may be that the governmental or public character of their acts is not seen to exist and thus the frustration of their proper functions results.[4]

If appropriate rules are to be evolved to deal with modern government, then modern government must be seen in the round and not fragmented, yet again history has proved to be an obstacle. Again, too, it must be emphasized that that history has its own sound justification. At a period when the full impact of modern government could not be clearly seen the issue of the treatment of government became acute in relation to tax exemption. Many bodies were claiming exemption which was sensibly enjoyed by the Crown. A convenient way of limiting these claims to exemption was to deny the character of a Crown servant. So, for example, the University of Edinburgh was (rightly) denied this character.[5] By these means the distinction was built into the law and has had enduring consequences. Once again, though the origins may be justified, the consequences can be deplored. The split which has been engendered affects all branches of the law. The servant of the local authority has some remedies when he is unjustifiably dismissed. The servant of the central government has none at law. An employee who changes between the two services does much more than change his master. The whole character of his relationship with his master is changed, even though the essential character of his duties is not. It is this aspect of public service which as much as anything shows the limiting effect on thought of this artificial division. Clearly it is impossible that all the developments in state activity should have left no mark in

[1] The rules (mentioned above) dealing with the disclosure of documents in litigation between the government and an individual are typical of this: see Mitchell, *Constitutional Law*, p. 261.

[2] *Rederiaktiebolaget Amphitrite* v. *The King* [1921] 3 K.B. 500.

[3] *Cory (William) and Sons Ltd.* v. *Corporation of London* [1951] 2 K.B. 476.

[4] *Western Heritable Investment Co.* v. *Glasgow Corporation*, 1956 S.C.(H.L.) 54.

[5] *Greig* v. *University of Edinburgh* (1868) 6 M.(H.L.) 97.

law. The advent of the National Health Service, which meant that hospitals became part of a service under the ultimate control of a Minister, was found to alter pre-existing rules relating to medical fault, particularly fault of consultants.[1] Yet the recognition of changed conditions has been slow and irregular. The fact of the existence of a National Health Service meant, among other things, that the potential employer of doctors in the hospital service was a near monopolist. Moreover, the conditions of employment of doctors bear strong marks of a service: they are for the most part governed by regulations. Yet in England the relationship of doctors to the hospital board has been regarded still as being the same as the relation ship between a private master and his servant, with the result that the remedies available to the wrongfully dismissed servant were unreasonably limited. The character of service was entirely neglected.[2] In Scotland, however, more recently[3] full weight was given to this service character with the result that remedies *were* appropriate to the condition of employment.

This aspect of employment in the public service is but one illustration of a further major consequence of the lack of generality of ideas. Here are to be seen the combined consequences of the dominance of private law (or its converse, the rejection of a specific public law) which has earlier been noted as one part of the revolution of 1688, and of the limitations upon thought imposed by the forms of action of judicial review. Ideas of general utility and significance such as that of *res extra commercium* or even ideas about the organization of a public service[4] have been lost, and appear too strange to be given effect.[5] As a result ideas of public contracts are ill-informed, so that although the compulsions of the needs of government may make themselves felt, the legal machinery to compensate the individual who has contracted with the government may be lacking.[6] The same may well be said to be true of delictual liability,[7] though it is probable that much less hardship arises on this score. More important is the fact that ideas about what will suffice to give a good title to

[1] *Hayward* v. *Edinburgh Board of Management*, 1954 S.C. 453.
[2] *Barber* v. *Manchester R.H.B.* [1958] 1 W.L.R. 181.
[3] *Palmer* v. *Inverness Hospitals Board of Management*, 1963 S.L.T. 124.
[4] *Farrier* v. *Elder and Scott*, 21 June, 1799 F.C.
[5] This emerges clearly in the opinions in the Inner House in the *Western Heritable Investment Co. Case*, 1956 S.L.T. 2.
[6] The *Amphitrite* case above is the outstanding example. A more recent one may be found in *Commissioners for Crown Lands* v. *Page* [1960] 2 Q.B. 274 See generally Mitchell, *The Contracts of Public Authorities*.
[7] *Hester* v. *MacDonald*, 1961 S.C. 370.

raise an action, particularly when general duties of public authorities are involved, are seriously underdeveloped. In part this is attributable to the fragmentary character of public law, to the absence of a system, since there has been little incentive to work out any general theory. In part this is again attributable to the ideas of property, and hence the insistence upon something akin to a proprietary right before the court's aid can be invoked.[1] That concern with property is readily understandable in the perspective of history, yet clearly the modern operations of government require, if law is to play its proper place in the regulation of society, a clarification and expansion of this particular concept.

In effect it is this question of the place of law in society that is at the heart of the matter. Some of the consequences of the absence of a system of public law which have been mentioned seem small and technical, but when all are cumulated the real problem becomes apparent. Other consequences which are more nearly constitutional could be mentioned. The relationship between central government departments and either local authorities or nationalized industries demonstrate limitations upon the use of law which have like causes to those limitations which have been discussed or mentioned in the context of the 'external' operations of government – its operations in relation to individuals. Enough, however, has probably been said to indicate the crisis which exists. Recently, there have been signs of the fact that recognition of the existence of a crisis is growing. 'We do not have a developed system of administrative law – perhaps because until recently we did not need it', said Lord Reid[2] recognizing in the same breath both the absence and the need. Earlier Lord Devlin had written,[3] 'I believe it to be generally recognized that in many of his dealings with the executive the citizen cannot get justice by process of law. The common law has now, I think, no longer the strength to provide any satisfactory solution to the problem of keeping the executive, with all the powers which under modern conditions are needed for the efficient conduct of the realm, under proper control'. Elsewhere the recognition is apparent in the continuing malaise which is felt by the public at large about the present situation. That malaise finds expression in pressures for further administrative or parliamentary remedies through a device akin to the Danish Ombudsman. The pressure for such an official may yet prove to be

[1] *D. and J. Nicol.* v. *Dundee Harbour Board*, 1915 S.C.(H.L.) 1.

[2] *Ridge* v. *Baldwin* [1964] A.C. 40 at p. 72.

[3] 'The Common Law, Public Policy and the Executive' (1956) 9 *Current Legal Problems* 1 at p. 14.

the most serious and damaging consequence of our lack of a system of public law. It is a consequence since in the absence of such a system the law has proved itself incapable of meeting the demands of a modern state and, because the inadequacies of the existing law are seen or felt, albeit instinctively, no longer do people turn to the law for relief but instead to administrative palliatives. But the problem to be solved, like the seventeenth-century problem of prerogative, can only be solved by courts and Parliament, by law and politics. Neither alone is effective, for as has been shown the popular remedy of an Ombudsman, operating of necessity in a parliamentary arena, could not deal with the central problems. Relief, in the end of the day, can be found only through law.

Thus, though much history enters into this theme, the theme is essentially modern. The crisis exists. It remains to be seen whether we must remain the prisoners of the unhappy consequences of some aspects of an otherwise happy history. Undoubtedly, the creation of an effective system of public law would be a major undertaking, involving as it would the rejection of many deep-seated ideas. It would probably require the creation of a new system of courts to break the fetters upon those which now exist. It is those fetters which have led to the acceptance by too many of a feeling of judicial impotence. Perhaps it is because the author is a lawyer that he does not accept the current despair about law. Recognition of the defects of the existing state of affairs need not lead to that despair. A description of the benefits that could flow from the reinstatement of public law as a means of social regulation would make this article too long, and in this publication might well be impertinent. It is enough if some idea has been given of the present crisis in the United Kingdom.

One further word might be added. Just as at the outset it was said that many of the good aspects of our constitutional arrangements would not be mentioned, though they exist, so in conclusion it should be said that the criticism in what has been said is aimed at law and lawyers. Overall the administrative morality, especially in the civil service, is remarkably high and it is not that which is criticized. It must, however, be recognized that the best of men need from time to time a stimulus to their conscience. That stimulus can best be provided by the law.

INDEX

483